Palgrave Studies in Economic History

Series Editor
Kent Deng
London School of Economics
London, UK

Palgrave Studies in Economic History is designed to illuminate and enrich our understanding of economies and economic phenomena of the past. The series covers a vast range of topics including financial history, labour history, development economics, commercialisation, urbanisation, industrialisation, modernisation, globalisation, and changes in world economic orders.

More information about this series at
http://www.palgrave.com/gp/series/14632

Daniel A. Tirado-Fabregat
Marc Badia-Miró • Henry Willebald
Editors

Time and Space

Latin American Regional Development in Historical Perspective

palgrave
macmillan

Editors
Daniel A. Tirado-Fabregat
Departament d'Anàlisi Econòmica
Universitat de València
València, Spain

Henry Willebald
Universidad de la República
Montevideo, Uruguay

Marc Badia-Miró
Departament d'Història Econòmica,
Institucions, Política i
Economia Mundial
Universitat de Barcelona
Barcelona, Spain

ISSN 2662-6497 ISSN 2662-6500 (electronic)
Palgrave Studies in Economic History
ISBN 978-3-030-47552-9 ISBN 978-3-030-47553-6 (eBook)
https://doi.org/10.1007/978-3-030-47553-6

Cover illustration: Instants/ GettyImages

This Palgrave Macmillan imprint is published by the registered company Springer Nature Switzerland AG.
The registered company address is: Gewerbestrasse 11, 6330 Cham, Switzerland

Acknowledgements

This book is the result of years of work, during which time we received invaluable help from various colleagues and institutions. As editors of the volume, the debts we owe are numerous since a great many researchers helped us out throughout the process, both informally and in seminars and conferences we shared. Particularly, most of the chapters that compose the volume have been presented and discussed at several seminars and academic conferences such as the following: Workshop: "*Reconstrucción de PIBs regionales en América Latina, 1890–2010*", Montevideo (2013); IV Congreso Latinoamericano de Historia Económica, Bogotá (2014); Foro Bienal Iberoamericano de Estudios sobre el Desarrollo, Montevideo (2015); Jean Monnet Action International Conference: "*Studying GDP regional imbalances for a better long-term analysis of European integration*", València (2016); European Social Science History Conference, València (2016); V Congreso Latinoamericano de Historia Económica, Sao Paulo (2016); International Conference in Regional Science, Sevilla (2018); International Economic History Association Congress, Boston (2018); International Conference in Regional Science, Castelló de la Plana (2019); VI Congreso Latinoamericano de Historia Económica, Santiago de Chile (2019). We want to thank all the participants for their insightful comments and advice in each of these meetings.

The area of Economic History (EH-València) of the Department of Economic Analysis at the University of València, the Department of Economic History, Institutions, Policy and World Economy at the University of Barcelona (UB) and the Instituto de Economía, Departamento de Economía, Facultad de Ciencias Económicas y

Administración, of the Universidad de la República, Uruguay, became the spaces that made the research task much easier and provided us with a permanent stimulus. We would also like to express our gratitude to all the team at Palgrave Macmillan, for both the production and the publishing processes. Our thanks also go to Kent Deng (series editor), to two anonymous referees for their suggestions, and to Laura Pacey, Ruth Jenner and Lavanya Devgun for their patience, endless inspiration and excellent editing. Finally, we are grateful for the financial support received from different institutions: Spanish Ministry of Economy and Competitiveness, projects ECO2015-65049-C12-1-P, ECO2015-65049-C12-2-P, ECO2015-71534-REDT, ECO2017-90848-REDT and EUIN2017-86001, Conselleria d'Educació, Universitats i Esport de la Generalitat Valenciana, project AICO/2018/130, Grup de Recerca consolidat de la Generalitat de Catalunya (2017SGR1466) and Proyecto de Investigación I+D CSIC 2012 "PIB y desarrollo regional en Uruguay: 1900–2010".

Contents

1 **Introduction: Time, Space and Economics in the History of Latin America** 1
Marc Badia-Miró, Daniel A. Tirado-Fabregat, and Henry Willebald

2 **Comparing Different Estimation Methodologies of Regional GDPs in Latin American Countries** 17
Alfonso Díez-Minguela and María Teresa Sanchis Llopis

3 **Productive and Regional Development Policies in Latin America Since 1890** 41
Luís Bértola

4 **Growth and Convergence Among Argentine Provinces Since 1895** 65
María Florencia Aráoz, Esteban A. Nicolini, and Mauricio Talassino

5 **From West to East: Bolivian Regional GDPs since the 1950s. A Story of Natural Resources and Infrastructure** 97
José A. Peres-Cajías

6 The Evolution of Regional Income Inequality in Brazil, 1872–2015 131
Justin R. Bucciferro and Pedro H. G. Ferreira de Souza

7 Spatial Inequality in Chile in the Long Run: A Paradox of Extreme Concentration in the Absence of Agglomeration Forces (1890–2017) 157
Marc Badia-Miró

8 Regional Economic Inequality in Colombia, 1926–2018 183
Adolfo Meisel Roca and Lucas Hahn

9 Regional GDP in Mexico, 1895–2010 211
José Aguilar Retureta, Marc Badia-Miró, and Alfonso Herranz-Loncán

10 Peruvian Regional Inequality: 1847–2017 241
Bruno Seminario, María Alejandra Zegarra, and Luis Palomino

11 Patterns of Regional Income Distribution in Uruguay (1872–2012): A Story of Agglomeration, Natural Resources and Public Policies 271
Julio Martinez-Galarraga, Adrián Rodríguez Miranda, and Henry Willebald

12 *Was the Oil Sown Evenly?* Long-Term Patterns of Regional Inequality in Venezuela (1881–2011) 309
Giuseppe De Corso and Daniel A. Tirado-Fabregat

13 Spatial Inequality in Latin America (1895–2010): Convergence and Clusters in a Long-Run Approach 343
Marc Badia-Miró, Esteban A. Nicolini, and Henry Willebald

14 Regional Inequality in Latin America: Does It Mirror the European Pattern? 375
Julio Martinez-Galarraga, Esteban A. Nicolini, Daniel A. Tirado-Fabregat, and Henry Willebald

Index 403

Notes on Contributors

José Aguilar Retureta graduated from the University of Veracruz and received his PhD in Economic History from the University of Barcelona under Alfonso Herranz-Loncán and Marc Badia-Miró's supervision. He is author of articles on Mexican regional income inequality over the long run published in *Revista de Historia Económica* and *Economic History of Developing Regions.*

María Florencia Aráoz is Associate Professor of Macroeconomics and Researcher in the Center for Economic Research for Human Development (Universidad del Norte Santo Tomás de Aquino, Tucumán, Argentina). She got her MSc in Economics at the National University of Tucumán (Argentina) and now is a doctoral student in Economic History at the University of Barcelona. Her research interests include regional development, institutions and the historical roots of economic development. She has published some of her research in journals like the *Revista de Historia Económica-Journal of Iberian and Latin America Economic History and Journal of Latin American Studies.*

Marc Badia-Miró is Associate Professor of Economic History at the University of Barcelona, Spain. He is also member of the Barcelona Economic Analysis Team. His research interests refer to economic geography, trade and natural resources in historical perspective, mainly focused in Latin America, during the First Globalization and Interwar period.

Luís Bértola (PhD in Economic History, University of Gothenburg) is Full Professor of Economic History and Development at the Faculty of

Social Sciences, Universidad de la República, Uruguay. He is a member of the Uruguayan Academy of Sciences. He taught postgraduate courses and seminars at more than 30 universities in Europe and the Americas, and was consultant at IDB, ILO, ECLAC, UNDP and many national institutions. He has widely published on Latin American long-run development, as well as on development and industrial policy.

Justin R. Bucciferro is A. Lindsay O'Connor Chair of American Institutions in the Economics Department at Colgate University and Associate Professor of Economics at Eastern Washington University. His research centers on the economic development and history of the Americas, addressing the interrelationships between demography, geography and inequality. He holds a PhD in Economics from the University of Colorado at Boulder and an MBA from Clarkson University. His research appears in the *Economic History Review, Economic Anthropology and the Journal of Iberian and Latin American Economic History.*

Giuseppe De Corso holds a PhD and a master's degree from the University of Simon Bolivar, Caracas. He is a graduate in Economics from the University of Tampa Florida USA. He has worked at the Central Bank of Venezuela in the department of Foreign Exchange Currency, as a professor of Economics at the Central University of Venezuela School of Management and Accounting. In Milan, he taught at the Ispi and the College of Milan, and in Colombia at Jorge Tadeo Lozano University. He published several books on Venezuela's economic growth and articles in *Revista de Historia Económica, Rivista Italiana di Geopolitica* and *Revista de Economía Institucional.*

Alfonso Díez-Minguela is Assistant Professor of Economic History at the Universitat de València (Spain). Having graduated at the University of Kent, UK, he then completed his PhD in Economics from the University of Warwick, UK. His broad research interests include history, economics and geography; in particular, he studies the historical roots of economic development in Spain. He has published refereed articles in *Papers in Regional Science, Historical Methods, Cliometrica, Journal of Interdisciplinary History, Journal of Economic History, Journal of Historical Geography* and *History of the Family*. Additionally, he has recently co-authored a book in the Palgrave Studies in Economic History series.

Pedro H. G. Ferreira de Souza is a tenured researcher at the Instituto de Pesquisa Econômica Aplicada, Ipea, the main research institute of the federal government in Brazil. He conducts academic and policy-oriented research on poverty, inequality and economic development. He holds a PhD in Sociology from the University of Brasília (2016). His PhD dissertation received the Capes/Ministry of Education Prize for Best PhD Dissertation in Sociology and the National Association of Graduate Studies and Research in the Social Sciences (ANPOCS) Prize for Best PhD Dissertation in the Social Sciences. His book *Uma História de Desigualdade: A Concentração de Renda entre os Ricos no Brasil* (1926–2013) (*A History of Inequality: The Concentration of Income at the Top in Brazil, 1926–2013*) was the Book of the Year in the 2019 Jabuti Awards, the most prestigious prize in the Brazilian publishing industry.

Lucas Hahn works as a research assistant in economics at Banco de la República in Cartagena, Colombia. His research has focused on the study of regional inequalities in the country using different methodological approaches, such as Stochastic Frontier Analysis and Input-Output matrices. Several of his articles have been published in peer-reviewed journals in Colombia. He holds a master's degree in Statistics from Columbia University.

Alfonso Herranz-Loncán is Professor of Economic History at the University of Barcelona and Director of the Research Centre "Antoni de Capmany" in Economics and Economic History. He has published extensively on the relationship between infrastructure and economic growth; the growth impact of railways in different countries; the political economy of infrastructure construction; market integration in Spain; and long-term economic growth in Latin America. He has published in journals including *Journal of Economic History, Economic History Review, European Review of Economic History* and *Cliometrica*. His book *Infraestructuras y crecimiento económico en España* (1850–1935) was awarded the Jaume Vicens-Vives prize of the Spanish Economic History Association.

Julio Martinez-Galarraga is Associate Professor of Economic History at the University of València, Spain. His research is focused on the fields of regional economics, economic geography, inequality and education from a historical perspective.

Adolfo Meisel Roca serves as the president of Universidad del Norte in Barranquilla, Colombia. He previously served as member of the Board of Directors at Banco de la República, the highest governing body in Colombia's central bank. Adolfo holds a PhD in Economics from the University of Illinois at Urbana-Champaign and a master's degree in Sociology from Yale University. His research studies regional disparities from a historical perspective, in particular regarding the persistence of social and economic inequalities in Colombia during the last two centuries.

Esteban A. Nicolini holds a master's degree in History from the National University of Tucumán (Argentina) and a doctorate in Economics from the Pompeu Fabra University (Spain). He is visiting professor at the Social Sciences Department, Carlos III University in Madrid, professor at the Economics Department in the Universidad Nacional de Tucumán (Argentina) and Director of the Center for Economic Research for Human Development (Universidad del Norte Santo Tomás de Aquino, Tucumán, Argentina). His main areas of research are growth and inequality in Europe in the eighteenth and nineteenth centuries and the Economic History of Argentina in the nineteenth and twentieth centuries. His research has been published in *Economic History Review, Explorations in Economic History, European Review of Economic History* and *Journal of Latin American Studies*, among other journals.

Luis Palomino is a research assistant at the Research Center of University of the Pacific, Peru. He holds a bachelor's degree in Economics from the National University of San Marcos, Peru. His research focuses on microeconomics, macroeconomics, mechanism design, regional growth and development.

José A. Peres-Cajías is Assistant Professor at the Economic History Department, University of Barcelona. He holds a PhD (Cum Laude) in Economic History from the University of Barcelona (2013) for a thesis on the evolution of Bolivian Public Finances from 1882 to 2010. His research aims at understanding the long-term economic development of developing regions by looking at the interplay of institutions, natural resources and trade. He published different articles in international journals including *Cliometrica, Economics and Human Biology, Journal of Latin American Studies, Sustainability, Revista de Historia Económica* and *Economic History of Developing Regions*. He also contributed to several chapters of books published by Palgrave, Routledge, Springer and Fondo de Cultura

Económica. One of his articles was awarded best article published in international journals by the Spanish Association of Economic History.

Adrián Rodríguez Miranda holds a PhD in Economic Development from the Universidad Autónoma de Madrid. He is a professor at the Faculty of Economic Sciences and Administration (FCEA) of the Universidad de la República, in Uruguay. At FCEA he is a senior researcher at the Institute of Economics and coordinates the Research Group on Local and Regional Development. His current research interests include local and regional development from a long-term perspective, local productive systems, social capital and local development as well as development policies at national and subnational levels. At the University of the Republic, he is coordinator of the Interdisciplinary Nucleus of Territorial Development Studies since 2012. He was coordinator of the Thematic Network of Development Studies from 2013 to 2015. He also was coordinator of the Ibero-American Network of Development Studies from 2011 to 2017.

María Teresa Sanchis Llopis holds a PhD in Economics from University of València (Spain). She is Associate Professor of Economic History at University of València and Associate Researcher of the Figuerola Institute of Social Sciences, University Carlos III. Nowadays, she is member of the editorial board of Revista de Historia Industrial. Economía y Empresa. Her research has been published in several journals such as *the European Review of Economic History, Cliometrica, Historical Methods, Journal of Interdisciplinary History, Papers in Regional Science, Revista de Historia Industrial* and *Revista de Historia Económica*, among others. She has contributed to collective books edited by prestigious international and national publishers. At this moment, her main research interest is focused in studying historical regional disparities, with special attention to the French case. Moreover, she has studied the Spanish industrialization by using growth accounting techniques, the impact of electrification on the Spanish economy and economic growth during the European Golden Age.

Bruno Seminario is a professor of Economics at University of the Pacific, Peru, and researcher at the Research Center of University of the Pacific. He is a member of the Peruvian Association of Economic History (APHE). His research focuses on macroeconomics, economic history, business cycles, space economics, regional development, regional inequality, demographics and pension systems.

Mauricio Talassino is a doctoral fellow in Economics by CONICET (Consejo Nacional de Investigaciones Científicas y Técnicas). His PhD dissertation (in progress) is about regional economic growth in Argentina in the twentieth century. He is a researcher at the Center for Economic Research for Human Development (Universidad del Norte Santo Tomás de Aquino, Tucumán, Argentina) and a professor at the National University of Tucumán, Argentina. He holds master's degrees in Applied Statistics and in Economics from the Universidad Nacional de Tucumán, Argentina.

Daniel A. Tirado-Fabregat is Professor of Economic History at the University of València, Spain. He has taught undergraduate and graduate courses on growth economics, Spanish economic history, world economic history and globalization at the Universities of València and Barcelona, Spain. His broad research interests include the historical roots of regional economic development and inequality.

Henry Willebald is Professor in Development Economics and Economic History at the Universidad de la República, Uruguay. His research interests refer to modern economic growth in settler economies and Latin American countries and, especially, about the evolution of income (from production and expenditure side), at national and regional levels, inequality, productive specialization, natural resources and sustainability.

María Alejandra Zegarra is an economist consultant at the Inter-American Development Bank in Washington D.C. She holds a master's degree in Economics from Brown University and is a former Fulbright Scholar. Her research focuses on the long-term consequences of inequality, pension systems, and the economic effects of tourism and mining.

List of Figures

Fig. 2.1 Historical reconstitution of regional GDP in Latin America by method. (Note: Bottom-up approaches red-coloured: ARG-1913; BRA-1895; BRA-1925; BOL-1950; BOL-1960) 24

Fig. 3.1 GDP (millions, left), population (thousands, left) and GDP per capita (thousands, right) in nine Latin American countries, 1890–2010 (international 1990 dollars). (Note: Argentina, Brazil, Bolivia, Chile, Colombia, México, Perú, Uruguay and Venezuela. Per capita GDP is a weighted average. Source: Bértola and Ocampo (2012) and for Bolivia, Herranz-Loncán and Peres-Cajías [2016]) 43

Fig. 3.2 Latin American (nine countries) relative GDP per capita (four developed countries = 100) (Source: Based on Fig. 3.1 and Maddison (2010) for the weighted average of France, Germany, the UK and the US) 44

Fig. 3.3 GDP per capita of nine Latin American countries (nine-year moving averages, at 1990 international dollars, semi-log scale). (Source: Bértola and Ocampo 2012 and for Bolivia, Herranz-Loncán and Peres-Cajías [2016]) 46

Fig. 4.1 Per capita GDP. (Income groups constructed using standard deviations from the simple average of the GDP per capita of the districts. E.g., Very Rich corresponds to districts with GDP per capita higher than the average GDP per capita plus a standard deviation, and so on). (Source: Table 4.2) 80

Fig. 4.2 Initial levels of GDP per capita and growth, Argentine provinces, period 1895–2004. (Note: BA: Buenos Aires; Cat: Catamarca; Cba: Córdoba; CF: Capital Federal; Cha: Chaco; Chu: Chubut; Corr: Corrientes; ER: Entre Ríos; For: Formosa; Juj: Jujuy ; LP: La Pampa; LR: La Rioja; Men: Mendoza; Mis: Misiones; RN: Río Negro; Sal: Salta; SC: Santa Cruz; SE: Santiago del Estero; SJ: San Juan; SL: San Luis; TF: Tierra del Fuego; Tuc: Tucumán. Source: Authors' elaboration) 86

Fig. 4.3 Initial levels of GDP per capita and growth Argentine provinces, selected periods. (Note: BA: Buenos Aires; Cat: Catamarca; Cba: Córdoba; CF: Capital Federal; Cha: Chaco; Chu: Chubut; Corr: Corrientes; ER: Entre Ríos; For: Formosa; Juj: Jujuy ; LP: La Pampa; LR: La Rioja; Men: Mendoza; Mis: Misiones; RN: Río Negro; Sal: Salta; SC: Santa Cruz; SE: Santiago del Estero; SJ: San Juan; SL: San Luis; TF: Tierra del Fuego; Tuc: Tucumán). (Source: Authors' elaboration) 87

Fig. 4.4 Coefficient of variation of per capita GDP. (Source: Authors' elaboration) 88

Fig. 5.1 Beta-convergence of departmental pc GDP, 1950–2012. (Sources: See text) 115

Fig. 5.2 Beta-convergence of department pc GDP, 1988–2012. (Sources: See text) 116

Fig. 5.3 Sigma-convergence of departmental pc GDP, 1950–2012. (Sources: See text) 117

Fig. 5.4 Departmental manufacturing GDP (%, the share of total manufacturing GDP), 1950–2017. (Sources: See text) 120

Fig. 6.1 Sigma-convergence: population-weighted coefficients of variation, 1872–2015. Note: Trend line fitted by a fourth-degree polynomial. (Sources: See Sect. 3) 142

Fig. 6.2 Unconditional β-convergence across time-consistent Brazilian states, 1872–2015. Note: Estimated speed of convergence (β) of 0.5% per year. (Sources: See Sect. 3) 145

Fig. 7.1 Standard deviation (weighted by population and non-weighted) for regions in Chile, 1895–2010. (Source: Own elaboration. See text) 170

Fig. 7.2 Beta-convergence for Chilean regions, 1895–2010. (Source: Own elaboration. See text) 172

Fig. 7.3 Concentration of economic activity in Chile, 1895–2010. (Source: GDP data comes from own elaboration from 1890 to 1973 and official sources from 1960 to 2010) 175

Fig. 8.1 Colombia: Correlations and Spearman correlations between bank deposits and regional GDP by sources (selected years, 1938–1990). (Source: Authors' calculations based on DNP, PUJ, CEGA and DANE. Numbers in the table are in the format correlation/Spearman correlation) 193

Fig. 8.2 Absolute β-convergence (1950–2018) 205
Fig. 9.1 Standard Deviation, 1895–2010. Mexico=1. (Source: German-Soto 2005; Aguilar-Retureta 2015; INEGI 2019) 226
Fig. 9.2 Beta convergence, regional GDP per capita of the Mexican states (1895–2010). (Sources: Aguilar-Retureta 2015; German-Soto 2005; INEGI 2019) 228
Fig. 9.3 Beta convergence, regional GDP per capita of the Mexican states (1895–1950). (Sources: Aguilar-Retureta 2015; German-Soto 2005; INEGI 2019) 229
Fig. 9.4 Beta convergence, regional GDP per capita of the Mexican states (1950–2010). (Sources: Aguilar-Retureta 2015; German-Soto 2005; INEGI 2019) 230
Fig. 9.5 Inequality indices: Theil, Gini, Williamson and coefficient of variation (1895–2010). (Sources: Aguilar-Retureta 2015; German-Soto 2005; INEGI 2019) 231
Fig. 9.6 Herfindahl-Hirschman Index (1895–2010) and share of Mexico City within national GDP. (Sources: Aguilar-Retureta 2015; German-Soto 2005; INEGI 2019) 233
Fig. 10.1 GDP per capita of Peru, 1795–2017 (PPP, 1990 international $). (Source: Seminario (2015). Own elaboration) 244
Fig. 10.2 Regional Williamson Coefficient in Peru, 1847–2017. (Sources: Seminario et al. (2019) and Seminario (2015). Own elaboration) 255
Fig. 10.3 Convergence between the regions of Peru, 1847–2017. (Sources: Seminario et al. (2019) and Seminario (2015). Own elaboration) 257
Fig. 10.4 Economic activity and regional inequality: North, Centre and South, 1847–2017 (%). (**a**) Distribution of the Peruvian GDP (%). (**b**) GDP per capita respect to the national average (Ratio indexed to 100). (**c**) Williamson Coefficient. (Sources: Seminario et al. (2019) and Seminario (2015). Own elaboration) 263
Fig. 10.5 Distributive evolution of GDP per capita in Peru, 1850–2017. (Sources: Seminario et al. (2019) and Seminario (2015). Own elaboration) 265
Fig. 11.1 Uruguay GDP per capita relative to US GDP per capita, 1870–2015. (Source: Maddison project database) 275
Fig. 11.2 Regional inequality in Uruguay (GDP per capita), 1872–2012. (Source: Own elaboration) 288
Fig. 12.1 GDP per capita of Venezuela as a percentage of GDP per capita of the United States, 1920–2016. (Source: Bolt et al. 2018) 316

Fig. 12.2 Weighed coefficient of variation (WCV). (Source: Main text) 325
Fig. 12.3 GDP per capita in 1881 vs. GDP per capita growth rate 1881–2011. (Source: Main text) 326
Fig. 12.4 GDP per capita in 1881 vs. GDP per capita growth rate 1881–1936. (Source: Main text) 327
Fig. 12.5 GDP per capita in 1936 vs. GDP per capita growth rate 1936–2011. (Source: Main text) 327
Fig. 12.6 Zulia GDP per capita as a share of Distrito Capital GDP per capita. (Source: Main text) 330
Fig. 13.1 Ratio between top 90% and bottom 10% regional GDP per capita. (Source: Authors' own) 349
Fig. 13.2 MLD components in Latin America, 1895–2010. (Source: Authors' own) 350
Fig. 13.3 Regional inequality by countries (MLD), 1895–2010. (Source: Authors' own) 352
Fig. 13.4 Regional inequality by countries (MLD), 1895–2010. (Source: Authors' own) 353
Fig. 13.5 Regional inequality by countries (MLD), 1895–2010. (Source: Authors' own) 354
Fig. 13.6 Convergence analysis in Latin America, 1895–2000. (Source: Authors' own) 357
Fig. 13.7 Convergence analysis in Latin America, 1895–1925. (Source: Authors' own) 360
Fig. 13.8 Convergence analysis in Latin America, 1935–1970. (Source: Authors' own) 361
Fig. 13.9 Convergence analysis in Argentina, Brazil and Mexico, 1935–1970. (Source: Authors' own) 362
Fig. 13.10 Convergence analysis in Latin America, 1980–2000. (Source: Authors' own) 363
Fig. 13.11 Regional GDP per capita in Latin America, 1895–2010. (Source: Authors' own) 365
Fig. 13.12 Local Indicators of Spatial Autocorrelation (LISA) maps, 1895–2000. (Source: Authors' own) 369
Fig. 14.1 Regional income dispersion (WCV) and GDP per capita (South West Europe, 1860–2010). (Source: Díez-Minguela et al. 2020) 388
Fig. 14.2 Regional income dispersion (WCV) and GDP per capita (Latin America, 1895–2010). (Source: Own elaboration based on footnote 10) 389

List of Tables

Table 2.1	National statistical offices in Latin America	20
Table 2.2	Official estimates of regional GDPs by country	21
Table 2.3	Historical reconstitution of subnational GDP	24
Table 2.4	Descriptive statistics	37
Table 3.1	GDP, population and GDP per capita growth rates in nine Latin American countries, 1890–2010 (international 1990 dollars)	43
Table 4.1	Share of regional GDP to total GDP (%)	77
Table 4.2	Per capita GDP (country current year GDP pc = 1)	79
Table 5.1	Sources and indicators used in the reconstruction of Bolivian regional GDPs	107
Table 5.2	Departmental population (%, the share of total population), 1846–2012	110
Table 5.3	Department population growth rates and immigration rates (%), 1950–2012	112
Table 5.4	Departmental pc GDP (Bolivian pc GDP = 1), 1950–2017	114
Table 5.5	Departmental GDP (%, the share of total GDP), 1950–2017	117
Table 6.1	Composition of Brazilian exports (%)—Brazil, 1850, 1875, and 1900	137
Table 6.2	Regional GDP per capita in Brazil, 1872–2015 (Brazil = 100)	146
Table 6.3	Regional GDP shares in Brazil, 1872–2015 (%)	149
Table 7.1	Evolution of sectorial GDP during the period 1890–2010 (%)	162
Table 7.2	Regional GDP per capita in Chile, 1895–2010 (average = 1)	169
Table 7.3	Share of regional GDP in Chile, 1895–2010 (%)	175
Table 8.1	Departments in the 16 regions of this study	194
Table 8.2	Regional share of bank deposits and GDP by decades (1926–2018)	196

Table 8.3	Regional share of population by decades (1926–2018)	197
Table 8.4	Standardized regional GDP per capita by decades (1926–2018)	198
Table 8.5	Colombia: population-weighted coefficient of variation of regional GDP per capita (1950–2018)	206
Table 9.1	Composition of Mexican GDP by sector, 1895–1929 (%)	213
Table 9.2	Regional GDP per capita in Mexico, 1895–2010 (Mexico = 1)	222
Table 9.3	Share of regional GDP, Mexican states (1895–2010)	232
Table 10.1	Sources and methods used to estimate the real GDP by department	248
Table 10.2	Regional GDP as a share of the total GDP, 1847–2017	253
Table 10.3	GDP per capita regional (Peru = 100)	258
Table 11.1	Regional shares in Uruguayan GDP (%) (Source: Own estimates)	286
Table 11.2	Relative GDP per capita for Uruguayan provinces, 1872–2012 (Uruguay = 100) (Source: Own estimates)	290
Table 12.1	Regional GDP as a percentage of national GDP	323
Table 12.2	Regional GDP per capita (Venezuela = 100)	329
Table 13.1	Convergence regression of Latin American regional growth (OLS)	358
Table 14.1	Regional inequality (WCV) South West Europe	384
Table 14.2	Regional inequality (WCV) Latin America	385
Table 14.3	Parametric estimates (pooled regressions) South West Europe 1860–2010	392
Table 14.4	Parametric estimates (pooled regressions) Latin America, 1895–2010	393

List of Maps

Map 5.1 Administrative division of Bolivia and ecological regions. (Sources: Maps of CIA, Central Intelligence Agency) 99

Map 5.2 The relative importance of Bolivian departments (Bolivian pc GDP = 1), 1950. (Sources: See text) 121

Map 5.3 The relative importance of Bolivian departments (Bolivian pc GDP = 1), 1980. (Sources: See text) 121

Map 5.4 The relative importance of Bolivian departments (Bolivian pc GDP = 1), 1988. (Sources: See text) 122

Map 5.5 The relative importance of Bolivian departments (Bolivian pc GDP = 1), 2012. (Sources: See text) 122

Map 6.1 Aggregated units and regions of Brazil. (Sources: Author's harmonization of state borders) 136

Map 6.2 Regional GDP per capita in Brazil: 1872, 1920, 1970, and 2015. N.B.: "very rich," state per capita GDP more than one standard deviation above the mean; "rich," between the mean and the mean plus one standard deviation; "poor," between the mean and the mean minus one standard deviation; "very poor," state per capita GDP lower than the mean minus one standard deviation. (Sources: See Sect. 3) 148

Map 8.1 Relief map of Colombia and the Andes Mountains. (Source: Geographical information provided by official institutions in Colombia [DANE, IGAC] and Natural Earth [http://www.naturalearthdata.com/]) 185

Map 8.2 Colombia: Aggregation of departments into 16 regions. (Source: Elaboration by the authors based on geographical information produced by DANE and Natural Earth [http://www.naturalearthdata.com/]) 195

Map 8.3	Colombia: standardized regional GDP per capita in 1950. (Sources: Authors' calculations based on estimates of population and GDP per capita, geographical information by DANE and Natural Earth [http://www.naturalearthdata.com/])	199
Map 8.4	Colombia: standardized regional GDP per capita in 1980. (Sources: Authors' calculations based on estimates of population and GDP per capita, geographical information by DANE and Natural Earth [http://www.naturalearthdata.com/])	200
Map 8.5	Colombia: standardized regional GDP per capita in 2018. (Sources: Authors' calculations based on estimates of population and GDP per capita, geographical information by DANE and Natural Earth [http://www.naturalearthdata.com/])	201
Map 9.1	Regional GDP per capita of the Mexican states, 1895–2010. (Source: Main text)	224
Map 10.1	Territorial administrative division of Peru (Regions and *Departmentos*). (Source: GEO GPS PERÚ. Own elaboration. Online: https://www.geogpsperu.com/p/descargas.html)	252
Map 10.2	GDP per capita by region, 1847 and 1890. (Sources: Seminario et al. (2019) and Seminario (2015). Own elaboration)	259
Map 10.3	GDP per capita regional—1930, 1990, and 2017. (Sources: Seminario et al. (2019) and Seminario (2015). Own elaboration)	260
Map 11.1	Provinces (*departamentos*) of Uruguay. (Source: Own elaboration based on Servicio Geográfico Militar (http://www.sgm.gub.uy))	282
Map 11.2	Maps by GDP per capita. Uruguayan provinces, 1872, 1961, 1990, 2012. (Note: Black: "High income" (income per capita $\geq$ mean + σ); dark grey: "Medium high income" (mean + σ > income per capita $\geq$ mean); grey: "Low middle income" (mean > income per capita $\geq$ mean − σ); white: "Low income" (mean − σ > income per capita))	294
Map 12.1	Map of the states of Venezuela	321
Map 12.2	Regional GDP per capita in 1881. (Source: Main text)	331
Map 12.3	Regional GDP per capita in 1936. (Source: Main text)	332
Map 12.4	Regional per capita GDP in 1981. (Source: Main text)	333
Map 12.5	Regional GDP per capita in 2011. (Source: Main text)	334

CHAPTER 1

Introduction: Time, Space and Economics in the History of Latin America

Marc Badia-Miró, Daniel A. Tirado-Fabregat, and Henry Willebald

1 Motivation

The recent edition of the New Oxford Handbook of Economic Geography states that in "economic geography the where, why, and so what questions are focused on understanding economy. The latter needs to be defined broadly as the totality of processes through which individuals, households and societies make a living and sustain themselves" (Clark et al. 2018: 46). "Where" is about the spatiality of economic processes and involves the key

M. Badia-Miró (✉)
Departament d'Història Econòmica, Institucions, Política i Economia Mundial
Universitat de Barcelona, Barcelona, Spain
e-mail: mbadia@ub.edu

D. A. Tirado-Fabregat
Departament d'Anàlisi Econòmica, Universitat de València, València, Spain
e-mail: daniel.tirado@uv.es

H. Willebald
Universidad de la República, Montevideo, Uruguay
e-mail: hwillebald@iecon.ccee.edu.uy

D. A. Tirado-Fabregat et al. (eds.), *Time and Space*,
Palgrave Studies in Economic History,
https://doi.org/10.1007/978-3-030-47553-6_1

concepts of location, place and territory. "What" helps economic geographers relate locations, places and territories to each other applying concepts of distance, proximity, diversity and scale. "Why" is about explaining the spatiality of economic processes and the diversity of economic life which is created in these relationships. Here, geographers can study a fascinating variety of forces ranging from economic standards such as demand-supply, through behaviour of agents (individuals and organizations), formal and informal institutions setting the rules of economic activities, to ethnicity, sex and all kinds of cultural factors.

As well stated in Ascani et al. (2012), with the phenomenon of globalization that progressively dominated the world economy since the last third of the twentieth century, many authors have argued about the existence of a "flat world" (Friedman 2005), the "end of geography" (O'Brien 1992) and the "death of distance" (Cairncross 1997). On the contrary, our contribution in this book—as economic geography in general—is "crucial in counteracting these hyper-globalist views, prominent in the 1990s, emphasizing homogenizing forces of globalization, envisaging a global society, and predicting the end of geography in economy, politics, and culture" (Clark et al. 2018: 48).

None of those factors and determinants are outside the field of economic history—also, scholars and professionals in this field do not believe that the last period of globalization was the first or the most intense of the last 500 years (O'Rourke and Williamson 2006; Obstfeld and Taylor 2006) and, on the contrary, the recognition of local realities constitutes common matter in our research. However, what can be presented as a new subject is the interest of quantitatively approaching these differentials to provide dimension and support the understanding of global performance.

Then, as economic historians, we consider that the trilogy of the economic geography of "where, why, and so what" would require another adverb that proves substantial for understanding economic development: "when". This is the reason why our book is titled *Time and Space* and we attempt to understand the evolution of the regional development of Latin America from a historical perspective.

Considerable attention has been paid to regional economics and human geography in order to tackle this issue and inform public policy. However, the problem has been approached as if regional imbalances were geographically determined or had been constructed in the recent past, rather than being historically rooted. This book supports the hypothesis that the current regional disparities are principally the result of a long and complex process in which historical, geographical, economic and political factors have all worked together.

Regional income inequality is a persistent feature of the global economic landscape and one of the central issues on the agenda of policymakers. Nevertheless, and as the chapters that form part of this book will show, the current imbalances are essentially the result of a long-term evolution that can be traced back to the origins of modern economic growth. In this respect, as has already been stressed in an abundant literature, economic growth of the last 250 years has been closely associated with the industrialization processes that originated in Britain in the eighteenth century. In this context, newly emerging technologies led to sustained growth in the productivity of the workforce and, eventually, to a substantial improvement in living standards. Even so, industrialization and economic growth did not occur everywhere, or at the same time.

Under these conditions, research on the evolution of regional inequality in the long run has received special attention within European and other developed countries. Much of the research has shown that the present-day economic landscape of Europe and the US has its roots in the origins and the evolution of national economic growth processes. From then on, despite all the socioeconomic changes that have occurred since the mid-1800s, reversals of fortunes and/or economic growth miracles have hardly been observed and, thus, spatial inequalities have been rather persistent over time (see, for instance, Wolf and Rosés 2019, which has a collection of most of the works for core economies).

However, albeit the research efforts carried out in the last decade, there is no comparable collective work for Latin American countries. In this respect, given that Latin American development differs widely across countries and regions, its diversity provides a set of excellent case studies in order to carry out a deep-rooted analysis of regional inequality in developing economies which might be useful for academics, professionals, policymakers and the general public, when comparing it with the performance of industrialized countries (Wolf and Rosés 2019). So, lessons from the Latin American past can be of much help and interest for current debates on regional inequalities, trade policies, territorial cohesion and public policies in developing and also developed countries.

The main objective of this book is to find out to what extent the stylized facts and explanatory hypotheses developed to explain regional inequality in industrialized countries can be applied to less developed economies. In contrast with European countries, Latin American economies largely specialized in commodity exports, showed higher levels of urbanization and high transports costs (both domestic and international) and experienced a lower pace of economic expansion and worse income distribution. New research with the focus on Latin America has the potential not only to provide a new perspective on the economic history of these regions but also to offer new insights on how those forces interact, moulding regional imbalances, in the non-core, peripheral countries. In that sense, the location of natural resources, industrial backwardness in most of these countries, areas with low population density, huge scarcities in infrastructure and logistics and a high degree of informal economy leads us to a new set of questions and tentative answers.

Our results indicate substantial differences in the historical trends of regional inequality in Latin America compared to Europe and the US. Latin American regional inequality did not follow the inverted-U pattern proposed by Williamson (1965). Each Latin American country experienced a specific path, although with a dominant trend towards convergence from high levels of inequality in the last third of the nineteenth century in parallel to market integration (both domestic and foreign). In addition, the variables determining the evolution of regional disparities in Latin America appear to be different from those in Europe. More specifically, our evidence indicates that aspects such as the inherited population distribution, the urbanization level, the location of natural resources, commodity price cycles, the unequal integration of the domestic market, the integration of the regions into international markets, the focus of public policies and the increasing intervention of the states in the economies had a much more relevant role than in the case of European countries.

Given that the main goal of the book is to offer the first quantitative description of Latin American modern economic development at a regional level, it brings together a group of leading American and European economic historians in order to build a new set of data on historical regional GDPs for nine Latin American countries: Argentina, Bolivia, Brazil, Chile, Colombia, Mexico, Perú, Uruguay and Venezuela. This new bulk of evidence allows us to undertake a new analysis of the long-term national development processes from a regional perspective. Besides, by doing so, the book also provides a transnational perspective on the Latin America economic development process.

2 Contents

One expression of Latin America's own regional disparity is the very different available information in territorial meaning. In most of the countries this means important limitations to proposing rigorous estimates, with changes in the coverage and scope and difficulties to get a consistent time evolution for particular economic activities and territories. Then, Chap. 2 refers to this issue. Alfonso Díez-Minguela and María Teresa Sanchis Llopis compare different estimation methodologies of regional GDP construction in Latin American countries. They offer a noteworthy overview of the different chapters that represent an additional contribution of our book in the methodological field.

Industrialization has played a central role in contributing to the evolution of regional inequality in the core economies. In Latin America, industrialization was a process based on substitution of imports and an active participation of the state in the economy. So, the aim of Chap. 3, written by Luís Bértola, is to identify the main stages of Latin American economic development with respect to the kind of industrial policy implemented by the states to promote growth and their implications for regional development. So, in this chapter industrial policy is considered not only as a sectoral policy, but also as a horizontal one. In this sense, the chapter gives context to the different case studies presented in this book.

After these two introductory chapters, the following nine chapters are devoted to analysing the evolution of regional imbalances across the bulk of national cases that are included in this volume.

María Florencia Aráoz, Esteban A. Nicolini and Mauricio Talassino study the case of Argentina. The economic development of Argentina since the end of the nineteenth century is a story of growth, *splendour* and then stagnation and relative decline. In this chapter, the authors present the first consistent formal quantitative analysis of the regional dimension of that story. By putting together estimations of the provincial GDPs for ten benchmark years between 1895 and 2004, they confirm the paramount importance of the city of Buenos Aires and the province of Buenos Aires in the national economy since the end of the nineteenth century. There are three new insights that the authors state about the evolution of regional disparities. First, there is a notable persistence in the relative positions of the provinces along the whole period under analysis. Second, this persistence is mainly due to the fact that the high levels of income per capita in some provinces of Patagonia and in Capital Federal—relative to provinces in the North—is a characteristic defined in the nineteenth century. Third, the explanation of a large share of regional inequality is related to the high productivity generated by an abundance of natural resources in some areas of *Pampa Húmeda* and Patagonia and by the presence of increasing returns in manufacturing and services in *Capital Federal.*

José A. Peres-Cajías deals with the Bolivian case since the 1950s due to the scarcity of data available for the previous decades. Economic history approaches to the study of Bolivian regions have been limited over the past two decades. Current economic research also tends to concentrate the analysis on the potentials and constraints of the regions themselves and gives little importance to how the economic differences between them affect the whole national economy. This is surprising given the magnitude of the differences. For example, over the last few decades, three of the nine departments have concentrated three quarters of the national production; the constant migration from the stagnant departments to the more dynamic departments also stands out. The chapter fills this gap through the reconstruction of a couple of indicators: departmental GDP for the period prior to the one covered by official statistics (1950–1988) and indices of economic concentration and productive specialization during the period 1950–2010. Unlike other cases in Latin America, the Bolivian case stands out by the low persistence in the relative importance of the regions and the high mobility in the top and bottom positions of the distribution of regional incomes. The chapter closes with an analysis of the possible causes of these regional experiences of relative success or failure where natural resources and infrastructure play central roles in the story.

Justin R. Bucciferro and Pedro H. G. Ferreira de Souza study the evolution of the largest country of our sample: Brazil (1872–2015). Regional inequality may hinder national development, which is disconcerting for Brazil as one of the world's most unequal countries. This chapter compiles new and existing provincial-level estimates of GDP per capita and examines their dispersion over time. Spatial inequality followed a cyclical pattern; it declined between 1872 and 1905/1920, reversed to an even higher level by 1940, stabilized until 1970 and, finally, has been falling. These trends were driven by commodity cycles (including coffee, rubber and soybeans), the supply of labour and capital (with abolition of slavery and mass immigration), reductions in transportation costs (from road and rail-line expansion), domestic and external trade policy (entailing import substitution industrialization or neoliberalism) and related processes of self-reinforcing structural change. The early estimates suggest a long-run succession of regional inequality in growth and contraction, though with an increasingly pronounced polarization between the North and the South.

Marc Badia-Miró studies the spatial inequality in Chile in the long run (1890–2017) and shows that it represents a paradox of extreme concentration in the absence of agglomeration forces around Santiago, the administrative capital. Despite this, and in contrast to what is found in most of the industrialized countries, GDP per capita in the capital has been below the country average and far from the levels in the wealthiest regions. Chile is a country where agglomeration economies seem to have had a marginal impact and where natural resource endowments have been crucial to explain the spatial location of economic activity (the nitrate mining cycle was extremely concentrated in space whereas copper mining has been much more disperse). Other characteristics to bear in mind are the impact of regional development policies in the 1960s, or the role played by infrastructure such as the railway through the Valle Central in boosting Santiago as a trade centre. This chapter describes the impact that all these elements had on the present-day layout of the country. At first glance, the new evidence shows that, in contrast to what we find in many of the developed countries, Chile shows a clear trend with regard to the reduction of GDP per capita concentration, interrupted only shortly by the expansion of Magallanes in 1960 (discovery of oil). This trend runs in parallel to the reinforcement of a process of extreme spatial concentration of the national GDP around Santiago (about 50% of the total GDP).

The regional economic inequality in Colombia (1926–2018) is presented by Adolfo Meisel Roca and Lucas W. Hahn de Castro. This chapter is devoted to the estimation of regional GDP of Colombia by decades between 1926 and 2018 (official figures since 1950). Then, the estimations are used to study several definitions of convergence. The main conclusion of this study is that Colombian regions did not converge in the twentieth century. Though poorer regions show higher growth rates, the dispersion of regional GDP per capita did not decrease. In fact, regional inequality has remained relatively stable with minor changes during the century. About the determinants of this behaviour, the authors argue that initially the geographic conditions of Colombia led to the development of isolated markets that concentrated in a few areas of the country, especially in the Andes Mountains. The integration of regional markets, undertaken through the construction of railroads and highways during the first half of the twentieth century, reinforced the patterns of regional economic inequality. The reduction of transport costs interacted with the presence of economies of scale and as a result produced a larger concentration of particular economic sectors, such as manufacturing, in the three largest cities (Bogotá, Medellín and Cali) located close to the geographic centre of the country. As a result, the economic significance of coastal regions declined. The adoption of import substitution industrialization (ISI) policies in the mid-twentieth century reinforced the development of this core-periphery pattern. While industrial sectors that were located in the central regions benefitted from these policies, peripheral regions did not due to the absence of manufacturing activities in their territories.

José Aguilar Retureta, Marc Badia-Miró and Alfonso Herranz-Loncán present the Mexican case from 1895 to 2010. Economic differences among Mexican regions are substantial and have been increasing for a long time. The study of the Mexican case confirms that regional inequality in low- and middle-income economies may have different trends and determinants from those of industrialized economies. It has followed a W-form in the long term, which largely reflects the alternation of different development models in the country since the late nineteenth century. Thus, between 1910 and 1940, or in the most recent period of economic openness (from the 1980s to the present), regional inequality has tended to increase. Divergence among Mexican regions was especially intense during the last period of the First Globalization (the 1920s). It was also in this period when the regional structure that has characterized the Mexican economy during the twentieth century was established, with a strong concentration of activity in Mexico City and a clear division between the rich North and the poor South. However, the period from 1940 to 1980 was characterized by regional convergence, although it was accompanied by sustained geographical concentration of industry. The main determinants of regional inequality changes have been different in each period. During the early twentieth century, a spatially uneven process of structural change explains the increase in regional inequality. By contrast, regional convergence during the state-led industrialization period was led by an intense process of factor mobility (and particularly labour flows) across the Mexican states and the concentration of economic activity around the main market (Mexico City) pushed by agglomeration economies in industry. Finally, since the mid-1980s divergence has been mainly driven by labour productivity differentials within each sector.

Bruno Seminario, María Alejandra Zegarra and Luis Palomino describe the evolution of regional inequality in Perú between the years 1847 and 2017 using the latest available statistics on the spatial distribution of population and economic activity. The main result observed is the transformation of the economic space of this country. Regional inequality steadily rose throughout the nineteenth century and the early decades of the twentieth century. Throughout the Colonial Era, most of the economic activity, population and infrastructure was concentrated in the Peruvian southern region. The prominence of the South had its roots on the population decline during the Spanish conquest and the economic activity driven by the mines located in the so-called "Alto Peru" (currently Bolivia). After the War of the Pacific, many structural changes took place, the modernization of Lima's manufacturing industry began and different mining cycles affected inner regions. Improvements in infrastructure integrated the coastal regions to the domestic market. Since 1950, regional inequality has witnessed a downward trend due to the expansion of the domestic economy and market integration. This dynamism created huge migration flows to these regions and consolidated a new regional distribution of economic activity, with the more dynamic zones located in the capital and in the depression of the highlands.

Julio Martinez-Galarraga, Adrián Rodríguez Miranda and Henry Willebald deal with the patterns of regional income distribution in Uruguay (1872–2012). In this chapter, the authors provide a new data set of regional GDP and GDP per capita for 16 benchmark years. As regards the long-term evolution of regional inequality, the authors find evidence of a persistent decline up to the 1960s with a reversal of the process from then on. The first decade of the twenty-first century, however, shows a new decreasing trend in regional inequality. Montevideo has represented a large share, both demographically and economically, over time as consequence of a privileged access to sea and agglomeration forces identified with a large market of skilled labour. However, inequality decreased; so other factors compensated for these centripetal forces until the 1920s. In particular, the integration of the domestic market with the construction of railways and the motor transport and infrastructure investments reduced trade costs and facilitated regional convergence. Since the 1930s, a high degree of state intervention in the economy meant relevant equalizer forces: altering relative prices/yields, taking advantage of strategic natural resources and promoting public enterprises and extensive presence of Public Administration in the territory. Inequality increased in the 1960s–1990s in the context of a new growth model based on low state intervention, with a greater emphasis on the development of financial and services sectors, and the deepening of international trade with neighbouring countries. After the 2001–2002 crisis, the pattern of regional development changed again and inequality decreased encouraged by a new wave of public-private institutions and the implementation of reforms to promote agro-industrial sectors supported by a notable boom in the commodity prices.

Finally, Giuseppe De Corso and Daniel Tirado-Fabregat present the long-term patterns of regional inequality in Venezuela (1881–2011). Given that the official statistical offices do not compile figures for regional GDP for the most recent period, calculating and presenting this new evidence is in itself an important contribution to our knowledge of the country's economic reality. The evidence on regional income inequality shows that its long-term evolution follows an inverted-U-shaped curve. However, although inequality today is no greater than it was in 1881, along the road a huge gap has opened up between the GDP per capita levels of the coastal regions and those of the interior. This dynamic is the result of two factors. The first of these is the export of natural resources, basically hydrocarbons. The production of these is limited to a few locations across the territory, and this has benefitted just a few coastal territories (first-nature geographical cause). The second is the actions of the state. Although they have not always had the desired results, government spending policies brought about the conditions whereby some territories were able to take advantage of their geographical location, in this case to supply the domestic market, thus boosting their relative growth (second-nature geographical cause). In this sense, the authors conclude that it might be said that "Venezuela sowed the oil, but unevenly".

All this evidence—quantitative and analytical—constitutes substantial inputs to understand the Latin American regional long-run evolution as a whole and to identify common patterns, different trajectories and the main stylized facts. This is the subject matter of the chapter entitled "Spatial Inequality in Latin America (1895–2010): Convergence and Clusters in a Long-Run Approach" written by Marc Badia-Miró, Esteban A. Nicolini and Henry Willebald. Likewise, this evidence opens the possibility to consider comparisons with other regions and this is the subject of the chapter written by Julio Martinez-Galarraga, Esteban A. Nicolini, Daniel Tirado-Fabregat and Henry Willebald titled "Regional Inequality in Latin America: Does It Mirror the European Pattern?"

3 Highlights, Stylized Facts and a Brief Discussion

So far, *Time and Space: Latin American Regional Development in Historical Perspective* represents a contribution in, at least, three dimensions: quantitative, historical and conceptual.

From a quantitative point of view, the volume presents an extensive data set corresponding to 9 countries, 182 regions (states, provinces, departments) and around 14 benchmark years from the end of the nineteenth century to the beginning of the twenty-first century. This constitutes a substantial contribution to quantitatively analyse the economic development of Latin America, identifying the evolution of regional inequality and studying economic convergence and the formation of convergence clubs (clusters of poor and rich regions).

We think that it also is a valuable contribution to the economic history of Latin America. In this respect, we must recognize that some doubts arose at the beginning of the project. Questions like "Did it make sense to propose these accounting efforts in peripheral economies?" "Were we able, in Latin America, to endorse this line of research?" Perhaps it seems futile to try to advance along this study given that several countries in the region had not yet completed their historical national accounts on the production side (while the complementary calculations on the expenditure and income side were still very incipient). However, we had the conviction that many of the distances, proximities, diversities and scale effects the theory deals with are key matters to understand the economic history of Latin America and our effort was much more than a mere academic whim. Is it possible to study the economic history of countries as huge as Argentina and Brazil or as varied as Chile and Bolivia without these considerations? It makes sense to study the economic history of Uruguay without integrating it with that of the Argentine *Pampa Húmeda* and that of Rio Grande do Sul in Brazil? How much of the economic history of northern and southern Mexican territories makes sense without considering the regional borders with the US and Central American countries? So far, it is in this sense that we consider our book a contribution to Latin American economic history.

Lastly, from a conceptual point of view, we think that the identification of true "economic territories" beyond political jurisdictions offers a renewed capacity of analysis and, therefore, having this type of accountability available means opening up new opportunities for explanation and interpretation, and renewed questions and hypotheses. Related to that, to some extent, we could refer to an old *cepalina* category that placed "structural heterogeneity" at the centre of the Latin American analysis of economic development. Traditionally, this idea was used to refer to the disparity between the levels of sectoral productivity, which denoted the coexistence of a small sector of high productivity with an extensive and diverse activities of low dynamism (Pinto 1965, 1970). In this conceptualization, the territorial dimension was naturally incorporated under the idea that economic growth can tend to be driven by the performance of a limited number of local economies within the nation-state, as well as transcending political boundaries in the constitution of true territories of production and consumption. A recent work of Economic Commission for Latin America and the Caribbean (ECLAC) states that "one of the particular manifestations of heterogeneity in Latin America and the Caribbean countries is the huge difference in the degrees of economic and social development shown by the different territories of each country, with localities with living standards similar to those of developed countries and places with a marked backwardness" (CEPAL 2014: 71). This is an ascertainment that has deep structural roots and that should not be neglected in any analysis of Latin American economic development.

Industrialization in Latin America was not the exclusive result of growing protectionism. The state acted in a multiplicity of fields—exchange market, labour relations, different taxation by type of good (exported and imported), research and development support, active role of public enterprises in utilities but also in companies typically owned by private agents—in countries where expressions of structural change were notorious in the production destined for the domestic market, but scarce in the external insertion of the economies. This "truncated" structural change (paraphrasing Fajnzylber 1983) and the preeminence of very restricted (duals) internal markets meant that Latin America continued to depend on its natural resources to participate in international markets for goods and services and this exposed it to recurring pressures of balance of payments. These substantial differences with the developed world do not invalidate the incidence of agglomeration forces, scales economies, transport costs, privileged locations and market potential—the main concepts of the NEG—to explain the economic development of Latin American economies but admit the possibility of introducing other analytical categories or a different hierarchical structuring of analysis. It is in this sense that our book opens, eventually, new spaces for conceptual discussions about the economic development of periphery economies.

Regional disparities in Latin America are among the highest in the world despite its long decline during the twentieth century. Industrialization, the exploitation of natural resources, trade and regional development policies in a context of domestic and regional market integration have been the drivers of this long declining pattern and a regional economic convergence, although its intensity has varied during the different historical periods.

First, during the export-led growth stage, convergence "between" countries explained most of the reduction in spatial inequality. Second, the expansion of industrialization and regional development policies, mostly in big and most industrialized countries (Argentina, Brazil and Mexico), but also in those that made industrial efforts during the 1950s and the 1960s, reduced the inequality "within" countries, maintained the differences between them and demonstrated the most intense period of convergence (in contrast with the experience of industrialized countries). Third, the oil shock in the 1970s and the debt crisis in the 1980s maintained regional differences, although the evolution of the countries was diverse (expansion in oil exporter regions and decline in the urbanized and industrial regions in parallel to the collapse of ISI policies and the progressive opening of markets). And finally, the re-globalization in the 1990s and the expansion of commodity prices at the beginning of the twenty-first century showed a new fall in inequality levels, both between and within countries.

But the result is not a simple process of convergence among Latin American regions. We observe a trend towards the emergence of clusters of regions, especially during the ISI years, in the 1950s and the 1960s, with similar levels of GDP per capita. On the one hand, there was the existence of agglomerations of rich regions in the extremes of the region that we call Latin America. In the North, there were richer regions close to the border with the US and, in the South, the Argentine provinces around the capital and the regions richer in natural resources (abundant land, livestock and oil) in the extreme of the continent. On the other hand, we identify agglomeration of poorer regions along the de Amazonas river in Brazil, Colombia and Perú. Rich regional clusters continued after the 1970s but poor regions dissipated, which would be evidence of a progressive predominance of factors of second nature on climate, roughness, rainfall and accessibility problems, together with a public policy with increasing focus on the regional matter ignored by previous development patterns.

Summing up, we have provided a narrative on the historical evolution of regional imbalances and the circumstances that cause them. By doing this, we feel that we have contributed to what is a current debate in literature on Geography and Economic History taken from both global and regional perspectives at the same time.

References

Ascani, A., Crescenzi, R. and Iammarino, S. (2012). Regional Economic Development: A Review. *European Commission European Research Area Search Working Paper* WP1/03, January.

Cairncross, F. (1997). *The death of distance.* Cambridge, MA: Harvard Business School Press.

Clark, G.L., Gordon, M. P., Feldman, M. P., Gertler, M. S., and Wójcik, D. (Eds.) (2018) *The New Oxford Handbook of Economic Geography.* United Kingdom: Oxford University Press.

Comisión Económica para América Latina y el Caribe (CEPAL) (2014). *Cambio estructural para la igualdad. Una visión integrada del desarrollo.* Santiago de Chile: CEPAL.

Fajnzylber, F. (1983). *La industrialización trunca de América Latina*, México DF: CET.

Friedman, T. (2005). *The world is flat: A brief history of Twenty-first Century.* New York: Farrar, Straus, and Giroux.

O'Brien, R. (1992). *Global financial integration: The end of geography.* London: Royal Institute of International Affairs.

Obstfeld, M., and Taylor, A. (2006). *Global Capital Markets. Integration, Crisis, and Growth.* Series: Japan-US Center UFJ Bank Monographs on International Financial Markets, Cambridge Press.

O'Rourke, K. and Williamson, J. G. (2006). *Globalización e historia: la evolución de una economía atlántica del siglo XIX.* Zaragoza, Prensas Universitarias de Zaragoza.

Pinto, A. (1965). Concentración del progreso técnico y de sus frutos en el desarrollo de América Latina. *El trimestre económico*, 32(1) 125, January–March.

———. (1970). Naturaleza e implicaciones de la 'heterogeneidad estructural' de la América Latina. *El trimestre económico*, vol. 37(1), 145, January–March.

Williamson, J. G. (1965). Regional inequality and the process of national development: a description of the patterns. Economic Development and Cultural Change, 13(4), 1–84.

Wolf, N., and Rosés, J. R. (eds.) (2019). *The economic development of Europe's regions. A quantitative history since 1900.* London: Routledge.

CHAPTER 2

Comparing Different Estimation Methodologies of Regional GDPs in Latin American Countries

Alfonso Díez-Minguela and María Teresa Sanchis Llopis

1 Introduction

Regional income disparities are a stylized fact observed since long in pre-industrial societies, developed and developing economies. In the aftermath of World War II (1939–1945), Western Europe witnessed a period of rapid economic growth, a golden age or *trente glorieuses*, and regional convergence, across and within countries, which came to a halt in the 1980s. Since then, and especially after the so-called Great Recession, there has been mounting territorial tensions in these developed and mature economies, resulting from, among other factors, diverging socioeconomic conditions.

Territorial cohesion has thus become a central theme in the political agenda, academia and press. In fact, it has recently been argued that "regional economic divergence has become a threat to economic progress,

A. Díez-Minguela (✉) • M. T. Sanchis Llopis
Universitat de València, València, Spain
e-mail: alfonso.diez@uv.es; m.teresa.sanchis@uv.es

D. A. Tirado-Fabregat et al. (eds.), *Time and Space*,
Palgrave Studies in Economic History,
https://doi.org/10.1007/978-3-030-47553-6_2

social cohesion and political stability in Europe" (Iammarino et al. 2018: 273). Interestingly, this "threat" has occurred in spite of the vast amount of resources devoted by the European Union to strengthen economic and social cohesion across territories. In short, it appears that policies cannot offset this diverging trend and, from a theoretical perspective, it also casts doubt on the predictive power of neoclassical growth theory.

Similarly, rapid socioeconomic change in China has also prompted discussion of regional inequality in the headlines, thereby bringing about the debate to developing economies. All in all, the regional inequality theme has stimulated research and discussion. Still, regional, namely, subnational, convergence or divergence is a process deep-rooted into the past. Economic historians have for long stressed the role played by industrialization in altering the pre-existing regional dynamics. Sidney Pollard, for instance, outlined the regional character of the industrialization take-off as well as its subsequent uneven development. Similarly, Williamson (1965) hypothesized that the relationship between national economic development and regional inequality would be inverted-U-shaped.

But, the lack of quantitative evidence at the subnational level has constrained research for long. In particular, it has not been possible to empirically test whether an inverted-U-shaped relationship emerged or not. The existing evidence was quite scarce, disperse and barely concluding. Even in developed economies, where national statistical offices have periodically published statistics since the 1950s, regional income or output has been somewhat neglected until the 1980s.[1] Consequently, and in order to go further back in time, some researchers have devoted a considerable amount of effort and resources to reconstitute subnational income.[2]

In Latin America, and in line with the recent experiences of other developing economies, this topic has recently been revived. Still, few countries publish regional or subnational statistics on a regular basis and,

[1] EUROSTAT has regularly published regional GDP since 1995. For earlier years see the REGIO-database, which follows ESA 1979 and dates back to 1979.

[2] There are estimates since the mid-nineteenth century for Great Britain (Crafts 2005; Geary and Stark 2016), for Spain (Martinez-Galarraga et al. 2010, 2015), for Italy (Felice 2011), for Portugal (Badia-Miró et al. 2012), for Belgium (Buyst 2010, 2011), for Sweden (Enflo et al. 2014) and for France (Combes et al. 2011; Díez-Minguela and Sanchis 2019; Caruana-Galizia 2013; Bazot 2014). Additionally, in a recent publication Rosés and Wolf (2019) have gathered some of these estimates and added those for other countries such as Austria, Denmark, Finland, Germany, the Netherlands, Norway, Switzerland and the United States.

at present, there is no harmonized system of regional accounts. Thus, the study of the deep-rooted causes of regional income disparities lacks a building platform, or infrastructure. This book thus presents novel evidence for a long list of countries: Argentina, Bolivia, Brazil, Chile, Colombia, Peru, Mexico, Uruguay and Venezuela. However, data limitations have not permitted the authors to follow a unique and harmonized approach to reconstitute subnational or regional Gross Domestic Product (GDP). This chapter thus briefly introduces and explains the distinct methodologies used.

In general, the estimation of regional GDPs is intimately connected to the estimation of national income or output and as such follows the rules and suggestions of the System of National Accounts (SNA). Normally, the publication of a population census or some sort of agricultural or industrial surveys is used to set a benchmark year. Whenever possible regional GDPs are estimated directly. However, in some cases, limitations in data availability do not permit a direct estimation, and national income is distributed across the territory using a wide array of ingenious approaches. Dearth of data has promoted ingenuity and originality, resulting in the use of a wide spectrum of approaches and proxy variables to construct the different regional datasets. That said, this chapter offers a survey of the methods used to assemble long-run income estimations for the Latin American regions. Our main aim is to alert on potential biases that can surface when comparing across countries.

The chapter is organized as follows. Section 2 briefly reviews the history of the different national statistical offices involved in the elaboration of national and regional accounts. Section 3 presents the different methodologies followed and discusses their advantages and disadvantages, while Section 4 provides a conclusion.

2 A Brief Overview of Latin American Official Estimates

The reconstitution of subnational income is closely linked to the estimation of the national output or Gross Domestic Product (GDP). In Latin America, national accounts were not published on a regular basis until the last quarter of the twentieth century. Following the rules and recommendations of the System of National Accounts (SNA), statistical offices had been in charge of the data collection, tabulation and publication of national and regional statistics. Although population counts and surveys were conducted in the nineteenth and early twentieth centuries, well before the development of the SNA, these historical statistics were, in most cases, scattered and isolated efforts.

Thus, apart from Brazil and Chile, the majority of the national statistical offices were established during the second half of the twentieth century, as Table 2.1 shows.[3] Delving deeper into the matter, it is worth remembering that counts, censuses and surveys, among others, were carried out by different governmental agencies or other entities (Church, …). All this corpus of historical statistics is fundamental because it provides a glimpse of the socioeconomic structure of each country in a period where the national statistics and the SNA were not expressed.[4]

Table 2.1 National statistical offices in Latin America

Country	*Entity*	*Acronym*	*Year of foundation*	*First census*
Argentina	Instituto Nacional de Estadística y Censos	INDEC	1968	1869
Bolivia	Instituto Nacional de Estadística	INE	1970	1950
Brazil	Instituto Brasileiro de Geografia e Estadística	IBGE	1937	1872
Chile	Banco Central de Chile	–	1925	1913
Colombia	Departamento Administrativo Nacional de Estadística	DANE	1953	1825[a]
Mexico	Instituto Nacional de Estadística y Geografía	INEGI	1983	1836
Peru	Instituto Nacional de Estadística e Informática	INE-INEI	1975	1827[b]
Uruguay	Instituto Nacional de Estadística	INE	1993	1852
Venezuela	Instituto Nacional de Estadística	INE	2001	1825[a]

[a]In 1825, a census was conducted in the former *Gran Colombia*, a territory that comprised parts of present Colombia, Panama, Venezuela and Ecuador. In Colombia, the following census is dated in 1835 and corresponds to the period of the *Republica de la Nueva Granada*

[b]In Peru, the first count of population took place in 1827, although the first census elaborated with modern criteria is dated in 1876

[3] In Chile, the Banco Central de Chile, founded in 1925, is in charge of national accounting.

[4] All the countries in this book have carried out census rounds since 1970 following the concepts, definitions and recommendations of the United Nations—Statistics Division (UNSD).

Concerning the estimation and publication of national Gross Domestic Product (GDP), Brazil is the country with the longest official and national time series, starting in the 1940s,[5] while the rest of the countries followed suit.[6] Certainly, most of these offices or centres benefitted enormously from a long and well-established statistical tradition that went back to the nineteenth century in most of these countries. In this context, socioeconomic data at the subnational level began to be published regularly, as Table 2.2 summarizes. In Brazil and Argentina there were early attempts

Table 2.2 Official estimates of regional GDPs by country

Country	*Years*	*Entity*
Argentina	1953	Consejo Federal de Inversiones (CFI)
	1965	INDEC
	1975	Consejo Federal de Inversiones (CFI)
Bolivia	1970	Comité de Obras Públicas de Santa Cruz (COPSCZ)
	1988; 1995; 2005; 2012; 2017	INE
Brazil	1939; 1950; 1970; 1980 1991; 2000; 2010; 2015[a]	Official estimates and Azzoni (1997)'s adjustments IBGE
Chile	1960–	Oficina de la Planificación Nacional (ODEPLAN)
	2008	Banco Central de Chile
Colombia	1980–2018	DANE
Mexico	1993–2010	INEGI
Peru	1970–2017	INEI
Uruguay	1961	Banco de la República Oriental de Uruguay (BROU)
	2008–2012	OPP-INE-BCU[b]
Venezuela[c]	–	–

[a]In Brazil, all the years with official GDP information since 1939 have also estimates at the state level, even if it is just retrospective or an extrapolation rather than direct estimates

[b]Oficina de Planeamiento y Presupuesto (OPP); Instituto Nacional de Estadística (INE); Banco Central de Uruguay (BCU)

[c]Although the Banco Central de Venezuela (BCV) estimates national output since 1950, there appears to be limited subnational information

[5]The first official estimate in Brazil dates back to 1939, while national accounting was annually published since 1947.

[6]The publication of official series of national GDP dates back to 1935 in Argentina, 1988 in Bolivia, 1939 in Brazil, 1960 in Chile, 1970 in Colombia, 1939 in Mexico, 1970 in Peru, 1983 in Uruguay and 1950 in Venezuela by Banco Central de Venezuela and the INE since 1997.

in the 1950s that were followed by Chile and Uruguay in the 1960s and then the remaining countries, except for Venezuela where there appears to be no official account at the subnational level.

Otherwise, dearth of official data does not necessarily mean that the national authorities were not interested in the productive capacity or income of their territories. Previous to the publication of official estimates of regional data, scattered information was published in certain countries. In Argentina, for instance, there were several efforts, one carried out by the *Consejo Federal de Inversiones* (CFI) and *Instituto Torcuato Di Tella* for 1953, another by the INDEC for 1965 and the third by the CFI for 1975. In Bolivia, the *Comité de Obras Públicas de Santa Cruz* systematized regional data gathered by the *Ministerio de Planificación y Coordinación* for 1970. In Chile, the office responsible for territorial planning and coordination (ODEPLAN), provides estimates since 1960 and Uruguay has two unique estimations, one corresponding to 1961 provided by the BROU (*Banco de la República Oriental de Uruguay*) and another for 2012 published jointly by the *Oficina de Planeamiento y Presupuesto*, the *Instituto Nacional de Estadística* and the *Banco Central de Uruguay*. In Colombia, three different institutions have made subnational output estimates to study regional income differences. The first one covers the period 1975–2000 and it was published by the *Centro de Estudios Ganaderos and Agrícolas* in 2004 and the second was made by the *Pontificia Universidad Javeriana* in 1992 for 1970–1990 and the third was produced by the *Departamento Nacional de Planeación* for 1960–1975. Besides, the *Banco Central de Peru* published during the 1950s studies for three regions (Costa, Sierra and Selva).

3 The Historical Reconstitution of Subnational GDP: Methods and Sources

In recent decades, there have been numerous efforts to reconstitute economic activity at the national and subnational level. The implementation of a set of concepts, definitions, classifications, accounting rules and recommendations (System of National Accounts) and the pioneering work of Angus Maddison set up a building platform for quantitative economic history. Eventually, several studies updated the original Maddison database with novel estimations of national income which, in turn, stimulated further research. In this process, historical research delved deeper into the sources to document and analyse regional dynamics, thereby opening a new avenue for research.

The main contributions of this line of research are threefold. On the one hand, it offers a comprehensive quantitative description of regional development for several countries. Rosés and Wolf (2019), for example, summarize the stories of 14 European countries throughout the twentieth century.[7] Second, this quantitative evidence raises further questions and expands our understanding regarding regional development. Finally, these studies have also contributed by creating novel and ingenious approaches to reconstitute several macroeconomic aggregates at the subnational level.

Nonetheless, the reconstitution of economic activity is a data-demanding task, and not all contexts offer reliable and consistent information. With the development of national statistical offices and the System of National Accounts (SNA) came the standardization of procedures and methods, thereby marking a turning point. But this will essentially limit research, in most cases, to the period that spans from World War II (1939–1945) to today. Therefore, in order to better understand regional dynamics along the process of economic development, considerable ingenuity must be employed in figuring out a method or approach to reconstitute economic activity in contexts where data are scarce, unreliable or inconsistent.

Table 2.3 sketches the main approaches used in the historical reconstitution of regional, namely, subnational, Gross Domestic Product (GDP). According to its nature, these can be organized into *bottom-up* or *top-down* methods. Following national accounting, and whenever data permit, economic activity can be reconstructed using a huge and wide array of sources. Although it is the preferred method, the *bottom-up* approach, however, is rarely used in historical contexts except for agrarian and non-complex economies in which a population count and an agricultural survey have been conducted. If data do not allow, several *top-down* methods can be used to distribute national income or output across regions.

As regards the historical reconstitution of regional GDPs in Latin America, Fig. 2.1 summarizes the main approaches employed. As expected, the *bottom-up* was conducted in a few cases. Out of the nine countries in this study, only in three (Argentina, Bolivia and Brazil) was a direct estimation carried out. This implies that the historical reconstitution of regional GDPs depended upon *top-down* methods. More detailed information about the several methods used to reconstitute regional GDPs is provided

[7] Rosés and Wolf (2019) also include a chapter on the long-run evolution of regional inequality in the United States.

Table 2.3 Historical reconstitution of subnational GDP

Estimation method	*Keyword*	*Historical information (main sources)*
Bottom-up (direct estimation)	Income	Wages and salaries, profits (censuses, surveys ...)
	Production	Production (censuses, surveys ...)
	Expenditure	Public and private expenditure (censuses, surveys ...)
		Population counts
Top-down (indirect estimation)	Parametric	Production
		Wages and salaries
		Business profits
	Non-parametric	Exports and imports
		Bank deposits
		Taxes

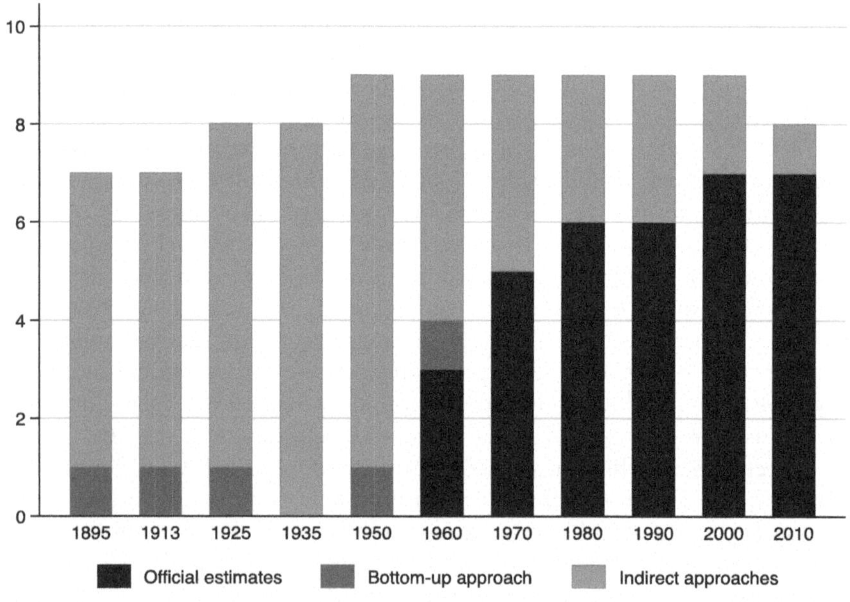

Fig. 2.1 Historical reconstitution of regional GDP in Latin America by method. (Note: Bottom-up approaches red-coloured: ARG-1913; BRA-1895; BRA-1925; BOL-1950; BOL-1960)

in Table A.1. Similarly, official estimates are, in general, derived from the direct estimation of economic activity by national statistical offices or related bodies. Having said that, it is worth stressing that Venezuela is the only country for which neither official estimates nor direct estimations were available. As a result, regional GDPs depend exclusively on indirect estimation methods.

3.1 *Bottom-Up or Direct Approach*

The *bottom-up* approach is essentially a direct estimation of the aggregate production, income or expenditure of a territory. Evidently, data availability is the main challenge since the vast amount of information required to reconstitute these macro-magnitudes is not always easy to gather, especially in historical contexts. Thus, and although data-demanding, whenever possible it is the preferred approach.

3.1.1 Direct Estimates Based on Production

A method based on the direct calculation of aggregate production leans upon a grained set of statistics collected at the subnational level. Besides, it relies on the structure of the economy and, as such, the information is organized by economic activity or sector. That said, sectoral output can thus be reconstituted for as many sectors as information permits, that is to say, depending upon how information is presented and published. Anyhow, most studies have often focused on three sectors (agriculture, manufacturing and services) and have used population counts and surveys (agriculture, industry) as the main sources.

In the specific case of Latin America, agricultural or industrial surveys were rarely published during the nineteenth century, becoming relatively more frequent in the twentieth century.[8] Still, one of the main challenges of this approach is the reliability and consistency of the sources. Industrial surveys often focused on large-scale establishments, thereby omitting the economic activity of small-scale establishments and craftsmen. Under these conditions, industrial value added is underestimated. Not only that,

[8] In Bolivia, for instance, the earliest agricultural census was conducted in 1950. Then, a similar effort was attempted in 1984, but it did not include information on the capital city of La Paz or information on the indigenous communities who mistrusted the data-collection process. In 2012, however, another agricultural census was carried out. Similarly, industrial surveys started to be regularly published since 1972. This anecdotal evidence illustrates the distinct challenges and difficulties faced by census-takers and national statistical offices.

it could be aggravated if there are heterogeneities in the economic structure and establishment size across territories. Thus, even if a direct estimation is preferred there are potential issues that can seriously bias the estimates.

Sometimes the limited coverage of surveys is corrected with historical information from other sources, such as registries. Nonetheless, in our case, Latin American countries were, generally speaking, exporters of foodstuffs and raw materials. As a result, trade statistics have been used profusely. Whenever agriculture was export-oriented and the extractive industry prevailed, the export of cash crops and/or mineral resources left a mark in the customs office, which has been often used to supplement agricultural and industrial surveys.

In the chapter on Bolivia, Peres-Cajías provides estimates based exclusively on the direct production approach for five sectors (agriculture, extractive industries, hydrocarbon, manufacturing and electricity, gas and water) in two benchmark years, 1950 and 1967. Likewise, Aguilar-Retureta (2015) directly estimates the production of the agriculture, livestock, forestry, mining and trade activities for Mexico in 1895–1930. In Uruguay, on the other hand, the population censuses are limited, but there are several agrarian and industrial censuses, thereby allowing the direct estimation of production for agriculture, fishing, mining and energy at different benchmark years throughout the period 1872–2005.[9] Notwithstanding the reliability of the estimates obtained by this way for the different countries, the remaining sectors could not be calculated directly. And, thus, the final datasets are a mixture of direct and indirect estimates.

3.1.2 *Direct Approach Based on Income*

The income-based approach consists of reconstituting labour, capital and land revenues by region. Usually, labour income is estimated using average wages and salaries from agricultural and industrial surveys, and population and employment from censuses or counts. In other cases, such as earnings realized by merchants or those employed in the liberal professions are often estimated using fiscal registers. Additionally, administrative

[9] In Uruguay the balance between the huge number of agrarian surveys (1852, 1900, 1908, 1916, 1924, 1937, 1943, 1951, 1956, 1966, 1970 and 1980) and the limited number of industrial surveys (1936, 1975, 1988, 1997) and population censuses (1850, 1860, 1908, 1963, 1985, 1996, 2011) is quite disproportionate.

information can be employed to reconstruct the labour income of public servants, army and navy personnel and even transport workers (railroads). For capital income, average profits for landowners, industrialists and real estate owners are sometimes calculated using fiscal sources. Anyway, the total number of individuals belonging to each group of factor owners (workers, capitalists and landowners) is extrapolated combining information derived from a wide array of censuses (population, dwellings, agrarian and industrial establishments …). In Argentina, the publication in 1914 of a census with economic and population information provided the researchers with rich data on agrarian and industrial activities that made it possible to estimate regional GDPs based on income directly.[10] In this case, the vast amount of additional sources used illustrates the huge effort in data compiling and pairing required to obtain a direct estimate.[11]

Notwithstanding the accuracy of the estimates provided by the income-based approach, the researchers hardly follow them to reconstruct historical regional GDPs. For instance, in this book, there are only two estimations based totally on income. One is by Araoz, Nicolini and Talassino for the GDP of Argentinian provinces in 1914; the other corresponds to Brazil in 1890 taken from Bértola et al. (2012).[12] Araoz, Nicolini and Talassino take into account the contributions from three productive factors (capital, land and labour). Wages paid to workers across different occupations; rents of physical capital in agriculture, livestock production and manufacturing and services establishments; and the rent paid to land in agriculture and livestock production constitute the basis for Argentinian income calculations. In the Brazilian case, Bértola et al. (2012) identify the occupational structure of the active population and then impute salaries and determine the income of each employment group. Sure, the effort in

[10] In Europe, in countries with agricultural and industrial surveys the researchers have tended to follow the direct approach based on production to estimate the regional value added for agriculture, livestock and manufacturing, as, for instance, Schulz (2000, 2007) does for the Austria-Hungary Empire, Combes et al. (2011) for France, Stohr (2018) for Switzerland, Ciccarelli and Fenoaltea (2009) for Italy.

[11] Several sources have been combined; among them are the *Tercer Censo Nacional de la República Argentina*, the *Boletín del Departamento Nacional del Trabajo* for 1907 and 1912, and the *Anuario Estadístico del Trabajo* for (1916).

[12] Bértola et al. (2012) provide estimates for 1872 and 1895. However, these data have been adjusted to 1895 according to the benchmark fit for this book's dataset.

terms of data compiling is so impressive that this task remains almost exclusively reserved for the teams of the national statistical offices.[13]

3.1.3 Direct Approach Based on Expenditure

Finally, the direct approach based on regional expenditures is rarely used to reconstitute long-run regional datasets. The expenditure approach is also highly data consuming. It usually combines data from different kind of sources, such as surveys on family budgets for consumption, data on investment, public budgets for government expenditure and trade statistics for net exports. It is almost exclusively affordable when there has been a previous task of data collection by national bureaus to elaborate official GDPs at the national level.

3.2 Top-Down or Indirect Approach

The amount of resources and effort required to directly estimate the aggregate income or output at the subnational level has encouraged researchers to look for alternative ways. As a result, several distinct *top-down* approaches have been carried out. Following a specific rationale, the aim is to distribute national income or output across the territory. Regional heterogeneities or variation is at the core of the issue, and national income or output has been distributed following distinct approaches, such as labour productivity, population density or taxes, among others.[14]

Internationally, indirect approaches have been the most prominently used, especially for manufacturing and services, but also for agriculture. They constitute the most suitable alternatives in those countries lacking agrarian and industrial surveys. The indirect approach not only brings to the researchers the chance to redistribute the national output across

[13] The most outstanding example of the income approach was offered by Delefortrie and Morice (1959) for France in 1954. These researchers assembled a well-stocked set of statistical sources to estimate regional incomes. A similar effort was made by Combes et al. (2011) to estimate the manufacturing and services value added for the French departments in 1860 and 1930. In both years agrarian and industrial surveys were available that were combined with fiscal sources, population and establishment censuses and government budgets, among other registers, to estimate the incomes by sector at the regional level.

[14] There is no evidence of the use of fiscal sources in the Latin American countries, but it has been used to estimate the historical databases of the European countries. Some examples are France (Bazot 2014; Combes et al. 2011; Delefortrie and Morice 1959), Spain (Martinez-Galarraga et al. 2019; Díez-Minguela et al. 2018), the United Kingdom (Crafts 2005).

regions by means of a wide set of proxy variables, but it also allows researchers to choose between alternative ways to express the distribution. The methods followed in the datasets gathered in this volume can be grouped into two broad categories: parametric and non-parametric methods.

3.2.1 Top-Down *Non-Parametric Approaches*

In this case, regional income is derived following a strategy that consists of distributing the national income according to a particular rule or norm. Thus, the first step is to calculate the coefficients of proportionality ρ_t for each year t as follows:

$$\rho_t = \frac{Y_t}{C_t}$$

where C_t is the total amount at the national level of the location factor and Y_t is the national income. The second step is to apply the coefficient of proportionality to the value of the location factor into the region i, C_{it} , to obtain $Z_{i,t}$ or the value added of region i in year t:

$$Z_{i,t} = \rho_t * C_{it} = \frac{C_{it}}{C_t} * Y_{t.}$$

The distribution could be done for as many sectors as possible, according to the sector composition of national value added and the availability of potential location variables. In this case, the regional income, $Z_{i,t}$, is calculated as the sum of the value added of the j sectors in the region i, namely, $Z_{ji,t}$. These values are obtained with the use of specific factors' location by each sector, ρ_{jt}, such as:

$$Z_{i,t} = \sum_j Z_{ji,t} = \sum_j C_{ji,t} \cdot \rho_{jt}$$

This approach has been used extensively for the Latin American regions. The datasets of Argentina, Bolivia, Chile, Peru, Mexico, Uruguay and Venezuela contain some benchmark estimates calculated total or partly in this way. Commonly, the value added for agriculture, mining, energy, transports, trade and services has relied on the use of proxy variables.

Throughout the entire book, it is possible to identify a wide battery of them varying according to the characteristics of the region, the sector, and the statistical sources available.

In agriculture, the most common are the share of a region in a selected group of crops, the share in agrarian exports, land productivity of selected crops, cattle stock or tithes payment, among others. Otherwise, the statistical yearbooks of the nations, the official trade customs statistics or the agrarian censuses constitute the main sources for extracting these proxy variables. The different bulk of crops reflects the specificity of each country's factor endowment. While cattle stock, cereals, vineyards and horticulture prevailed in Uruguay, in Brazil cocoa, coffee, sugar and cotton were the most representative; in Chile, however, cereals, vines, potatoes and cattle represented approximately 80% of the agricultural value added, but there were marked regional differences. In Peru, the lack of production statistics has been overcome by using the data for exports. Under the assumption that crop exports are a good proxy, wool, sugar and cotton captured a large share of the agricultural value added.

The extractive industry, mining and hydrocarbons, jointly with utilities such as gas, water and electricity, have also played a relevant role in the socioeconomic development of Latin America. Besides, the value of production has been recurrently used to shed further light on regional inequality. The two proxies most commonly used are the share in value exports of specific commodities and the share in physical production. In Bolivia, the value of exports declared is used to estimate the value added of extractive industries, while the regional production of electricity in thousands of kWh in each department capital is used to compute the subnational value added. Similar proxies are used for Chile and Mexico. In the services sector, the population size, population density, capital cities' size and employment by industry are the usual variables; meanwhile for the transport sector it is possible to count the kilometres of roads or railroads to convert the national values into regional ones.

The main drawbacks of this approach are associated with the representativeness of the variables used as proxies.[15] The closeness to the concept

[15] An interesting example that demonstrates a lack of representativeness is the use of fiscal revenues to make the distribution. Usually, in the past taxes related with the exercise of agrarian or manufacturing activities were levied on individuals. Thus, the individuals subject to the tax did not represent the whole population of active establishments. There used to be some income or size establishments exempt from the fiscal levy and also a high level of tax evasion. In these cases, the fiscal revenues overestimate the output of the richest regions, usually bet-

represented and the degree of coverage are the basic points to question. For instance, in agriculture or mining where the participation in a selected group of crops of exports is used as proxy, the regions heavily specialized in these products will tend to be overrepresented while the regions with a natural endowment not suitable for them will be underrepresented. An interesting example is the region of Magallanes in Chile. This region is highly specialized in sheep cattle, a product with a trifling presence in the national agrarian output. In the same way, the output of the less outward-oriented regions will also be underestimated. Researchers have tried to correct this bias by taking as many proxies as possible or by correcting them with the use of complementary indicators.

One of the most commonly used approaches was introduced by Geary and Stark (2002), called the G&S method thereafter. It is a particular case of indirect distribution based on the use of location factors. Most of the databases on regional income constructed by economic historians over the last decade rely heavily on it.[16] It becomes a good option when direct estimates based on production are not viable. The G&S method distributes national value added of each sector over different regions according to regional employment, correcting by regional relative wages. It departs from the fact that national GDP, namely, Y_n, equals the sum of regional GDPs (Y_i):

$$Y_n = \sum_i Y_i$$

Then, each region GDP (Y_i) can be expressed as:

$$Y_i = \sum_j y_{ij} L_{ij}$$

ter represented by the tax, and underestimate that of the poorest regions where low-size activities predominate (Díez-Minguela and Sanchis 2019). Activities not subject to fiscal levies in the past included the army, public services, professional activities, household activities and small size establishments (Delefortrie and Morice 1959). To correct the biases the tax information should be combined with other sources, such as population, land and manufacturing censuses.

[16] Geary and Stark (2002, 2016) for Great Britain, Martinez-Galarraga et al. (2010, 2013, 2015) for Spain, Felice (2005a, b) for Italy, Badia-Miró et al. (2012) for Portugal, Buyst (2010) for Belgium, Sweden, Enflo et al. (2014), Díez-Minguela and Sanchis (2019) and Rosés and Sanchis (2019) for France, Enflo (2014) for Finland.

where y_{ij} represents the value added per worker in region i and industry j and L_{ij} represent the corresponding number of workers. The historical population censuses allow the extraction of L_{ij}, but labour productivity in each industry, y_{ij}, remains unknown. To solve this problem, Geary and Stark (2002) propose to proxy y_{ij} using the sector productivity at the national level, y_j, rescaled with the relative wages between region *i* and the national average for industry *j* (ω_{ij}/ω_j), according to this equation:

$$Y_i = \sum_j \left[y_j \beta_j \left(\frac{\omega_{ij}}{\omega_j} \right) \right] L_{ij}$$

where β_j is a scalar introduced to guarantee that the national level is equal to the sum of the regions. Hence, this method relies on two big assumptions: first, regional production depends on the number of employees, and, second, the differences in regional wages in specific sectors reflect differences in productivity. Therefore, the allocation of national GDP is not exclusively based on employment, but it is corrected by the relative wages as indicators of productivity.

Compared to the direct approaches, the G&S method is less data-demanding and easier to implement. It only requires data on historical national GDP (Y_n), GDP per worker by industry at the national level (y_j), regional wages by industry (ω_{ij}) and the corresponding number of workers (L_{ij}). However, it presents important limitations closely related with data availability, well with the underlying assumptions on which it rests. The lacking of regional wage data is possibly one of the main obstacles found in most Latin American countries for applying the pure G&S method, along with the difficulty to pair population censuses with nearby wage surveys. But not only that, the use of relative wages to proxy productivity differentials is also subject to criticism. The assumption of labour market integration across regions is not always sustainable, especially when there are serious obstacles to factor mobility or when there is a high presence of non-tradable activities in the economy.

The presence of natural barriers, such as high transport costs, as well as artificial barriers linked to differences in language, culture, local institutions or illiteracy, among others, hinder factor mobility across regions with different development levels. This is the reason why some researchers have decided not to use relative wages as a proxy for relative productivity, even when it is affordable. Another reason to question relative wages as a good proxy of labour productivity is the high presence of the non-tradable economy in less developed regions. Seminario and Zegarra (2016), the authors of the Peruvian dataset, consider that this kind of imperfection is not evenly distributed across regions and it could bias the regional wages. In the more traditional agrarian regions made up predominantly of small size and familiar farms it used to be a higher proportion of peasant family members that do not stand in a regular employment relation, while more institutionalized employment relations were the rule in more developed regions. This fact will tend to reduce the wages of the poorest regions, and hence, to underestimate their output. Aguilar-Retureta (2015) outlined this trait of the Mexican labour market and opted for the direct approach in agriculture; similarly, Badia-Miró (this book) does the same for Chile and adopts an indirect approach based on the economically active population employed in some representative products and land productivity.

At the same time, the wages reflect other spatial specificities apart from productivity. For example, Geary and Stark (2002) do not take into account differences in regional prices, and instead they use nominal wages instead of real wages. Thus, it is impossible to distinguish which part of the increase in nominal wages responds to increases in productivity and which to local price inflation. For instance, the Latin American regions have been unevenly shaken by periods of exports booms of raw materials. Thus, higher nominal wages in the exporter regions are not necessarily a sign of higher productivity and, consequently, the output of the exporter regions can be overestimated if nominal wages are not properly deflated by the regional inflation rate. Geary and Stark (2015) consider that higher inflation rates in a single region do not invalidate their method because they could be a sign of local dynamism and hence of higher productivity. To test the accuracy of their method, Geary and Stark (2015) compare their regional GDP estimates with official data published for the United Kingdom for the last decades and conclude that, given the adequate wage and employment data, their approach yields quite accurate GDP estimates. Díez-Minguela and Sanchis (2019) arrive at similar conclusions comparing their estimates for French departments using the Geary and Stark method with those obtained by Combes et al. (2011) for 1860 and 1930 using the direct production approach.

Notwithstanding these shortcomings, one of the most valuable properties of the G&S method is its flexibility, as outlined by Missiaia and Enflo (2020). The G&S approach separately estimates each of the three big sectors of the economy, and even allows descending to higher levels of disaggregation. In this way, this method is able to produce quite precise estimates of value added by sector, or industry, and also to merge estimates based on the pure G&S method for some industries, with estimates based on other approaches for others. Several researchers have relied on the flexible character of the G&S approach to construct historical regional GDPs.[17] Hence, they follow the finest estimates procured by the direct approach, where possible, and reserve the G&S method for those sectors with more limited information.

The Latin American regions' dataset gathered in this volume presents a lot of benchmark estimates following a mixed approach that merges the pure G&S with other strategies, as, for instance, the direct approach based on production. This way, the benchmark estimates for Brazil in 1872 and 1920 taken from Bértola et al. (2012) are a mixture of G&S and direct estimates. Similarly, the estimates for Mexico in 1895–1930 taken from Aguilar-Retureta (2015) are made up of direct estimates based on production for agriculture, livestock, forestry, mining and commerce, while manufacturing, construction, energy, government, transport and other services are estimated following G&S. In the case of Uruguay, a country abundant in agrarian censuses, estimates for agriculture follow a direct approach, while the standard G&S is used in the manufacturing and service sectors. Hence in the case of Uruguay, three datasets inspired by similar distributive criteria have been assembled: Castro and Willebald (2019) for 1872–1908, Martinez-Galarraga et al. (this book) for 1908–1975 and Rodríguez-Miranda and Goinheix (2018) for 1986–2005.

3.2.2 Top-Down *Parametric Approach*

This method was first proposed by Crafts (1983) to estimate historical income or output for the United Kingdom at the national level. Eventually, this approach was further adapted for other purposes such as the estimation of economic activity at the subnational level. In short, it is a two-step methodology. First, using information for a particular year where regional output or income is available, the following equation is estimated:

$$\mathrm{Y}_{it} = \alpha + \beta_1 \mathrm{K}_{it} + \beta_2 \mathrm{Z}_{it} + \beta_3 \mathrm{X}_{it} + \varepsilon_{it}$$

[17] Some datasets of European historical estimates have been constructed combining direct estimates based on production for some industries with others based on Geary & Stark. For instance, Schulze (2007, 2019) for Austria-Hungary, Felice (2011, 2019) for Italy, Martinez-Galarraga et al. (2011) for Spain.

where Y_{it} is the GDP of region i, and K_{it}, Z_{it}, X_{it} are a set of proxy variables. The second step consists of regressing this equation with the estimated coefficients, $\widehat{\beta_1}, \widehat{\beta_2}, \widehat{\beta_3}$, over the corresponding proxy variables K_{it}, Z_{it}, X_{it} for those years with no available regional GDPs.

Bucciferro and Ferreira de Souza (this book) used a two-step parametric approach in order to estimate subnational GDP in 1905 Brazil, using as benchmark a regression based on information for 20 states in 1920. They used as explanatory variables state and municipal expenditures, the value of exports of seven major commodities (cocoa, coffee, cotton, mate, rubber, sugar and tobacco), the population aged 15 to 59 and a regional dummy variable to distinguish states in the South and in the Southeast. It is worth remembering that this methodology assumes that regional shares were constant from 1905 to 1920. In this way, German-Soto (2005) follows this logic to estimate regional income for Mexico from 1940 to 1992.

The criticisms of this approach have focused on the validity of the explanatory variables, the misspecification of the equation and the rigidity of the coefficients. The representativeness of the explanatory variables is usually addressed by introducing additional variables into the equation. The examples in this book follow this strategy; however, the different level of development of the regions presented a challenge for guaranteeing that the selected variables had the same explanatory power for all the regions. One classical example arises when the share of manufacturing employment is introduced as regressor. In general, this variable suits the most industrialized regions rather than the less developed regions better.[18] But this bias could also be present in other variables such as the population aged 15–59, bank deposits, public expenditure, exports and so on. In general, most of them represent the state of the economy in a modern region than in a traditional one better.

More questionable is the rigidity of the coefficients. A fundamental assumption of this approach is that the parameters remain stable over time. Additionally, the approach also neglects current potential differences across regions with regard to the elasticity of the same explanatory variables. This is a strong assumption, particularly in long periods of substantial socioeconomic change.[19] The bias will be larger the longer the length

[18] This criticism has been tested for the Austria-Hungary Empire by Pammer (1997) with reference to the work of Good (1994).

[19] The stability of the parameters across time has been tested by Díez-Minguela and Sanchis (2019) for France in 1911. They compare regional income estimates obtained using param-

between the benchmark year and the current estimation year. And, consequently, the final results could be quite misleading depending on the intensity of the changes between the current and the reference dates.

4 Concluding Remarks

In the above discussion, we have briefly presented how the dataset has been constructed and the potential concerns. In Table 2.4 we illustrate three outstanding heterogeneities that should be taken into account when reading each case study. First, not all countries in the sample have estimates for all years. Some have a longer statistical tradition than others while historical statistics have "survived the test of time" better in some places. Since historical research relies heavily upon the availability of counts, censuses and surveys it is worth remembering the diverging fortunes of each country, particularly in the years before the development of national accounting.

Another significant heterogeneity is the size and territorial organization of each country. As Table 2.4 shows, there are sizable differences in surface areas. Whereas in Brazil, the average region is 425.787 km^2, in Uruguay it is 9.275 km^2, around 45 times less. Regrettably, the territorial administration is "what it is" and cannot be changed, but it should be borne in mind, especially when comparing regions from different countries.

This, in turn, leads us to the third issue. The above heterogeneities could have biased the results, since there appears to be substantial variation regarding the maximum and the minimum coefficient of variation (CV) found. This bias could have resulted from the above-mentioned heterogeneities and also from the distinct approaches employed in the reconstitution of subnational economic activity. This chapter has addressed some of the main issues. In sum, the indirect non-parametric approach, combined sometimes with direct estimations for agriculture and extractive industries, has been the most recurrent way to estimate output. Out of the nine countries in the sample, seven followed this "mixed approach" and in four of these (Argentina, Brazil, Mexico, Venezuela) the coefficient of variation ranges between 0.25 and 0.80. In Bolivia and Uruguay,

eters estimated for different benchmark years. These results clearly confirm the instability of the estimated parameters and, therefore, question the consistency of regional income estimates.

Table 2.4 Descriptive statistics

Country	*Period of study*	*Number years*	*Number regions*	*Area*	*Area*	*Coefficient of variation*	
				country	*region*	*Max.*	*Min.*
Argentina	1895–1975	7	24	2,780,400	115,704	0.616	0.248
Bolivia	1950–2017	8	9	1,098,581	137,322	0.326	0.169
Brazil	1872–2015	12	20	8,515,770	425,787	0.680	0.288
Chile	1890–2017	64	13[a]	756,102	30,249	1.287	0.322
Colombia	1926–2018	92	16	1,142,748	71,421	0.633	0.528
Mexico	1895–2010	57	32	1,964,375	61,296	0.815	0.471
Peru	1850–2012	162	25	1,285,216	51,408	0.853	0.552
Uruguay	1872–2012	16	19	176,215	9,275	0.456	0.267
Venezuela	1881–2011	12	24	916,445	38,185	0.860	0.257

Note: Coefficient of variation refers to a population-weighted coefficient of variation. The maximum and minimum values are for the period 1895–2010

[a]In Chile there is an administrative change in the number of provinces considered in 1973, from 25 to 13, but there is not a way to establish correspondences between the two classifications in order to maintain the number of regions across the whole period constant

however, regional disparities were less significant, which could be the result of a shorter time span (Bolivia) or smaller regions (Uruguay). In Chile, where a "mixed approach" was followed, regional inequality ranged from 1.287 to 0.322, which can be partly explained by a change in the number of regions, from 25 to 13 in 1973, and dissimilar regional impact of the exporting booms are on the basis of these huge disparities.

Finally, in Colombia and Peru, the reconstitution of economic activity at the subnational level was based on specific approaches. The Peruvian estimates are based on a parametric approach and the Colombian estimates on backwardly discounting the regional growth rates of proxy variables to current official regional estimates. In both cases, it is questionable whether the evolution of regional inequality can be attributed to the economic dynamics of the regions or to the estimation method. Notwithstanding all these issues, the novel dataset presented in this book is an extraordinary leap in the economic history of Latin America, which will hopefully set in motion further research and efforts to better understand the economic geography of the continent.

References

Aguilar-Retureta, J. (2015). The GDP per capita of the Mexican regions (1895–1930): New estimates. *Revista de Historia Económica*, 33 (3): 387–423.

Azzoni, C. (1997). Concentração Regional e Dispersão das Rendas Per Capita Estaduais: Análise a partir de Séries Históricas Estaduais de PIB, 1939–1995. *Estudos Econômicos*, 27 (3): 341–393.

Badia-Miró, M., Guilera, J., and Lains, P. (2012). Regional incomes in Portugal: Industrialization, integration and inequality, 1890–1980. *Revista de Historia Económica*, 30 (2): 225–244.

Bazot, G. (2014). Interregional inequalities, convergence, and growth in France from 1840 to 1911. *Annals of Economics and Statistics*, 113/114, 309–345.

Bértola, L., Castelnovo, C. and Willebald, H. (2012). "*Income Distribution in Brazil, 1870–1920.*" Montevideo: Banco Central del Uruguay, XVII Jornadas Anuales de Economía.

Buyst, E. (2010). Reversal of fortune in a small, open economy: Regional GDP in Belgium, 1896–2000. *Rivista di Storia Economica*, 26, 75–92.

———. (2011). Continuity and change in regional disparities in Belgium during the twentieth century. *Journal of Historical Geography*, 37, 329–337.

Caruana-Galizia, P. (2013). Estimating French regional income: Departmental per capita gross value added, 1872–1911. *Research in Economic History*, 29, 71–95.

Castro, P. and Willebald, H. (2019). "Producto PIB regional en Uruguay durante la Primera Globalización (1872–1908): menor desigualad y convergencia entre regions". *Serie Documento de Trabajo, Instituto de Economía*, Facultad de Ciencias Económicas y de Administración, Universidad de la República, Montevideo.

Ciccarelli, C. and Fenoaltea, S. (2009). *La produzione industrial delle regioni d'Italia., 1861–1913: Una ricostruzione quantitative. La industrienon-manifatturiere.* Roma: Banca d'Italia.

Combes P. P., Lafourcade M., Thisse J. F. and Toutain, J. C. (2011). The rise and fall of spatial inequalities in France: A long run perspective. *Explorations in Economic History*, 48, 2, 243–271.

Crafts, N.F.R. (2005). Regional GDP in Britain, 1871–1911: Some estimates. *Scottish Journal of Political Economy*, 52, 1, 54–64.

Delefortrie, N., and Morice, J. (1959). *Les revenus départementaux en 1864 et 1954.* Paris: Armand Colin.

Díez-Minguela, A. and Sanchis, M.T. (2019). Regional income inequality in France: What does history teach us? *Historical Methods: Journal of Quantitative and Interdisciplinary History*, 52, 1, 1–14.

Díez-Minguela, A., Martinez-Galarraga, J., Tirado, D. A. (2018). *Regional inequality in Spain, 1860–2015.* Palgrave Macmillan, London.

Enflo, K. (2014). Finland's regional GDPs: estimates, sources and interpretations. *Lund Papers in Economic History*. General Issues. N. 135. Department of Economic History. Lund University.

Enflo, K., Henning, M. and Schön, L. (2014). Swedish Regional GDP 1855–2000: Estimations and general trends in the Swedish regional system. *Research in Economic History*, 30, 47–89.

Felice, E. (2005a). Il reddito delle regioni italiane nel 1938 e nel 1951. Una stima basata sul costo del lavoro. *Rivista di Storia Economica*, XXI(1), 3–30.

Felice, E. (2005b). Il valore aggiunto regionale. Una stima per il 1891 e per il 1911 e alcune elaborazioni di lungo periodo (1891–1971). *Rivista di Storia Economica*, XXI(3), 273–314.

Felice, E. (2019). The roots of a dual equilibrium: GDP, productivity and structural change in the Italian regions in the long run (1871–2011). *European Review of Economic History*, 23, 4, 499–528.

Felice, E. (2011). Regional value added in Italy, 1891–2001, and the foundation of a long-term picture. *Economic History Review*, 64, 3, 929–950.

Geary, F., and Stark, T. (2002). Examining Ireland's post-famine economic growth performance. *Economic Journal*, 112, 919–935.

Geary, F., and Stark, L. (2015). Regional GDP in the UK, 1861–1911: New estimates. *Economic History Review*, 68, 123–144.

Geary, F., and Stark, T. (2016). What happened to regional inequality in Britain in the twentieth century? *Economic History Review*, 69, 1, 215–228.

German-Soto, V. (2005). Generación del producto interno bruto Mexicano for entidad federativa, 1940–1992. *Trimestre Economico*, 72, 287, 617–653.

Good, D.F. (1994). The economic lag of Central and Eastern Europe: Income and estimates for the Habsburg successor states, 1870–1910. *Journal of Economic History*, 45(4): 869–891.

Iammarino, S., Rodríguez-Pose, A. and Storper, M. (2018). Regional inequality in Europe: Evidence, theory and policy implications. *Journal of Economic Geography*, 19, 2, 273–298.

Martinez-Galarraga, J., Rosés, J. R. and Tirado, D. A. (2010). The upswing of regional income inequality in Spain, 1860–1930. *Explorations in Economic History*, 47, 2, 244–257.

———. (2015). The long-term patterns of regional income inequality in Spain (1860–2000). *Regional Studies*, 49, 4, 502–517.

Martinez-Galarraga, J., Paluzie, E., and Tirado, D. A. (2013). Trade policy and wage gradients: evidence from a protectionis turn. *Cliometrica*, 7, 3, 295–318.

Martinez-Galarraga, J., Rodríguez Miranda, A., Siniscalchi, S. and Willebald, H. (2019). La distribución regional de la producción en Uruguay, 1908–1975: propuesta metodológica y fuentes. *Documentos de Trabajo, DT 13/2019. Instituto de Economía*, Facultad de Ciencias Económicas y Administración, Universidad de la República, Uruguay.

Missiaia, A. and Enflo, K. (2020). Regional GDP before GDP. A methodological survey of historical regional accounts. In: Molena, M. and Svensson, S. (eds.)

Regional Economic development and history. Regions and Cities. Oxon and New York: Routledge, 82–97.

N.F.R Crafts, N. F. R. (1983). Gross national product in Europe 1870–1910: Some new estimates. *Explorations in Economic History* 20, 2, 387–401.

Pammer, M. (1997). Proxy data and income estimates: The economic lag of central and eastern Europe. *Journal of Economic History*, 57, 2, 448–455.

Rodríguez-Miranda, A. and Goinheix, S. (2018). Estimación del VAB departamental en Uruguay y evolución en el período 1981–2011. Documentos de Trabajo, DT 03/2018. Instituto de Economía, Facultad de Ciencias Económicas y Administración, Universidad de la República, Uruguay.

Rosés, J. R. and Wolf, N. (2019). "Regional economic development in Europe, 1900–2010: A description of the patterns". In: Wolf, N. and Rosés, J. R. (eds.) *The Economic Development of Europe's regions: A quantitative history since 1900,* 3–41. London: Routledge Explorations in Economic History, Routledge.

Rosés, J. R. and Sanchis, M. T. (2019). A long run perspective on French Regional Income Inequalities, 1860–2010. In: Wolf, N. and Rosés, J. R. (eds.), *The Economic Development of Europe's regions. A quantitative history since 1900.* London: Routledge Explorations in Economic History, Routledge, 129–148.

Seminario, B. and Zegarra, M. A. (2016). *La evolución de la desigualdad regional en el Perú: Estimación del PIB de las distintas regiones del Perú, 1795–2012.* https://bit.ly/2xiVCDx

Schulz, M. S. (2000). Patterns of growth and stagnation in the late nineteenth century Habsburg economy. *European Review of Economic History*, 4, 3, 311–240.

Schulze, M.-S. (2007). Regional income dispersion and market potential in the late nineteenth century Hapsburg Empire. *Economic History Working Papers 106/07. Department of Economic History*, London School of Economics and Political Science.

Schulze, M.-S (2019). From empire to republic: regional inequality in Austria, 1870-2014, chapter 3.1, 42–69 in Rosés and Wolf (ed.). *The economic development of Europe's regions. A quantitative Economic history since 1900.* Routledge Explorations in Economic History, London, Routledge, 42–69.

Stohr, C. (2018). Multiple Core Regions: Regional Inequality in Switzerland, 1860–2008. *Researh in Economic History*, 34, 135–198.

Valecillos, H. (1998). *Impactos regionales del crecimiento y la contracción económica en Venezuela, 1936–1990.* Caracas: Banco Central de Venezuela.

Williamson, J. G. (1965). Regional inequality and the process of national development. *Economic Development and Cultural Change,* 13, 1–84.

CHAPTER 3

Productive and Regional Development Policies in Latin America Since 1890

Luís Bértola

1 Introduction

The aim of this chapter is to identify the main stages of Latin American economic development with respect to the kind of productive policy implemented by the states to promote growth and their implications for regional development. Productive or industrial policy is considered in this chapter not only as a sectoral policy, but also as a horizontal one. The relation between industrial and development policy and regional development is not obvious. Regional and local development has become a particular approach to development, departing from the fact that development always takes place in particular territorial environments. There has always been a tension in development studies between theories that emphasize the existence of some universal development trends and those that emphasize the specific features of different regions. Development studies, and local development theories, have always emphasized the limits of very general theories to understand the situation of less developed regions, which

L. Bértola (✉)
Facultad de Ciencias Sociales, Universidad de la República,
Montevideo, Uruguay
e-mail: luis.bertola@cienciassociales.edu.uy

D. A. Tirado-Fabregat et al. (eds.), *Time and Space*,
Palgrave Studies in Economic History,
https://doi.org/10.1007/978-3-030-47553-6_3

have not only different positions in the international or national arena, but also different social structures in general. Thus, policy must be specially designed according to the particular circumstances, given that there is an important difference between development policies inspired by general theories and applied to a territory and policies that depart from the particular features of a territory.

The chapter gives context to the different case studies presented in this book. However, this chapter should not be interpreted as an outcome of the others. The state of our knowledge on regional development is, in spite of the important achievements of the following chapters, still limited. A systematic study of the relation between regional development and state policy should still be performed. Again, this chapter must be seen as an ex ante contextualization rather than an ex post synthesis.

I will mainly use data and information for the nine countries under scrutiny: Argentina, Bolivia, Brazil, Chile, Colombia, México, Perú, Uruguay and Venezuela, but I will often refer to Latin America as a whole.

The nine countries adequately represent the Latin American typology proposed by Bértola and Ocampo (2012): Argentina, Chile and Uruguay constitute the so-called Euro-American societies, Brazil and Venezuela stand for the Afro-American and Bolivia, Colombia, Perú and México stand for the Indo-American ones. The large countries show regions of three kinds, but the dominant feature is assumed as above. Recently, Bértola (2018) included Chile as a particular case, known as Indo-Euro-American. In terms of size, a relevant aspect when discussing industrialization policies is that among the Afro- and Indo-Americans, Bolivia represent the small ones, Colombia, Perú and Venezuela the medium-sized and Brazil and México the big ones.

2 The Big Long-Run Picture

Modern economic growth is a process in which productivity growth progressively surpasses growth due to accumulation of productive factors. In particular, per capita GDP growth tends to be higher than population growth.

If we look at Fig. 3.1 and Table 3.1, we see that this has not been the case for Latin America. The only period in which GDP per capita growth slightly surpassed population growth was the one between 1945 and 1980, in spite of a very fast population growth, the highest during the whole period. That population grew more than GDP per capita during the

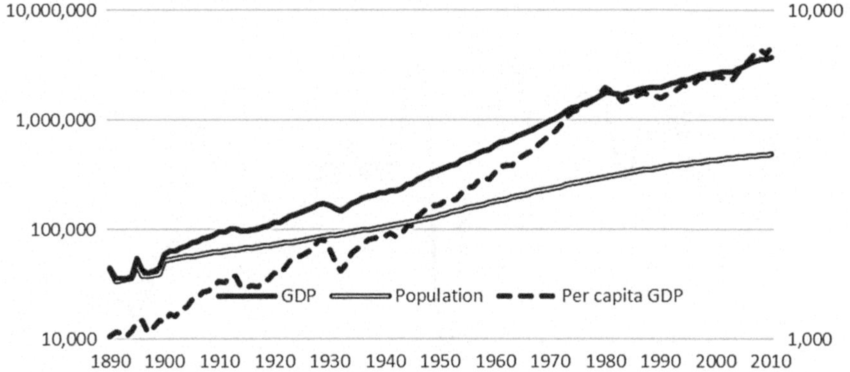

Fig. 3.1 GDP (millions, left), population (thousands, left) and GDP per capita (thousands, right) in nine Latin American countries, 1890–2010 (international 1990 dollars). (Note: Argentina, Brazil, Bolivia, Chile, Colombia, México, Perú, Uruguay and Venezuela. Per capita GDP is a weighted average. Source: Bértola and Ocampo (2012) and for Bolivia, Herranz-Loncán and Peres-Cajías [2016])

Table 3.1 GDP, population and GDP per capita growth rates in nine Latin American countries, 1890–2010 (international 1990 dollars)

	GDP	*Population*	*GDP per capita*
1890–1929	3.5	1.8	1.7
1829–1945	2.6	2.0	0.6
1945–1980	5.6	2.7	2.8
1980–2010	2.6	1.6	1.0
1890–2010	3.8	2.0	1.7

Source: Bértola and Ocampo (2012) and, for Bolivia, Herranz-Loncán and Peres-Cajías (2016)

Note: Argentina, Brazil, Bolivia, Chile, Colombia, México, Perú, Uruguay and Venezuela. Per capita GDP is a weighted average

whole period may not be surprising. What is really a matter of concern is that the last period, 1980–2010, showed the same pattern and reversed the "modern" trend of 1945–1980.

This may be one of the underlying explanations for the fact that the Latin American countries steadily lagged behind the leaders of the world economy, as shown in Fig. 3.2.

Fig. 3.2 Latin American (nine countries) relative GDP per capita (four developed countries = 100) (Source: Based on Fig. 3.1 and Maddison (2010) for the weighted average of France, Germany, the UK and the US)

Relative performance depends on what happens on both ends. The WWII period witnessed extraordinary growth in the US; the 1970s were critical years for developed countries. A short story can be told like this: on average, these Latin American countries showed a clearly lower GDP than did the leading world countries, but could keep growing and even making some modest relative progress until the 1920s; from the 1930s and up to the 1970s, they could manage to grow fast and not diverge, in spite of the explosive growth in post-WWII US and the golden age of capitalism experienced by other leading countries in the 1950s and 1960s. Since the 1980s the divergent trend is clearly noticeable.

As can be clearly seen in Fig. 3.2, and even in Fig. 3.1, Latin American growth is subject to strong cyclical fluctuations. These fluctuations are mainly due to the particular productive structure of the Latin American countries. Their export sectors are concentrated on very few products, live stuff and raw materials, with relatively little value added and highly volatile prices. Besides, exports are concentrated in a few markets (for a concise discussion and evidence of this see Bértola and Ocampo 2012, chap. 1).

In spite of the shallow and scarcely diversified productive structure, the Latin American countries are able to appropriate important rents from natural resources, when world demand is booming. Thus, the economic cycle is speeded up, as the rents from natural resources attract foreign and native investment, domestic demand grows and idle capacity is occupied, with important short-run increases in productivity as an outcome. However, in the medium to long term, technological development tends to erode the rents from natural resources, and the expansive cycle comes to an end. This is a pattern that prevailed since Latin America was incorporated in the world markets, and is still at work now, particularly in South America.

The acceleration of population growth until the 1980s went hand in hand with radical changes in its distribution. During the late nineteenth and early twentieth century, the scarcely populated areas of the Atlantic coast grew the most, due to the combination of high natural growth rates and immigration, particularly in the Euro-American countries. Immigration was also important in some regions of the Afro-American countries, particularly in the Brazilian South-East. However, the Euro-American countries, particularly Argentina and Uruguay, went through an early demographic transition. Together with the interruption of immigration flows since the 1930s, the demographic dynamic of the continent changed, with the Indo- and Afro-American countries showing the highest growth rates of population. In all countries, but at different moments, population growth was followed by an intense process of urbanization (Fig. 3.3).

3 Latin America: One and Many

Following Bértola and Ocampo (2012), the Latin American countries can be divided into three groups: Indo-, Afro- and Euro-Americans. The main feature of this typology is not ethnic origin per se, but the social relations which prevailed in the different societies. As the twentieth century advanced, the main difference between the Afro- and Indo-Americans became the size of the country, an important determinant of inward-looking industrialization. Nevertheless, a recent paper by Bértola (2018) finds that ethnic typology still plays an important role in the twentieth century, especially when considering human development and income distribution.

The three Euro-American countries (all present in our sample) achieved, at the end of the nineteenth century, significantly higher per capita income, real wages, levels of industrialization, literacy rates and many other indicators of social and economic development than did the other two groups.

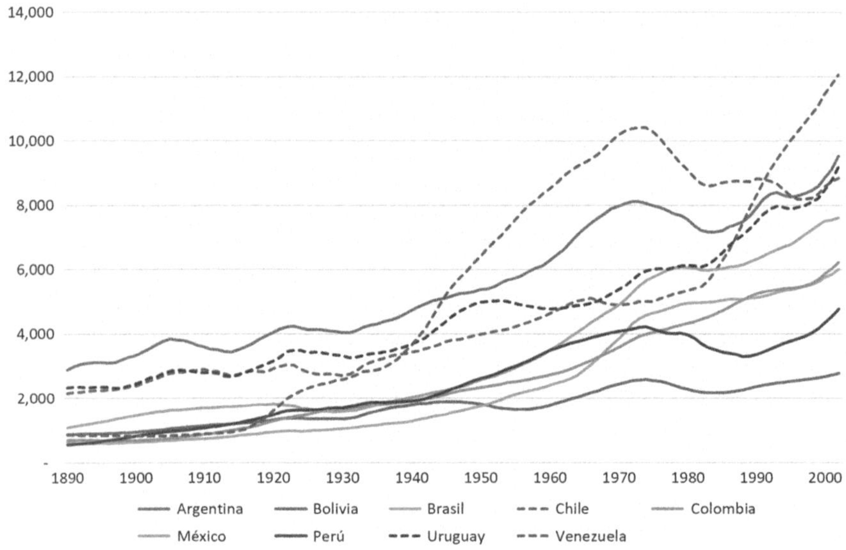

Fig. 3.3 GDP per capita of nine Latin American countries (nine-year moving averages, at 1990 international dollars, semi-log scale). (Source: Bértola and Ocampo 2012 and for Bolivia, Herranz-Loncán and Peres-Cajías [2016])

They also showed, especially in relation to Afro-American regions, lower inequality levels. It is in this respect that Chile departs from the Euro-American pattern, as it showed, throughout its modern history, much higher income inequality levels than Argentina and Uruguay (Rodríguez Weber 2017). These three countries showed an early decline of export-led growth since WWI. Moreover, a paradox found by Bértola (2018) is that these three countries showed, during the industrialization period, the most important achievements in terms of inequality reduction, human development and the creation of social states, while their GDP growth rates were among the lowest.

On the contrary, the Indo- and Afro-American countries did grow more, producing partial convergence among the Latin American countries. Brazil could even narrow the gap with world leaders, even if the gap remained huge. On the other hand, these countries witnessed only modest achievements in terms of human development and inequality reduction. That is why Bértola (2018) characterizes their growth model as a Lewis-like one, as labor abundance, in spite of populist policies, pressed real wages down. México (Indo-American) and Brazil (Afro-American) are the best examples in our sample. Colombia, Perú and Venezuela are good examples of medium-size countries, with important geographical diversity, with important reserves of natural resources and diverse ethnical composition too. A good example of the role of the size of the country is Bolivia. Together with its complex geography and its insular character, Bolivia, in spite of its important natural resources, showed all the time, until recently, the lowest per capita income levels of the region, and remained peripheral to the continent's convergence trend.

4 State Policies During the First Globalization Boom and Their Impact on Regional Development

Our typology also differentiates between countries that produce renewables, mainly agricultural production, and non-renewable minerals. In turn, there is an important difference among the agrarian products: tropical countries do not compete with developed regions, but with other peripheral regions, often labor abundant, which determines the structure of markets and costs, particularly of labor. Countries with temperate climate, often the Euro-Americans, produce the same products as the developed regions, and their labor markets are rather integrated.

Did industrial policy play any role during the export-led era until the 1920s? Yes, in many respects. Nevertheless, it is possible to say that no regional development policy was developed, if we, by that, mean some kind of endogenous local development policies.

First of all, the export-led era was characterized by the consolidation of the central power of the state. The long-lasting conflicts that followed Independence implied the construction of new borders, new capabilities, new authorities and, nonetheless, new identities. It is worth remembering that the Argentine Republic, for instance, was not created until the 1860s. Most of the times, the state was consolidated in authoritarian ways, which often led historians to label the new republics as oligarchic: controlled by the military and political elite, landowners, miners, British capitals and an internationalized merchant class.

The consolidation of the power of the state and the enforcement of property rights made it possible for foreign capital to invest in infrastructure (railways, trams, insurance, banking, telegraphs), in strategic productive activities (mining, slaughterhouses, sugar mills) and in state liabilities.

Even the agricultural sector attracted important investment in irrigation systems, race-breeding, fencing and the like. The main goal of infrastructure was to link the places where natural resources were produced and extracted to world markets. This policy had obvious outcomes in terms of regional development. Large new areas that were previously completely isolated were integrated into the world economy. Infrastructure was crucial: the cost of trading products with Bogotá, Chuquisaca, México City, Quito and Sucre was nine to twenty-seven times that of trading with Buenos Aires and Montevideo, both well placed on either side of the Rio de la Plata (Brading 1969: 243–4).

It is possible to say that the main outcome of this period was the expansion of the frontier. Huge amounts of land were incorporated into the world economy. Sometimes, the process took place within the limits of the newly created national states. The expansion to the north of México, the conquest of the desert in Argentina (in the 1880s) and the conquest of the *Araucania* in Chile are among the most outstanding examples. Expansion, however, also took place by international conquest. The most outstanding one was probably the War of the Pacific, through which Chile conquered the nitrates-abundant North, previously Bolivian and Peruvian territory. We cannot forget the conquest of Northern México by the US.

As an outcome of this process, a completely new map of regional economies appeared, and new social structures were created, hand in hand with radical changes in power distribution in the old areas. The main outcome was the strengthening of the landowning classes, as well as that of merchants and foreign capital, particularly the British ones.

An intensively debated topic is whether there existed a protectionist policy during this period. By the end of the nineteenth century, the Latin American countries had the highest ratio of tariffs to imports, only after the US and similar to other Western offshoots (Coatsworth and Williamson 2004; Bértola and Williamson 2003). This fact cannot simply be interpreted as the prevalence of a protectionist doctrine.

The main aim of import duties was to finance the state budget. Import duties damaged the interests of the export sectors only marginally and were often resisted by the labor movements and the early socialists, as they increased the cost of living. Of course, duties had some impacts on the domestic industry. Moreover, in many countries the dominant liberal ideas were not that radical as to avoid the construction of pacts with some local elites. One example is sugar production in Northern Argentina, which remained protected even during the heydays of the *Belle Époque*. Here and there, industrialist ideas were present, but their importance was small in relation to the fiscal needs of the state, which were mainly related to defense, domestic order and administration.

Notwithstanding that, as time went by and well into the twentieth century, the so-called strategic tariffs were increasingly incorporated into a set of industrial policies in different countries.

As Bulmer-Thomas put it, liberalism in the nineteenth century in Latin America was mainly concerned with the "relations between Church and State, the degree of personal freedom from state interference and the constitutional arrangements between central and local governments", while the arguments for economic liberalism were much less. The most important reasons for that were "the limitations imposed on economic policy by the demands of state finance, the behavior of trade partners and the difficulty of finding fiscal alternatives to tariff revenues" (Bulmer-Thomas 2017).

In Brazil, the well-known expansion of coffee production to the South implied radical changes. Together with the abolition of slavery, an important flow of mainly Italian *colono* immigrants produced radical social transformations, which combined with fast economic growth in that region would create the conditions for one of the most important regional processes of industrialization: that of Sao Paulo.

The so-called liberal reforms, that is, the creation of a free market of land, capital and labor, advanced at a different pace in different regions. The Indo-American regions were the most conservative ones. There, the colonial elites resisted Independence with particular strength and the Independency wars lasted long and destroyed infrastructure and capital. The new republics had to rely on colonial institutions to finance state expenses and the local elites continued to extract different kinds of rents from the peasant communities. Some local traditional economic activities were protected with high tariffs, thus hindering the development of modern industries. However, this is not the same as to protect the creation of a new modern industry.

México is a particular case. The Porfiriato regime promoted a process of modernization and fast growth, in which industrial growth played an important role. Tax exemptions and tariffs were used to promote the expansion of a modern industrial sector that, due to the limited domestic market, could only survive with protection and a high concentration of market power by a few powerful entrepreneurs. The state was directly involved in the creation of enterprises and in the financial sector. The highly concentrated structure of power and wealth that went hand in hand with economic growth was one of the reasons behind the Mexican Revolution (Moreno-Brid and Ros 2009; Haber 2010).

Colombia and Venezuela combined the protection of tariffs and the very limited integration of their domestic markets, particularly fragmented by their geographies, to develop local industries in different regions (Ocampo 2012). While helping to spread production over the territory, the limited size and levels of income of these local markets did not allow them to develop a modern industry and to benefit from economies of scale. For that, they had to wait until the second part of the twentieth century.

Perú is a good example of the role played by investment in infrastructure to develop regional economies based on the exploitation of natural resources. After the guano boom and after the loss of the nitrates in the South in favor of Chile, new regional economies developed thanks to domestic and international investments. Railroads, roads end engineering, and the opening of the Panama Canal, allowed the expansion of the plantation economy in the North, oil production in Piura, rubber in the Amazônia and mining in the Central Coast and *Sierra*, producing increased regional inequalities. While these inequalities reflect different levels of modernization (Seminario et al., this volume), the main explanation behind the process was the possibility to extract rents from natural resources.

In the Euro-American economies, where domestic taxation was very difficult to arrange, due to dynamics of demographic change and the expansion of the frontier, foreign trade duties were the main source to finance the state. Duties were imposed on imports, and only rarely on exports, with the exception of the Chilean nitrates, as this country has the monopoly of world production and could transfer duties to the final consumer. This, as mentioned, was also the case with other settler economies, including the US.

5 State-Led Growth: Strategies and Policies and Their Impact on Regional Development

It is not easy to give a simplified picture of what happened in Latin America between the 1929 crisis and the so-called lost decades of the 1980s. We have already seen that the 1930s and WWII were periods of slow growth. However, they were periods of important structural change.

The measures adopted by the different Latin American countries to meet the crisis combined devaluations (the Gold Standard was finally abandoned), the introduction of multiple exchange rates (originally to favor the export sector, later to promote industrialization), adjustment and the increase of tariffs, import controls and limits to import from different currency zones, currency controls and sometimes state monopoly of currency exchange, defaults on external debt obligations and banning of capital remittances.

Whether intentional or unintentional, most of these measures altered relative prices in favor of local production of consumer goods, both agricultural and manufactured. This is an important point, as not only was the manufacturing industry the winner of structural change, but many crops for domestic consumption or as inputs for local industries were also winners. The degree to which different countries could develop industrial production depended on their previous development. The Euro-Americans, with higher per capita income, had already diversified their economies to some extent, and had experimented with some kind of protectionism to promote modern industry. The same can be said of the two big countries, Brazil and México. In all these cases there already existed important entrepreneurial groups and capital investment, so as to allow industrial growth. However, the contraction of the traditional export sectors counteracted the growth process as much as it promoted the growth of new sectors.

Bolivia was an outstanding case. Without particular conditions to direct growth toward the domestic market, different forces converged to an old-fashioned strategy of conquest of new territory. The Chaco war was a complete disaster, with huge costs in terms of human lives and in terms of economic destruction. The combined effects of the 1929 crisis, the new defeat in the international arena, the enormous disappointment of the population and the deep economic crisis and stagnation were the underlying explanations of the Bolivian Revolution of 1952, one of the most radical in the continent.

During the depression and WWII, the manufacturing sector of Colombia and Venezuela did not grow significantly. In 1950 the share of the manufacturing industry of GDP was around 12% in both countries. Industrial growth was still limited to the sectors that had developed before the big crisis and remained local in character.

The period 1945–1980 witnessed one of the higher growth rates and more structural transformation. It was the result of mainly two factors: the new international environment characterized by high growth rates in the Western economies and more trade-friendly policies, and the existence of more systematic policies in Latin America with the explicit goal of industrializing the economy and promoting related changes. As usual, the results were not homogeneous. The structuralist approach that came to dominate Latin American developmentalism and best represented by ECLA went through a first phase in which external links were seen as critical. However, since the 1960s a similar emphasis was laid on the different domestic factors that hindered development: landownership, state capabilities, the educational system, trade structures and more. As industrialization advanced, the increasing regional differences opened the way for the development of theories and policies of regional development. They played an increasing role as time went by, but they were never dominant and regional development was mainly the outcome of national and sectoral policies.

Brazil was the champion of industrialization: Brazilian manufacturing production made important progress and reduced the productivity gap with the leading world in a significant way (from about 30% to 80% of the Swedish productivity level, Lara 2019). Industrialization was originally developed under populist regimes, under which attempts were made to increase real wages and apply policies with important social components. However, after State Cup 1964, the pattern shifted significantly toward a Lewis-like model, in which domestic demand was driven by middle and upper classes, and at the time industrial production became more export orientated.

The story of the Euro-American countries showed many similarities, even if the timing differed somewhat. Argentina and Chile had a big push in the 1960s, while Uruguay had its golden age about a decade earlier. However, the country's very narrow domestic market, the limits of structural change (Lara 2019) and the attempts to develop an ambitious welfare regime, combined with the deterioration of the terms of trade in the late 1950s, constituted a perfect storm, which led to increasing social and political conflict. The Argentine and Chilean cases, even with nuances, were similar: both, as well as Uruguay, ended in military dictatorships that would radically change the growth model, producing drastic shifts in relative prices, export orientation and later, in the 1990s, a process of de-industrialization.

Colombia, Perú and Venezuela showed important contrasts. Colombia had already started a process of industrial growth in the 1930s. The process deepened in 1950–1970 with the development of new branches, such as paper industries, metal and mechanics, chemicals. In any case, Colombian industrialization was never a real success. The Venezuelan case was worse. Venezuela was part of the Gold Standard well into the 1930s, which meant, for example, a revaluation of the bolivar by more than 60% in relation to the dollar, which implied the collapse of the previously developed industries and showed the weakness of social sectors linked to exports. This seems to be a very early version of the Dutch disease. Developments after WWII included two new orientations. First, to expand state control over oil rents, and second to *sembrar petróleo*, that is, to use the oil rents to promote the expansion of other sectors of the economy, through several institutional innovations. The first one has an important benchmark in 1960, when the state-owned company known today as PDVSA was created, and when oil was nationalized in 1976.

The Peruvian case also shows rather limited development of the domestic industrial sector and its development continued to be significantly influenced by the ups and downs of different primary sectors in different regions. Public policy was mainly aimed at easing private investment in primary production, through legal security, fiscal exemptions and other economic benefits. It led to an important modernization of these export sectors. Mining and oil extraction experienced a steady growth, while fisheries showed a boom until early 1972 and then shrunk to a third of the top levels. As Kuramoto and Glave (2014), state, these processes implied significant technological improvements. However, they were mainly developed by foreign companies and had very limited spillovers in the domestic economy. Thorp and Bertram (2013) point to the fact that national capitals used to play an important role in times of crisis and depression, while foreign capital tended to concentrate property and investment in expansive cycles. As a result, the process of development was spasmodic, uneven and with relatively low productive integration across the country. Different from other Latin American countries, Perú did not experience an inward-looking industrialization. On the contrary, industrial growth was mainly export-led, very much based on natural resource processing, and produced deep inequalities, not only between the regions, but also within them.

The Mexican case is outstanding. The Mexican Revolution implied a radical change in its development, but there is a lively debate on whether the new industries that sustained post-WWII growth were new or the natural continuation of the Porfiriato growth.

By 1940, México was still an overwhelmingly rural society. Since the Revolution, growth has been modest; industrial growth was the leading sector, but its share of GDP did not surpass 15%. However, bad performance seems to have been concentrated during the 1930s, mainly due to procyclical policies and the negative impact of the recession in the US. The industrial process that started with the Porfiriato continued up to the 1920s (Moreno-Brid and Ros 2009: 89–92).

During the thirty years from 1940 to 1970, the Mexican population more than doubled; GDP grew at 3.2% and manufacturing at 8.2% a year. Urbanization increased from 35% to 58%. Many other connected changes can be mentioned. In order to stimulate industrial growth, a protectionist doctrine was clearly adopted, using similar tools as in other Latin American countries. Once light industry developed, policy was orientated toward the development of durable consumer, heavy intermediate and capital goods. As mentioned by Moreno-Brid and Ros (2009), it was not agriculture that subsidized the manufacturing sector, but mainly mining and oil.

The result of these policies in terms of regional development has not been a subject of particular interest in the literature. A study of the most important economic history books of the different countries during the industrialization period reveals that the topic of regional or local development is almost not existent. The main questions had to do with domestic or foreign markets, industry versus agriculture, the origin of finance and technology, macroeconomic policy and industrial policy. Regional development was not a problem per se.

Initially, during the late 1960s and 1970s this was a matter of concern, but regional policies did not have an important impact. It is possible to say that there were two main reasons behind the interest in regional development. On the one hand, one related to the particular pattern of development of Latin America, very much based on natural resources. The negative trend of the terms of trade since the mid-1950s and 1960s, similar to what happened in the 1930s, had an important impact on some regional economies. The second one is military or geopolitical, that is, the concern of different states with their borders, the security over the territory and the regional balance of power.

The first one is the most important and is also two-fold. The extractive model was featured by enclave production in mining activities, with relatively modest spillovers to the rest of the economy. In regions where peasant communities prevailed, they were scarcely integrated into the national and world economy. The main gains of production were concentrated in the big cities or even sent abroad. Thus, increasingly there was some concern about how the benefits of development could reach the majority of the population. In particular, the question was how to create dynamics of regional and local development. This topic came to the agenda very slowly. It is possible to say that, as a matter of fact, this is something that really took an important place in the agenda in the twentieth-first century. And this is one of the reasons behind the research presented in this book. In other words, the concern with local development became important first when Latin America de-industrialized, and the results of a new wave of natural resource-based growth did not reach the wide majorities of the population, and because social policies failed to solve poverty and poor growth prospects. Industrialization promoted regional development, to some extent, as it demanded increasing amounts of foodstuffs and raw materials for the urban population and industries. Some regional cities which were the core of less developed regions hosted important industries, mainly those processing raw materials produced in the regional countryside. These cities were the support for some regional development. At times, they were particularly stimulated by regional governments. Most of the cases included in this volume show that regional inequalities were reduced between 1930 and 1970. In spite of that, urbanization per se is a process of concentration of population, income and wealth, as well as political power in the big cities. Therefore, reduced regional inequality may go hand in hand with high income inequality.

Then we turn to the second topic, that of national security. Since the nineteenth century, investment in infrastructure and logistics had not only an economic but also a military goal, to be able to reach and defend the frontiers. To occupy the landscape was also important, for that matter. Probably, one of the most important projects in order to promote regional development was the creation of Brasilia as Brazil's new capital city in 1960. The original idea dated from the early nineteenth century but was first put into action by the developmentalist regime of Juscelino Kubitschek. The Brazilian economy and population were strongly concentrated in the coastal regions, increasingly in the South. Brazil still had a huge frontier to explore, and a huge territory to defend. However, during the whole period 1930–1980, the federal government could not do too much to revert the process of concentration of wealth, income and population in the more dynamic areas around the Sao Paulo-Minas Gerais axis.

Notwithstanding that, since the 1950s, Brazil took important initiatives to develop the backward regions of the North and North-East. In

1952, during the Vargas regime, the Banco do Nordeste (BNB) was created and, in 1956, during the Kubitschek regime, and with the leadership of Celso Furtado, the working group *Grupo de Trabalho para o Desenvolvimento do Nordeste (GTDN)* was created, which led to the creation of the *Superintendência do Desenvolvimento do Nordeste (SUDENE)*, in 1959, and later the *Superintendência do Desenvolvimento da Amazônia (SUDAM)* and the *Superintendência de Desenvolvimento do Centro-Oeste (SUDECO)*.

However, as compared to the impact of national industrialization policies on the development of cities in peripheral regions, the impact of the specific regional policies was marginal (Monteiro Neto et al. 2017).

In Argentina, industrialization policies had a direct impact on the development of the urban concentrations of the provinces of the Central Area. However, peripheral provinces were incorporated into the industrialist process following the path developed during the previous period, that is, the production for the domestic market of single agrarian goods, on the basis of an alliance between traditional local elites and investors from the core areas, consolidating the minifundia-latifundia pattern of landownership and on the basis of protection to local production. This was the case for sugar and tobacco in Tucumán, Salta and Jujuy, vineyards in Mendoza and San Juan, cotton in Chaco and Formosa, yerba mate and tea in Corrientes and Misiones. The economic and social alliance behind these regional economies secured the investment of federal resources in regional infrastructure. In spite of that, there were important differences in the development of these provinces. A particular situation, similar to the Brazilian West, were the Southern provinces and the territory of *Tierra del Fuego*. There, military reasons were behind the settlement policy, many times accompanied with productive investment for the exploitation of natural resources, as oil. They became rich regions in terms of per capita income, mainly due to the scarce population and the relative abundance of natural resources (Cao and Vaca 2006).

In México, one important policy with an impact on regional development was the border industrialization program. The establishment of Maquila industries in the North was the result of an agreement with the US, which allowed importing inputs to México tax free, if the production was exported. In turn, the US only charged duties over the value-added share.

Other policies of similar character are the free zones. In Brazil, the Manaus Free Zone was first proposed during the Kubitschek regime but was finally created during the military dictatorship in 1967, as an industrial enclave. This free zone now covers a large area of three different estates of the Amazônia. In Chile, in the late 1960s, under the leadership of President Frei, the Iquique Free Zone was first proposed, because of demographic and geopolitical reasons. It was institutionalized during the Allende regime and finally became operational during the military dictatorship in 1975. In other words, the project survived many different ideological orientations as a policy of common national interest. Quite on the contrary, the Arica Free Zone motor vehicle cluster, developed during the 1950s and 1960s, was closed during the Pinochet dictatorship (Gwynne 1978).

In Venezuela, during the post-WWII period, specific funds were created to promote regional development, together with the selection of strategic industries to be developed. According to Moncayo Jiménez (2013), Venezuela was the first Andean country to explicitly introduce regional considerations in its *II Plan de la Nación* 1963–1966. Also, in Colombia, and inspired by the French model, the government of Lleras Restrepo presented a regionalization model in order to articulate development policies and, in 1968, passed a constitutional reform in order to decentralize public administration. In the 1970s the spatial dimension of development was present in almost every development plan, as in the *IV Plan de la Nación* in Venezuela and the *Plan Estrategia Socio-económica del Desarrollo 1971–1991* in Bolivia. The main outcome in the Bolivian case was the steady development and economic weight of the Santa Cruz province.

6 Structural Reforms and the Reactions Against Them: Recent Regional Development Policies

Recent development has been full of different policy measures directed toward regional and local development. Increasing interest in the topic is the result of important theoretical changes in development theory and policy.

Many strands of thought contribute to that. Human Development theory stresses the role of capabilities, the achievement of goals beyond monetary income and the role of institutions. Mainstream theories of development have been challenged on many fronts. Neo-institutionalism stresses the role of democracy, equality, property rights and civil rights. Endogenous growth theories, evolutionism, Neo-Schumpeterians and neo-structuralists stress the role of domestic capabilities in order to take advantage of technological spillovers. These theories are combined with local development theories, which stress that development always take place within certain territories, with particular natural, economics, social and institutional conditions. Thus, success is the result of complex combinations of factors. Economic development, on its own, tends to reproduce important inequalities at the regional level, a reason why development policies must be strongly anchored in the particularities of every territory.

These particular ideas found fertile ground in Latin America due to three processes. First, Latin Americas divergence was deepened since the 1980s. Second, in the countries which did not experience a profound process of industrialization, regional inequality decreased depending on natural resource endowments, but inequality within the dynamic regions remained very high, as social transformation was limited and wealth highly concentrated. Policy was needed to produce spillovers. Third, the countries in which structural change advanced more, regional disparities increased, but, at the same time, social inequalities were reduced or controlled and living standards had increased for most of the population. After the structural reforms, the more industrialized regions faced de-industrialization, increasing unemployment and increasing inequality. Inequality increased within the regions. Natural resource-based development per se did not guarantee improvements in living conditions and the benefits of export-led growth reached a minority.

During the first decade of the twenty-first century, many Latin American countries were governed by leftist regimes that tried to reduce the social gap developed particularly during the period of structural reforms. In doing that, people from less developed regions were benefited. However, it is not clear whether these regions could develop economic and social structures able to make these new benefits sustainable in time.

In Argentina, the dominant discourse was the substitution of efficiency for subsidy. The territories should depend on their rate of return. State enterprises, regional elites, the old industrial elite gave place to a new financial elite and the entrepreneurial sector linked to agrobusiness in the *Pampa Húmeda*. A general increase in inequality took place. In the Southern provinces, and after the democratic transition, a significant reduction of resources direct toward national security took place, as the confrontation with Chile was significantly reduced. Privatization of state-owned enterprises, such as *Yacimientos Petrolíferos Fiscales (YPF)*, led to the paradox of increased production but a significant reduction of re-investment in the territory, reproducing the old enclave economy model. The peripheral regions experienced a dual process: the deregulation process left them without the benefits to their productive sector. On the other side, the reintroduction of democracy gave them institutional stability and legitimacy to bargain federal resources for investment in infrastructure (Cao and Vaca 2006).

In Brazil, the crisis of the 1980s and the *Plano Real* of 1995 implied a significant reduction of the state budget and state policies directed toward productive development. The impact on the regional economies was huge and negative. The *superintendencias* were transformed into regional development agencies, with reduced attributions (Monteiro Neto et al. 2017).

Two different factors helped to produce an important policy change in favor of regional development policies: the new expansive economic cycle that lasted until the beginning of the 2010s and the new government of the *Partido dos Trabalhadores*.

The new policy present in the *Política Nacional de Desenvolvimento Regional (PNDR)* tried to overcome the shortcomings of the previous policy: the increased disparities in the per capita income of different states; the concentration of resources in the metropolitan areas of the backward regions; the failure of development policies in the arid regions of the North-East; the failure of the industrialization policies in the Amazônia. The new policy had very ambitious goals and a wide conceptual base, full of considerations on human development, trans-scale and multidimensional approaches, transparency, social participation and more. The priority regions were the North-East, the frontier regions and the depopulated regions.

However, the resources available for this policy were limited; the *Fundo Nacional de Desenvolvimento Regional (FNDR)* was never implemented and regional policy continued to be highly dependent on national and sectoral policies (Monteiro Neto et al. 2017).

Perú has experienced, since the 1990s, a process of profound economic liberalization, especially in relation to trade. Free Trade Agreements with the US, Chile and Canada coincided later with the commodity price boom, which attracted significant foreign investment in the mining sector. This process went hand in hand with a decentralization policy that transferred to the regional and local governments much of the responsibilities in terms of social policy and services. The different territories have quite different capabilities and economic resources, and many regional economies, such as Huancavelica and the Amazônia, are scarcely integrated. The public sector, on the other side, is extremely fragmented and organized in unnecessarily small local units, with very little institutional capabilities (Neyra 2011).

Bolivia followed a similar path. The New Economic Policy of Paz Estensoro was clearly in line with the liberalizing trend: reduce state intervention to investment in infrastructure and social services, promote the private sector and foreign direct investment. In terms of regional development, it substituted the idea of decentralization for that of regional development policy. The leftist reaction of the Evo Morales government and its development plans did not have territory as a particular issue. The emphasis was rather on the pluri-national character of the state, strengthening the autonomy of the indigenous people in different regions. The *Complejos Productivos Integrales*, inspired by the concept of endogenous local development, had important implications in terms of regional development. They emphasized the role of coordination of local actors, together with the role of the central government to promote redistribution of wealth and income. Not even in the second development plan of Morales was territory one of the four development axes.

Precisely as the previously radical developmentalist Paz Estensoro performed the neo-liberal agenda in Bolivia, the previously state capitalism defender Carlos Andrés Pérez was the one that led the neo-liberal turn in Venezuela. Accepting that market economy implies unequal regional development, the negative outcomes were to be counteracted by transfers of public funds to the backward regions. Regional development policies were thus weakened. In contrast with Bolivia, and even Ecuador, the leftist turn in Venezuela recovered the pre-liberalization era's orientations, promoting a wide set of institutions that aimed to achieve an even development in the territory. However, this process, far from empowering local and regional authorities, was strictly led by the central state, thus weakening the capabilities of local authorities.

Colombia followed a similar path of substitution of decentralization for regional development policies, but in this case, policies were tainted and dyed by the increasing role of military insurrection, a reason why decentralization was mainly directed toward the empowerment of local elites in order to strengthen the presence of the state. While since the period of structural reforms regional development policies lost their significance, they never completely disappeared; they mainly continued as the territorial expression of sectoral policies. However, the Santos government, 2010–2014, placed regional development as a pivotal element. As in many other countries, Colombia also experienced, even if marginally, different initiatives of development policies, based on the territory, as industrial parks, productive clusters and the like (Moncayo Jiménez 2013).

7 Concluding Remarks

This chapter aimed to give some context to the following studies on regional development in some Latin American countries. The focus was on the main dynamics of the development of the different countries and on the main productive policies implemented, considered in bold terms. We paid particular attention to the existence of development policies that considered regional development as a particular policy approach.

During the first globalization boom, up to 1930, the most important policies with an impact on regional development were the set of policies directed toward the consolidation of the central power of the state to enforce property rights and to invest in infrastructure and logistics. This set of policies made it possible to exploit the natural resource base. In terms of regional development, it can be labeled as a passive policy, as the regions were developed according to their natural endowments, the availability of labor extracted under different social forms and depending on international demand and prices. However, regional development always had a political, military component, in terms of the defense of the territory. Moreover, the consolidation of the national states often went over the national borders and ended in international conflicts, such as the Pacific War. In terms of productive policy, tariffs played an important role as they, during a long period of time, were the main source of resources for the state. In more conservative countries, the protectionist tradition was inherited from the logic of the colonial times. In more liberal regions, they were a fiscal need, but they were increasingly used as a systematic protectionist policy for domestic industries.

After the 1929 crash and during the depression, the Latin American countries were forced to be much more active in terms of productive policy. The initial reactions were spontaneous, with the aim to recover equilibrium in the context of a drastic reduction of world trade. It was first after WWII that more articulated industrialization policies took place. By then, regional development was not a problem of particular concern. On the contrary, industrialization, urbanization and the development of services implied an important concentration of income, wealth and political power in the big cities. Some development of regional centers took place, processing new agricultural and mineral products, and in minor cities, but this was not a priority of development policies. Toward the 1960s more clear attempts were made to develop some regional economies, particularly through the creation of free zones, as in the Brazilian Amazônia, Northern México and Northern Chile. The outcomes were the result of national and sectoral policies, rather than of regional development policy, as we understand it today. In many cases, geopolitical considerations were present. In any case, the 1960s and 1970s saw a slow and continued process of planning activity in which regional development was taking an increasing role.

The structural reforms interrupted this process. Together with the bet to rely on private and foreign investment and reduce the sphere of engagement of the state in the development process, decentralization policies were stimulated. However, decentralization did not mean regional development policy, but local administration of reduced resources, limited to social expenses and infrastructure. In turn, local governments became more and more dependent on the national budget. The regional development policy did not attempt to counteract the disparities arising from allocation according to market mechanisms.

Many intellectual reasons may lie behind the increased interest in local and regional development during the last decades. It coincided partly with the change of political winds in the region, where many countries moved to the left. However, I want to emphasize the fact that the outcomes of industrialization in terms of concentration of power and income, and the process of de-industrialization, both created severe problems for the development of different regions of the Latin American countries. During the so-called structural reforms, and as the agricultural commercial sector improved productivity, and industrial employment receded, an increasing share of the Latin American population enlarged the informal sector, with many of them living in miserable conditions. While the recent commodity boom helped to alleviate these conditions and reduce inequality and poverty, the current situation is pressing many families into poverty again. In spite of its increasing intellectual and policy role, regional development policies are still lacking a powerful impact in Latin America.

To combine export-led growth with increasing diversity of exports, based on more complex and deeper productive structures, with an expansion of domestic demand, including a more ambitious supranational regional integration, seems to be the goals that local and regional development policies should aim for. On the other side, national development policies need to be deeply rooted in the different particularities of the territory and its complex composition.

References

Bértola, L. (2018). Viewed up close nobody is normal: industrialization and income inequality in Latina America, Paper presented at the presidential session, *World Economic History Congress*, Boston 2018.

Bértola, L. and Ocampo, J. A. (2012). *The Economic Development of Latin America since Independence*, Oxford University Press.

Bértola, L. and Williamson, J. G. (2003). Globalization in Latin America before 1940. In Bulmer-Thomas, V., Coatsworth, J. H. and Cortés-Conde, R. (eds.), *The Cambridge Economic History of Latin America, Volume II The long Twentieth Century*, Cambridge University Press.

Brading, C. W. (1969). Un analisis comparativo del costo de la vida en diversas capitales de Hispanoamérica. *Boletín Histórico de la Fundación John Boulton* 20 (March): 229-63.

Bulmer-Thomas, V. (2017). *Freedom to Trade, Free Trade and Laissez-faire: economic liberalism in 19th century Latin America*, Conference at the Doctoral Program in Economic History, Faculty of Social Sciences, Montevideo.

Cao, H. and Vaca, J. (2006). Desarrollo regional en la Argentina: la centenaria vigencia de un patrón de asimetría territorial. *EURE*, Vol. XXXII, 95, 95-111.

Coatsworth, J. H. and Williamson, J. G. (2004). The roots of Latin American protectionism: looking before the Great Depression. In Estevadeordal, A., Rodrik, D., Taylor, A. M. and Velasco, A. (eds.). *Integrating the Americas: FFTA and Beyond*. Harvard University Press.

Gwynne, R. N. (1978). Government planning and the location of the motor vehicle industry in Chile. *Tijdschrift Voor Economische En Sociale Geografie*, *69*, 130–140.

Haber, S. (2010). Mercado interno, industrialización y banca, 1890–1929. In Kuntz, S. (ed.). *Historia Económica General de México. De la colonia a nuestros días*, El Colegio de México.

Herranz-Loncan, A. and J.A. Péres-Cajías (2015), "Tracing the reversal of fortune in the Americas: Bolivian GDP per capita since the mid-nineteenth century", Cliométrica.

Herranz-Loncán, A. and Peres-Cajías, J. A. (2016). Tracing the Reversal of Fortune in the Americas. Bolivian GDP per capita since the mid-nineteenth century. *Cliometrica*, 10 (1), 99–12

Kuramoto, J. and Glave, M. (2014). Extractivismo y crecimiento económico en el Perú, 1930–1980. In Contreras, C. (ed.). *Compendio de historia económica V: la economía peruana entre la gran depresión y el reformismo militar, 1930–1980*. Instituto de Estudios Peruanos, Lima.

Lara, C. (2019), *Manufacturing performance in international perspective: New evidence for the Southern Cone*, Ph.D. Dissertation in Economic History, Faculty of Social Sciences, Universidad de la República, Uruguay.

Maddison, A. (2010). Historical Statistics. PIB and population data. Recuperat de http://www.ggdc.net/maddison/Historical_Statistics/horizontal-file_02-2010.xls

Moncayo Jiménez, E. (2013). La Evolución de las Polítias Regionales en los países andinos: una visión comparativa. *Documentos y Aportes en Administración Pública y Gestión Estatal*, 13, 21, 7–39.

Monteiro Neto, A, Costa, M. A., Mendes Resende, G., Cronemberger Mendes, C. and Pereira Galindo, E. (2017). Desenvolvimento Territorial no Brasil: Reflexöes sobre políticas e instrumentos no periodo recente e propostas de aperfeiçoamento. In Monteiro Neto, A., Nunes de Castro, C. and Brandão, C. A. (eds.). *Desenvolvimento Regional no Brasil: políticas, estratégias e perspectivas*. IPEA.

Moreno-Brid, J. C. and Ros, J. (2009). *Development and Growth in the Mexican Economy. A Historical perspective*. Oxford University Press.

Neyra, G. (2011). *Propuestas para la política nacional de desarrollo regional en el Perú*. CIES, Lima.

Ocampo, J. A. (2012). La Historia Divergente de las Economías Grancolombianas. In Bértola, L. and Gerchunoff, P. (eds.), *Institucionalidad y Desarrollo Económico en América Latina*, CEPAL, Santiago de Chile.

Rodríguez Weber, J. (2017). *Desarrollo y Desigualdad en Chile (1850–2009)*, Centro de Investigaciones Diego Barros Arana, Santiago de Chile.

Thorp, R. and Bertram, G. (2013). *Perú 1890–1977: crecimiento y políticas en una economía abierta*. Lima: Mosca Azul Editores, Fundación Friedrich Ebert, Universidad del Pacífic.

CHAPTER 4

Growth and Convergence Among Argentine Provinces Since 1895

María Florencia Aráoz, Esteban A. Nicolini, and Mauricio Talassino

1 Introduction

The changing evolution of income per capita in Argentina in the last 150 years generates one of the best-known puzzles in the economic history of Latin America. Growth rates of real per capita Gross Domestic

M. F. Aráoz (✉)
CIEDH—Universidad del Norte Santo Tomás de Aquino, Tucumán, Argentina

Universitat de Barcelona, Barcelona, Spain
e-mail: faraoz@unsta.edu.ar

E. A. Nicolini
CIEDH—Universidad del Norte Santo Tomás de Aquino, Tucumán, Argentina

INVECO—Universidad Nacional de Tucumán, Tucumán, Argentina

M. Talassino
CIEDH—Universidad del Norte Santo Tomás de Aquino, Tucumán, Argentina

CONICET, Buenos Aires, Argentina

Universidad de San Andrés, Buenos Aires, Argentina

D. A. Tirado-Fabregat et al. (eds.), *Time and Space*,
Palgrave Studies in Economic History,
https://doi.org/10.1007/978-3-030-47553-6_4

Product (GDP) fluctuate around a trend of 1.2% per year between the second half of the nineteenth century and the 1970s and then decrease dramatically to zero until the end of the century (Ferreres 2010; Buera et al. 2011). In relative terms, Argentina's level of income per capita showed a clear deterioration vis-à-vis both developed economies and other land-abundant offshoots like Australia and Canada (Hofman 2001; Sanz Villarroya 2009). While in 1895, Argentina was at the very top of the global distribution of national incomes per capita, today it is a middle-income economy in the group of developing countries.

Until very recently, it was impossible to make any precise assessment of the regional dimension of this process of economic transformation before the 1950s. The first available consistent estimation of the GDP of the provinces in Argentina was for 1953 showing that the three richest districts in the country were Tierra del Fuego, Santa Cruz (both in the very south of Patagonia) and the city of Buenos Aires (CFI-ITDT 1965) (*Consejo Federal de Inversiones-Instituto Torcuato Di Tella*). For the period before that year, we have some individual estimations of the GDP for a few provinces,[1] but there is no comparable estimation of their per capita incomes or any other macromagnitude. There are hypotheses and qualitative evidence that, since pre-colonial times, there was a process of reversal in the relative economic affluence of regions within the current boundaries of Argentina. The south of the country, sparsely populated and relatively poor in the sixteenth century, would have become the richest and more affluent area in the twentieth century (Maloney and Valencia Caicedo 2016); however, the timing of this process of reversal is not completely clear.

During colonial times the northwest of the country was the most densely populated and probably the richest area because of its proximity to the mining areas of Alto Perú (today Bolivia). The mountainous areas close to the Andes, in the West, specialised in artisanal wine, liquors and raw textiles, and some of them exploited their comparative advantage in cattle raising for both transportation (mules) and meat (cows) (Sempat Assadourian 1982). Since the eighteenth century, the regional history of Argentina is dominated by the expansion of Buenos Aires and its prevalence over the other provinces in both economic and political terms.

After independence in 1816, internal conflicts arose because of the unbalanced power of Buenos Aires in the decision-making process of the

[1] For Mendoza, see Coria López (2008); for Salta, see Antonelli et al. (2011).

former territories of the Viceroyalty of Río de la Plata and over the newly designed policies on external trade and the control of customs. The end of the civil wars and the process of constitutional and political organisation initiated in 1853 was the result of the predominance of Buenos Aires over the other provinces combined with compromises with some economies of the interior.[2] The export-led process of growth, dominant during the second half of the nineteenth century, confirmed the relative importance of the areas close to the River Plate and suitable for cereal cultivation and cattle raising. The incorporation of new territories previously occupied by native populations in the north and the south of the country generated a kind of a frontier economy where the very low population density generated, initially, high labour productivity.[3]

The political and economic changes in the central decades of the twentieth century with a more inward-looking development strategy reinforced the process of industrial growth, mostly concentrated in the city of Buenos Aires, that consolidated its role as the main economic and political pole in the country. During the twentieth century, many provinces in the south of the country also experienced high growth rates, at least partially due to the oil boom after the 1940s and, particularly, in the 1960s (Maloney and Valencia Caicedo 2016; Rapoport 2008).

In this chapter, we put together the results of a collective effort that generated the first complete set of consistent estimations of the GDPs of the Argentine provinces for selected benchmarks since 1895. These estimations do not only open the possibility to reconstruct the regional history of the GDP per capita since the nineteenth century but also generate, as a by-product, a long run view of a broad set of measures of the

[2] In the national Constitution of 1853, the legislative power was split between a Senate (with fixed representation by province) and a Representative Camera (*Cámara de Diputados*) where the representation of each province was proportional to its population. This solution tried to minimize the conflict between the "large" provinces like Buenos Aires and the "small" provinces like many of the traditional provinces in the North. See Gallo and Cortés Conde (1995).

[3] In the current distribution of the provinces in Argentina, we can distinguish the fourteen "traditional" provinces (Buenos Aires, Entre Ríos, Corrientes, Santa Fe, Córdoba, San Luis, Mendoza, San Juan, La Rioja, Catamarca, Santiago del Estero, Tucumán, Salta and Jujuy), the nine national territories that were incorporated into the national political control only at the end of the nineteenth century and will eventually become provinces with all their rights in the middle of the twentieth century (Misiones, Chaco, Formosa, La Pampa, Neuquén, Río Negro, Chubut, Santa Cruz, Tierra del Fuego) and the city of Buenos Aires (or Capital Federal). See political division of Argentina in maps on Figure 4.1, in Sect. 4 of this chapter.

economic structure of the provinces and regions like wages, occupational structure, capital stock in industries and services, agricultural land use and production, among others. The analysis of these figures confirms some intuitions that economic historians had about the regional characteristics of the process of Argentine economic development and suggests new insights that open some interesting avenues for further research.

The rest of the chapter is organised as follows. In Sect. 2, we present the main characteristics of the historical evolution of Argentina since the second half of the nineteenth century. In Sect. 3, we describe the methodology to generate completely new estimations of regional GDP between 1895 and 1946, and a description of the sources used by official and semi-official statistical offices for estimating provincial GDPs for the benchmarks 1953, 1965, 1975, 1986, 1993 and 2004. In Sect. 4, we discuss the main results. The conclusions of Sect. 5 close this chapter.

2 The Economic Evolution of Argentina Since 1895

Argentina was born as an independent country in the year 1816. However, the first National Constitution was sanctioned in 1853. The previous period was dominated by generalised conflicts and struggles, both internal and external, that postponed any attempt of political and economic organisation. The year 1880 marked both an institutional and an economic starting point for Argentina (Gerchunoff and Llach 2009). In the subsequent years, Argentina enthusiastically joined the global markets of goods, services and productive factors and became an example of rapid income growth based mainly on the exploitation of abundant fertile land and comparative advantages in the production of primary goods (wool, meat, cereals) for international markets.

After the military expansion of *Conquista del Desierto* (1879–1885)[4] that incorporated the territories of the south of the country to the national economy, the 1880s brought the first massive immigration explosion, allowing a significant increase in the labour supply. At the same time, a

[4] The Campaigns to the Desert, often known as "The Conquest of the Desert", were a set of military actions carried out by the Argentine government in the northern (Chaco) and southern territories (current areas of La Pampa, Neuquén, Río Negro, Chubut, Santa Cruz and Tierra del Fuego) of the country. The objective was to recover the sovereign dominance of those territories mainly occupied by aborigines and to subdue them (Bandieri 2009).

substantial inflow of foreign investment, mostly in infrastructure and railways, increased productive capital and reinforced the expansion of agro-pastoral lands. The conjunction of these factors gave rise to an enormous growth of the production of maize, wheat, meat and wool; production in the primary sector accounted for 36.5% of the Argentine GDP in 1895 (Cortés Conde 1994).

Secondary and tertiary sectors also expanded during this period until World War I (WWI) but at a slower pace. The industries processing local raw materials for both exports (chilled meat and grain processing) and domestic consumption (food and beverages) led the growth of manufactures, with a high concentration in the city of Buenos Aires. In 1914 these branches accounted for 42% of total industrial production (Aráoz and Nicolini 2020).

This model of economic development changed after WWI and the worldwide recession of the 1930s. The international flow of goods, services and productive factors shrunk, and the country responded to the international context with higher levels of public intervention in the economy, higher and selective tariffs, control of the exchange rate, stimulus to the industrial sector and a process of import substitution. In 1936, Argentina had the second-largest industrial sector in South America (in relative terms), encompassing not only the traditional sectors of food processing but also other sectors oriented to the internal market, such as textiles, metals and electricity (Gerchunoff and Llach 2018).

The promotion of the national industries was an explicit goal of the military government that arose in the revolution of 1943, reinforced later during the Peronist government (1946–1951; 1951–1955). It can be considered that this policy was partially successful: while in 1929, 45% of manufactures consumed in the country were imported, twenty years later, that proportion was 15%. Notwithstanding, industrial manufacturing was characterised by high relative costs and low export possibilities (Gerchunoff and Llach 2018).

In the 1950s, this model of high state intervention showed clear signs of decline. The economic tensions due to the scarcity of reserves, the deficit, both fiscal and external, as well as inflation would be constant throughout this period. A significant crisis in 1952 forced the Peronist government to reformulate the policies that had been in force since 1946 and had had great initial success. Higher support to primary activities and exports were granted, the government expenditure was reduced, the expansive wage policy was restrained and the policy of subsidised credit for the manufacturing sector was moderated. Perhaps one of the most innovative policies regarding investment was the intent of the Peronist government to subscribe to international agreements to exploit oil production. However, the strong pressure from pro-government and opposition sectors, highly influenced by nationalist ideas, meant that this could only be materialised in 1958, with Frondizi at the head of the Executive Power. That year, exploitation contracts with foreign oil companies were signed (Gerchunoff 1989; Belini and Korol 2012).

Between 1955 and 1973 there was an alternation of dictatorial governments and civil governments democratically elected but with a banned Peronist movement. Economic policies were unstable and erratic. There were periods combining stabilisation policies with strong incentives to some industrial sectors considered fundamental and a more favourable disposition towards foreign investments (presidency of Frondizi, between 1958 and 1962). Other periods were characterised by fiscal and monetary expansionary policies, freezing of public service, tariffs and exchange controls (presidency of Illia, between 1963 and 1966).

The expansion of the light industries decelerated after the 1950s, partly because of the strong constraint generated by a persistent deficit in the balance of payments; the most critical items in imports were oil, capital goods and inputs. The evolution of terms of trade (mostly exogenous to a small economy like Argentina) was another central variable to understand the external constraints.

The period starting in the 1950s is known as the "stop-and-go" crisis (Braun and Joy 1968). During the government of Frondizi, there was a significant liberalisation of the oil sector, a rapid increase in foreign investment, expansion of production and a sizeable reduction of imports in this item. Between 1957 and 1962, the national oil production was tripled and by 1962 it was strongly concentrated in only six provinces (31% of total national production in Santa Cruz, 23% in Chubut, 18% in Mendoza, 9% in Salta, 6% in Neuquén and 6% in Tierra del Fuego). However, during the Illia administration oil contracts were annulled and production barely maintained the levels of previous years (Belini and Korol 2012).

The decade between the years 1963 and 1973 is called by Cortés Conde (2005) as "the decade of growth", while Gerchunoff and Llach (2009) denote it as the "economic spring". The world was increasingly influenced by accelerated technological innovation, the expansion of world trade and the international movements of capital and commercial agreements.

Despite the turbulent domestic context in political matters, Argentina benefitted from that friendly global context.

Economic instability, extremely high inflation, continued fiscal deficit, currency overvaluation and some attempts to return to world markets are features that typify the evolution of the Argentine economy in the period that begins after the 1976 military coup. One of the main characteristics of the economic policy of the military government (1976–1983) was the deliberate attempt to dismantle many of the key elements of the industrialist strategy of import substitution industrialisation (ISI); the new policies included reduction of subsidies and tariffs, labour and financial market liberalisation and a large capital inflow from both the international organisation and the private sector. The opening up to international capital markets ended with the debt crisis of the 1980s, but in the 1990s many standard liberal recipes were reinforced (privatisation of many public companies, reduction of the public sector, liberalisation of markets and reduction of tariffs) and implemented together with a fixed exchange rate. After considerable economic expansion, in 2001, the combination of currency overvaluation and persistent public and current account deficits generated an explosive cocktail that ended with a severe political crisis, social unrest, default in public debt and the deepest recession in Argentina since the 1930s.

3 New Data: Methodology and Descriptive Analysis

Official estimations for the Argentine provinces' GDP are available since 1953. For the period before, the data comes from previous contributions from Aráoz and Nicolini (2016, 2020) and Talassino (2015, 2019). In order to analyse the evolution of regional growth and regional inequality since the end of the nineteenth century, we will use figures for the years 1895, 1914, 1937, 1946, 1953, 1965, 1975, 1986, 1993 and 2004. The estimation for 1895, 1914, 1937 and 1946 have been elaborated by the authors of this chapter while the other benchmark years are taken from official and semi-official statistics.

The estimates for the year 1895 are obtained by using an indirect approach in which the total national GDP of each sector is distributed among the twenty-four provinces based on the share of each one in an economic variable that proxies the total value-added of the sector. For instance, the national aggregate value-added in livestock production is distributed according to the share of each province in the total national value of cattle. The national figures for the sectoral GDPs come from Cortés Conde (1994), with an opening of eight sectors.[5] The primary source used to distribute the value-added of each sector among provinces is the *Segundo Censo de La República Argentina* (República Argentina 1898), which provides provincial information about the cultivated area by crops, the number of people employed and the value of the stock of capital in manufacturing and services,[6] among others. Because the census only provides information relative to the cultivated area, to estimate the value of the production (which is used to allocate the Argentine agricultural GDP between the provinces), we have also used complementary sources, like Correa and Lahite (1898), to assess the prices and yield per hectare for tobacco, sugar cane and forestall trees, Seguí (1898) to determine the prices and yield per hectare for alfalfa and *Ministerio de Agricultura de la República Argentina* (1916) to estimate the prices and yield for wheat, linen, maize and barley.[7]

For 1914 we have used direct estimation, based on the identity between the GDP and the sum of the retributions to productive factors (capital, land and labour). In particular, we assumed that the provincial GDP (Y) for each province is:

$$Y = \sum_{i=1}^{N} L_i w_i + \left[r_A K_A + r_C K_C + r_I K_I + r_S K_S \right] + \left[q_A T_A + q_C T_C \right] + s_C C \quad (4.1)$$

The first term on the right-hand side of the equation is the remuneration to labour that is equal to the sum of all the wages paid to workers across the N different occupations. The second term in brackets includes

[5] The sectors analysed by Cortés Conde in 1895 are manufacturing, trade, construction, transport, agriculture (crops and livestock) and government; in 1914 he adds energy and services. This means that Cortés Conde does not include explicitly the participation of energy and services in 1895; given that the sum of the sectoral participations in 1895 does not add to 100% (Cortés Conde, 1994: 6, Table 1), Aráoz and Nicolini (2016) assumed that the difference corresponds to these two sectors jointly included in 1895 in one sector called "energy and services".

[6] The distribution of the total value-added of manufacturing and trade sectors among the provinces was based on the value of capital and number of workers in each occupational category in those sectors in each province.

[7] For further details, see Aráoz and Nicolini (2016).

the rents (r) paid to physical capital (K) in agriculture (A), livestock production (C) and in establishments in the industry (I) and services (S). The third term is the rent (q) paid to land (T) in agriculture and livestock production, and the last term is the flow of income generated by livestock (C).[8] The rate of return is different across sectors. The most important sources of information in which we base our estimation are the *Tercer Censo Nacional de La República Argentina* (República Argentina 1916b), Departamento Nacional del Trabajo (1907, 1913), the *Anuario Estadístico del Trabajo* (República Argentina 1916a) and Bunge (1917).

To estimate the figures for 1937 and 1946, we have followed the same strategy of indirect estimation as the one for 1895. The national sectoral value-added for both years comes from *Banco Central de la República Argentina* (1976), which is a revised version of that presented in Secretaría de Asuntos Económicos (1955) and is disaggregated in fourteen economic sectors.[9] The main sources used are Ministerio de Agricultura (1939) to determine the allocator from the agricultural and livestock sectors,[10] Dirección General de Estadística de la Nación (1940) for wages (used in the construction) and industrial value-added (used in manufacturing, mining and electricity, gas and water), the *IV Censo General de la Nación* (República Argentina n.d.), which provides data on the number of sectoral workers, cattle stock, value-added of the secondary sector, commercial sales, among others, Anuario Estadístico de la República Argentina (Ministerio de Asuntos Técnicos n.d.; Dirección Nacional de Estadística y Censos n.d.) for agricultural production, cattle prices and so on. Other sources like provincial budgets of the public sector, memories and statistical sectoral yearbooks provided information for fishing, railways, post office, telephone and others.

The estimations of provincial GDPs for 1953 were reported by CFI-ITDT (1965), and they are disaggregated in fourteen sectors. To produce these figures, CFI-ITDT uses a mixed approach, depending on the

[8] We assume that the value of the livestock (C) generates a return (s_c) to its owners.

[9] The quantity of economic sectors considered in each benchmark year is not always equal because the sources and methodology are not similar. For the years 1937, 1946 and 1953, the sectors are crops, livestock, fishing, mining, manufacturing, electricity, gas and water, construction, transport, communications, finance, housing, commerce, government and other services.

[10] To distribute the livestock value-added among the provinces, the allocator used was the value of the livestock in each province. The agricultural value-added was distributed proportionally to the gross value of each crop in each province.

availability of information. In some cases (for instance, agriculture, livestock production, manufacturing and services), they calculate the added value in each sector in each province while for other sectors (like commerce, finance, transportation and communications), they use the indirect approach or descending method, which involves allocating the national GDP between the provinces, using appropriate allocators.

In 1975 the official statistical agency in Argentina, INDEC (1975a) (*Instituto Nacional de Estadística y Censos*), published a report which provides the provincial GDPs for 1965, disaggregated in ten economic sectors. This report excludes the provinces of Salta, Santa Cruz and Tucumán. However, the *Anuario Estadístico de la República Argentina* (INDEC 1974), also published by this office, offers information for these provinces. Even though these are official statistics, we do not have any information regarding the methodology used to estimate the provincial GDPs in 1965, so these figures should be taken with caution. The sectoral GDP for 1975 came from CFI (1983) and was calculated by direct estimation, for nine economic sectors.[11]

The 1986 and 1993 estimates come from Martínez (2004), who uses estimates and interpolations based on data from CFI, SAREP (*Secretaría de Asistencia para la Reforma Económica Provincial del Ministerio del Interior de la Nación*) and *Ministerio de Economía*. Finally, the 2004 figures are from INDEC (2016) and were estimated by the descending method, for fifty-three branches of activity.

All the estimates for the benchmarks are nominated in current prices of each year. However, since the end of the nineteenth century, there were several changes in the denomination of the Argentine monetary unit (*Peso Moneda Nacional, Peso Ley, Austral, Peso Convertible*). In addition, there was no available set of consistent provincial deflators covering the whole period. This situation constitutes a problem for the calculation of the growth rates of provincial GDPs in real terms. So, for calculating growth rates of real provincial GDPs, we generated provincial GDPs at constant prices by distributing the real GDP at 1993 prices from Ferreres (2010) among provinces according to their share in the sum of the GDP of all the

[11] The economic sectors considered for 1975 are agriculture, forestry, hunting and fishing; mines and quarries; manufacturing; electricity, gas and water; construction; wholesale, retail, and restaurants and hotels; transport, storage and communications; financial establishments, insurance, real estate and services provided to companies; community, social and personal services.

districts in each benchmark year. In that way, we solve the problem of changes in the denomination of the legal tender and the lack of provincial deflators.[12]

Regarding the population, we use census data for 1895 and 1914, and official interpolations and projections for the remaining years. For 1937 and 1946, we use Dirección Nacional de Estadística y Censos (1956); for 1953, CFI-ITDT (1965); and for 1965, 1975, 1986, 1993 and 2004, INDEC (1975b, 1989, 1993, 1996, 2008).

The borders and geographic configuration of some provinces and national territories changed during the period of this study. In this regard, it is necessary to deal with the case of the national territory of Los Andes that existed between 1900 and 1943 in the northwest of Argentina, and it was part of the current areas of the provinces of Jujuy, Salta and Catamarca. At the administrative level, Los Andes was made up of four departments: San Antonio de los Cobres, Antofagasta de la Sierra, Pastos Grandes and Susques. In our data, Los Andes is present in the estimates of the years 1914 and 1937. So, the proportion of inhabitants of Susques was used to assign the GDP percentage of Los Andes to Jujuy, Pastos Grandes and San Antonio de los Cobres to Salta and Antofagasta de la Sierra to Catamarca.[13] Another very relevant issue is the Military Area of Comodoro Rivadavia in the south of Argentina, which between 1943 and 1955 covered parts of Chubut and Santa Cruz. This administrative unit is important because a lot of oil production in Argentina came from there (69% in 1946). In the estimation of 1946, the value-added in oil production from Comodoro Rivadavia was distributed between Chubut and Santa Cruz proportional to the production of oil in each province (for more information see Talassino 2019).

[12] A possible alternative to this approach would be to transform all the nominal provincial GDPs to real terms using the deflator of the national GDP. This would not affect the results in terms of convergence obtained in this chapter, only the scale on the vertical axis of Figs. 4.2 and 4.3.

[13] Criteria based on the Decree that establishes the dissolution of the National Territory of the Andes (Decree No. 9375, September 21, 1943), which in Article 1 states: "*The national territory of the Andes will be divided into three fractions which will include: 1st) Department of Susques or the North, that will pass to the jurisdiction of the Province of Jujuy, 2nd) Department of Pastos Grandes or the Center, and San Antonio de Los Cobres, which will make up the territory of the Province of Salta, and 3rd) Department of Antofagasta de la Sierra, which will become part of the Province of Catamarca*" (authors' translation).

There is a non-trivial caveat about the quality and precision of the measurement of economic activity and even population in the censuses of the beginning of the period, and particularly in 1895, for the national territories. The director of the *Segundo Censo Nacional, Gabriel Carrasco,* notes: “the national territories, except Misiones, can be considered depopulated, since, on average, they do not reach one inhabitant for every 10 km^2 of surface” (*Segundo Censo de La República Argentina*: p. cxxv, vol. 2; translation by the authors). So, the records for the distant territories are probably not very reliable. However, given that these territories’ main economic characteristics emerging from the first set of estimations are confirmed by the more recent, and probably reliable, censuses, we are confident that the information of the census is a reasonable approximation of the real numbers.

4 Long-Term Patterns of Regional Inequality

In general, the regional pattern of economic activity is characterised by the large and expanding importance of the province of Buenos Aires and the district of Capital Federal during the first half of the twentieth century and by the opposite process since the 1990s. Also, there is a remarkable persistence in the relative positions of provinces and regions, in a context of slow and clear reinforcement of the division between a poor North and a rich South—with the particular exception of Capital Federal, in the centre of the country. Finally, the secular expansion of the regional dispersion of income per capita is clearly observable.

Since colonial times, the city of Buenos Aires and its agrarian hinterland in the province of Buenos Aires have played a dominant role in the economic process and the political events of the country. The estimation of regional GDPs for 1895 confirms that the concentration of economic activity in Buenos Aires and Capital Federal was already noticeable at the end of the nineteenth century. Table 4.1 shows that the participation of these two districts in the national valued-added is more than 45% at the end of the nineteenth century, and it expands to more than 60% in the 1980s. Comparing Tables 4.1 and 4.2 it is possible to see that the expansion of Buenos Aires is extensive in the sense that its share of total GDP increased but its relative income per capita stagnated; in Capital Federal both variables increased.

In 1895, most of the provinces with relevant participation in the national GDP are located in the *Pampa Húmeda*,[14] a region in the centre

[14] The *Pampa Húmeda* extends over most of the province of Buenos Aires and Entre Ríos, centre and south of Santa Fe, a major share of Córdoba and some extension of La Pampa.

Table 4.1 Share of regional GDP to total GDP (%)

Provinces	*Year*									
	1895	*1914*	*1937*	*1946*	*1953*	*1965*	*1975*	*1986*	*1993*	*2004*
Buenos Aires	24.63	29.04	27.18	28.02	31.47	37.57	32.21	39.14	34.39	32.95
Capital Federal	22.27	25.87	31.71	33.77	30.02	24.97	27.61	23.56	23.94	20.65
Catamarca	0.91	0.58	0.29	0.35	0.32	0.27	0.40	0.39	0.53	0.85
Chaco	0.29	0.46	1.22	1.44	1.78	1.62	1.14	0.89	1.26	1.30
Chubut	0.07	0.29	1.15	1.04	0.95	0.88	1.46	1.61	1.30	2.23
Córdoba	6.95	8.61	8.89	6.56	6.57	7.77	6.56	7.11	7.92	7.84
Corrientes	3.68	2.67	1.78	1.69	1.40	1.26	1.32	1.09	1.35	1.18
Entre Ríos	6.72	4.25	3.14	2.79	2.88	2.21	2.33	1.66	2.17	2.43
Formosa	0.15	0.22	0.46	0.44	0.47	0.35	0.54	0.30	0.59	0.51
Jujuy	0.77	0.87	0.63	0.69	0.83	0.64	1.04	0.69	0.87	0.84
La Pampa	0.63	1.50	1.25	1.02	0.95	0.97	0.60	1.03	0.85	0.88
La Rioja	0.80	0.74	0.27	0.30	0.28	0.21	0.38	0.51	0.53	0.58
Mendoza	3.49	2.93	2.44	3.65	3.88	3.83	4.44	2.64	3.90	3.92
Misiones	0.64	0.30	0.61	0.91	0.82	0.80	1.50	1.34	1.35	1.25
Neuquén	0.14	0.26	0.36	0.39	0.35	0.37	1.06	0.98	1.70	3.11
Río Negro	0.18	0.50	0.58	0.74	0.93	0.94	1.29	1.48	1.42	1.34
Salta	1.79	1.15	1.12	1.07	1.14	1.25	1.36	1.50	1.47	1.75
San Juan	2.55	0.97	0.74	1.31	1.14	1.17	0.98	0.94	1.09	1.10
San Luis	0.96	1.35	0.56	0.48	0.51	0.53	0.45	1.08	1.02	1.07
Santa Cruz	0.05	0.26	0.37	0.43	0.47	0.89	0.65	0.74	0.95	1.71

(continued)

Table 4.1 (continued)

Provinces	*Year*									
	1895	*1914*	*1937*	*1946*	*1953*	*1965*	*1975*	*1986*	*1993*	*2004*
Santa Fe	14.03	12.70	11.82	9.60	9.13	9.20	8.53	8.21	7.86	8.82
Santiago del Estero	1.72	1.43	1.02	1.07	1.09	0.69	1.02	0.60	0.91	1.17
Tierra del Fuego	0.02	0.06	0.08	0.08	0.10	0.12	0.21	0.75	0.66	0.80
Tucumán	6.59	2.99	2.34	2.17	2.49	1.46	2.92	1.76	1.99	1.74
Total	**100.00**	**100.00**	**100.00**	**100.00**	**100.00**	**100.00**	**100.00**	**100.00**	**100.00**	**100.00**

Source: See text

Table 4.2 Per capita GDP (country current year GDP pc = 1)

Provinces	*Year*									
	1895	*1914*	*1937*	*1946*	*1953*	*1965*	*1975*	*1986*	*1993*	*2004*
Buenos Aires	1.06	1.11	1.01	1.04	1.06	1.04	0.84	0.99	0.89	0.87
Capital Federal	1.33	1.29	1.67	1.80	1.77	1.87	2.44	2.50	2.68	2.62
Catamarca	0.40	0.45	0.29	0.38	0.35	0.34	0.54	0.53	0.64	0.91
Chaco	1.08	0.77	0.54	0.53	0.65	0.64	0.46	0.35	0.49	0.49
Chubut	0.73	0.98	2.19	1.80	1.39	1.16	1.67	1.62	1.17	1.94
Córdoba	0.78	0.92	0.94	0.70	0.71	0.88	0.75	0.82	0.94	0.93
Corrientes	0.61	0.61	0.52	0.51	0.46	0.49	0.54	0.46	0.55	0.46
Entre Ríos	0.91	0.79	0.63	0.56	0.63	0.59	0.69	0.52	0.70	0.77
Formosa	1.22	0.92	0.74	0.62	0.59	0.37	0.52	0.28	0.47	0.38
Jujuy	0.61	0.88	0.62	0.66	0.74	0.51	0.75	0.45	0.55	0.50
La Pampa	0.96	1.17	0.92	0.95	1.01	1.28	0.80	1.37	1.06	1.06
La Rioja	0.45	0.73	0.35	0.43	0.41	0.35	0.66	0.85	0.77	0.71
Mendoza	1.19	0.83	0.67	0.99	0.99	0.92	1.05	0.61	0.90	0.90
Misiones	0.76	0.45	0.48	0.59	0.47	0.43	0.75	0.60	0.55	0.47
Neuquén	0.39	0.72	0.71	0.72	0.63	0.60	1.39	1.01	1.35	2.32
Río Negro	0.75	0.93	0.72	0.87	1.36	0.90	1.04	1.04	0.90	0.88
Salta	0.60	0.64	0.64	0.58	0.58	0.59	0.60	0.60	0.54	0.58
San Juan	1.20	0.64	0.48	0.80	0.66	0.69	0.59	0.57	0.68	0.64
San Luis	0.46	0.91	0.47	0.46	0.52	0.65	0.59	1.41	1.14	1.02
Santa Cruz	1.89	2.09	1.33	1.59	2.00	2.75	1.69	1.65	1.87	3.11
Santa Fe	1.40	1.11	1.06	0.89	0.90	1.00	0.95	0.94	0.92	1.07
Santiago del Estero	0.42	0.43	0.35	0.36	0.40	0.31	0.48	0.29	0.44	0.54
Tierra del Fuego	1.66	1.91	2.18	2.55	2.48	2.45	2.89	4.20	2.82	2.72
Tucumán	1.21	0.71	0.64	0.58	0.65	0.41	0.85	0.50	0.57	0.47
Total	**1.00**	**1.00**	**1.00**	**1.00**	**1.00**	**1.00**	**1.00**	**1.00**	**1.00**	**1.00**

Source: See text

of the country, naturally endowed for the production of cereals and meat, the two most important items in Argentine exports. The only other province that is close to this group is Tucumán, which contributed with more than 6% to the total national income. In this case, the specialisation in sugar cane cultivation and industrial sugar production generated a considerable expansion of economic activity since the 1870s and suffered a very acute crisis of overproduction, precisely in 1895, that marked the beginning of a deceleration (Juarez-Dappe 2010).

The evolution of the spatial configuration of the regional distribution of incomes per capita is summarised in Table 4.2 and maps in Fig. 4.1.

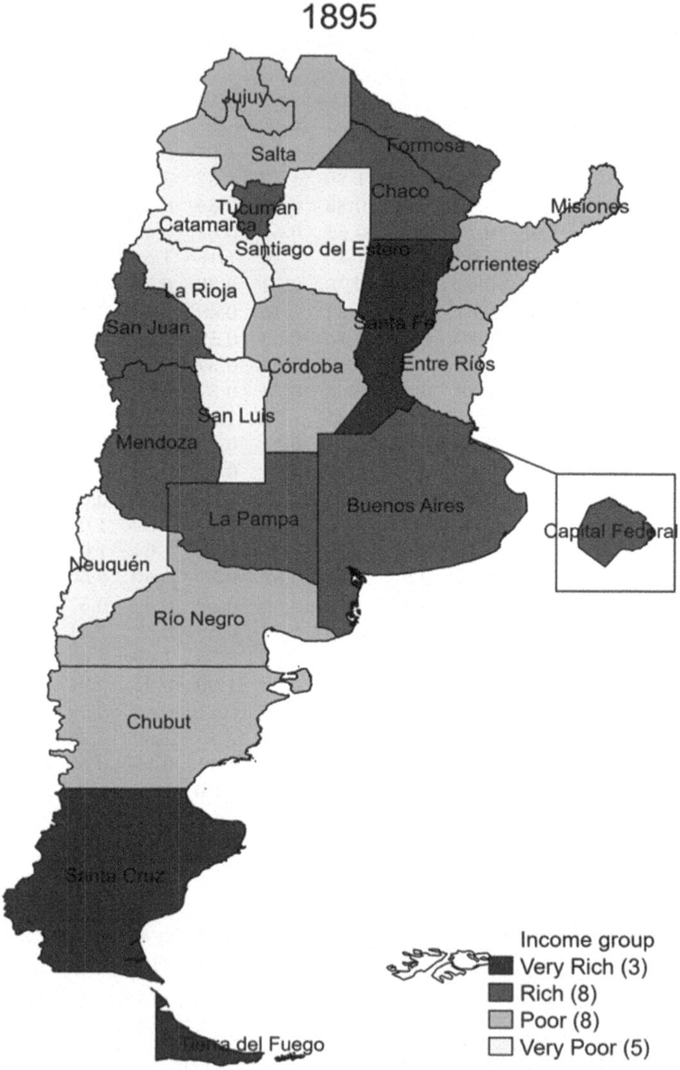

Fig. 4.1 Per capita GDP. (Income groups constructed using standard deviations from the simple average of the GDP per capita of the districts. E.g., Very Rich corresponds to districts with GDP per capita higher than the average GDP per capita plus a standard deviation, and so on). (Source: Table 4.2)

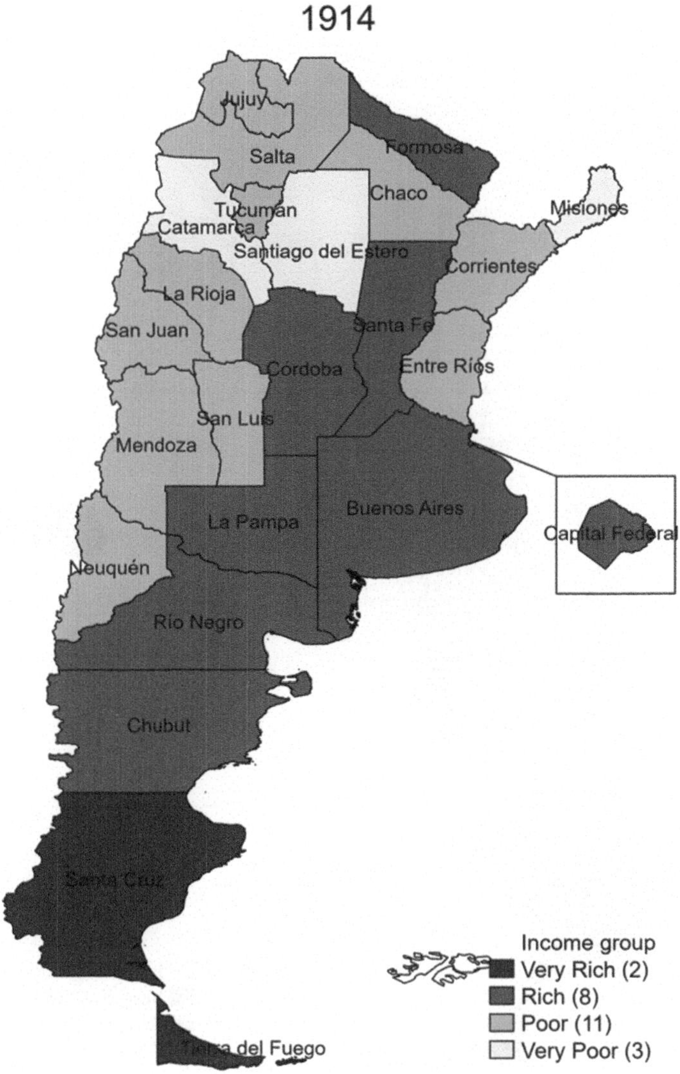

Fig. 4.1 (continued)

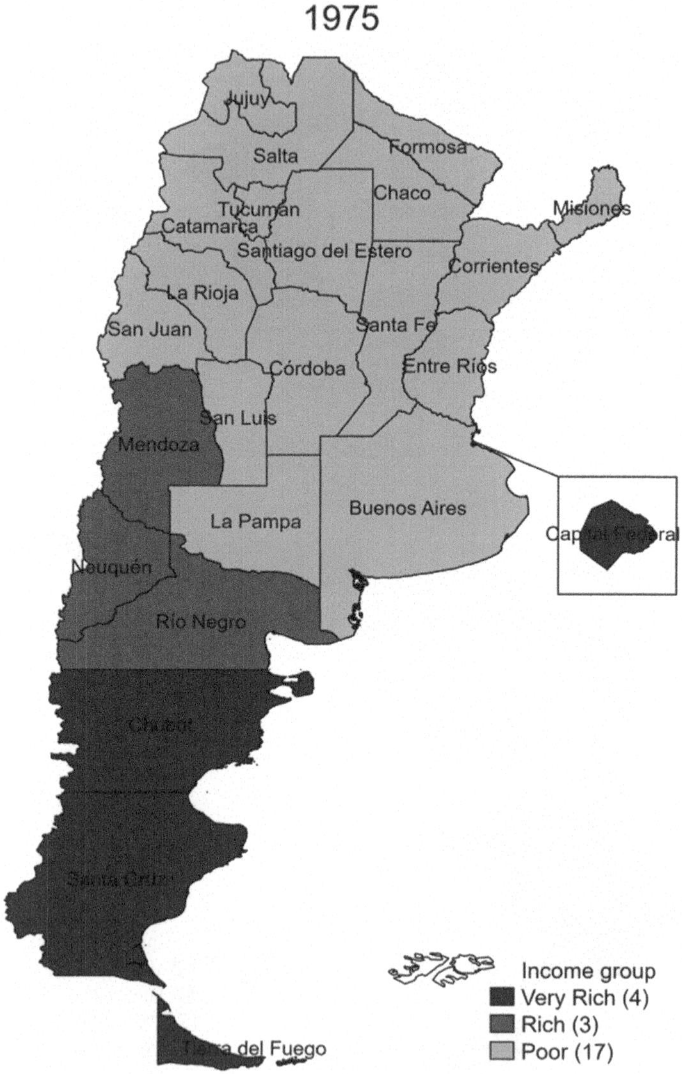

Fig. 4.1 (continued)

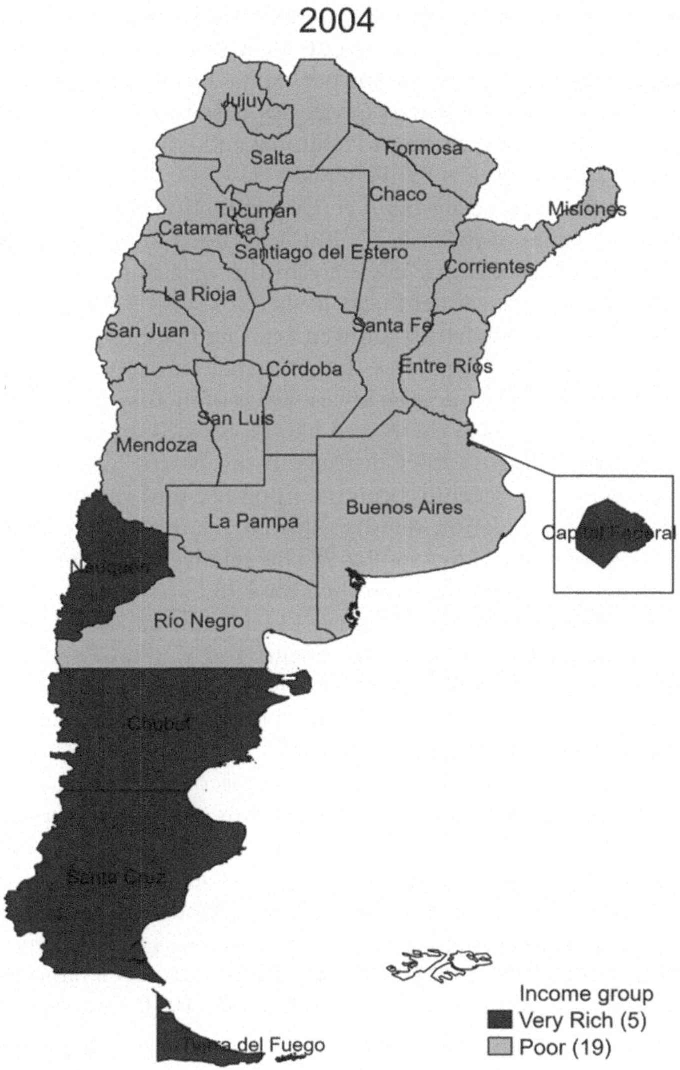

Fig. 4.1 (continued)

One of its most remarkable features is that some provinces in Patagonia[15] (Tierra del Fuego, Santa Cruz and eventually Chubut) and Capital Federal are the ones with the highest income per capita during most of the period. This is related to complementary processes based on extensive exploitation of land and oil production in Patagonia and concentration of manufacturing and services in Capital Federal.

In 1895 Santa Fe, specialising in cereal production, had the third highest income per capita of the country but it declined in relative terms after 1914. The other high-income areas are in the very south of the country like Santa Cruz and Tierra del Fuego (where extensive sheep production and very low population density allowed very high labour productivity) or in Capital Federal, where most of the industrial and services sector were located. On the opposite side, the lowest levels of income per capita dominate in several provinces of the North like La Rioja, Catamarca, Misiones and Santiago del Estero. Other districts in the North like Formosa and Chaco have only very recently been incorporated into the national economy and its low population density allowed relatively high income per capita in a frontier-economy context.[16] This relatively affluent position of these districts in the Northeast vanished for 1937.

Between 1895 and 1914 we observe (1) a confirmation of the leading positions by Santa Cruz, Tierra del Fuego and Capital Federal; (2) an expansion of the relative affluence to other provinces in Patagonia (confirmed later); and (3) a conformation of a block of high-income provinces in the area of *Pampa Húmeda*.

The three decades after 1914 are characterised by a strong persistence in the relative positions of the provinces in terms of GDP per capita (Aráoz and Nicolini 2020). Again, very high growth rates are noticeable in Capital Federal and are quite common among Patagonian provinces like Río Negro, Chubut and Tierra del Fuego. Also, Mendoza experienced high growth to get into the group of rich districts (in terms of the groups of the Maps in Fig. 4.1) where it remained until 1975; the consolidation of wine production in the industrial sector until the 1940s followed by an

[15] The Argentine Patagonia include the contemporary provinces of Chubut, Neuquén, part of the province of La Pampa, part of the province of Buenos Aires, the southern tip of the province of Mendoza, Río Negro, Santa Cruz and Tierra del Fuego, Antarctica and South Atlantic Islands.

[16] In Chaco and Formosa agriculture was the predominant activity together with a rather primitive production of sugar. The very low population density recorded by the official census in 1895 (less than one inhabitant per square kilometre) explains the relatively high income per capita.

expansion of oil production in the 1950s were relevant components of growth in this province.[17] Additionally, in this period, the impact of the inward-looking process of development is distinguishable in the relative decline of the *Pampa Húmeda*. This geographic area, in the centre of the country, with the most important comparative advantages in internationally tradable goods (cereals and meat), had in 1946 a smaller per capita GDP compared to the national average than in 1914.

Few changes in the relative positions took place between 1946 and 1965, and for 1975 the most important characteristics of the regional income distribution in the second half of the twentieth century were already defined and eventually became more pronounced. There was a very high income per capita in Capital Federal up to 2.68 times the national average in 1993. In the rich club, together with the city of Buenos Aires, Tierra del Fuego and Santa Cruz stand out in 2004 with incomes 2.72 and 3.11 times the national average. At the opposite extreme, all the provinces in the North are in the poor group, with Formosa showing only 38% of the national average income per capita in 2004.

The case of Neuquén is remarkable, which started at the lowest place in the ranking of per capita GDPs and finished in the rich club in 2004. The expansion of oil production and gas was a relevant component of growth in this province.

The distance between the richest and the poorest districts increased in the long run. In 1895, the three richest provinces (Tierra del Fuego, Santa Cruz and Santa Fe) had an unweighted average of 1.65 relative to the national average of 1, while the three poorest (Catamarca, Neuquén and Santiago del Estero) an unweighted average of 0.40. In 2004 the three richest districts (Capital Federal, Tierra del Fuego and Santa Cruz) had an unweighted average of 2.82, while the three poorest (Formosa, Corrientes and Misiones) an unweighted average of 0.44. The ratio between the averages increases from 4.12 to 6.41.

Figure 4.2 shows that there is beta-convergence among the Argentine provinces between 1895 and 2004.[18] These results do not coincide with

[17] The subsequent relative lag of Mendoza is partially explained by a significant drop in the demand for wine and the stop on oil investment (Coria López 2008, 2014).

[18] In general, beta-convergence does not imply sigma-convergence. If the initial dispersion of incomes is low relative to the random shocks that are pushing them apart, we can observe beta-convergence and sigma-divergence (Young et al. 2008). In our context, this would imply that the dispersion of provincial incomes per capita in 1895 was unusually low, suggesting that the development process in Argentina during the nineteenth century generated unusually low levels of regional inequality. This opens some interesting hypotheses for further research depending on the availability of new estimates of regional levels of income before 1895.

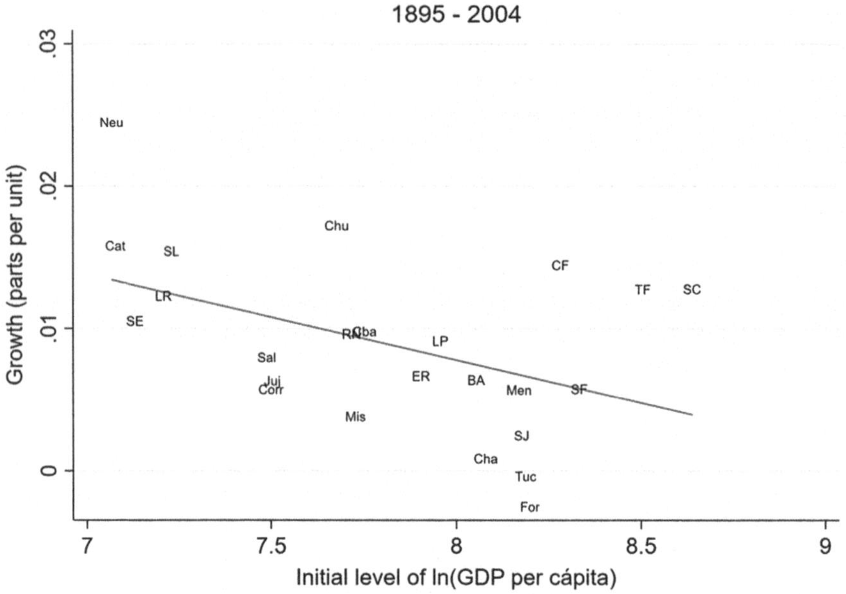

Fig. 4.2 Initial levels of GDP per capita and growth, Argentine provinces, period 1895–2004. (Note: BA: Buenos Aires; Cat: Catamarca; Cba: Córdoba; CF: Capital Federal; Cha: Chaco; Chu: Chubut; Corr: Corrientes; ER: Entre Ríos; For: Formosa; Juj: Jujuy ; LP: La Pampa; LR: La Rioja; Men: Mendoza; Mis: Misiones; RN: Río Negro; Sal: Salta; SC: Santa Cruz; SE: Santiago del Estero; SJ: San Juan; SL: San Luis; TF: Tierra del Fuego; Tuc: Tucumán. Source: Authors' elaboration)

others, like Marina (2001), Elías (1995) and Grotz and Llach (2013), but the benchmarks used by them (they generally start in the 1950s) are different from ours.

This convergence, in the long run, is the result of different patterns in the different sub-periods (see Fig. 4.3). The first sub-period, 1895–1914, corresponds to the second part of the period of consolidation of the national markets and integration into the international markets; this period is characterised by beta-convergence, indicating that the poorest provinces tend to grow faster than the richest ones. Tucumán and Mendoza, two archetypical examples of regional economies integrated into the national market with products for domestic consumption, had a relatively high per capita income in 1895 but experienced a relative decline afterwards, as we

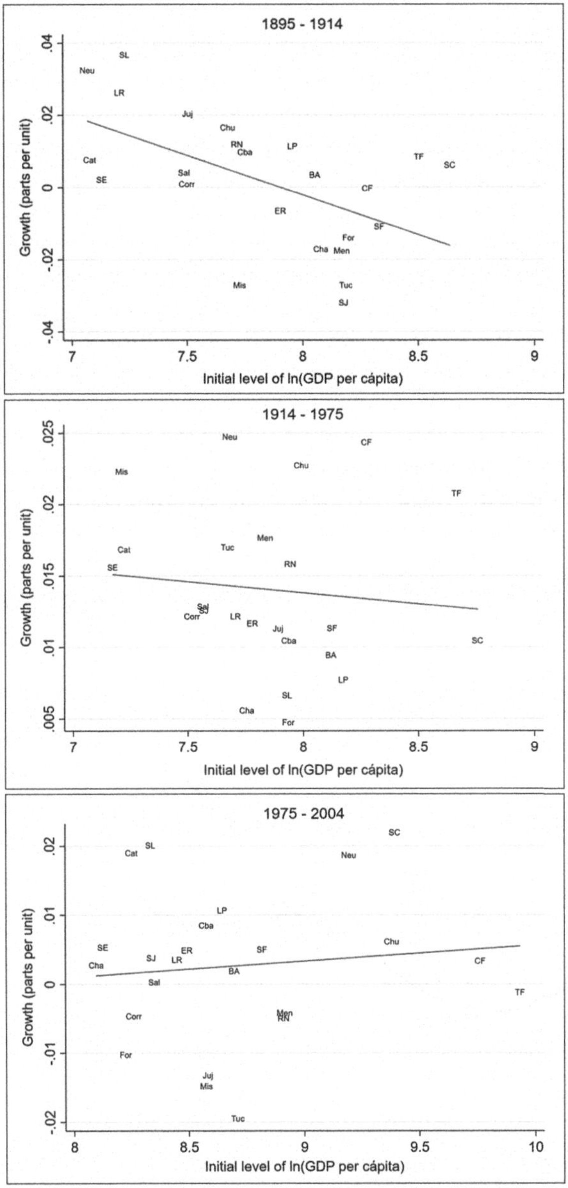

Fig. 4.3 Initial levels of GDP per capita and growth Argentine provinces, selected periods. (Note: BA: Buenos Aires; Cat: Catamarca; Cba: Córdoba; CF: Capital Federal; Cha: Chaco; Chu: Chubut; Corr: Corrientes; ER: Entre Ríos; For: Formosa; Juj: Jujuy ; LP: La Pampa; LR: La Rioja; Men: Mendoza; Mis: Misiones; RN: Río Negro; Sal: Salta; SC: Santa Cruz; SE: Santiago del Estero; SJ: San Juan; SL: San Luis; TF: Tierra del Fuego; Tuc: Tucumán). (Source: Authors' elaboration)

can see in Table 4.2 and Fig. 4.1. Santa Fe, another high per capita income province, also loses its relative position because it was strongly specialised in agro-pastoral activities and did not participate in the growing diversification of the national economy.

The analysis of sigma-convergence (see Fig. 4.4) shows a decline in the dispersion of incomes per capita between 1895 and 1914, which is the last part of the period of integration into the world markets before World War I.

The central decades of the century show the opposite situation. Between 1914 and 1975, there is no convergence and a notorious increase in the dispersion in average incomes (see Figs. 4.3 and 4.4). The import substitution industrialisation (ISI) in Argentina generated a complex system of stimulus for the industrial sector focused on those branches considered strategic for national development (basic production of metals, oil, electricity) rather than on the potential impact over the regional and personal distribution of income. Given that these branches tended to emerge and expand in the geographic areas with an already relatively high income per capita (mainly Capital Federal for manufacturing and electricity and some provinces in

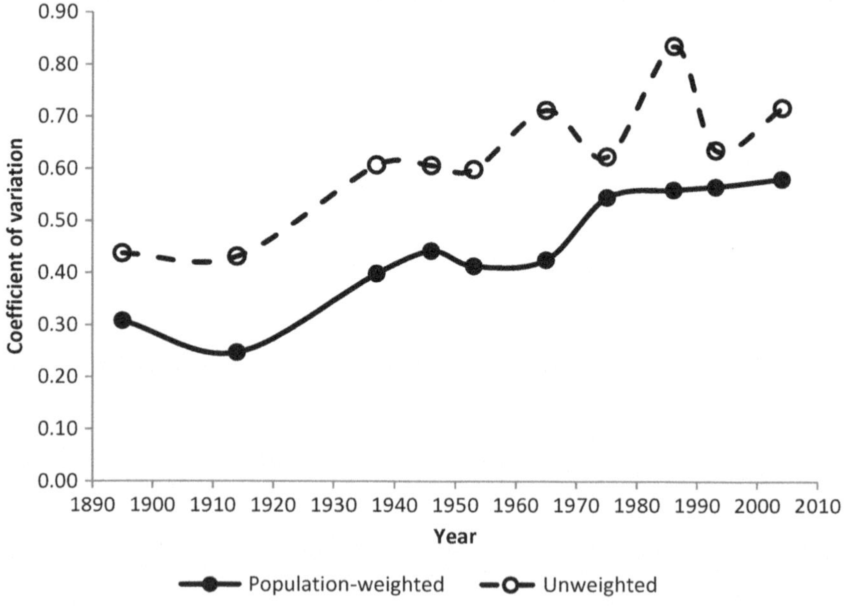

Fig. 4.4 Coefficient of variation of per capita GDP. (Source: Authors' elaboration)

Patagonia for oil), these economic interventions did not contribute to regional cohesion but instead reinforced the process of augmenting inequalities. The highest growth rates in this period correspond to Capital Federal, where most of the expansion of the industrial production took place, and Patagonia oil districts (Neuquén, Chubut and Tierra del Fuego).[19] As usual, in the general pattern of persistence, the provinces in the North (Chaco and Formosa) lagged behind with very low growth rates. Between 1914 and 1975 the coefficient of variation of GDP increased substantially (Fig. 4.4).

Lastly, between 1975 and 2004, we cannot reject the non-beta-convergence hypothesis (see Fig. 4.3), and Fig. 4.4 suggests a weak sigma-divergence. The poorest provinces do not show a homogeneous growth pattern: there is high growth in Catamarca and San Luis, but almost zero growth in Formosa and Corrientes. The high growth rates of some rich districts, like Santa Cruz and Neuquén, help to expand the regional dispersion.

5 Conclusions: Forces Behind Regional Inequality

The spatial profile of the Argentine economy was shaped by three main forces. The first one is comparative advantage in agro-pastoral production, mediated by national trade policies and the international context. This force is relevant in the period before 1914 to understand the dominance of *Pampa Húmeda* and the surprisingly high income per capita in some provinces in Patagonia. The second force is the expanding demand in the domestic market for manufactured goods characterised by increasing returns, mostly in Capital Federal. The third one is the availability of oil and gas deposits that generated a very relevant growth in income per capita in some provinces—particularly in Patagonia—after the 1930s. These two latter forces are particularly relevant to understand the process of divergence and persistence in relative positions in the period 1914–1975. The poorest provinces, all of them in the north of the country, lagged unrelentingly behind during most of the twentieth century with some exceptional periods of catch-up and convergence (1895–1914) when the other forces were not dominant.

[19] Oil extraction started in 1907 in Chubut, in 1918 in Neuquén, in 1946 in Santa Cruz and in 1949 in Tierra del Fuego.

The economic and political history of Argentina is permanently traversed by the extraordinary weight of the urban conglomerate of Buenos Aires, one of the largest in Latin America today, which covered Capital Federal and some districts in the province of Buenos Aires. Its traditional importance as the administrative centre and main port since the colonial period only grew with time. The affluence of the city of Buenos Aires during the globalisation era was mainly a by-product of the extraordinary economic expansion of the *Pampa Húmeda* in the centre-east of the country, covering the provinces of Buenos Aires, Santa Fe, La Pampa and some areas of Córdoba. In 1914 the geographic block formed of these provinces, plus Capital Federal, generated more than 77% of the national GDP and most of them have per capita incomes higher than the national average.

The traditional role of the city of Buenos Aires as the main centre of commercial and financial services and light manufacturing products was reinforced when the inward-looking process of development started. The state-led industrialisation dominant in the central decades of the twentieth century was based on a battery of policies, tariffs, exchange rate controls, subsidies, and so on, that intended to expand manufactures. The impact of economic intervention in the geographic distribution of economic activity has not been studied in depth. However, we know that the public stimulus was mostly sectoral rather than geographic (Belini 2012) and probably boosted specific sectors in regions and provinces with some initial industrial networks and some scope for exploiting economies of scale and networks effects. This expansion of industrial activity took place mainly in Capital Federal although the data for 1953 shows that some important industrial activity spilled over to the Conurbano, those municipalities in the province of Buenos Aires limited to Capital Federal (CFI-ITDT 1965: 213).

Another important element to understand the evolution of regional inequality is a strong path dependence on population distribution. At the end of the nineteenth century, the "traditional" provinces were all based in cities founded by Spanish conquerors in the sixteenth century while many of the national territories were recently incorporated into the national markets and administrative control in 1895. The national territories have some characteristics of a frontier economy with very low population density and high labour productivity in extensive agriculture or cattle farming. Two national territories in the North (Formosa and Chaco) started with high incomes per capita because of this nature of the frontier economy but quite rapidly converged to the other poor provinces in this area when the advantages of low population density vanished. On the other hand, some districts in Patagonia (Santa Cruz and Tierra del Fuego) started with high income per capita because of a large land-labour ratio at the end of the nineteenth century but they maintained their privileged economic positions in the second half of the twentieth century as a result of the stream of incomes generated by oil and gas deposits.

The contemporary regional distribution of income can be summarised by a wealthy capital city, a poor North and a rich South and an increasing distance between the two tails of the distribution. With few exceptions the evolution of regional inequality is dominated by tendencies that only reinforced the privileged positions of some districts: the city of Buenos Aires enjoyed a role of commercial intermediary and administrative centre at the beginning to move to an industrial pole with scale economies afterwards; in the case of Patagonia, there were comparative advantages because of land abundance for extensive sheep raising first and mineral deposits afterwards. Some provinces in the *Pampa Húmeda* exploited comparative advantages in agro-pastoral production with variable success depending on the dominant set of policies. Neither the location fundamentals nor the public policies prevented the provinces in the North from falling behind and stagnating in relative terms.

References

Antonelli, E., Carrazán Mena, G. and Romero, F. (2011). *La Economía de Salta Entre Finales Del Siglo XIX y Comienzos Del Siglo XX*. Salta: Enfoques Alternativos.

Aráoz, M. F. and Nicolini, E. A. (2016). "The Evolution of Regional GDPs in Argentina during the Period of Globalization at the End of the 19th and Beginning of the 20th Century." In *LI Reunión Anual de La Asociación Argentina de Economía Política*, edited by Asociación Argentina de Economía Política. San Miguel de Tucumán.

Aráoz, M. F. and Nicolini, E. A. (2020). "Regional Growth and the Persistence of Regional Income Inequality in Argentina in the First Half of the Twentieth Century." *Journal of Latin American Studies*, 52, 293–316. Doi:10.1017/S0022216X19001299

Banco Central de la República Argentina. (1976). "Series Históricas de Cuentas Nacionales de La Argentina." Banco Central de la República Argentina.

Bandieri, S. (2009). *Historia de La Patagonia*. 2ª Edición. Buenos Aires: Sudamericana.

Belini, C. (2012). “Industrial Exports and Peronist Economic Policies in Post-War Argentina.” *Journal of Latin American Studies* 44, (2): 285–317.

Belini, C. and Korol, J.C. (2012). *Historia Economica de La Argentina En El Siglo XX.* 1ª Edición. Buenos Aires: Siglo Veintiuno Editores S.A.

Braun, O. and Joy, L. (1968). “A Model of Economic Stagnation-A Case Study of the Argentine Economy.” *The Economic Journal* 78, (312): 868–87. Doi:10.2307/2229183.

Buera, F., Navarro, G. and Nicolini, J. P. (2011). “The Argentine Economy after Two Centuries.” *Latin American Journal of Economics* 48 (2): 133–56.

Bunge, A. E. (1917). *Riqueza y Renta de La Argentina, Su Distribucion y Su Capacidad Contributiva.* Buenos Aires: Agencia General de Libreria y Publicaciones.

Consejo Federal de Inversiones. (1983). “Producto Bruto Geográfico 1970–1980.” Buenos Aires: Consejo Federal de Inversiones.

Consejo Federal de Inversiones and Insituto Torcuato Di Tella. (1965). “Relevamiento de La Estructura Regional de La Economía Argentina. Tomo II—Investigaciones Estadísticas.” Buenos Aires: Consejo Federal de Inversiones.

Coria López, L. A. (2008). “El PBG de Mendoza Para 1914. Algunos Aspectos Metodológicos.” In *XXI Jornadas de Historia Económica de La Asociación Argentina de Historia Económica.* Caseros.

Coria López, L. A. (2014). “El Producto Bruto Geográfico de Mendoza de Los Últimos 100 Años.” In *XLIX Reunión Anual de La Asociación Argentina de Economía Política.* Posadas: Asociación Argentina de Economía Política.

Correa, A. and Lahitte, E. (1898). *Investigación Parlamentaria Sobre Agricultura, Ganadería, Industrias Derivadas y Colonización. Anexo G: Tucumán y Santiago Del Estero.* Buenos Aires: Taller Tipográfico de la Penitenciaría Nacional.

Cortés Conde, R. (1994). “Estimaciones Del Producto Bruto Interno de Argentina 1875–1935.” Unpublished.

Cortés Conde, R. (2005). *La Economía Política de La Argentina En El Siglo XX.* Buenos Aires: Edhasa.

Departamento Nacional del Trabajo. (1907). “Boletín Del Departamento Nacional Del Trabajo N° 3.” Buenos Aires.

Departamento Nacional del Trabajo. (1913). “Boletín Del Departamento Nacional Del Trabajo N° 25.” Buenos Aires.

Dirección General de Estadística de la Nación. (1940). “Estadística Industrial de 1937.” Buenos Aires: Ministerio de Hacienda de la República Argentina.

Dirección Nacional de Estadística y Censos. (n.d.) “Anuario Estadístico de La República Argentina 1957.” Buenos Aires: Dirección Nacional de Estadísticas y Censos.

Dirección Nacional de Estadística y Censos. (1956). “Informe Demográfico de La República Argentina 1944–1954.” Buenos Aires: Dirección Nacional de Estadísticas y Censos.

Elías, V. J. (1995). "Regional Economic Convergence: The Case of Latin American Economies." *Estudios de Economía* 22 (2): 159–76.

Ferreres, O. J. (2010). *Dos Siglos de Economía Argentina—Edición Bicentenario.* Buenos Aires: Fundación Norte y Sur.

Gallo, E. and Cortés Conde, R. (1995). *Argentina: La República Conservadora.* Buenos Aires: Paidós.

Gerchunoff, P. (1989). "Peronist Economic Policies, 1946–55." In *The Political Economy of Argentina, 1946–83*, edited by Guido di Tella and Rudiger Dornbusch, 1st ed., 59–88. Houndmills, Basingstoke, Hampshire RG21 2XS and London: Macmillan Press Ltd.

Gerchunoff, P. and Llach, L. (2018). *El Ciclo de La Ilusión y El Desencanto. Políticas Económicas Argentinas de 1880 a Nuestros Días.* 1ª Edición. Ciudad Autónoma de Buenos Aires: CRITICA (Paidós SAICF).

Gerchunoff, P. and Llach, L. (2009). "Equality or Growth: A 20th Century Argentine Dilemma." *Revista de Historia Económica* 27 (3): 397–426.

Grotz, M. and Llach, J. J. (2013). "Coparticipación Casi Sin Convergencia, 1950–2010." In *Consecuencias Económicas y Políticas Del Federalismo Fiscal Argentino*, edited by Carlos Gervasoni and Alberto Porto. La Plata.

Hofman, A. A. (2001). "Long Run Economic Development in Latin America in a Comparative Perspective: Proximate and Ultimate Causes." Macroeconomía Del Desarrollo. Santiago de Chile.

Instituto Nacional de Estadística y Censos. (1974). "Anuario Estadístico de La República Argentina 1973." Buenos Aires: Instituto Nacional de Estadística y Censos.

Instituto Nacional de Estadística y Censos. (1975a). "Producto Bruto Geográfico".

Instituto Nacional de Estadística y Censos. (1975b). "Serie Anual de La Población de La Capital Federal y Las Provincias Por Sexo y Grupo de Edades, 1960–1975." Buenos Aires: Instituto Nacional de Estadística y Censos.

Instituto Nacional de Estadística y Censos. (1989). "Proyecciones Provinciales Por Sexo y Edad. Período 1970/1990".

Instituto Nacional de Estadística y Censos. (1993). "Proyecciones Provinciales Por Grupos de Edad. Período 1985–1990".

Instituto Nacional de Estadística y Censos. (1996). "Estimaciones de La Población Por Departamento. Período 1990–2005".

Instituto Nacional de Estadística y Censos. (2008). *Estimaciones de Población Total Por Departamento y Año Calendario. Período 2001–2010.* Buenos Aires: Instituto Nacional de Estadística y Censos.

Instituto Nacional de Estadística y Censos. (2016). *Cuentas Nacionales: Metodología de Estimación: Base 2004 y Serie a Precios Constantes y Corrientes.* Ciudad Autónoma de Buenos Aires: Instituto Nacional de Estadística y Censos.

Juarez-Dappe, P. (2010). *When Sugar Ruled: Economy and Society in Northwestern Argentina, Tucuman, 1876–1916.* Ohio University Press.

Maloney, W. F. and Valencia Caicedo, F. (2016). "The Persistence of (Subnational) Fortune." *The Economic Journal* 126: 2363–2401.

Marina, A. (2001). "Convergencia Económica En Argentina ¿Qué Nos Dice La Evidencia Empírica?" In *Convergencia Económica e Integración: La Experiencia En Europa y América Latina*, edited by Tomás Mancha-Navarro and Daniel Sotelsek-Salem, 147–62. Ediciones Pirámide.

Martínez, R. G. (2004). "Estimaciones Preliminares Del Producto Interno Provincial a Precios Constantes. Periodo 1980/2002." Unpublished.

Ministerio de Agricultura de la República Argentina. (1916). "Estadística Agrícola 1914–1915." Buenos Aires: Talleres Gráficos del Ministerio de Agricultura de la Nación.

Ministerio de Agricultura de la República Argentina. (1939). "Censo Nacional Agropecuario 1937." Buenos Aires: Guillermo Kraft Ltda.

Ministerio de Asuntos Técnicos. (n.d.) "Anuario Estadístico de La República Argentina 1949–1950." Buenos Aires: Dirección Nacional del Servicio Estadístico.

Rapoport, M. (2008). *Historia Económica, Política y Social de La Argentina, 1880–2003.* 2da Edición. Buenos Aires: Emecé.

República Argentina. (1898). *Segundo Censo de La República Argentina*. Buenos Aires: Taller Tipográfico de la Penitenciaría Nacional.

República Argentina. (1916a). *Anuario Estadístico Del Trabajo.* Buenos Aires: Talleres Gráficos A. de Martino.

República Argentina. (1916b). *Tercer Censo Nacional de La República Argentina.* Buenos Aires: Talleres gráficos de L.J. Rosso y Cia.

República Argentina (n.d.). *IV Censo General de La Nación.* Dirección Nacional del Servicio Estadístico.

Secretaría de Asuntos Económicos. (1955). Producto e Ingreso de la República Argentina en el periodo 1935–1954. Buenos Aires: Secretaría de Asuntos Económicos, Poder Ejecutivo Nacional, República Argentina.

Sanz Villarroya, I. (2009). "Macroeconomic Outcomes and the Relative Position of Argentina's Economy, 1875–2000." *Journal of Latin American Studies* 41: 309–46.

Seguí, D. F. (1898). *Investigación Parlamentaria Sobre Agricultura, Ganadería, Industrias Derivadas y Colonización. Anexo B. Provincia de Buenos Aires.* Taller Tipográfico de la Peninteciaría Nacional.

Sempat Assadourian, C. (1982). *El Sistema de La Economía Colonial. Mercado Interno, Regiones y Espacio Económico.* Edited by Estudios Históricos. 1ª edición. Lima: Instituto de Estudios Peruanos.

Talassino, M. R. (2015). "Producto Bruto Geográfico de 1946 de Las Provincias Argentinas: Una Estimación Preliminar." In *L Reunión Anual de La Asociación Argentina de Economía Política*, edited by Asociación Argentina de Economía Política. Salta.

Talassino, M. R. (2019). "Producto Bruto Geográfico de Las Provincias Argentinas Durante La Primera Mitad Del Siglo XX: Estimación y Análisis de Convergencia." In *XVII Jornadas Interescuelas/Departamentos de Historia*. San Fernando del Valle de Catamarca.

Young, A. T., Higgins, M. J. and Levy, D. (2008). "Sigma Convergence versus Beta Convergence: Evidence from U.S. County-Level Data." *Journal of Money, Credit and Banking* 40, (5): 1083–93.

CHAPTER 5

From West to East: Bolivian Regional GDPs since the 1950s. A Story of Natural Resources and Infrastructure

José A. Peres-Cajías

1 Introduction

This volume analyzes the evolution of the location of economic activity in Latin America through time and seeks to identify its main determinants. The present chapter on Bolivia's regional GDPs offers additional insights to this general effort given the landlocked nature of the country. Indeed,

The author acknowledges funding from Generalitat de Catalunya-AGAUR through the Beatriu de Pinós program (BP2016-00407). The author thanks suggestions and comments made by authors of the present volume to former versions of the chapter, particularly those by Marc Badia-Miró, Esteban Nicolini, Daniel Tirado, and Henry Willebald. The generous provision of information by Pablo Mendieta and Rafael Vera on regional GDPs during the 1970s and early 1980s and the invaluable cooperation of the staff at the Biblioteca Departamental/Gobernación de Santa Cruz are also highly appreciated.

J. A. Peres-Cajías (✉)
Universitat de Barcelona, Barcelona, Spain
e-mail: joalperes@ub.edu

D. A. Tirado-Fabregat et al. (eds.), *Time and Space*,
Palgrave Studies in Economic History,
https://doi.org/10.1007/978-3-030-47553-6_5

it has been suggested several times that economic activity in landlocked countries could be highly determined by investments in infrastructure such as roads or bridges (Limao and Venables 2001; *United Nations* 2014; Wilmsmeier and Sánchez 2009). This is undoubtedly the case for the Bolivian economy, which, in addition to the lack of sea access, offers a vibrant set of ecological regions (with a considerable ruggedness to some of them), and does not have navigable rivers that connect the most populated areas.

The analysis of Bolivia's regional GDPs is also illustrative of Bolivian historiography. On the one hand, a very influential interpretation stresses that Bolivian history is not the result of class clashes, but that of regional confrontations (Roca 1999). It is argued that despite a centralized framework being adopted by the country since Independence (1825), territorial conflicts have been constant throughout history. The civil war, which took place at the end of the nineteenth century and determined a change of the Legislative and Executive seats from Sucre to La Paz, was the most dramatic example. Another recent illustration lies in the political turmoil fueled by regional demands at the beginning of the twenty-first century.[1] On the other hand, except a book published several decades ago (Fifer 1972), most historical studies have focused on specific regions of the country (Langer and Conti 1991; Rodríguez Ostria 1994; Sandoval et al. 2003).

The current chapter overcomes the above mentioned limitation by offering a general assessment of the economic activity in Bolivian regions thanks to an estimation, for the first time, of regional GDPs in Bolivia since 1950 onwards.[2] In contrast to most works in this volume, the analysis of Bolivia's regional GDPs starts in 1950. This limitation is related to the inability to allocate agriculture production (see the methodological section) between the different Bolivian *departamentos* (see the discussion

[1] Political instability increased dramatically in Bolivia at the beginning of the twentieth-first century because of different reasons. One of them was the demand for higher political and administrative autonomy by the east and south departments. Moreover, separatist claims were also sometimes expressed, even if its relative relevance in the political debate is debatable.

[2] Urquiola et al. (1999) study the evolution of economic activity from 1950 to 1992 by using population statistics. Machicado et al. (2012) and Pereira et al. (2012) offer a general assessment of regional growth by using regional GDPs from 1988 to 2009. Recently, Mendieta (2019) offered an analysis of regional GDPs that starts earlier than previous work (the 1970s) but not earlier than the present one.

in Herranz-Loncán and Peres-Cajías 2016).[3] Departments will be the unit of analysis of this chapter due to two features: (a) no significant border changes have taken place since the late 1930s; (b) there is evidence of a wide range of economic indicators for the administrative unit from the 1950s onwards, something that does not hold for provinces or municipalities—the latter were importantly reorganized in the early 1990s. Map 5.1 shows the nine Bolivian departments and the ecological diversity previously noted.

The new quantitative evidence shows the economic upsurge and consolidation of new regions beyond the traditional economic zones, which were located to the west of the country since colonial times. This process took place in the second half of the twentieth century and is in stark contrast with other case studies covered in this volume, where economic activity has tended to be concentrated continuously in the same regions since

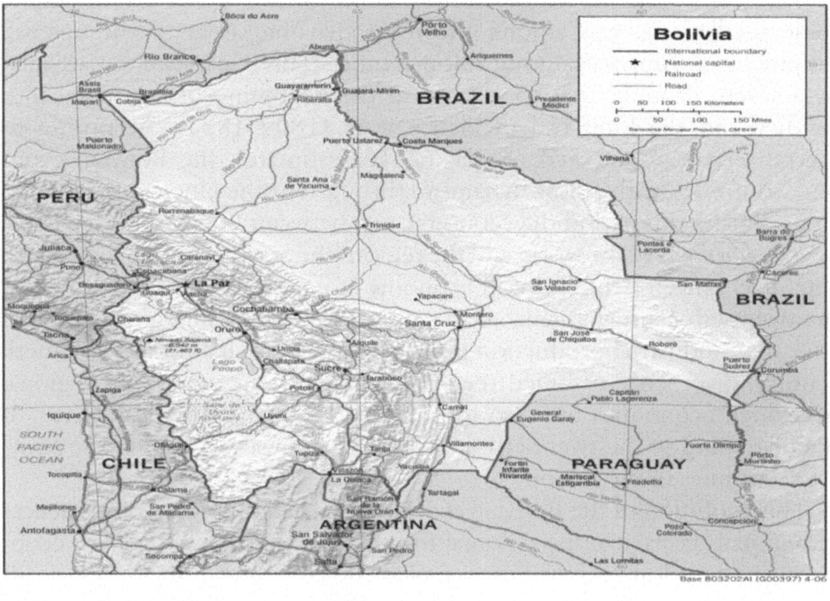

Map 5.1 Administrative division of Bolivia and ecological regions. (Sources: Maps of CIA, Central Intelligence Agency)

[3] Bolivia is divided into nine *departamentos*, which are composed of provinces which, in turn, are composed of municipalities.

the mid-nineteenth century. This changing pattern is first explained by the availability of rich natural resource endowments. However, given the landlocked nature of the country and the relevance of transports costs, it is argued that natural resources may act as potent engines of regional economic growth only when a minimum network of public infrastructure is available.

After this introduction, the rest of the chapter is organized as follows. Section 2 presents an overview of the evolution of regional economic growth in Bolivia since Independence to the present day. Section 3 explains the methodology and sources used in the reconstruction of regional GDPs. Section 4 presents the main results, and Sect. 5 concludes.

2 Regional Growth in Bolivia Since Independence

The current economic space of Bolivia has been integrated into the world economy since the sixteenth century thanks to silver exports and, despite some oscillations, was among the most dynamic areas of the Spanish Empire in the Americas during colonial times. This dynamism was affected by a severe drought that took place at the beginning of the nineteenth century and the long Independence wars (1809–1825). According to Herranz-Loncán and Peres-Cajías (2016) estimates, the Bolivian economy continued with a slow dynamism throughout the nineteenth century. Thus, during this period the economic gap between Bolivia and the developed economies of the world and the region (the Southern cone) increased. The divergence of the Bolivian economy stopped during the first half of the twentieth century thanks to the consolidation of mining exports and, after that, industrial production. During the second half of the twentieth century, divergence resumed regarding not only the world and regional developed economies but also most countries in the Americas. Thus, at the beginning of the twentieth-first century, Bolivia was among the poorest economies in the region.

This evolution of the Bolivian economy has had different consequences in regional terms. During colonial times, far away from an enclave economy, silver exploitation in Potosí fueled the economic integration of different economic regions (Assadourian 1982). In effect, either by the supply of currency or by demand effects, the economic behavior of Potosí profoundly influenced cereal production in Cochabamba or sugar production in Santa Cruz, to name a couple of examples. This market integration was not uniform across the different regions or through time. However, it persisted until the last decades of colonial rule (Menegus Bornemann 1999).

Once Independence was achieved (1825), these colonial markets remained integrated (Mitre 1986). Nevertheless, they were affected by the new political and economic context (Gelman 2009; Prado 1995). On the one hand, silver production in Potosí was unable to recover from the sharp decrease that took place at the beginning of the nineteenth century. On the other hand, de-urbanization, the consolidation of foreign competitors, and the direct and indirect costs of Independence created new restrictions. In spite of this low economic dynamism, the relative importance of Bolivian regions remained more or less similar to that of colonial times, the departments of La Paz, Cochabamba, Potosí, and Chuquisaca being the most important (Dalence 1851; Pentland 1975). The former two because of their agricultural centrality, the third for mining and agriculture production, and the latter for its administrative importance.

Some decades later and in spite of the general slow dynamism of the economy, some critical changes must be considered to understand future regional differentiation. First, after a slow but constant recovery since the 1850s, silver production in Potosí overcame colonial records during the early 1870s (Mitre 1981). Second, whereas the coastal region was a marginal one in terms of population density or state presence, the loss at the War of the Pacific against Chile (1879) determined the landlocked nature of Bolivia. Third, disadvantageous trade agreements with neighbor countries and the arrival of railways to the mining centers of Uyuni (1888) and Oruro (1892) improved the competitiveness of imports to the west of the country (Peres-Cajías 2017).[4] Consequently, contrary to colonial times, the rebound in mining production witnessed during the last decades of the nineteenth century did not necessarily improve production levels to those Bolivian regions specialized in agricultural or manufacturing production (Rodríguez Ostria 1994).

Further changes took place during the last decade of the nineteenth century. Indeed, the fall in the international price of silver and the

[4] The most relevant of the mentioned bilateral trade agreements were those signed with Chile and Peru. The treaties included different elements such as transit fees or administrative clauses. However, they also implied virtual free trade agreements between Bolivia and these countries. The liberalization was disadvantageous for Bolivia since few products were exported from this country to the remained two. By contrast, different Chilean and Peruvian products, such as wheat or sugar, competed directly with Bolivian local production (Peres-Cajías 2017).

consequent crisis in the sector was offset by a rapid transition to tin exploitation, which was located once more in the west (Mitre 1993). At the same time, there was a rapid rise in rubber production in the north-east of the country, which reached international markets through the networks of Amazonian rivers that end up in the Atlantic Ocean (Gamarra Téllez 2007); these routes were transited both by traditional boats and by steamships. Thus, for the first time, a Bolivian commodity was located beyond the Andes, and its exploitation fueled new economic interactions between the departments of Santa Cruz, Beni, and Pando (Orsag 2019). Last but not the least, the victory of the liberals in the so-called Federal War (1898–1899) determined the transfer of the Executive and Legislative seats from Sucre to La Paz and, with it, the consolidation of new political elites.

On the eve of the twentieth century, these new elites promoted an export-led growth strategy through different schemes that looked at the restrictions that affected a landlocked economy. For instance, separate peace and boundary treaties were signed with all neighboring countries (Paraguay being the exception) to reduce transaction costs, such as the payment of transit fees (Peres-Cajías 2017). Likewise, new railway lines were built, which allowed connecting western locations to the world economy (through the Ocean Pacific) and between them. In this context, La Paz and Oruro consolidated as the leading economic poles of the Bolivian economy, the latter because of mining production and the former for being the new seat of government and that of modern services such as banking or retailing. In contrast, local suppliers in the east had greater difficulties in reaching the old western colonial markets. Thus, not surprisingly, the representatives of eastern departments protested against the existence of a so-called "railways regionalism" and asked for the spread of railways to their regions (Barragán and Peres-Cajías 2007).

In the context of economic growth at the country level, the years of World War I witnessed new changes in this regional divide. As a result of Asian competition, the rubber boom ended abruptly in 1914, which affected exports and the regional dynamism generated in the east by this commodity. After that, a railway line between Cochabamba and Oruro was inaugurated in 1917, which allowed the connection of the former to the most dynamic regions. Mainly due to this line, railway expansion also became crucial to the transport of local products inside the country and not only in export commodities to international markets (Contreras 2017). Meanwhile, price and production increases allowed the expansion of mining exports. Thus, tin consolidated as the most important export, representing at least two-thirds of Bolivian exports since the late 1910s to the early 1950s (Peres-Cajías and Carreras-Marín 2017). It was also noticed that during that same period, 80% of Bolivian exports transited through Chilean ports (Arica and Antofagasta) before reaching world markets (Agramont and Peres-Cajías 2016).

The Great Depression represented the first major crisis that the Bolivian economy suffered in the twentieth century (Herranz-Loncán and Peres-Cajías 2016). Its effects were increased by the Chaco War (1932–1935), and it was not until 1938 that the GDP per capita recovered to the pre-crisis level. As a consequence of these shocks and changes in the political status quo, state intervention in the economy became increasingly important. This was reflected, for instance, in higher taxes on mining (Contreras 1990; Peres-Cajías 2014) or the nationalization of oil resources, a sector located in the south-east of the country that was growing tentatively since the 1920s (Klein and Peres-Cajías 2014). The trauma of the war also brought anxiety about the need to integrate the country. This was reflected in a railway project to connect Santa Cruz with Argentina and Brazil and the centralization of road investment, an alternative that begun to be considered in the 1930s (Contreras 2017). However, the lack of connection between Cochabamba and Santa Cruz persisted and maintained the division of the Bolivian internal market and the economic supremacy of western departments (Peres-Cajías 2017). This division was amplified by an industrialization process that started in the late 1920s and was highly concentrated in the department of La Paz (CEPAL 1958; Rodríguez Ostria 1999).

The 1952–1985 period is one of the most exciting and paradoxical in Bolivian economic history: whereas it began and ended with major financial crises (which explains the Bolivian divergence), it presented the highest economic growth rates in the middle years (Herranz-Loncán and Peres-Cajías 2016). The period is associated with state capitalism, given that, after the 1952 Revolution, state intervention in the economy became critical, either by the increase of public investment or by the creation of new public companies (Wilkie 1969; Zondag 1966). The 1952 Revolution also fostered the so-called "East March", an economic strategy that presented the following objectives: (a) the connection of the east and west of the country through the construction of a new highway between Cochabamba and Santa Cruz; (b) the substitution of agricultural imports by promoting agrarian projects in the east; (c) the replacement of oil imports by investing directly or facilitating private investment in the hydrocarbon industry.

Progressively, the "East March" modified the regional divide. In effect, Santa Cruz became connected to Brazil and Argentina through railways since 1953 and 1957, respectively, and to Cochabamba through the highway inaugurated in 1954. Likewise, imports of several agricultural products such as sugar or rice were substituted, and agro-industrial production increased. Whereas the results were less successful in terms of exports (for instance, cotton sales in the early 1970s were not sustainable [Demeure 1999]), products of Santa Cruz (such as sugar) regained prominence in western markets. More critically, price differentials between Santa Cruz de la Sierra (the capital city of Santa Cruz) and the rest of department capitals tended to disappear toward the 1960s (Peres-Cajías 2017). As for the hydrocarbon sector, oil self-sufficiency was achieved in 1954, and progressive improvement continued until the 1970s when the industry became central at a national level in terms of both its size over GDP and its contribution to total exports (Klein and Peres-Cajías 2014).

Despite the impulse of national integration through road construction, large areas of the country remained isolated. This was particularly true for the departments of Beni and Pando. In effect, in contrast to Santa Cruz, price differentials between Trinidad and Cobija (the capitals of Beni and Pando) and the rest of capitals remained significant during the 1960s. Likewise, it was not until the 1980s that a paved road between Santa Cruz de la Sierra and Trinidad was inaugurated. Thus, the increase in meat production in Beni that started in the late 1940s was possible only because of the existence of airplane facilities (De Marchi et al. 2018). Indeed, the creation of public companies and the proliferation of private services allowed the transportation of meat from several places in Beni to west markets, particularly the city of La Paz and the mines in Oruro and Potosí.

The limits of state capitalism became evident in the early 1980s. On the one hand, although the development of so-called medium-sized mining (in private hands) generated some dynamism and diversification, nationalized mining represented almost two-thirds of the sector (Espinoza 2010). Production levels in this subsector remained stagnant, so its financial sustainability ended up depending exclusively on the evolution of international prices. As for manufacturing production, the sector did not surpass 15% of the Bolivian GDP since the 1940s, depended on foreign inputs, and was concentrated in the so-called light areas (Luna 1995). Worse still, there was an exceptional drought in 1982 that affected agricultural production, especially in the western departments (Luna 1995). Likewise, Bolivian public finances depended on external resources (Peres-Cajías 2014). In this context, state intervention ended up as an engine of macroeconomic instability that was reflected in a sharp hyperinflation process (Kehoe et al. 2019). Thus, during these years, the only economic activities that maintained some dynamism were oil and gas production in the southeast of the country, and cocaine production (which in contrast to coca leaf production is not accounted for in official statistics) in the tropical valleys of Cochabamba and Beni (SEAMOS 1992).

Hyperinflation ceased in 1985 through a shock policy that was accompanied by several structural reforms that were in line with the Washington Consensus. These policy changes were effective in curbing macroeconomic instability, but not so much in promoting economic growth: between 1985 and 2004, growth rates were not particularly high and were affected by the various financial crises that took place in Latin America. Moreover, the change in the role of state intervention very often created social tensions and fostered regional differentiation. This was particularly clear in the case of the public mining company, whose closure generated around 20,000 unemployed in the departments of Potosí and Oruro; this shock was worsened by a general crisis in the mining sector led by the sharp decrease of international prices that took place in the mid-1980s.[5] In the same vein, the end of state protection affected the traditional industrial sector.

In stark contrast, thanks to a partnership between the Bolivian government, private companies, and foreign aid, a soybean complex was developed in Santa Cruz, and exports of these products became relevant immediately (Montenegro and Guzmán 1999). Similarly, thanks to a gas trade agreement between Brazil and Bolivia (which started in the mid-1970s and was finally reached in the early 1990s), and the subsequent construction of a pipeline, natural gas became the most critical Bolivian export since 2000, representing around 40% of total exports.

During the 2004–2014 period, the Bolivian economy was benefited by the commodities super cycle. In regional terms, the benefited regions were widespread. For instance, it helped the hydrocarbon departments (Tarija, Chuquisaca, and Santa Cruz), the mining regions (Potosí, Oruro, north of La Paz), soybean producers (Santa Cruz), and, at the end of the period, quinoa producers located in La Paz, Oruro, and Potosí. In spite of

[5] Notice that other public companies were also closed or privatized.

these improvements, there is still evidence pointing to the low integration of the Bolivian economy, a phenomenon that especially affects Beni and Pando.[6] Indeed, whereas there has been a noticeable increase in public investment in roads over the past years, the most important cities of Pando and Beni (Cobija, Trinidad, and Riberalta) are not connected by a paved road or to the national system (see De Marchi et al. 2018).[7]

Summing up, this overlook of Bolivian regional growth suggests the existence of some stylized facts: (a) the Bolivian economy has been integrated into the world economy through the export of a few commodities; (b) the construction of the Bolivian internal market has been painful and is still an ongoing process; (c) changes in Bolivian exports were in line with changes in the relative importance of Bolivian regions; (d) these changes were determined by natural resource endowments and investment in transport infrastructures such as railways or roads. The analysis of Bolivia's regional GDPs will allow the identification of the size and timing of these changes.

3 The Estimation of Bolivian Regional GDPs

"Historical GDP reconstructions are the result of ad hoc efforts by individual scholars who had to make the best possible use of available incomplete sources" (Felice 2019: 8). So, this section aims to present the methodology and sources used in the estimation of Bolivia's regional GDPs. This allows identifying the potentialities and restrictions of the new quantitative evidence. First of all, the reconstruction is based on the production approach, by which sectoral GDPs at the national level are allocated between the nine Bolivian departments: regional GDPs are obtained as an aggregation once all national-sectoral GDPs have been distributed between the nine departments. The reconstruction considered six different sectors: agriculture, mining, hydrocarbons, manufactures, electricity and gas, and the rest of services (which aggregates construction, financial establishments, trade, transport, communal services, restaurants, and hotels, and public administration services). The inability to allocate

[6] This has been proved by looking at the correlation of regional GDP growth from 1988 to 2009 (Pereira et al. 2012) or a spatial correlation matrix from 1970 to 2015 (Mendieta 2019).

[7] Truly, the network of Amazonian rivers has been widely used for Bolivian internal trade during and after the rubber boom. However, this system is still under the control of the state and is not a reliable alternative to road transport (see de Marchi et al. 2018).

agricultural production before 1950 (because of the inexistence of reliable information on *national production levels* and the inexistence of indicators to map the output of the leading products *by regions*) explains why the reconstruction of Bolivia's regional GDPs starts in 1950.

Secondly, given the relevance of the so-called "Gerschenkron effect" (the changing results that may derive from linking series calculated in different base years, Felice 2019: 12), sectoral GDPs were in current prices. This, however, may generate other sources of bias when comparing the economic importance of regions. Specifically, it may increase the size of resource-rich regions just because of increases in international prices.

Thirdly, the distribution of the sectoral GDP has been based mostly on direct indicators (Felice 2019) (see Table 5.1). To this end, the reconstruction used the current methodological guidelines of the official estimations of Bolivia's regional GDPs (INE 2004). For instance, it has been based on some of the same indicators used to allocate sectoral GDPs, or, has been achieved through the use of national average prices (i.e., uniform prices across the regions).

Table 5.1 Sources and indicators used in the reconstruction of Bolivian regional GDPs

Sectors	*1950*	*1967*	*1970*	*1980*	*1988–2017*
Agriculture	Direct: gross value of production	Ministerio de Planificación (1970a)	COPSCZ (1982)	Ministerio de Planificación (1992)	Official estimations
Mining	Direct: value exported	Direct: gross value of production			
Hydrocarbon	Direct: production	Ministerio de Planificación (1970a)			
Manufactures	Direct: gross value of production	Direct: gross value of production			
Electricity	Direct: production	Ministerio de Planificación (1970a)			
Rest of sectors	Indirect: urban population	Indirect: urban population			

Sources: Author's own elaboration

Along with the use of some previously unexplored secondary sources (which were first presented by Mendieta 2019), the original contribution of this chapter is the estimation of Bolivia's regional GDPs in 1950 and 1967. The following paragraphs explain the indicators and sources used in this reconstruction. To begin with, the agricultural sector (which represented 31% of Bolivian GDP in 1950) was allocated over the nine departments by estimating the share of each department in the value of production of a sample of products.[8] For this, information on quantities were obtained from the National Agrarian Census of 1950, and that of prices from CEPAL (1958). The agricultural GDP of 1967 was then allocated to each department by the Ministerio de Planificación y Coordinación (1970a).

Secondly, two different extractive subsectors were reconstructed: mining and hydrocarbons. In 1950, the mining GDP (13% of Bolivia's GDP) was allocated over five departments (La Paz, Oruro, Potosí, Cochabamba, and Chuquisaca) by using the value of exports declared in the Bolivian official trade statistics; the allocation was based on the average relative importance of mining exports of each department in 1950 and 1951. In 1967, the distribution took into account the relative importance of each department (La Paz, Oruro, Potosí, and Cochabamba) in the value of production presented by Ministerio de Planificación y Coordinación (1970b). The hydrocarbon sector was distributed by using the produced quantities of oil in each department in 1950;[9] for 1967, the estimations by the Ministerio de Planificación y Coordinación (1970a) were used.

[8] Given the diversification of the Bolivian agricultural sector and differences in the productive aptitude of the various regions of the country, several products have been considered: nine crops (maize, potatoes, wheat, coffee, yucca, rice, barley, coca, sugar cane), three fruits (oranges, raisins, and peaches), and three livestock products (beef, lamb, and pork meat). The value of production obtained with this sample of products is equivalent to 84% of the value of production of the agricultural sector estimated by CEPAL (1958). Furthermore, the sample of products used allows obtaining a structure of agricultural production that is very similar to that of official statistics: in our estimation the total agricultural value of production is distributed between crops (55%), fruits (5%), and livestock products (40%); in that of official statistics it is distributed between crops (43%), fruits (9%), livestock products (42%), forestry (4%), and exports (1%). See CEPAL (1958).

[9] These were obtained from *Estadísticas económicas de la actividad petrolera* (www.ine.gob.bo/indice/indice.aspx?d1=0201&d2=6). The distribution according to production figures by the department assumes the absence of large differences in operating costs and/or in the level of productivity of the different oil fields. This assumption can be accepted as valid for

Thirdly, manufacturing production (15% of Bolivia's GDP in 1950) was allocated based on the share of each department on the value of production provided by CEPAL (1958) for 1950, and by the Ministerio de Planificación y Coordinación (1970b) for 1967. In the case of 1950, the value of production used was that of each department in 1954.[10]

Fourthly, Bolivian statistics include in a single sector the value added by electricity, water, and gas production. Due to the lack of information on the water sector and practically zero gas production, the distribution of this sectoral GDP in 1950 (1.4% of total GDP) was carried out considering electricity production in thousands of kWh on each department capital in 1954.[11] In the case of 1967, the estimations by the Ministerio de Planificación y Coordinación (1970a) were used.

Finally, the rest of the sectors were added into a single category due to the lack of indicators that allow for its regional distribution. Thus, following Badia-Miró (2015), the distribution of this remnant was operationalized considering the relative importance of each department in the urban population.

Before presenting the main results, it is also necessary to clarify the sources of population figures. Total population figures for the years 1846, 1900, and 1950 were obtained from Herranz-Loncán and Peres-Cajías (2016).[12] The share of department population was obtained from Dalence

the period and, given the low relative importance of the hydrocarbon sector, does not affect the main conclusions of the chapter.

[10] Bolivian regional GDP statistics consider seven different subsectors: food; drinks and tobacco; textiles, clothing and leather products; wood and wood products; other manufacturing industries; petroleum refining products; and non-metallic mineral products. The use of the 1954 value is justified by the "inertia that normally tends to be created in terms of location" (CEPAL 1958: 131). Furthermore, the original source does not record the information related to industrial production in the departments of Tarija, Beni, and Pando. However, the source reports the production value of "Other Departments", which has been distributed among these three departments taking into account their relative importance on urban population in 1950.

[11] The original source also presented electrical production generated by the "Great Mining" and electrical production generated in the "Rest of the country". The former has been distributed among the mining departments by applying the mining GDP ratios of 1950 previously presented; the electrical production of the "rest of the country" was assigned to the nine departments considering their relative importance for urban population. The use of urban population is justified by the fact that there was no interconnected national system of electricity. So, consumption should be strongly correlated with production.

[12] In this work, total population is the result of the aggregation of the census population, the "non-subject" population, and the population added by census omission.

(1851), and the population censuses of 1900 and 1950; these same sources were used for the estimation of urban population (people living in locations with more than 2000 inhabitants). For 1976, 1992, 2001, and 2012, Bolivian total population figures were obtained from ECLAC (Economic Commission for Latin America and the Caribbean) estimates, which apply a correction factor by census omission (which is common in most censuses) on the original census data. In each of these four years, shares of both department population and urban population were obtained from the original figures offered by national censuses. Lastly, population figures between census years were obtained by geometric interpolation.

4 The Relative Importance of Bolivian Regions, 1950–2017

This section presents the evolution of economic activity in Bolivian departments through time. Department population figures allow an initial insight into the relative importance of Bolivian regions since Independence onwards (Table 5.2). The data shows that despite a small reduction over the last decades, the relative importance of La Paz has been maintained since the nineteenth century, being the most populated department until

Table 5.2 Departmental population (%, the share of total population), 1846–2012

%	*1846*	*1900*	*1950*	*1976*	*1992*	*2001*	*2012*
La Paz	29.0	25.6	30.6	31.8	29.6	28.4	27.0
Oruro	6.4	5.0	6.9	6.7	5.3	4.7	4.9
Potosí	16.4	18.9	18.2	14.3	10.1	8.6	8.2
Cochabamba	19.0	19.1	16.3	15.6	17.3	17.6	17.5
Chuquisaca	11.1	11.9	9.5	7.8	7.1	6.4	5.8
Tarija	6.2	5.4	4.2	4.1	4.5	4.7	4.8
Santa Cruz	6.6	11.1	9.5	15.4	21.2	24.5	26.4
Beni	4.8	1.8	4.1	3.6	4.3	4.4	4.2
Pando		1.3	0.6	0.7	0.6	0.6	1.1
Litoral	0.3						

Sources: See text

Notes: No information is presented for Litoral from 1900 onwards because this department was lost during the War of the Pacific (1879). The department of Beni was created in 1842, and the population information for 1846 includes data from the current department of Pando. Indeed, Pando was founded only in 1938, so the 1900 information refers to what was called "National Territory of Colonies"

very recent years (according to official projections around 2015). In the case of Oruro, there have been continuous oscillations around a mean of 5% of the total Bolivian population. In contrast, the relative importance of Potosí remained high during the nineteenth century and the first half of the twentieth century but declined after that: from a peak of 18% of the total Bolivian population in 1950, it decreased to 8% in 2012. In Valles, the relative importance of Cochabamba and Tarija fell slightly during the first half of the twentieth century but also recovered after that. Furthermore, Cochabamba has been the second/third most populated department in Bolivia throughout this time, absorbing 15–20% of the Bolivian population. As for Chuquisaca, it stands out for having a continuous decline during the twentieth century, reducing from 12% (1900) to 6% (2012) of the total Bolivian population.

To understand the changes above, Table 5.3 presents information on rates of population annual average growth and net immigration by department since 1950—that is, during the period of the most dramatic changes.[13] Indeed, the table shows that the decline in the relative importance of Potosí over total population can be explained by low population growth rates (they have systematically been among the lowest), and the relevance of negative immigration rates (they have been the most negative during the entire period under scrutiny). A favorite destination of Potosí emigrants was La Paz (particularly before the debt crisis of the 1980s), Cochabamba, and Santa Cruz (in both cases, particularly after the debt crisis of the 1980s).

In the same vein, the decline in the relative importance of Chuquisaca over total population is also linked with low population growth rates (except the 1976–1992 period, consistently among the lowest), and the relevance of negative immigration rates (systematically, the second most

[13] Figures on population annual average growth rates depicted in Table 5.3 are different to those presented by official Bolivian statistics (see, for example, INE 2012: 13) since, as previously stated, I introduce the CEPAL figures on total population that includes census omission. During the 1950–1976 period, my estimates on department population growth rates are generally 0.2 percentage points higher; the only exception is Beni where the INE figure presents a growth rate of 3.3% per year. During the 1976–1992 period, my estimates are 0.1 percentage points higher. The 1992–2001 period is more problematic since my estimates are 0.5 percentage points lower. Differences in the 2001–2012 period are not significant. In spite of these differences between my estimates and those of INE, the relative importance of each department in terms of population growth rates remains similar, which is in keeping with the conclusions of the analysis.

Table 5.3 Department population growth rates and immigration rates (%), 1950–2012

	1950–1976		*1976–1992*		*1992–2001*		*2001–2012*	
	Population growth	*Net immigration*	*Population growth*	*Net immigration*	*Population growth*	*Net immigration*	*Population growth*	*Net immigration*
La Paz	2.3	3.3	1.8	0.0	1.8	−2.5	1.3	−3.9
Oruro	2.0	−6.4	0.8	−18.6	1.0	−20.5	2.1	−13.5
Potosí	1.2	−10.2	0.1	−22.8	0.5	−27.3	1.3	−24.8
Cochabamba	2.0	−2.3	2.9	8.2	2.5	6.6	1.7	6.9
Chuquisaca	1.4	−9.8	1.7	−12.0	1.2	−15.0	0.7	−16.3
Tarija	2.0	5.7	3.0	9.2	2.7	14.4	1.9	13.3
Santa Cruz	4.1	18.4	4.3	22.2	3.9	27.2	2.4	19.4
Beni	1.7	−6.9	3.3	−5.9	2.5	−10.9	1.3	−11.8
Pando	2.7	4.8	0.8	−3.8	3.0	10.5	6.9	44.2

Sources: For population growth figures, see text. Net immigration rates were calculated by using total population figures by place of birth and place of residence originally offered in national censuses

Notes: Immigration rates are measured as the difference between total immigrants and total emigrants in the department i over total population originally born in department i between census years without considering foreign immigrants or Bolivians that migrated abroad

negative during the period analyzed). It was noticed that most of the Chuquisaca emigrants (around 50%) went to Santa Cruz. Table 5.3 also shows low population growth rates and negative immigration rates in the case of Oruro (particularly during the 1976–2001 period), which may help to understand the oscillations in the relative importance of its population over total population. Throughout this time, Oruro's population migrated to La Paz (particularly before the debt crisis of the 1980s) and Cochabamba (particularly after the debt crisis of the 1980s).

The dramatic increase in the population in Santa Cruz represents the other side of the coin. Indeed, Table 5.2 shows that there has been considerable stability, as well as a marginal role in the relative importance of Beni (around 4%) and Pando (below 1%) over the total Bolivian population. In contrast, the decline of Santa Cruz during the first half of the twentieth century was recovered after that, jumping from 10% (1950) to 26% (2012) of total population. Moreover, according to up-to-date estimations, Santa Cruz is nowadays the most populated Bolivian department.

This increase is explained by the achievement of the highest population growth rates during the second half of the twentieth century (around 4% per year) and the significance of favorable immigration rates (approximately 20% of the population initially born in the department) (see Table 5.3). Whereas Santa Cruz received immigrants from all over the country, most of them initially came from Cochabamba, Chuquisaca, and Potosí; after the debt crisis of the 1980s, immigration fluxes from these departments remained significant, and those from La Paz became relevant.

Overall, population figures stress changes in the relative importance of Bolivian regions that, since 1950, negatively affected western departments in favor of Santa Cruz. The estimation of regional GDPs per capita offers new evidence that goes in this same direction (Table 5.4). Indeed, it is true that, despite some loss in their relative importance during the last quarter of the twentieth century, La Paz and, overall, Oruro have maintained their economic relevance. However, there is an apparent reversal of fortune in the case of Potosí: whereas its GDP per capita was similar to the national average in 1950, it has tended to be below the national average since the 1960s, and it has been among the lowest until the last commodity boom. In contrast, the regional GDP per capita of Santa Cruz has been above the national average since the 1960s. Similarly, whereas the regional GDP per capita of Tarija was among the lowest in the 1950s, it has increased since the mid-1970s. Not surprisingly, once natural gas

Table 5.4 Departmental pc GDP (Bolivian pc GDP = 1), 1950–2017

	1950	*1967*	*1970*	*1980*	*1988*	*1995*	*2005*	*2012*	*2017*
La Paz	1.13	1.04	1.04	0.94	0.92	1.01	0.88	0.93	1.09
Oruro	1.40	1.08	1.29	1.40	1.02	1.13	1.02	1.03	1.11
Potosí	0.99	0.81	0.90	0.66	0.56	0.51	0.54	0.71	0.83
Cochabamba	0.83	0.99	1.02	0.97	1.09	1.04	0.96	0.81	0.85
Chuquisaca	0.80	0.64	0.77	0.77	0.91	0.76	0.71	0.78	0.89
Tarija	0.69	0.75	0.73	1.18	1.08	0.95	2.36	2.81	1.62
Santa Cruz	1.00	1.49	1.21	1.37	1.30	1.23	1.17	1.07	1.02
Beni	0.93	0.90	0.58	0.84	1.00	0.90	0.71	0.60	0.64
Pando	0.36	0.39	0.77	0.54	1.17	1.25	1.21	0.82	0.72
Bolivia	1	1	1	1	1	1	1	1	1

consolidated as an essential Bolivian export since the early 2000s, the regional GDP per capita of Tarija tended to double the Bolivian average.

Are these changes the result of a general process of convergence among Bolivian departments? The new GDP per capita series also allows the testing of this hypothesis. For this, two different concepts of convergence were used: β-convergence (more impoverished regions grow at higher rates than more affluent regions) and σ-convergence (a reduction in the dispersion of GDP per capita).[14] To begin with, Fig. 5.1 could suggest the existence of an unconditional β-convergence from 1950 to 2012: poorer departments in 1950 tended to grow in real terms at higher rates than richer departments. However, the small sample size (nine departments) should be taken into consideration and, therefore, the amplified impact that specific regions may have on the results. Indeed, if Pando and Tarija are removed from the analysis there is no more convergence, changing the R^2 from 0.47 to 0.16.

In the same context, if the analysis is split into two periods (1950–1980 and 1988–2012), an unconditional β-convergence remains in the first case (not shown) but not in the second one (see Fig. 5.2). This is in line with different works that have rejected the hypothesis of an unconditional convergence among Bolivian regions during this last period (Caballero-Claure and Caballero-Martínez 2016). Furthermore, by using a non-parametric framework, a recent paper suggests the existence of a clear divergence

[14] It is said that β-convergence is a precondition of σ-convergence. However, the existence of β-convergence does not necessarily mean that there is σ-convergence; in contrast, if there is σ-convergence, there will also be β-convergence.

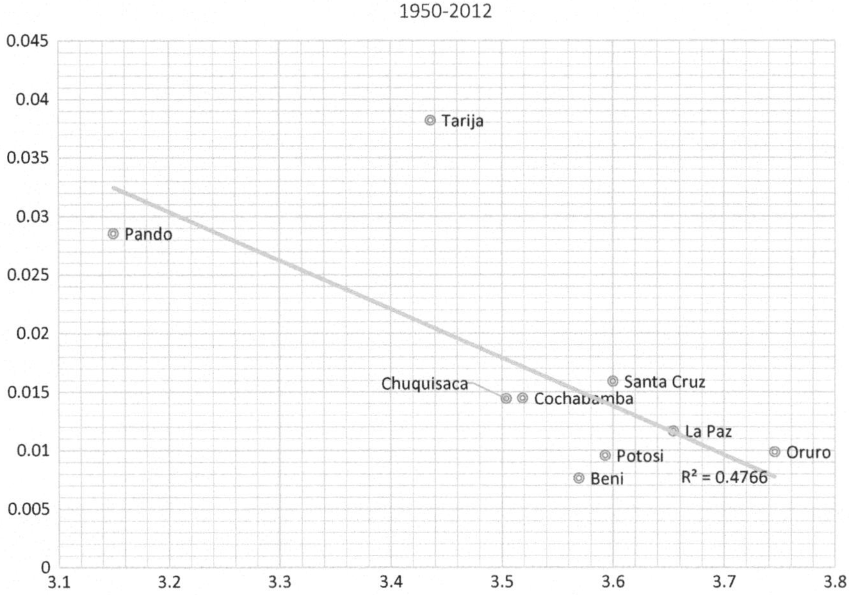

Fig. 5.1 Beta-convergence of departmental pc GDP, 1950–2012. (Sources: See text)

during the 1988–2000 period and another one for the 2000–2014 period where two groups of convergence would have consolidated (Mendez-Guerra 2017).

The analysis of σ-convergence (which is measured as the standard deviation of GDP per capita) allows going further into this debate (Fig. 5.3). If all regional GDPs have the same weight, a σ-convergence is identifiable during the 1960s and 1980s; after that, there is a divergence that stops with the end of the commodity boom in 2014. This trend is also identifiable when regional inequality is measured either by Gini (presented in Fig. 5.3) or by Theil (not shown in Fig. 5.3) coefficients: differences between regional pc GDPs tended to decrease during the state capitalism period and increased after that, particularly since the 1990s. However, if regional GDPs are adjusted by their relevance to the total Bolivian population, there is a constant process of σ-divergence. At the same time, when Gini or Theil indicators (the former presented in Fig. 5.3) are also weighted

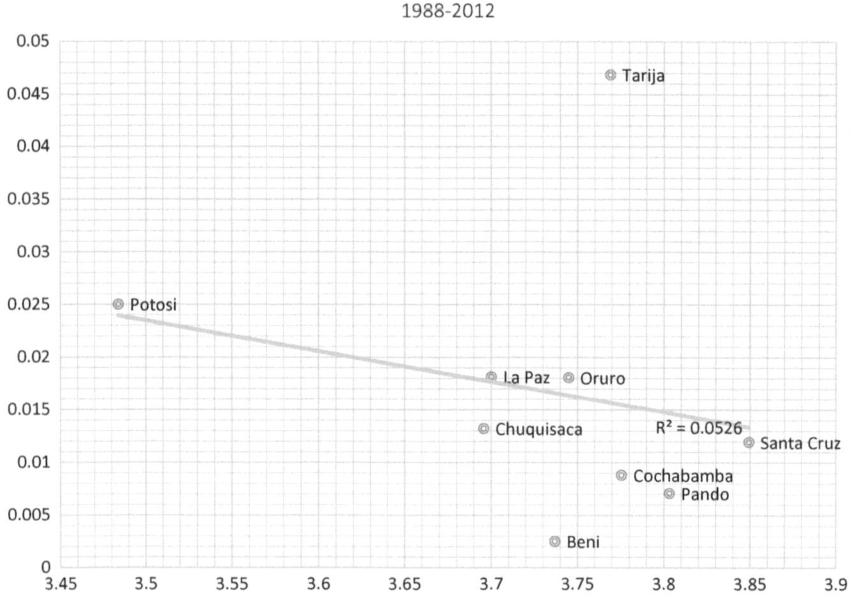

Fig. 5.2 Beta-convergence of department pc GDP, 1988–2012. (Sources: See text)

by population shares, regional inequality tends to remain stable at high levels throughout the entire period.

Overall, all convergence indicators suggest the lack of convergence between Bolivian departments after the 1980s. The lack of convergence holds for the 1950–1980 period if β-convergence is analyzed without certain specific regions or if σ-convergence is measured with population-weighted pc GDP. Table 5.5 presents further evidence on the existence of significant differences between Bolivian departments from the 1950s onwards. Indeed, it shows that the relative importance of the aggregate GDP of the three biggest departments (La Paz, Cochabamba, and Santa Cruz) over total GDP increased from 58% in 1950 to 70% in 1988, where it has stabilized since then.

Therefore, the changes above in the relative importance of Bolivian department population, or those of the ratio of department GDP per capita to the national average, should not be understood as a general process of convergence, but as an output of specific crises and booms in particular

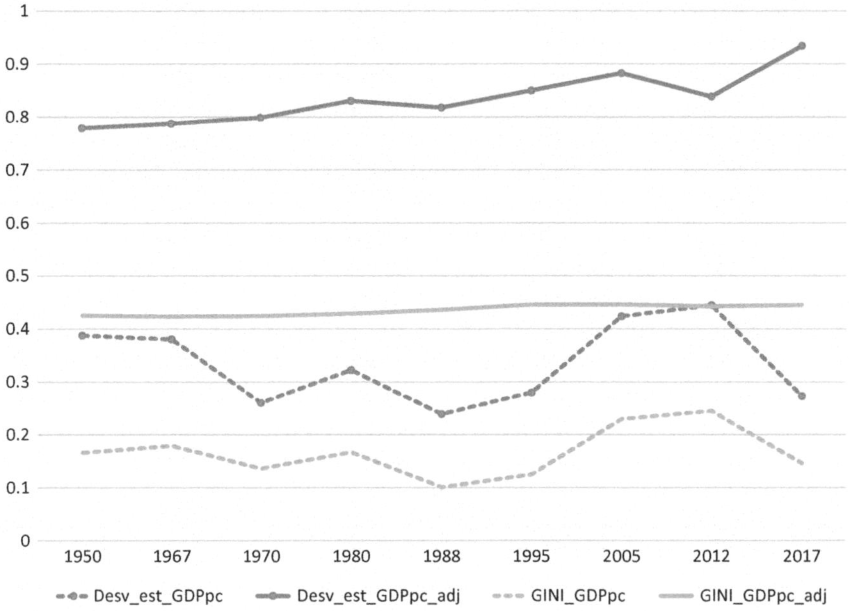

Fig. 5.3 Sigma-convergence of departmental pc GDP, 1950–2012. (Sources: See text)

Table 5.5 Departmental GDP (%, the share of total GDP), 1950–2017

	1950	*1967*	*1970*	*1980*	*1988*	*1995*	*2005*	*2012*	*2017*
La Paz	34.8	32.7	32.8	29.4	27.8	29.5	24.5	25.2	28.1
Oruro	9.6	7.4	8.8	8.9	5.8	5.8	4.9	5.1	5.3
Potosí	18.0	12.6	13.6	8.6	6.2	4.9	4.5	5.9	6.6
Cochabamba	13.5	15.8	16.2	15.7	18.5	18.1	16.9	14.2	14.8
Chuquisaca	7.6	5.3	6.3	5.9	6.6	5.2	4.4	4.5	5.0
Tarija	2.9	3.1	3.0	4.9	4.8	4.4	11.2	13.5	8.0
Santa Cruz	9.5	19.5	16.7	22.9	25.5	27.5	29.5	28.2	28.7
Beni	3.8	3.4	2.2	3.2	4.1	3.9	3.1	2.5	2.7
Pando	0.2	0.3	0.6	0.4	0.7	0.8	0.9	0.9	0.9
	100.0	100.0	100.0	100.0	100.0	100.0	100.0	100.0	100.0

Sources: See text

regions. Indeed, Table 5.5 confirms a decline in the relative importance of the three western departments during the second half of the twentieth century: the relative importance of La Paz, Oruro, and Potosí decreased from 35%, 10%, and 18% of GDP in 1950, to 25%, 6%, and 8% during the last years. Likewise, the aggregate relative importance of these economies fell from 62% of total GDP in 1950 to 40% in recent years. Although in a minor range, Table 5.5 also shows the decline in the relative importance of Chuquisaca. On the other hand, the progression of Santa Cruz is evident: from less than 10% of total GDP in 1950, it became the second most crucial regional economy in the 1960s, and the biggest since the mid-1990s, absorbing almost 30% of the Bolivian GDP in recent years. The increase is also noticeable in Tarija: from 3% of total GDP until the 1970s, the department has come to represent 14% of GDP during the last commodity boom, and 8% in the post-commodity context. In contrast, the relative importance of the other eastern economies (Beni and Pando) remained marginal. It also points out the stability of the relative importance of Cochabamba with around 15% of total GDP, which consolidated as the third most crucial regional economy.

The boom and crises of Bolivian departments are critically linked with their natural resource endowments, the ability to transport these products, and their prices in international markets. For instance, the dynamism in the north-west of the country on the eve of the twentieth century was linked to rubber exports (that transited through the network of Amazonian rivers up to the Atlantic) and ended when the international price of this commodity fell because of the Asian concurrence. At the same time, the predominance of western departments before the 1950s was importantly determined by their mineral resource endowments and the existence of a relatively well-developed railway network that connected these departments with Chilean and, to a lesser extent, Peruvian and Argentinean ports. The three western departments remained the most relevant in terms of mineral production during the second half of the twentieth century (95% of the total output before the 1980s crisis and 80% after that). This relevance and the particular virulence of the 1980s crisis on the international price of tin is also critical to understand the decline of Oruro and Potosí from the 1980s to the beginning of the twentieth-first century (see below).

Natural resource endowments and public infrastructure are also critical to understand the success stories of Santa Cruz and Tarija. On the one hand, the fertile soils of Santa Cruz could be increasingly exploited since the mid-1950s thanks to the highway between Cochabamba and Santa Cruz; it allowed the transportation of agriculture products from the east to the west and moving migrants from the west to the east. Furthermore, additional road improvements in the east, as well as an increase in public and private investments, generated a reconfiguration of the location of agricultural production in Bolivia: in 1950, 24% of this sectoral GDP was generated in La Paz and just 14% in Santa Cruz; in 1980 the ratios moved to 17% and 22%, respectively; in recent years, it was around 17% in La Paz and increased to 43% in Santa Cruz.

The behavior of Santa Cruz is also linked to hydrocarbon production; in the 1950s, when the Bolivian economy became self-sufficient in oil production, 80% of the hydrocarbon GDP was generated by this department. In the 1970s, with the transition of Bolivian exports from mining to hydrocarbon products, the relevance of Santa Cruz remained unchanged. At the beginning of the twentieth-first century, when natural gas consolidated as the main Bolivian export, two-thirds of hydrocarbon production originated in Tarija and a quarter in Santa Cruz. In the former case, spectacular increases in the department's GDP were witnessed during the last commodity boom. These changes were undoubtedly related to the evolution of the international price of oil but would be impossible without the existence of previous investments in infrastructure such as pipelines or refineries.

Natural resource endowments are even essential to understand changes in the regional predominance of manufacturing production (Fig. 5.4). As previously stated, the Bolivian industrialization process started in the late 1920s and was predominantly located in La Paz, which in 1950, according to our estimates, represented 65% of the manufacturing GDP. In 1980, the relative importance of La Paz and Santa Cruz was roughly similar, around 27% of the sectoral GDP. Over the last decades, the relative importance of La Paz in the manufacturing GDP reduced to 23%, but it increased to 40% in Santa Cruz.

This consolidation of Santa Cruz as the manufacturing engine of the Bolivian economy is related to the increasing predominance of Santa Cruz in the production of food and, to a lesser extent, petroleum refining products. For instance, the relative importance of La Paz and Santa Cruz in food production in 1967 (which represented 26% of the gross value of manufacture production) was somewhat similar (around 35% of total food production). In 1995, food production (which represented 33% of total manufacturing production) originated mostly in Santa Cruz (43%), and

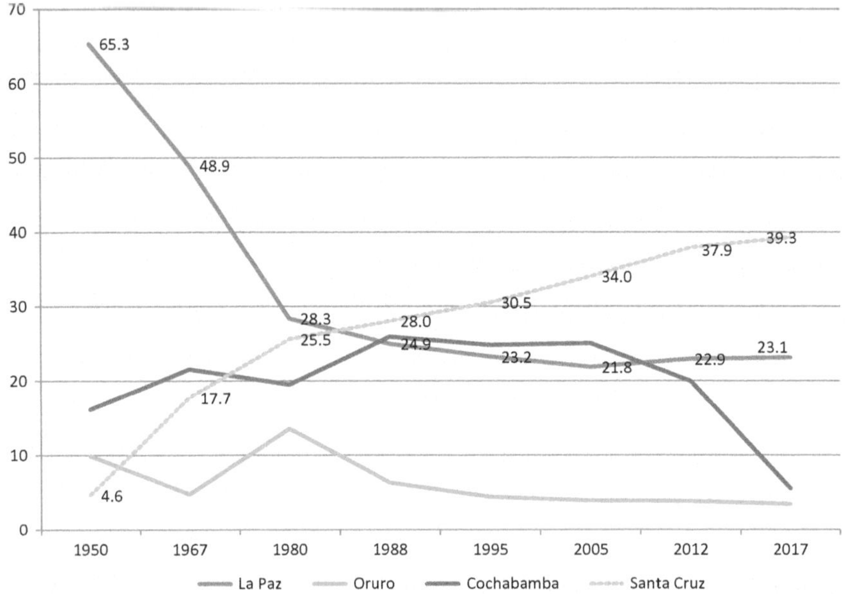

Fig. 5.4 Departmental manufacturing GDP (%, the share of total manufacturing GDP), 1950–2017. (Sources: See text)

the relevance of La Paz was much lower (13%). In 2017, food production still represented 36% of total manufacturing production, and half of it came from Santa Cruz (a share that can be traced back to 2008) and just 12% from La Paz.

Overall, the new quantitative evidence points to a change to the center of gravity of the Bolivian economy, from a north-south axis located in the west to a western-eastern one, where Santa Cruz gets increasing preeminence. This transition can be visualized by different maps that group the nine departments into four quartiles before the National Revolution of 1952 (Map 5.2), during state capitalism (Map 5.3), after the hyperinflation process (Map 5.4), and during the last commodity boom (Map 5.5).

Indeed, according to Map 5.2, the wealthier departments in 1950 were in La Paz and Oruro. They were followed by Potosí and Santa Cruz which, however, presented very different features; the relative importance of the former both in total population and in total GDP was double that of the latter. The similarities between Cochabamba and Beni also mask very

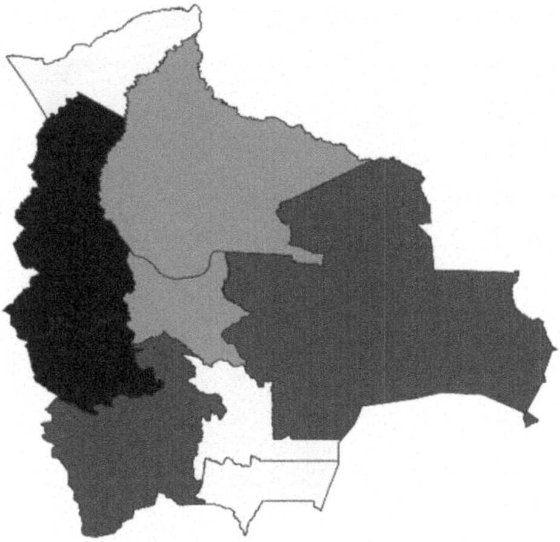

Map 5.2 The relative importance of Bolivian departments (Bolivian pc GDP = 1), 1950. (Sources: See text)

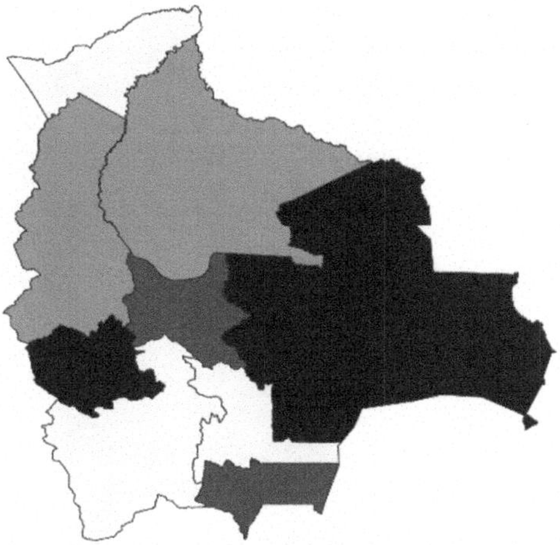

Map 5.3 The relative importance of Bolivian departments (Bolivian pc GDP = 1), 1980. (Sources: See text)

different situations; the former was among the more significant departments in terms of population and production, and the latter was among the smaller. Finally, the map stresses the marginality of Chuquisaca (one of the most critical departments in the nineteenth century) in 1950 and that of Pando and Tarija.

During the state capitalism period, and thanks to the East March, Santa Cruz became one of the more vibrant regional economies; the other one was Oruro (Map 5.3). They were followed by Cochabamba and Tarija,

Map 5.4 The relative importance of Bolivian departments (Bolivian pc GDP = 1), 1988. (Sources: See text)

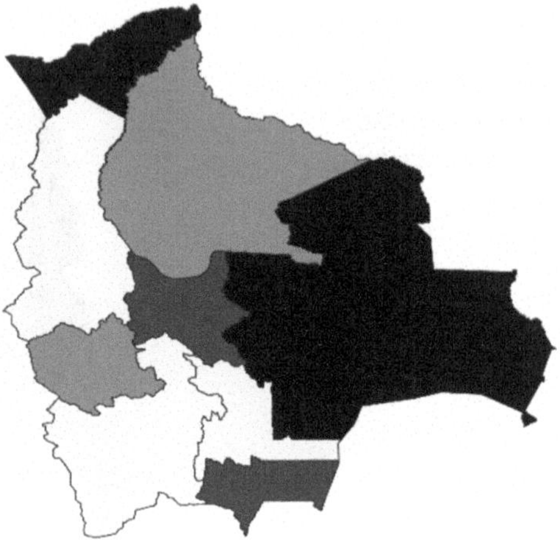

Map 5.5 The relative importance of Bolivian departments (Bolivian pc GDP = 1), 2012. (Sources: See text)

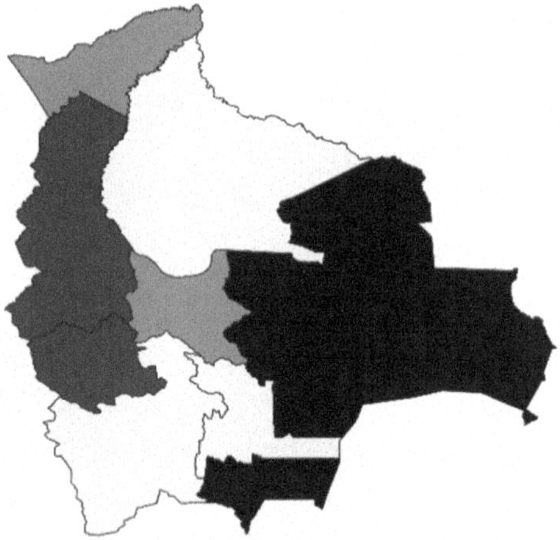

which, thanks to hydrocarbon production, shed its previous marginality. The map also points to the relatively small size of the GDP per capita of La Paz toward the national average. This "marginality" suggests the existence of low levels of productivity, given that this department was the biggest in terms of population and regional GDP. Indeed, the GDP per capita of La Paz concerning the national average is grouped with that of Beni, a department whose total population and GDP was around 10% of those of La Paz. Pando and Chuquisaca remained in the group of weaker departments, a cluster that was also reached by Potosí, a department whose relative importance over total population and total GDP has reduced steadily since the 1950s.

The 1980s crisis affected not only the evolution of the Bolivian economy but also the relative importance of each region. Indeed, the regional GDP in 1986 (when the reduction of the Bolivian GDP that started in the early 1980s stopped) was above its pre-crisis level (1980) in Pando and Cochabamba, was somewhat similar to the pre-crisis level in Chuquisaca, and was below the pre-crisis level in the rest of the departments. However, the distance between the GDP level of 1986 and that of 1980 was below 10 percentage points in the case of Santa Cruz and Beni, was around 13 percentage points in La Paz and Tarija, and was approximately 40 percentage points in Oruro and Potosí.

The severity of the crisis in these two departments was heavily influenced by the behavior of the mining sector; the mining GDP in Potosí in 1986 was equivalent to 46% of its level in 1980, and in the case of Oruro, it was equal to 40% of its pre-crisis level. The reduction of mining GDP was also noticeable in the case of La Paz (in 1986 equivalent to 37% of the 1980 level), but its impact on the total GDP was milder given the lower relevance of the sector in this department. Essential reductions in the agricultural sector were also witnessed during this period. However, the shock was mostly as a consequence of the 1982 drought and, except Oruro where the agricultural GDP in 1983 was equivalent to 46% of the 1980 level, was not as severe as in the mining sector. Other significant reductions in sectoral GDPs took place in manufacturing production in La Paz, Oruro, and Potosí; manufacturing production also reduced in Tarija and Santa Cruz, but the gap was narrower than in the previous cases.

The different effects of the crisis should be borne in mind when analyzing the regional configuration of the Bolivian economy in 1988 (Map 5.4). Indeed, the relevance of Santa Cruz is explained by the progressive strength of the economy acquired since the 1950s, but that of Pando is more a result of the milder effects of the crisis and low rates of population growth. Given the softer impact of the crisis, it does not come as a surprise that Cochabamba and Tarija maintained their previous rank. In contrast, the noticeable effects of the crisis on mining production explain the fall of Oruro toward the mid-lowest levels, where it is grouped with Beni. Interestedly, La Paz joined the poorest economies (Potosí and Chuquisaca) in spite of being the most populated and having the highest regional GDP. Once more, this points to the existence of noticeable restrictions in terms of productivity in this department.

The regional configuration of the Bolivian economy also changed as a result of the last commodity boom (Map 5.5). Santa Cruz remained in the group of more prosperous economies, where it was joined by Tarija thanks to the consolidation of natural gas as the main Bolivian export and the evolution of the international price of this commodity. La Paz and Oruro recovered their previous relevance; in the last case, once more, thanks to mineral production (in 2012, it represented a third of the GDP of Oruro). The significance of Cochabamba reduced somewhat as did that of Pando, whose relative position is more in line with what could be expected given its relative importance over total population and GDP. During these years, the departments of Beni, Chuquisaca, and Potosí remained as the poorest, the last case being particularly worrisome given the noticeable increase in international mining prices and the relevance of the sector in this department (44% in 2012).

Summing up, the analysis of the relative importance of each department over the total population and total GDP stresses the existence of significant changes from the 1950s onwards. There is relative stability in the position of La Paz and Cochabamba, an apparent reversal of fortune in the case of Potosí (something that could have also happened in the case of Chuquisaca during the first half of the twentieth century), and a definite improvement in the case of Santa Cruz. When the analysis focuses on the relative position of each regional pc GDP over the national pc GDP average, it points out the leadership of Santa Cruz since the 1960s, the lower ranks of La Paz in spite of being the most populated and for a long time the biggest economy, and the consolidation of Chuquisaca and Potosí among the poorest even before the 1980s crisis. It also points out the improvements of Tarija during the 1970s and the last commodity boom. However, the reduction in the relative weight of the regional economy over total GDP in the post-boom context questions the sustainability of these upward movements. In short, western economies such as La Paz and Cochabamba remain critical, but Santa Cruz undoubtedly consolidated as the most dynamic.

5 Conclusions

This chapter has analyzed the evolution of the location of economic activity in Bolivia. In contrast to most cases covered in this volume, it shows a significant change in the relative importance of regions. To begin with, the early connection (sixteenth century) of the current Bolivian economic space to the world economy through silver exports gave economic prevalence to the current western departments. This configuration persisted once Independence was achieved (1825), the relatively short-lived dynamism of rubber exports in the north-west (1890s–1910s) being an exception. Furthermore, the prevalence of western departments was particularly noticeable during the 1888–1954 period, given that the configuration of the Bolivian railway network connected the western departments with each other and to the world economy but divided the Bolivian internal market.

This configuration changed dramatically during the second half of the twentieth century, when the relative importance of Santa Cruz increased markedly. Previous studies have analyzed this process by looking at population figures. This chapter provides additional evidence thanks to the estimation for the first time of regional GDPs since 1950. In effect, either by studying the regional GDP per capita or by looking at the regional participation in the total GDP, there is no doubt that Santa Cruz consolidated as the most crucial regional economy. Interestedly, the relevance of Tarija has also changed from one of the most marginal to one of the most relevant over the last decades. In contrast, there is an apparent reversal of fortune in the case of the famous colonial center of Potosí.

Thus, since the 1950s, there has been a progressive change to the center of gravity of the Bolivian economy, from a north-south axis located in western departments to a west-east axis where Santa Cruz gained increasing prevalence. Undoubtedly, these changes are explained by the availability of natural resources. In effect, the early prevalence of western departments was highly influenced by mineral endowments. Similarly, the upsurge of Santa Cruz cannot be understood without considering its fertile soils and the hydrocarbon resources. This is also true in the case of Tarija, the region that has produced two-thirds of the hydrocarbon GDP since the early 2000s.

However, given the landlocked nature of the country, previous investments in infrastructure were critical to making these endowments economically valuable. Indeed, the prevalence of Santa Cruz is also linked to the highway between Cochabamba and Santa Cruz which was inaugurated in 1954. Thanks to this road, retail prices in Santa Cruz de la Sierra tended to converge to those of the rest of the capitals in western departments. Likewise, this road allowed the arrival of immigrants from the rest of the country and the achievement of population growth rates of around 4% per year. Similarly, it should be remembered that hydrocarbon sales depend on previous substantial investments in capital goods and transport infrastructure, as well as political bargaining with potential customers. This suggests that regional economic growth in Bolivia is determined not only by a resources lottery but also by active public policies.

References

Agramont, D. and Peres-Cajías, J. (2016). *Bolivia: un país privado de Litoral.* La Paz: Oxfam/Plural.

Assadourian, C. S. (1982). *El Sistema de La Economía Colonial. Mercado Interno, Regiones y Espacio Económico.* Lima: Instituto de Estudios Peruanos.

Badia-Miró, M. (2015). The Evolution of the Location of Economic Activity in Chile in the Long Run: A Paradox of Extreme Concentration in Absence of Agglomeration Economies. *Estudios de Economía* 42 (2): 143–67.

Barragán R., R. and J. A. Peres-Cajías. (2007). El Armazón Estatal y Sus Imaginarios. Historia Del Estado. In *Informe Nacional de Desarrollo Humano 2007. El Estado Del Estado*, edited by PNUD, 127–218. La Paz.

Caballero-Claure, B. and R. Caballero-Martínez. (2016). Sigma Convergencia, Convergencia Beta y Condicional En Bolivia, 1990–2011. *Economia Coyuntural,Revista de Temas de Perspectivas y Coyuntura* 1 (1): 25–59.

CEPAL. (1958). *Análisis y Proyecciones Del Desarrollo Económico. IV. El Desarrollo Económico de Bolivia.* México: Naciones Unidas, Departamento de Asuntos Económicos y Sociales.

Contreras, M. E. (1990). Debt, Taxes, and War: The Political Economy of Bolivia, c. 1920–1935. *Journal of Latin American Studies* 22 (2): 265–87.

———. (2017). El Desarrollo Del Transporte En Bolivia, Una Aproximación Al Impacto Económico y Social de Los Ferrocarriles y Carreteras 1900–2015. In *Un Siglo de Economía En Bolivia (1900–2015) Tópicos de Historia Económica*, edited by Iván Velásquez-Castellanos and Napoleón Pacheco Torrico. La Paz: Konrad Adenauer Stiftung.

COPSCZ. (1982). *Diagnóstico Agropecuario Del Departamento de Santa Cruz.* Santa Cruz de la Sierra: Comité de Obras Públicas de Santa Cruz.

Dalence, J M. (1851). *Bosquejo Estadístico de Bolivia.* La Paz: Universidad Mayor de San Andrés.

Demeure, J. (1999). Agricultura. De La Subsistencia a La Competencia Internacional. In *Bolivia En El Siglo XX. La Formación de La Bolivia Contemporánea*, edited by Fernando Campero. La Paz: Harvard Club Bolivia.

Espinoza, J. (2010). *Minería Boliviana: Su Realidad.* La Paz: Plural.

Felice, E. (2019). GDP and Convergence in Modern Times. In *Handbook of Cliometrics*, edited by C. Diebolt and M. Haupert (eds.), 263–93. Berlin Heidelberg: Springer-Verlag.

Fifer, V. (1972). *Bolivia: Land, Location and Politics since 1825.* New York: Cambridge University Press.

Gamarra Téllez, M P. (2007). *Amazonía Norte de Bolivia, Economía Gomera (1870–1940). Bases Económicas de Un Poder Regional. La Casa Suárez. Bolivia, Estudios En Ciencias Sociales. N° 5.* La Paz: CIMA.

Gelman, J. (2009). ¿Crisis Postcolonial En Las Economías Sudamericanas?. In *Latinoamérica y España, 1800–1850: Un Crecimiento Económico Nada Excepcional*, Enrique Llopis and Carlos Marichal. Madrid: Instituto Mora/ Marcial Pons.

Herranz-Loncán, A. and J.A. Peres-Cajías. (2016). Tracing the Reversal of Fortune in the Americas: Bolivian GDP per Capita since the Mid-Nineteenth Century. *Cliometrica* 10 (1).

INE (2004). Cuentas Nacionales. Metodología Cuentas Regionales. La Paz.

Kehoe, T., Machicado, C. and J. A. Peres-Cajías. (2019). The Monetary and Fiscal History of Bolivia, 1960–2017. *NBER Working Paper* 25523.

Klein, H. S. and J. A. Peres-Cajías. (2014). Bolivian Oil and Natural Gas under State and Private Control, 1910–2010. *Bolivian Studies Journal/Revista de Estudios Bolivianos.*

Langer, E. D. and V. E. Conti. (1991). Circuitos comerciales tradicionales y cambio economico en los Andes Centromeridionales (1830–1930). *Desarrollo Economico* 31 (121): 91–111.

Limao, N. and A. J. Venables. (2001). Infrastructure, Geographical Disadvantage, Transport Costs, and Trade. *The World Bank Economic Review* 15 (3): 451–79.

Luna, J. (1995). El Sector Productivo Boliviano Durante El Período Inflacionario. In *Inflación, Estabilización y Crecimiento. La Experiencia Boliviana de 1982 a 1993*, edited by J. A. Morales and G. La Torre, 143–243. La Paz: IISEC/UCB.

Machicado, C. G., Nina, O. and L. C. Jemio. (2012). *Factores que inciden en el crecimiento y desarrollo en Bolivia. Análisis Nacional y Regional, 1989–2009.* La Paz: PIEB.

Marchi, B. De, Morales, H. and C. Machicado. (2018). El territorio desde las redes de transporte en la Amazonía Norte de Bolivia. *Revista Boliviana de Investigación* 13 (2): 13–33.

Mendez-Guerra, C. (2017). Heterogeneous Growth and Regional (Di) Convergence in Bolivia: A Distribution Dynamics Approach. *Economía Coyuntural, Revista de Temas de Coyuntura y Perspectivas* 2 (4): 81–108.

Mendieta, P. (2019). A Regional Landscape of Bolivian Economic Growth. *Revista Latinoamericana de Desarrollo Economico*, 31: 77–98.

Menegus Bornemann, M. (1999). *Dos décadas de investigación en historia económica comparada en América Latina: Homenaje a Carlos Sempat Assadourian*. México, D.F.: Colegio de México.

Ministerio de Planificación y Coordinación. (1970a). *Cuentas Nacionales, 1958–1969. Cuentas Regionales, 1965–1969*. La Paz.

———. (1970b). *Estrategia Socioeconómica Del Desarrollo Nacional, 1971–1991*. La Paz.

———. (1992). *Cuentas Regionales de Bolivia Por Actividad Económica (Serie 1980–1986)*. La Paz.

Mitre, A. (1981). *Los Patriarcas de La Plata: Estructura Socioeconómica de La Mineria Boliviana En El Siglo XIX*. Lima: Instituto de Estudios Peruanos.

———. (1986). *El Monedero de Los Andes: Región Económica y Moneda Boliviana Enel Siglo XIX*. La Paz: Hisbol.

———. (1993). *El enigma de los hornos: La Economía Política de La Fundición de Estaño. El Proceso Boliviano a La Luz de Otras Experiencias. Biblioteca Minera Boliviana*. Vol. 7. La Paz, Bolivia: Asociación Nacional de Mineros Medianos.

Montenegro, D. and Á. Guzmán. (1999). *Inversión y Productividad En El Sector Agrícola-Agroindustrial Boliviano: Caso de La Agricultura Comercial Período 1985–1998*. Santiago de Chile: CEPAL.

Orsag, J. O. (2019). Regional trade networks during the Bolivian rubber boom (1880–1910). Unpublished manuscript.

Pentland, J. B. (1975). *Informe Sobre Bolivia*. Potosí: Editorial Potosí.

Pereira, M., R., Sheriff, B., H. E. and V. Salinas Maceda. (2012). *Finanzas Públicas: Comportamiento e Impacto En El Desarrollo Nacional y Regional (1990–2010)*.

Peres-Cajías, J. A. (2014). Bolivian Public Finances, 1882–2010. The Challenge to Make Social Spending Sustainable. *Revista de Historia Económica* 32 (1): 77–117.

———. (2017). Bolivian Tariff Policy during the Late Nineteenth and Early Twentieth Centuries: High Average Tariff and Unbalanced Regional Protection. *Journal of Latin American Studies* 49 (3): 433–62.

Peres-Cajías, J. A. and A. Carreras-Marín. (2017). The Bolivian Export Sector, 1870–1950. In *Latin America's First Export Era Revisited*, edited by Sandra Kuntz. London: Palgrave.

Prado, G. (1995). Efectos Económicos de La Adulteración Monetaria En Bolivia, 1830–1870. *Revista de Humanidades y Ciencias Sociales* 1: 35–76.

Roca, J. L. (1999). *La Fisonomía Del Regionalismo Boliviano*. La Paz: Plural.

Rodríguez Ostria, G. (1999). Producción, Mercancías y Empresarios. In *Bolivia En El Siglo XX. La Formación de La Bolivia Contemporánea*, edited by F. Campero, 291–304. La Paz: Harvard Club de Bolivia.

———. (1994). *Elites, Mercado y Cuestion Regional En Bolivia*. Quito: Facultad Latinoamericana de Ciencias Sociales FLACSO.

Sandoval, C. D., Sandoval, A. V., del Rio, M. A., Sandoval, F., Mertens, C. and C. Parada. (2003). *Santa Cruz: Economía y Poder, 1952–1993. Investigaciones Regionales. Santa Cruz*. La Paz: Pieb.

SEAMOS. (1992). *La Economía de La Coca En Bolivia. Análisis Macro y Microeconómico*. La Paz: Seamos.

United Nations. (2014). *The Development Economics of Landlockness: Understanding the Development Costs of Being Landlocked*. New York: United Nations.

Urquiola, M., Andersen, L., Antelo, E., Evia, J. L. and O. Nina. (1999). Geography and Development in Bolivia Migration, Urban and Industrial Concentration, Welfare, and Convergence: 1950–1992. *A Study for the Inter-American Development Bank Research Network*.

Wilkie, J. W. (1969). *The Bolivian Revolution and U.S. Aid since 1952; Financial Background and Context of Political Decisions. Latin American Studies*. Vol. 13. Los Angeles: Latin American Center, University of California.

Wilmsmeier, G. and R. J. Sánchez. (2009). *Landlocked Countries in South America: Transport System Challenges Recursos Naturales e Infraestructura*. Santiago de Chile: CEPAL.

Zondag, C. H. (1966). *The Bolivian Economy, 1952–65; the Revolution and Its Aftermath. Praeger Special Studies in International Economics and Development*. New York: Praeger.

CHAPTER 6

The Evolution of Regional Income Inequality in Brazil, 1872–2015

Justin R. Bucciferro and Pedro H. G. Ferreira de Souza

1 Introduction

Brazil is among the largest countries in the world in both area (8.5 million square kilometers) and population (over 200 million inhabitants), and also one of the most unequal. It comprises 26 states and a Federal District, yet, as of 2015, just three states in the southeast region made up a combined 40% of the national population and 52% of its income; in contrast, the 11 states located in the north and northeast regions correspond to almost 36% of the Brazilian population but just 19% of the Gross Domestic

J. R. Bucciferro (✉)
Colgate University, Hamilton, NY, USA

Eastern Washington University, Cheney, WA, USA
e-mail: jbucciferro@colgate.edu

P. H. G. Ferreira de Souza
Department of Social Policy, Instituto de Pesquisa Econômica Aplicada, Brasilia, Brazil
e-mail: pedro.ferreira@ipea.gov.br

D. A. Tirado-Fabregat et al. (eds.), *Time and Space*,
Palgrave Studies in Economic History,
https://doi.org/10.1007/978-3-030-47553-6_6

Product (GDP).[1] The persistence of such high levels of spatial inequality has elicited a wide array of regional development policies, ranging from fiscal incentive programs to free trade zones.[2] However, while most scholars agree that such disparities have distant historical roots, few studies provide a consistent global overview of regional inequality from the late-nineteenth century to the present.[3]

The case of Brazil provides insights into the relative causes of development, including the interplay between inequality and episodes of rapid economic, social, and political change. The north and south regions had a reversal of fortune that began during the colonial period and was completed by the turn of the twentieth century. Real wages in the Southeast were already one and a half times higher than those of the Northeast in 1920, mirroring, to some extent, the North-South disparity found in contemporary United States (Pereira 2019). Within regions of Brazil inequality was also pronounced, but its impact on later development would vary according to states' political and economic institutions: in Minas Gerais and São Paulo, for instance, high inequality in 1920 correlates positively with measures like income and schooling as of 2000, though the relationship is apparently negative for Pernambuco and Rio Grande do Sul (Funari 2017). Musacchio et al. (2014) likewise emphasize Brazil's heterogeneous regional experience, finding positive trade shocks to be associated with increased educational expenditures and better outcomes between 1889 and 1930, yet the connection is weaker for states that had relied more extensively on slavery prior to abolition.

This chapter investigates how income inequality has varied across Brazilian states (or provinces, prior to 1889) over the past nearly 150 years—a timeframe that encompasses not only the formative period of the Republic just mentioned, but also the late Imperial Era. Specifically, we examine trends in the dispersion of per capita incomes for 12 reference years spanning from 1872 to 2015 (1872, 1905, 1920, 1939, 1950,

[1] The average unweighted GDP per capita (purchasing power parity) of states in the Southeast, South, and Center-West (\$19,546; $n = 9$) is more than two times that of states in the North and Northeast (\$8621; $n = 11$). Authors' calculations based on the sources described in Sect. 3 and state aggregates listed in the Appendix; likewise, for all GDP and population references to follow. Map 6.1 illustrates the states making up each region of Brazil.

[2] Diniz (2009) and Ferreira (2004) offer detailed reviews of such regional policy efforts.

[3] For alternative perspectives on regional incomes and their dispersion as far back as 1872, the year of Brazil's first official census, see Monasterio and Reis (2008), Monasterio (2010), and Reis (2014).

1960, 1970, 1980, 1991, 2000, 2010, and 2015). Because census data on incomes only part from 1960 and official income series extend from no earlier than 1939 (Azzoni 1997), we consolidate official figures and other authors' estimates for preceding years back to the first national census of 1872, including our own for the year 1905.

The detailed results provide a novel perspective on regional inequality over this timespan. Trends in the population-weighted coefficients of variation indicate a cyclical pattern of per capita income inequality across states: there were two peaks, in the late-nineteenth and mid-twentieth centuries, followed by noticeable equalizations of income. This apparently contradicts any broader laws of motion—in particular, what is known as σ-convergence—though at this point data for the nineteenth century remain tentative. There is, nonetheless, evidence of so-called β-convergence, as measured by negative correlations between states' initial levels of per capita GDP and their subsequent rates of growth.

Regional inequality ebbed and flowed over the course of Brazilian development as a result of the unique interplay of geographical, institutional, and market-related factors. The coffee boom and the onset of industrialization meant São Paulo rapidly surpassed wealthier states in the late-nineteenth century. Subsequently, as government policy strongly favored industrial growth, the concentration of manufacturing in southeastern states became a major driver of regional inequality. The debt crisis of the 1980s, however, forced a change of course: regional inequality receded as partial trade liberalization and stagflation severely hurt manufacturing, and other regions profited from improved world market conditions for agribusiness exports, among other changes. In this chapter, we document these trends and discuss their origins in a specific interplay of structural constraints and historical processes.

Ours are certainly not the first estimates of national GDP for Brazil spanning this extended period. For instance, Goldsmith (1986), building on the work of Contador and Haddad (1975) and others, presents an uninterrupted series of aggregate GDP projections for Brazil after 1850 based on good exports plus imports, central government expenditures, and money supply. Neither are they the first of regional incomes for Brazil in the nineteenth century, although these are certainly rarer (and probably less reliable). The year 1872 has received particular attention, being the date of the first national census, by authors including Reis (2008), Monasterio (2010), and Bértola et al. (2009). Unlike previous work, here we consider regional (as opposed to national) trends, and between- (versus within-) state inequality; moreover, we present benchmark figures for at least every two or three decades, permitting a careful analysis of long-run shifts in inequality and their proximate causes.

The remainder of this chapter is organized as follows. Section 2 provides an overview of the major political and economic events in Brazilian history since the mid-nineteenth century. Section 3 describes our data sources and methodology. Section 4 presents our estimates for regional inequality in Brazil across 12 periods (1872–2015). Finally, Sect. 5 discusses our main findings and outlines directions for future research.

2 Historical Background

The rough century and a half between 1872 and 2015 transformed Brazil from a collection of slave-based, export-oriented rural societies separated by high transportation costs into a modern, developing urban country. Independence from Portugal was gained only in 1822; 50 years later, the Empire of Brazil was a Constitutional Monarchy still ruled by a branch of the Portuguese Brigantine dynasty. Although the Atlantic slave trade had *de facto* ended more than 20 years earlier, in 1872 slaves comprised 16% of a population of roughly 10 million people, and GDP per capita was only about $1120 (in 2017 PPP US dollars, $). By 2015, the Brazilian population exceeded 202 million, mostly in urban areas, democracy was firmly established, and GDP per capita was 15 times higher, at almost $16,500 (in 2017 PPP$).

The average income of Brazil today nearly coincides with that of Latin America as a whole; inequality across countries is substantial though, with Brazil closer in terms of PPP-adjusted GDP per capita to Peru, Colombia, the Dominican Republic, and Costa Rica.[4] Though many countries have no available data prior to 1950, there were likely substantial shifts in

[4] For 2017, the World Bank reports GDP per capita (PPP, current international dollars) of $15,662 for Brazil compared to $16,160 for all of Latin America and the Caribbean (data downloaded from the World Development Indicators, updated 09/24/19). Two close pairs of countries below and above, respectively, Brazil in the income ranking for Latin America are Peru ($13,772) and Colombia ($14,507), and the Dominican Republic ($16,452) and Costa Rica ($16,976).

relative income rankings over time—how does Brazil compare in this regard? In 1870, to use the estimates of Bértola and Ocampo (2012), the GDP per capita of Brazil was also not far below the (nine-country) average for Latin America and, likewise, similar to that of Colombia or Peru; by 2010, alternately, Brazil's average income had converged somewhat with Argentina's and Uruguay's (though it stayed fairly constant at about half of Chile's).[5]

The closing decades of the nineteenth century were a turning point in Brazilian history. Economic growth had until then been sluggish, but conditions were ripe for faster growth. Slavery was abolished in 1888 and the monarchy overthrown in 1889. Government policy and subsidies after 1850 stimulated the rapid construction and expansion of the railroad network, especially in the Southeast, which aided in lowering the country's prohibitive transportation costs.[6] Aside from difficult terrain and poor infrastructure, another historical impediment to market integration was high taxes on domestic trade: the prices of labor and goods varied widely across regions before the 1950s (Pereira 2019), and even the authority to set taxes on exports belonged to states during the Republic (Musacchio et al. 2014). Given such barriers, the need to replace slave labor led to bolder government policy promoting large-scale European immigration as the rise of coffee powered a new boom in exports.

At first, coffee was cultivated by slaves in large plantations in the Vale do Paraíba region comprising the east of São Paulo and south of Rio de Janeiro (see Map 6.1). Soil exhaustion pushed producers to the west of São Paulo, where the coffee boom took place due to the better soil, as well as improved technology and an extensive railroad network that also benefited production for the domestic market. São Paulo thus became the

[5] The per capita GDP (in international 1990 Geary-Khamis dollars) reported by Bértola and Ocampo (2012: 292–295) is $694 for Brazil in 1870, compared to an average of $790 for Latin America, $676 for Colombia, and $840 for Peru. Between 1870 and 2010, the ratio of Brazil's per capita GDP to Argentina's changed from 47.3% to 57.2%; to Uruguay's, from 33.0% to 57.8%; and to Chile's, from 52.6% to 51.1%.

[6] The first railroad concessions were granted in 1835 but failed to attract investors. After 1850, the Imperial government offered subsidies, including dividend guarantees, to investors. The first Brazilian railroad, the *Estrada de Ferro Mauá* (Mauá Railway), was inaugurated in 1854 and linked Rio de Janeiro to the nearby *Porto da Estrela* (Estrela Port). Railway construction accelerated over the second half of the nineteenth century, so that by the early 1910s the system had more than 24,000 kilometers of lines, with almost 65% of tracks in the Southeast (Summerhill 2018: 64, 68).

Map 6.1 Aggregated units and regions of Brazil. (Sources: Author's harmonization of state borders)

focal point of the Brazilian industrialization process. Profits from coffee, the influx of immigrants with relatively high human capital, institutional changes, and the integration of markets and agglomeration effects fostered by railroads opened possibilities unavailable during the previous export booms (Luna and Klein 2003: 53–78; Summerhill 2005, 2018).

Thus, the economic geography of the country was thoroughly reshaped over the course of the nineteenth century, as the Southeast took off while the Northeast stagnated. Indeed, coffee exports surpassed sugar exports in value by 1830 and soared over the next few decades (Abreu and Lago 2014). As is visible in Table 6.1, by 1875 coffee alone accounted for over half of the value of Brazil's exports. Notwithstanding the brief competition from rubber at the peak of the Amazon rubber boom (roughly from

Table 6.1 Composition of Brazilian exports (%)—Brazil, 1850, 1875, and 1900

	Cacao	*Coffee*	*Cotton*	*Hides*	*Rubber*	*Sugar*	*Other*	*Total*
1850	1.3	45.0	7.8	6.2	1.2	26.8	11.6	100
1875	0.8	61.4	8.3	5.1	4.9	11.5	8.0	100
1900	3.3	58.0	2.6	3.4	21.5	2.7	8.5	100

Source: Absell and Tena-Junguito (2016) corrected free-on-board (FOB) prices

N.B.: Figures refer to the share of each commodity in total export value

1880 to 1910), coffee would remain the most important crop well into the twentieth century, taking the place held by sugar during the colonial era. In general, one might understand Brazil's economic history in terms of the different regional specializations afforded by geography, which influenced how these regions would (or would not) integrate into international markets and be affected by the global commodity cycle—insomuch, there are many "Brazils."

The so-called First Republic toppled the Brazilian Empire in 1889 and effectively worked as a liberal and oligarchic compromise led by *Paulista* coffee planters. As the country kept urbanizing and industrializing, the regime was increasingly fractionalized by internal dissent. In the wake of the Great Depression, Vargas' 1930 Revolution brought about another turning point in Brazil's history, ultimately paving the way for decades of import substitution industrialization (ISI), to be pursued both by democratic presidents between 1945 and 1964 and by the right-wing military dictatorship inaugurated in 1964.[7] Between 1930 and 1980, Brazil was one of the fastest-growing countries in the world: real GDP was multiplied by 23 and GDP per capita increased by a factor of 7. Manufacturing, heavily concentrated in São Paulo, quickly surpassed agriculture as the main economic sector: in the early 1950s, each contributed about 25% to GDP, and by the early 1980s, industry was four times as important (44% versus 11%).[8]

[7] There is a vast literature on the First Republic, the 1930 Revolution, and Getúlio Vargas' corporatist dictatorship, the *Estado Novo* (1937–1945). Bethell (2008a), Carvalho (2008), Fausto (1988), and Gomes (2005) provide excellent summaries and analyses.

[8] All figures on the sectoral composition of GDP in this chapter come from Ipeadata (http://www.ipeadata.gov.br, accessed 02/13/2019).

High growth rates were financed by either high inflation or external debt, giving rise to social tensions and recurrent balance of payments crises.[9] The first oil shock in 1973 posed a challenge to the dictatorship's economic model, but unexpected defeats in semi-competitive legislative elections and unrest among military hardliners forced the regime to double down on ISI, now hoping to use it to remedy personal and regional inequalities (e.g. Brazil 1974). The second oil shock in 1979 proved even more devastating, as Brazil's terms of trade plunged and interest rate hikes in developed countries caused a balance of payments collapse and a deep recession. GDP contracted 6.3% between 1980 and 1983 and inflation soared from about 40% per year in 1978–1979 to 85% in 1980, and 164% in 1983.[10] The 1980s were a "lost decade": following a 4.4% contraction in GDP in 1990, the Brazilian economy entered the 1990s only 17% larger than it was in 1980, while the total population had grown by 21%. Meanwhile, inflation spiraled out of control, peaking at almost 2500% per year in 1993. In 1985, Brazil made the transition back to democracy, enacting in 1988 a strongly social-democratic constitution amid macroeconomic woes.[11]

ISI was definitely abandoned in the 1990s. The *Plano Real* of 1994 finally curtailed inflation, and fiscal responsibility became a cornerstone of economic policy (at least until the mid to late 2010s). Deep sectoral changes unfolded in tandem with (limited) trade liberalization and the privatization of public companies: de-industrialization meant an expansion of services and a 20% decline in the share of manufacturing in GDP (from 44% in 1980 to 25% in 2013).[12] The result was only moderate growth between 1994 and 2003 (on average, 2.7% per year), but the

[9] Due to space limitations, this chapter deliberately glosses over some nuances of the period, such as the early 1960s stagflation and the austere structural adjustment imposed by the military between 1964 and 1967. See Bethell (2008b), Bethell and Castro (2008), Resende (1982), and Villela (2005) for more information.

[10] Inflation rates refer to the IPC-Fipe price index because Brazil's current official consumer price indices (INPC and IPCA) are only available from 1980 onwards; in any case, they show the same trend as the IPC-Fipe. Data for all three indexes are available at http://www.ipeadata.gov.br (accessed 02/13/2019).

[11] See Abreu (2008) and the volume organized by Giambiagi et al. (2005) for a detailed overview of the period.

[12] Dix-Carneiro and Kovak (2017) provide a summary of the major changes in Brazilian trade policy since the 1980s. Their empirical analysis finds that trade liberalization had large and growing effects on regional formal earnings and employment.

economy accelerated afterwards, averaging 4% per year from 2003 to 2013. The turnaround happened as previous institutional reforms—for example, the adoption of inflation and fiscal targets—aligned with more favorable international conditions, namely, a major run-up in commodity prices.

Brazilian exports increased four-fold from 2002 to 2012, from 60 to 242 billion US dollars, led by commodities such as iron ores and concentrates, oils from petroleum and bituminous minerals, sugar, coffee, and soybeans.[13] Such conditions gave the government leeway to pursue expansionist economic policies that sought to tackle the country's high poverty and inequality levels as well as foster consumption-driven growth. This arrangement worked well until existing idle capacity was depleted. By 2014, failed attempts to boost investment rates resulted in renewed inflationary pressures and rising fiscal deficits and public debt; even worse, the government was engulfed by a series of major corruption scandals. The stage was set for the steepest three-year economic contraction in Brazil's recorded history, as GDP fell by 6.4% from 2013 to 2016, while President Rousseff was impeached and removed from office in 2015.

The period from 1872 to 2015 was, by any standard, marked by major change. During the "first globalization" from 1870 to 1913—when the world experienced relatively free exchange of goods and people (Williamson 1995: 148)—slavery within Brazil was abolished, the Empire was replaced by a Republic, and European labor fueled the booming southeastern coffee economy. The shift in the country's traditional economic center of gravity from the Northeast, during the colonial era, to the Southeast, after Independence, was consolidated in the early twentieth century by domestic industrial policies adopted from the 1930s through the 1970s. The balance of payments collapse amid global economic crisis in the 1980s marked a return to trade openness, though with little resulting growth until a new cycle of rising commodity prices had begun after the millennium. Living standards across regions have improved over the past two decades; however, renewed financial and political stress threatens to reverse the progress made.

[13] Figures expressed in nominal "free on board" (FOB) US dollars. Data available at http://comexstat.mdic.gov.br/ (accessed 02/14/2019).

3 Data Sources and Methodology

This section briefly describes the data sources on population, GDP, and GDP shares by state, as well as the methodology employed in construction of the dataset, particularly the estimation of regional GDP shares for the year 1905. From 1872 onwards, figures on the overall population and its distribution across states are from official census records available through the Instituto Brasileiro de Geografia e Estatística (IBGE, Brazil's central statistics agency) website.[14] Estimates for years between censuses were obtained by cubic-spline interpolation until 2010, and extrapolated for 2015 assuming the continuation of average 2000–2010 growth rates.

Brazilian GDP estimates prior to 1890 were calculated for benchmark years by Tombolo and Sampaio (2013). We adjusted the results for those years that did not exactly coincide (e.g. 1872) by chaining their estimates with the growth rates listed in the Maddison Project Database (Bolt et al. 2018). For 1900–1962, we used the numbers from Ipeadata.[15] From 1963 to 2015, we relied on the time series provided by the Brazilian Central Bank.[16]

State GDP shares come from several sources. For 1872 and 1920, we used estimates from the social tables computed by Bértola et al. (2012); from 1939 to 1980, the figures come from the regional series harmonized by Azzoni (1997); and from 1985 onwards, the source was IBGE's official System of Regional Accounts.[17] Regional GDP shares for 1905 were calculated in two steps. First, the following regression was run for states ($n = 20$) in 1920:

$$\ln(GDP) = \alpha + \beta_1 \ln(expenditure) + \beta_2 \ln(exports) + \beta_3 \ln(depratio) + \beta_4 \ln(population_{15-59}) + \beta_5 southern + \varepsilon \quad (1)$$

where *expenditure* is the sum of state and municipal government expenditures, *exports* is the value of exports of seven major commodities (cocoa, coffee, cotton, mate, rubber, sugar, and tobacco), *depratio* is the dependency ratio of individuals under 14 or over 60 years to the total population

[14] See http://sidra.ibge.gov.br, Tables 1209 and 1286 (accessed 12/30/2018).

[15] See http://www.ipeadata.gov.br (accessed 10/10/2018).

[16] See http://www3.bcb.gov.br/sgspub (accessed 09/28/2018).

[17] See https://www.ibge.gov.br/estatisticas-novoportal/economicas/contas-nacionais/9054-contas-regionais-do-brasil.html?=&t=downloads (accessed 10/09/2018).

with reported age, *population*$_{15-59}$ is the population aged 15 to 59, and *southern* is a dummy for states in the South and Southeast. The yield by state of each commodity in 1920 was obtained from Brazil (1923). We assumed each state's participation in the exports of each commodity was proportional to its total output, and regional shares were constant from 1905 to 1920. All monetary variables are expressed in 2017 PPP US dollars. In the second step, we applied the estimated coefficients to values observed for the same independent variables in 1905, computed predicted values, and, thus, GDP shares.

4 Regional Income Inequality in the Long Run

How did the contours of regional income inequality in Brazil change over the long run? This section combines estimates from the well-known and/or official sources just described, and our newly computed figures for 1905, to present data on real state-level GDP per capita for 12 reference periods (1872, 1905, 1920, 1939, 1950, 1960, 1970, 1980, 1991, 2000, 2010, and 2015) spanning the 143 years from 1872 to 2015. Granted that the states (provinces) comprising Brazil have changed over time as new areas were settled and boundaries shifted, we consider a total of 20 homogenous regional units (shown in Map 6.1) that allow for consistent comparison.[18] The path of spatial inequality is found to be somewhat unexpected, namely, because it apparently contradicts (taken altogether) established theory.

Figure 6.1 summarizes the main results for so-called σ-convergence by plotting the evolution of the population-weighted coefficients of variation (CV) for real GDP per capita over time (results for other common measures of inequality, such as the Gini Coefficient or Generalized Entropy indices, show similar patterns; unweighted figures likewise replicate both the trends and levels seen in Fig. 6.1). The figure shows a polynomial trend line that should not be interpreted literally; the data, nonetheless, suggest that regional inequality in Brazil followed neither a linear nor an inverted-U-shaped trajectory, at least in the long run.

[18] Brazil is a federative republic currently divided into 26 states and a Federal District. Temporal consistency demands that the more recently settled areas of the country in the North and Center-West be aggregated: the states of Acre, Rondônia, and Roraima are grouped with Amazonas; Amapá is joined with Pará; Tocantins and the Federal District are grouped with Goiás; and Mato Grosso do Sul is included with Mato Grosso.

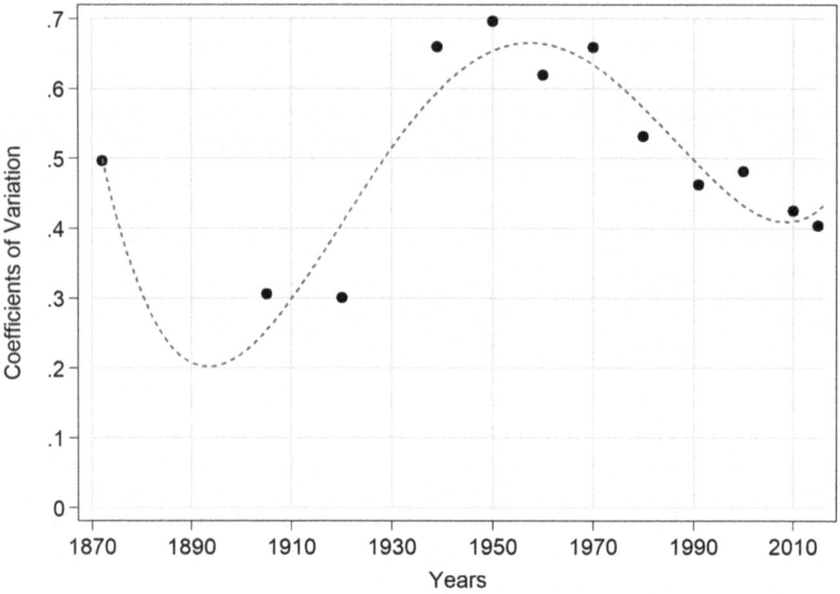

Fig. 6.1 Sigma-convergence: population-weighted coefficients of variation, 1872–2015. Note: Trend line fitted by a fourth-degree polynomial. (Sources: See Sect. 3)

There appear to be three distinct phases over this period. The *Belle Époque* of 1870–1905 saw a significant decline in inequality amid rapid political and economic change as the country transitioned from the Brazilian Empire to the First Republic. The value of the CV in 1872 is 0.5, substantially higher than the next value of 0.3 in 1905. It should be noted, however, that the former is the product of a different estimation technique—the social tables approach by Bértola et al. (2009)—that weighs heavily on the wage distribution in one particular region. More confidence is needed before making absolute statements, though new evidence compiled by the authors (not shown) suggests that the CV was, in fact, much higher during the mid-nineteenth century.

From 1920 to 1939, this apparent downward trend was reversed and regional income dispersion surged in a period marked by the 1930 Revolution, considered a turning point in the modernization of the country, and Vargas' quasi-fascist *Estado Novo* (New State, 1937–1945). In economic terms, the turn of the twentieth century was about when the coffee boom peaked, which also spurred the industrial development of São Paulo: coffee profits, lower transportation costs due to the subsidized construction of railways, and the government-sponsored influx of European immigrants hastened the transformation of the region into Brazil's manufacturing hub (for brief overviews of the literature on this topic, see Monasterio and Reis [2008] and Reis [2014]).

Neither re-democratization in 1945 nor the military coup of 1964 provoked large changes in inequality, as the CV plateaued at a very high level between 0.6 and 0.7 during the heyday of ISI. In fact, its protectionist push helped entrench regional inequalities insofar as poorer regions could not compete with the interplay of regionally biased policies and the positive externalities, spillovers, and agglomeration effects found in São Paulo and in the Southeast. Poorer regions effectively subsidized the industrialization of the Southeast, as ISI policies entailed: (1) import controls on manufactured goods and overvalued exchange rates for the acquisition of industrial inputs and capital goods; and (2) massive direct investments and easier access to credit in well-established industrial hubs.[19] Public education was largely neglected and underfunded relative to more developed countries like the United States (Kang 2011), so the concentration of human capital in the Southeast persisted. The decade of the 1970s, toward the latter stages of ISI, would inaugurate a prolonged reduction in the dispersion of GDP per capita among states.

The final phase began in the waning years of the military dictatorship (1964–1985) and lasted through the first 30 years of the *Nova República* (New Republic), when the CV reached its lowest level since 1920 (0.4). As noted, the 1980s were a decade of severe macroeconomic imbalances and deep recessions that signaled the end of ISI. Economic policy in the 1990s was steered toward trade liberalization, privatization, and a new focus on fiscal responsibility. Rich industrial regions endured significant losses as local manufactures were less efficient than competing imports. Meanwhile, the decentralization of economic activity was furthered in the long term through the expansion of the highway network from the 1960s, the transfer of the capital to Brasília (in 1960), the large increase in educational investment after re-democratization in 1985, and the agricultural

[19] For more information, see Abreu et al. (2000) for an overview of ISI in Brazil since the turn of the twentieth century; and Maimon et al. (1977) and Baer (2003) on the regional effects of ISI plans.

development of the Center-West. Mechanization, technology, the introduction of new crops (such as soybeans), and particularly the commodity boom of the 2000s worked to improve Central-Western states' relative ranks.

Consequently, our overall finding is that regional inequality in the long run followed a wave-like trajectory, ebbing and flowing without displaying any secular trends toward either increasing or decreasing income dispersion. Granted, if one restricts attention to the period from 1905 on (dropping the one observation for 1872), there is a clear inverted-U-shaped trend like that posited by Williamson (1965). The absence of a uniform pattern in the dispersion of regional incomes per capita (σ-convergence) does not mean that there was no convergence whatsoever between Brazilian states. For instance, poorer states might indeed have grown faster over the long run (β-convergence), but random exogenous shocks could have increased their cross-sectional dispersion; thus, unconditional β-convergence is a necessary but not sufficient cause for σ-convergence (Young et al. 2008).

Figure 6.2 addresses this issue by depicting visually the relationship between annual real growth rates and the logarithm of real GDP per capita at the start of the period (real variables are calculated using the IPC-Fipe price index). The downward-sloping regression line shows that, on average, states that were poorer in 1872 grew faster than richer ones, with an estimated speed of convergence (β) of 0.5% per year. Unsurprisingly, β-convergence was much stronger since World War II than in the period from 1872 to 1950 (result not shown). In any case, the estimated coefficients are somewhat low, yet they are fully consistent with the theoretical insight that poorer regions tend to experience catch-up growth due to the diminishing returns of capital.

Table 6.2 presents a closer look at each regional unit from 1872 to 2015: the columns list the GDP per capita of Brazilian states and regions relative to overall GDP per capita for Brazil in those years. Rankings are somewhat predictable over time: for instance, northeastern states always have below-average per capita incomes, whereas São Paulo, Rio de Janeiro, and states in the South are usually close to the top of the distribution. Still, there were some marked changes which largely coincide with the early take-off of manufacturing in São Paulo and the rise and fall of state-sponsored ISI.

The century between 1872 and 1970 saw São Paulo continuously increase its relative GDP per capita, while almost all other states lost

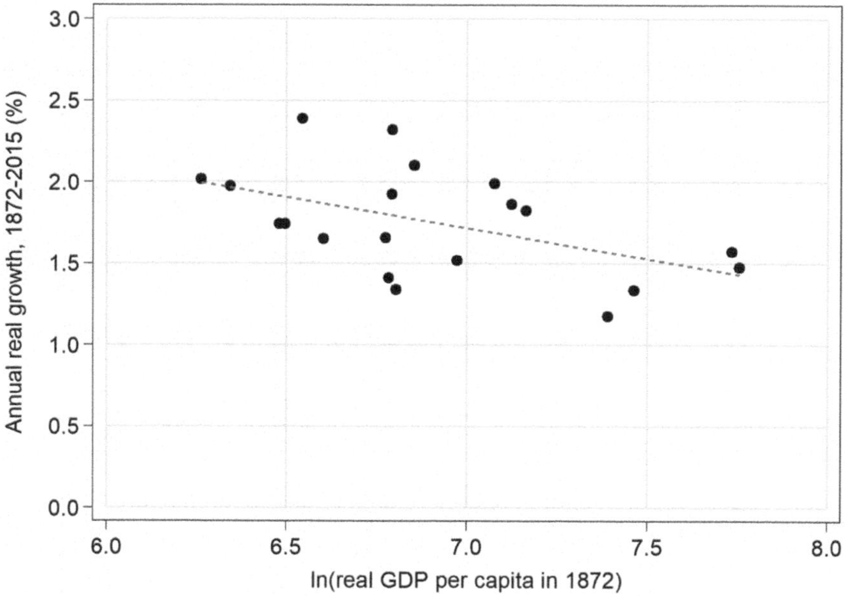

Fig. 6.2 Unconditional β-convergence across time-consistent Brazilian states, 1872–2015. Note: Estimated speed of convergence (β) of 0.5% per year. (Sources: See Sect. 3)

ground. The one partial exception was Goiás, which rapidly increased its relative income after the capital was transferred to Brasília (the new Federal District) in 1960.[20] At its peak, São Paulo had a GDP per capita more than two times greater than the country as a whole: the state climbed from tenth to first place in the income ranking. In contrast, relative losses were very large elsewhere, particularly in the North, which stagnated following the end of the rubber cycle post-1910.

[20] In 1960, the Brazilian capital was transferred from the city of Rio de Janeiro to Brasília, a planned city built from scratch in an unpopulated region split off from Goiás. Brasília became the new Federal District, while the city of Rio de Janeiro first became the state of Guanabara and then merged with the state of Rio de Janeiro in 1975. For the sake of temporal consistency, the new Federal District and Goiás had to be grouped together.

Table 6.2 Regional GDP per capita in Brazil, 1872–2015 (Brazil = 100)

Region	*1872*	*1905*	*1920*	*1939*	*1950*	*1960*	*1970*	*1980*	*1991*	*2000*	*2010*	*2015*
North	**147**	**104**	**87**	**76**	**48**	**63**	**57**	**67**	**73**	**59**	**65**	**61**
Amazonas	156	111	88	88	54	63	70	83	89	76	79	72
Pará	145	100	87	69	45	63	50	57	62	46	54	53
Northeast	**75**	**74**	**70**	**48**	**42**	**46**	**40**	**42**	**46**	**44**	**48**	**51**
Maranhão	81	95	74	41	25	31	27	26	24	30	35	37
Piauí	79	76	71	43	21	22	21	22	26	31	35	41
Ceará	59	63	60	42	39	41	32	35	42	44	46	49
Rio Grande do Norte	47	79	63	46	48	54	33	40	48	47	56	57
Paraíba	58	64	54	38	44	48	29	29	39	39	44	48
Pernambuco	78	79	73	70	60	60	53	50	60	49	54	57
Alagoas	66	66	69	39	40	44	41	40	42	40	43	48
Sergipe	51	80	84	48	39	45	46	41	63	53	63	58
Bahia	95	75	75	47	40	49	48	56	54	51	54	57
Southeast	**114**	**115**	**114**	**141**	**152**	**145**	**152**	**143**	**137**	**137**	**133**	**129**
Minas Gerais	80	82	91	59	66	66	68	85	89	81	88	85
Espírito Santo	111	122	114	65	76	60	71	88	94	108	119	109
Rio de Janeiro	204	137	145	236	214	180	167	140	141	140	138	132
São Paulo	80	147	126	180	202	198	207	180	164	165	154	150
South	**165**	**128**	**140**	**111**	**107**	**103**	**96**	**108**	**114**	**111**	**111**	**119**
Paraná	85	147	152	99	118	100	74	91	102	104	106	117
Santa Catarina	106	120	138	80	80	84	89	112	113	116	121	125
Rio Grande do Sul	209	124	138	127	111	113	122	123	124	116	111	118
Center-West	77	**86**	**121**	**69**	**51**	**55**	**66**	**79**	**89**	**115**	**118**	**121**
Mato Grosso	115	113	124	90	60	77	65	82	73	82	93	107
Goiás	62	74	120	59	48	46	67	78	98	134	132	129
BRAZIL	**100**	**100**	**100**	**100**	**100**	**100**	**100**	**100**	**100**	**100**	**100**	**100**

Sources: See Sect. 3

The debt-fueled crisis of ISI in Brazil since the mid to late 1970s entailed a very different pattern. Once the industrial powerhouse of the country, São Paulo's relative economic standing declined steeply (though until today it remains the richest state in Brazil). Rio de Janeiro, the second in this list, continued its long-run decline toward the national average, and so did Rio Grande do Sul, the third-wealthiest state in 1970. In turn, all other states made inroads. The major relative growth miracle took place in the Center-West, where per capita GDP was just two-thirds of the national average in 1970, but is now 21% higher. Both the move of the federal capital and the expansion of export-oriented agribusiness played important roles.

The four panels of Map 6.2 illustrate these trends. The different colors correspond to four relative income groups based on the real, weighted national average per capita GDP and its year-specific, unweighted standard deviations: very rich, state per capita GDP more than one standard deviation above the mean; rich, between the mean and the mean plus one standard deviation; poor, less than one standard deviation beneath the mean; and very poor, state per capita GDP lower than the mean minus one standard deviation.

Panel A shows relative incomes in 1872, when the regional pattern of inequality was not as pronounced as it would come to be. In relative terms, the sparsely populated northern states (then on the eve of the rubber boom), Rio de Janeiro (then home of the federal capital), and Rio Grande do Sul were far wealthier than the rest of the country. The end of the boom in *borracha* (rubber) and the onset of industrialization created a different situation by 1920 and the North-South divide became clearer (Panel B), with states in the Center-West, Southeast (including São Paulo), and South (notably Paraná) having incomes up to one standard deviation above the mean or more.

Decades of state-led industrialization made the contrast grow starker by 1970 (Panel C). São Paulo, Rio de Janeiro, and Rio Grande do Sul were the only states with incomes above the national average; apart from Santa Catarina, all other states failed to reach just 80% of national GDP per capita (see Table 6.2). Such polarization has weakened since then, but the regions that benefited most were not the poorest in relative terms. Thus, while not as differentiated as in Panel C, in 2015 there was still a clear-cut divide between poorer (North and Northeast) and richer (South/East or Center-West) regions.

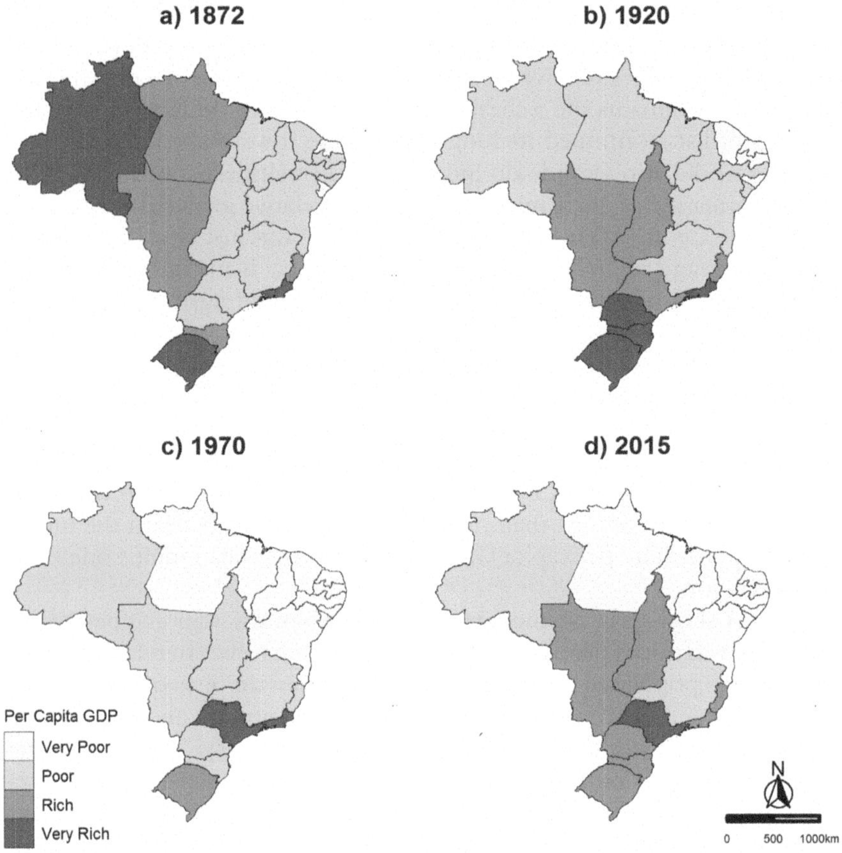

Map 6.2 Regional GDP per capita in Brazil: 1872, 1920, 1970, and 2015. N.B.: "very rich," state per capita GDP more than one standard deviation above the mean; "rich," between the mean and the mean plus one standard deviation; "poor," between the mean and the mean minus one standard deviation; "very poor," state per capita GDP lower than the mean minus one standard deviation. (Sources: See Sect. 3)

Finally, Table 6.3 provides an alternative view of regional inequality, setting aside GDP per capita and focusing on each state's share of aggregate GDP. The results amplify previous trends discussed for GDP per capita, since major economic changes spurred massive within-country

Table 6.3 Regional GDP shares in Brazil, 1872–2015 (%)

Region	*1872*	*1905*	*1920*	*1939*	*1950*	*1960*	*1970*	*1980*	*1991*	*2000*	*2010*	*2015*
North	**4.9**	**4.6**	**4.1**	**2.7**	**1.7**	**2.3**	**2.2**	**3.3**	**4.5**	**4.1**	**4.9**	**4.9**
Amazonas	0.9	1.7	1.3	1.1	0.7	0.9	1.0	1.6	2.3	2.3	2.6	2.5
Pará	4.0	2.9	2.8	1.6	1.0	1.4	1.2	1.7	2.2	1.8	2.3	2.4
Maranhão	2.9	2.7	2.1	1.2	0.8	1.1	0.9	0.9	0.8	1.0	1.2	1.3
Northeast	**35.1**	**28.1**	**25.7**	**16.8**	**14.4**	**14.7**	**12.0**	**12.2**	**13.3**	**12.5**	**13.5**	**14.2**
Piauí	1.6	1.5	1.4	0.8	0.4	0.4	0.4	0.4	0.5	0.5	0.6	0.7
Ceará	4.3	2.9	2.6	2.1	2.0	1.9	1.5	1.5	1.8	1.9	2.0	2.2
Rio Grande do Norte	1.1	1.2	1.1	0.9	0.9	0.9	0.6	0.6	0.8	0.8	0.9	1.0
Paraíba	2.2	1.8	1.7	1.3	1.4	1.4	0.7	0.7	0.8	0.8	0.9	0.9
Pernambuco	6.6	5.4	5.1	4.5	3.9	3.5	3.0	2.6	2.9	2.3	2.5	2.6
Alagoas	2.3	2.4	2.2	0.9	0.8	0.8	0.7	0.7	0.7	0.7	0.7	0.8
Sergipe	0.9	1.5	1.3	0.6	0.5	0.5	0.4	0.4	0.6	0.6	0.7	0.6
Bahia	13.2	8.7	8.2	4.5	3.7	4.2	3.8	4.4	4.4	3.9	4.0	4.1
Southeast	**46.6**	**52.0**	**50.9**	**63.0**	**66.1**	**63.6**	**65.2**	**62.1**	**58.8**	**58.3**	**56.1**	**54.1**
Minas Gerais	16.3	16.6	17.5	9.8	10.0	9.5	8.4	9.6	9.5	8.5	9.0	8.7
Espírito Santo	0.9	1.6	1.7	1.2	1.3	1.0	1.2	1.5	1.7	2.0	2.2	2.0
Rio de Janeiro	22.7	13.3	12.8	20.7	19.3	17.0	16.1	13.2	12.3	11.8	11.6	11.0
São Paulo	6.7	20.5	18.9	31.3	35.5	36.1	39.5	37.8	35.3	36.0	33.3	32.4
South	**11.8**	**13.4**	**16.2**	**15.4**	**16.1**	**17.4**	**17.0**	**17.3**	**17.1**	**16.5**	**16.0**	**16.9**
Paraná	1.0	2.9	3.4	2.9	4.8	6.1	5.5	5.9	5.9	5.9	5.8	6.3
Santa Catarina	1.7	2.2	3.0	2.3	2.4	2.6	2.8	3.4	3.5	3.7	4.0	4.2
Rio Grande do Sul	9.1	8.3	9.8	10.2	8.9	8.7	8.7	8.0	7.7	6.9	6.2	6.4
Center-West	**1.7**	**1.9**	**3.0**	**2.1**	**1.7**	**2.3**	**3.6**	**5.0**	**6.3**	**8.7**	**9.6**	**10.2**
Mato Grosso	0.7	0.8	1.0	0.9	0.6	1.0	1.1	1.7	1.9	2.2	2.7	3.2
Goiás	1.0	1.1	2.0	1.2	1.1	1.3	2.5	3.3	4.4	6.5	6.9	7.0
BRAZIL	**100**	**100**	**100**	**100**	**100**	**100**	**100**	**100**	**100**	**100**	**100**	**100**

Sources: See Sect. 3

migration flows over the course of the twentieth century. Indeed, the figures clearly show how the rise of São Paulo was a major independent source of the concentration of economic activity in the Southeast: its GDP share multiplied six-fold between 1872 and the 1970 peak, with almost 40% of the total economy entirely offsetting the sluggish performance of Minas Gerais and Rio de Janeiro. The north and northeast regions—the wealthiest in the country during colonial times—also struggled, leading to a seismic shift in the economic center of gravity of the country. As a result, the gap in GDP shares between these two most populated regions (Southeast versus Northeast) climbed from 12 to 53 percentage points in just one century.

Again, 1970 was a turning point, though changes were not so dramatic as to completely upend the prevailing economic geography of the country. The three leading states (São Paulo, Rio de Janeiro, and Rio Grande do Sul) experienced a combined 15 percentage point loss in their GDP share. The decline in the concentration of economic activity favored the Center-West above all, to an even greater degree than before: its GDP share almost tripled by 2015. The North and the Northeast also benefited modestly.

The results paint a complex picture of the evolution of regional income inequality in Brazil. Cross-sectional dispersion of incomes per capita evolved in waves, but on average poorer states did grow slightly faster than richer ones. The rise and fall of São Paulo as the foremost economic driver of national growth reshaped the country's economic geography, spurring the concentration and subsequent de-concentration of economic activity in the southeastern states. Still, notwithstanding the ascent of the Center-West, some stylized facts remain valid for the whole period: the Northeast's economic disadvantage and a deepening North-South cleavage that plausibly has few direct parallels in modern world history.

5 Discussion and Conclusion

In this chapter, we have combined new estimates and results from well-known sources to construct consistent long-run time series on GDP per capita by state in Brazil, spanning 12 reference periods across nearly 150 years. More specifically, we use consolidated data from official and scholarly sources for 11 benchmark years from 1872 to 2015, plus our own estimates for the year 1905. This wealth of data allows us to complement previous research by providing a long-term view ranging from the waning years of the Imperial Era to the present.

Our results defy simplified narratives. Dispersion in income per capita across states (σ-convergence), as measured by population-weighted coefficients of variation, resembles a sigmoid function over time, falling and rising (and returning to fall) over successive periods of convergence and divergence. Hence, inequality declined in the late-nineteenth century before rising markedly in the first half of the twentieth century and then finally receding to levels similar to those at the start of the period. Growth regressions, in turn, point out that there was indeed unconditional (β) convergence across states, albeit at a slow pace (0.5% from 1872 to 2015). As stated, the estimate for 1872 is less robust and the narrative is therefore still subject to revision.

The detailed analysis of relative GDP per capita and GDP shares shows some patterns despite the volatility of the nineteenth century. First, there was increased market integration and the economic rise of the Southeast, which would have been even greater in per capita terms were it not for fast population growth and both European (between 1870 and 1920) and internal (in the twentieth century) migration. Second, rapid economic growth in São Paulo deepened the North-South divide, especially during the heyday of ISI. Third, economic liberalization following the stagflation of the 1980s caused another shift in relative fortunes and pushed down regional inequality, as formerly vibrant industrial hubs in the Southeast lagged and commodity exports in the Center-West surged. Finally, these major trends coexisted with occasional, oft-ignored local booms and busts, usually linked to international market conditions, such as the rubber cycle in Amazonas and Pará, or the cotton boom in Maranhão and Alagoas.

Geography, markets, and institutions go a long way in explaining these trends. From the outset, the Portuguese settlement of Brazil focused on the production or extraction of in-demand commodities near coastal areas in a country where topography and a lack of navigable waterways in the hinterlands made transportation costs very high. This implied limited inter-sectoral factor mobility, a very fragmented domestic market, and stagnant productivity, except in the export-oriented sector. In a sense, Brazil really comprises many countries in one.

The Northeast specialized in the production of sugar on large-scale plantations powered by slave labor; as sugar exports stagnated, the Southeast acquired increasing economic significance. As coffee exports soared in the late-nineteenth century, conditions were set for the region's economic take-off, especially for the state of São Paulo: government-sponsored European immigration provided abundant and relatively better-skilled labor, profits from coffee after the end of the slave trade meant abundant capital, and railways dramatically lowered transportation costs and opened possibilities for economies of scale and agglomeration effects.

The rest of the country mostly missed out on these momentous changes. Though the domestic slave trade was quickly re-routed to the Southeast, high transportation costs and imperfect capital markets meant limited North-South mass migration in the late-nineteenth century, while currency appreciation due to coffee exports essentially priced producers out of traditional northeastern commodity markets. Likewise, railroad construction was heavily concentrated in the emerging southeastern areas of the country, so the Northeast also largely failed to benefit from the spillover and agglomeration effects caused by lower transportation costs that boosted economic growth at the turn of the century (Summerhill 2005, 2018). Setting aside brief regional booms (e.g. the rubber cycle in the North), regional polarization was already present in Brazil at the start of the twentieth century.

The transition to an urban economy and deliberate government efforts toward industrialization only accentuated these processes. Coffee profits, better infrastructure, and higher incomes gave São Paulo (and Rio de Janeiro, to a lesser extent) a head start that was subsequently reinforced by ISI policies. Protectionism meant poorer regions had to buy more expensive manufactured goods produced in the Southeast, which in turn faced a virtuous circle, concentrating most public and private investment. An alternative interpretation of the findings, however, is that ISI policies may have eventually stimulated the development of the North and Center-West, and at least slowed the widening of the Northeast-Southeast gap.

The decline and fall of ISI following the debt crisis of the 1980s eventually led to an inevitable (and incomplete) liberalization of trade and macroeconomic policy in the 1990s that reversed this trajectory. Brazilian manufacturing was severely outcompeted by imports and shrank rapidly as a percentage of GDP, while other regions benefited from greater investments in education, increased policy awareness to regional inequalities, better transportation networks, and improved technology and world market conditions for agribusiness exports. The Center-West fared particularly well, being the most successful region of the country since the federal capital was moved from Rio de Janeiro to Brasília in 1960. The stimulus provided by the influx of hundreds of thousands of well-paid civil servants and improved infrastructure was complemented by the rise of agribusiness. Thus, regional inequality in Brazil fell since the 1970s, regressing back to similar levels as seen in the early-nineteenth century.

Taken together, Brazil did not experience any secular trend toward either increasing or decreasing regional inequality. The interaction of geography, markets, and institutions set off path-dependent processes that caused inequality to ebb and flow over time, often with sudden, unforeseen turning points. Consequently, any attempts to predict future trends are exceedingly risky. Further work is needed to extend the regional GDP estimates back to the early-nineteenth and into the eighteenth century, which would make it possible to assess the regional effects of the gold rush and compare them with the subsequent rise of coffee. Additional historical data on wages and occupations would be welcome to evaluate and further refine our estimates.

Appendix: Correspondence Between Present-Day States and Historical Regional Units

Harmonization 1872–2015	*Actual Name*	*Status*
Alagoas	Alagoas	Present-day state
Bahia	Bahia	Present-day state
Ceará	Ceará	Present-day state
Espírito Santo	Espírito Santo	Present-day state
Goiás	Distrito Federal	Present-day state; split off Goiás in 1960
	Goiás	Present-day state
	Tocantins	Present-day state; split off from Goiás in 1988
Maranhão	Maranhão	Present-day state
Mato Grosso	Mato Grosso	Present-day state
	Mato Grosso do Sul	Present-day state; split off from Mato Grosso in 1977
Minas Gerais	Minas Gerais	Present-day state
Amazonas	Acre	Present-day state; territory purchased from Bolivia in 1903, granted statehood in 1962
	Amazonas	Present-day state
	Rondônia	Present-day state; federal territory split off from Amazonas and Mato Grosso in 1943, granted statehood in 1981[21]
	Roraima	Present-day state; federal territory split off from Amazonas in 1943, granted statehood in 1988

[21] Rondônia was grouped with Amazonas because its most populated areas were formerly part of that state.

Harmonization 1872–2015	*Actual Name*	*Status*
Pará	Amapá	Present-day state; federal territory split off from Pará in 1943, granted statehood in 1988
	Pará	Present-day state
Paraíba	Paraíba	Present-day state
Pernambuco	Pernambuco	Present-day state
Piauí	Piauí	Present-day state
Rio de Janeiro	Court	Capital of the Portuguese Kingdom, 1808–1820
	Neutral Municipality	Capital of the Brazilian Empire, 1834–1889
	Federal District	Federal District of the Brazilian Republic, 1889–1960
	Guanabara	City of Rio de Janeiro granted statehood after capital was transferred to Brasília in 1960, merged with state of Rio de Janeiro in 1975
	Rio de Janeiro	Present-day state
Rio Grande do Norte	Rio Grande do Norte	Present-day state
Rio Grande do Sul	Rio Grande do Sul	Present-day state
Santa Catarina	Santa Catarina	Present-day state
Paraná	Paraná	Present-day state; split-off from São Paulo in 1853
São Paulo	São Paulo	Present-day state
Sergipe	Sergipe	Present-day state

Source: Elaborated by the authors

References

Abreu, M. de P., Bevilaqua, A. S. and Pinho, D. M. (2000). "Import substitution and growth in Brazil, 1890s–1970s". In Cárdenas, E., Ocampo, J. A. and Thorp, R. (Ed.). *An Economic History of Twentieth-Century Latin America*, Vol. 3, 154–175. New York: Palgrave Macmillan.

Abreu, M. de P. and Correa do Lago. LA. (2014). "A economia brasileira no Império, 1822–1889". In Abreu, M. de P. *A Ordem do Progresso: Dois Séculos de Política Econômica no Brasil*, 2nd edition, 1–28. São Paulo: Elsevier Campus.

Abreu, M. de P. (2008). "The Brazilian economy, 1980–1994". In *The Cambridge History of Latin America IX—Brazil since 1930*, Bethell, L. (Ed.). 395–429. New York: Cambridge University Press.

Absell, C. D. and Tena-Junguito, A. (2016). "Brazilian Export Growth and Divergence in the Tropics during the Nineteenth Century". *Journal of Latin American Studies* 48(4): 677–706.

Azzoni, C. R. (1997). "Concentração Regional e Dispersão das Rendas Per Capita Estaduais: Análise a partir de Séries Históricas Estaduais de PIB, 1939–1995". *Estudos Econômicos* 27(3): 341–393.

Baer, W. (2003). *A Economia Brasileira*. São Paulo: Nobel.

Bértola, L., Castelnovo, C., Rodríguez Weber, J. and Willebald, H. (2009). "Income Distribution in the Latin American Southern Cone during the First Globalization Boom and Beyond". *International Journal of Comparative Sociology* 50(5–6), 452–485.

Bértola, L., Castelnovo, C. and Willebald, H. (2012). "Income Distribution in Brazil, 1870–1920". *XVII Jornadas Anuales de Economia, Banco Central del Uruguay*, 1–25.

Bértola, L. and Ocampo, J. A. (2012). *The Economic Development of Latin America since Independence*. Oxford: Oxford University Press.

Bethell, L. (2008a). "Politics in Brazil under Vargas, 1930–1945". In Bethell, L. (Ed.). *The Cambridge History of Latin America IX—Brazil since 1930*, 3–86. New York: Cambridge University Press.

———. (2008b). "Politics in Brazil under the Liberal Republic, 1945–1964". In Behell, L. (Ed.) *The Cambridge History of Latin America IX—Brazil since 1930*, 87–164. New York: Cambridge University Press.

Bethell, L. and Castro, C. (2008). "Politics in Brazil under Military Rule, 1964–1985". In Bethell, L. (Ed.). *The Cambridge History of Latin America IX—Brazil since 1930*, 165–230. New York: Cambridge University Press.

Bolt, J., Inklaar, R. Jong, H. and van Zanden, J. L. (2018). "Rebasing 'Maddison': New Income Comparisons and the Shape of Long-Run Economic Development". *Maddison Project Working Paper* 10.

Brazil, Directoria Geral de Estatistica. (1923). *Recenseamento do Brasil—1920 Vol. III*. Rio de Janeiro: Ministerio da Agricultura, Industria e Commercio.

Brazil. (1974). *II Plano Nacional de Desenvolvimento (1975–1979)*. Brasília: Imprensa Oficial.

Carvalho, J. M. (2008). *Cidadania no Brasil: O Longo Caminho*. Rio de Janeiro: Civilização Brasileira.

Contador, C. R. and C. L. Haddad. "Produto real, moeda e preços: a experiência brasileira no período 1861–1970." *Revista Brasileira de Economia*, 36 (1975):407–440.

Diniz, C. C. (2009). "Celso Furtado e o desenvolvimento regional". *Nova Economia*, 19(2): 227–249.

Dix-Carneiro, R. and Kovak, B. K. (2017). "Trade Liberalization and Regional Dynamics". *American Economic Review* 107(10): 2908–2946.

Fausto, B. (1988). "Estado, classe trabalhadora e burguesia industrial (1920–1945): uma revisão". *Novos Estudos* 20: 6–37.

Ferreira, P. C. (2004). *Regional policy in Brazil: a review*. Unpublished manuscript.

Funari, P. P. P. 2017. "Inequality, Institutions, and Long-Term Development: A Perspective from Brazilian Regions". In Bértola, L. and Williamson, J. (Ed.), *Has Latin American Inequality Changed Direction?*, 113–142. Cham: Springer International Publishing.

Giambiagi, F., Villela, A., de Castro, L. de C. and Hermann, J. (2005). *Economia Brasileira Contemporânea*. Rio de Janeiro: Elsevier Campus.

Goldsmith, Raymond W. Brasil 1850–1984: *Desenvolvimento Financieiro sob um Século de Inflação*. São Paulo: Harper and Row, 1986.

Gomes, A. de C. (2005). *A Invenção do Trabalhismo*. Rio de Janeiro: Editora Fundação Getúlio Vargas.

Kang, T. (2011). "Descentralização e Financiamento da Educação Brasileira: Uma Análise Comparativa, 1930–1964". *Revista Estudos Econômicos* 41(3): 573–598.

Luna, F. V. and Klein, H. S. (2003). *Slavery and the Economy of São Paulo, 1750–1850*. Stanford, CA: Stanford University Press.

Maimon, D., Baer, W. and Geiger, P. P. (1977). "O Impacto Regional das Políticas Econômicas no Brasil". *Revista Brasileira de Geografia* 39(3): 3–53.

Monasterio, L. M. (2010). "Brazilian Spatial Dynamics in the Long Term (1872–2000): 'Path Dependency' or 'Reversal of Fortune'?". *Journal of Geographic Systems* 12: 51–67.

Monasterio, L. M., Reis, E. (2008). "Mudanças na Concentração Espacial das Ocupações nas Atividades Manufatureiras no Brasil—1872–1920". *Instituto de Pesquisa Econômica Aplicada (Ipea) Working Paper* 1361: 1–36.

Musacchio, A., Fritscher, A. M. and Viarengo, M. (2014). "Colonial Institutions, Trade Shocks, and the Diffusion of Elementary Education in Brazil, 1889–1930". *Journal of Economic History* 74(3): 730–766.

Pereira, T. Z. (2019). "The North-South Divide: Real Wages and Welfare in Brazil during the Early 20th Century". *Revista de Historia Económica*.

Reis, E. (2008). "A renda per capita dos municípios brasileiros circa 1872". Unpublished manuscript.

———. (2014). "Spatial Income Inequality in Brazil, 1872–2000". *EconomiA*, 15: 119–140.

Resende, A. L. (1982). "A Política Brasileira de Estabilização: 1963–1968". *Pesquisa e Planejamento Econômico* 12(3): 757–806.

Summerhill, W. (2005). "Big Social Savings in a Small Laggard Economy: Railroad-led Growth in Brazil". *The Journal of Economic History* 65(1): 72–102.

———. (2018). *Trilhos do Desenvolvimento: As Ferrovias no Crescimento da Economia Brasileira 1854–1913*. São Paulo: Alfaiatar.

Tombolo, G. and Sampaio, A de V. (2013). "O PIB brasileiro nos séculos XIX e XX: duzentos anos de flutuações econômicas". *Revista de Economia* 39(3): 181–216.

Villela, A. (2005). "Dos 'anos dourados' de JK à crise não resolvida". In Giambiagi, F., Villela, A., de Castro, L. de C. and Hermann, J. (Ed). *Economia Brasileira Contemporânea*, 45–68. Rio de Janeiro: Elsevier Campus.

Williamson, J. G. (1965). "Regional Inequality and the Process of National Development: A Description of the Patterns". *Economic Development and Cultural Change* 13(4): 3–84.

———. (1995). "The Evolution of Global Labor Markets since 1830: Background Evidence and Hypotheses". *Explorations in Economic History* 32: 141–196.

Young, A. T., Higgins, M. J. and Levy, D. (2008). "Sigma Convergence versus Beta Convergence: Evidence from U.S. County-Level Data". *Journal of Money, Credit, and Banking* 40(5): 1083–1093.

CHAPTER 7

Spatial Inequality in Chile in the Long Run: A Paradox of Extreme Concentration in the Absence of Agglomeration Forces (1890–2017)

Marc Badia-Miró

1 Introduction

Chile is characterized as a country with an extreme concentration of economic activity around Santiago, the administrative capital. Despite this, and in contrast to what is found in most of the industrialized countries,

This chapter is mostly based on previous works already published as Badia-Miró (2015). I would appreciate the comments received by C. Ducoing, D. A. Tirado-Fabregat, H. Willeballd and A. Herranz-Loncán. I also acknowledge the financial support offered by the project PGC2018-095821-B-I00 and ECO2015-65049-C12-1-P, funded by the *Ministerio de Ciencia, Innovación y Universidades* (MCIU), to the *Agencia Estatal de Investigación* (AEI) and the *Fondo Europeo de Desarrollo Regional* (FEDER). I also thank the financial support of the Catalan Government (2017SGR1466).

M. Badia-Miró (✉)
Departament d'Història, Institucions, Política i Econòmica Mundial
Universitat de Barcelona, Barcelona, Spain
e-mail: mbadia@ub.edu

D. A. Tirado-Fabregat et al. (eds.), *Time and Space*,
Palgrave Studies in Economic History,
https://doi.org/10.1007/978-3-030-47553-6_7

income levels per inhabitant in the capital have been below the country average and far from the levels in the wealthiest regions. In this context it is relevant to understand the evolution and the dynamics that lie behind both results, in a country where agglomeration economies seem to have had a marginal impact and where natural resource endowments have been crucial to explain the spatial location of economic activity (the nitrate mining cycle was extremely concentrated in space and labour-intensive, whereas copper mining has been much more disperse and capital-intensive). Other factors to bear in mind are the industrialization favoured by Import Substitution Industrialization (ISI) policies during the 1940s and the 1950s, the impact of regional development policies around the 1960s, the impact of liberalization economies during the 1980s or the role played by infrastructures such as the railway through the *Valle Central* in boosting Santiago as a trade centre.

This chapter describes the impact that all of these and other factors had on the present-day layout of the country. Moreover, it also measures the real impact that these and other factors could have to answer some of the relevant questions which arise, such as, Was the effect of the capital and the enormous market potential of the central region of the country the real driver of spatial distribution in the twentieth-century Chilean economy? What was the spatial impact of the persistently high transport costs in domestic and foreign trade? Furthermore, the relevance of the Chilean case increases as a case study to understand the location of the economic activity where industry played a secondary role in the transformation of these economies.

The Chilean case is also interesting because the study of the spatial distribution of the economy goes beyond mere description and the chapter focuses on the determinants behind this long-term performance. For this reason, it determines the importance of the interrelation between primary factors, following the models of Heckscher-Ohlin of comparative advantage, and comparing them with the factors of the New Economic Geography (NEG), which emerge around the effects derived from the market potential and the agglomeration economies.

When Sala-i-Martin (1996) presented the existence of β-convergence in most of the European regions and in the United States, from 1960 onwards, he did not consider the fact that much of the initial divergence of GDP per capita among the regions occurred around the transition to the twentieth century. During those years, the impact of the agglomeration economies, due to the industrial revolution, was more intense.[1] Those results clearly followed the predictions of the Solow model, where comparative advantage determines the location of economic activity (Barro and Sala-i-Martin 1992).

Considering this long-term view, an inverted-U evolution fit perfectly with the predictions of Williamson (1965) and Krugman (1991) and the NEG: pushed by the existence of scale economies, a reduction of transport costs favoured first the increase and then the reduction of regional inequality, in the presence of agglomeration economies.[2] Recent studies for most of the European countries clearly show the existence of this curve, during the early years of industrialization, such as in England before 1910 (Crafts 2005), in France during the period 1860–1930 (Diez-Minguela et al. 2018), in Spain for the same period (Rosés et al. 2010) and in Portugal from 1970 on (Badia-Miró et al. 2012).

However, the Chilean case does not show the same pattern observed for these countries. Even though the process of concentration of economic activity took place around Santiago and Valparaíso, neither industry nor services benefited excessively from the emergence of agglomeration economies in these leading regions. The lack of such spatial forces would explain why the reduction of inequality, observed in the long run, was the result of counterbalancing forces. On the one hand, the increase in the dispersion of regional income was related with the existence of several mining cycles (first nature or H-O forces). On the other hand, the reduction in regional dispersion was in parallel to the expansion of industry and services in the capital (second nature or NEG forces).

In this chapter we are going to check the existence of first nature forces and go deeper testing the reliability of the predictions of the NEG framework, specifically the interaction between trade policies and the spatial dynamic of economic activity, through its impact on transport costs. The Chilean case was characterized by the existence of huge differences in trade policies since the Pacific War. An initial stage of export-led growth

[1] The introduction to the book by Combes et al. (2008) makes a thorough review of the impact of industrialization as the main driver of the generation of regional inequalities during the industrial revolution. Other references to bear in mind when considering the evolution of regional income inequality are Barro and Sala-i-Martin (1992), Fujita and Krugman (2004) and Fujita et al. (1999).

[2] The integration of domestic markets and the opening of the economy to international markets explain most of the reduction in transport costs during the late nineteenth century and the beginning of the twentieth century.

during the First Globalization, with higher import and exports tariffs as main fiscal revenues, was pushed by the nitrate cycle. A second stage was shaped by the drastic protectionist shift, which influenced efforts to industrialize the country during the period of Import Substitution Industrialization (ISI), coinciding with the emergence of the copper cycle, until the 1970s. Subsequently, a third stage was characterized by a marked trade openness in the post-1973 liberalization process after the coup d'état, leading to a strong de-industrialization, in parallel to economic expansion driven by mining and agro-industrial exports, pushed by the commodity boom price cycle at the beginning of the twenty-first century.[3]

In order to answer all these questions, I have estimated values for the regional GDP per capita of the 13 present-day regions for the period 1890–1960 and compared them with the official estimations from 1960 onwards. To do that I have grouped previous estimations of regional GDP shares for 25 Chilean provinces from Badia-Miró (2008), for the period 1890–1973. At first glance, the new evidence shows that, in contrast to many of the developed countries, Chile shows a clear tendency towards the reduction of GDP per capita concentration, only interrupted shortly by the expansion of Magallanes in 1960 due to the discovery of oil in that region. This trend runs in parallel to the reinforcement of a process of extreme spatial concentration of the national GDP around Santiago.

This chapter is organized as follows. The second section provides the historical background. The third section describes the data and the methodology considered to obtain regional GDP figures. The fourth section analyses the evolution of the spatial distribution of the economy in the long run. The fifth section concludes.

2 From Nitrate Cycle to the Commodity Boom in the Early Twenty-First Century

After the Pacific War the Chilean economy became strongly linked with the evolution of the nitrate sector, until the Great Depression. The expansion of saltpetre exports connected the Tarapacá and Antofagasta regions, in the north, with the international markets and boosted the Chilean economy through the increase of fiscal revenues and the expansion of aggregate demand of the northern regions. Nevertheless, this windfall reduced diversification that caused an extreme dependence on these

[3] Díaz and Wagner (2004) offers an interesting survey for Chilean trade policies.

resources (Gallo 2008). The result was that the crisis in the sector extended its impact to the rest of the economy. The manufacturing sector expanded its activity as a response to this demand expansion while the agrarian sector stagnated (Cariola Sutter and Sunkel 1983).

World War I and the 1920s consolidated the expansion of the manufacturing sector as a result of an import substitution process, near Santiago, Valparaíso and the south, with a rise in tariffs, natural protection (due to the difficulties of international trade during the war) and urban expansion (Badia-Miró and Ducoing 2015; Palma 1984). In parallel, during the first decades of the twentieth century, the so-called "Gran Minería"[4] pushed copper production after the stagnation observed with the depletion of high-grade deposits at the end of the nineteenth century (Badia-Miró and Ducoing 2015). The 1920s were also a period of public debt expansion to finance structural budget deficits. In the mid-1920s, the Kemmerer mission advised the reform of the fiscal system and the creation of a Central Bank which favoured foreign investment. Nevertheless, fiscal equilibrium was never achieved (Collier and Sater 2004).

The Great Depression deeply affected the Chilean economy due to the fall in copper prices, the rise in copper import taxes in the US (one of the main importers) and the collapse of the nitrate sector. Occupation in mining fell and foreign investment suddenly stopped. Moreover, despite efforts to reduce the fiscal deficit through spending cuts, fiscal balance could not be achieved during the 1930s.

From the mid-1930s onwards, the Chilean economy recovered due to an increase in copper prices and industry promotion policies, by using differential exchange rates, and favoured a deepening of the import substitution process which had been started a decade before (Bulmer-Thomas 2003). In 1939, the CORFO (*Corporación de Fomento Fabril*) was created to reinforce industrial promotion and domestic demand to become an alternative source of sustained growth.

World War II and the subsequent import collapse consolidated this manufacturing expansion based on domestic demand. Import shortages for raw materials and machinery affected the industry at first, but US aid, in the warlike context, allowed the industry to continue its recovery and lay the foundations for sustained growth.

[4] *Gran Minería* describes three North American-owner mines of low-grade copper ores which started to produce copper after huge investments in machinery and infrastructure at the beginning of the twentieth century.

The 1950s and the 1960s are known as the ISI period decades, where industrialization led by the state policies were deeply implemented in the country. Higher import tariffs, differential exchange rates, investment facilities and expansion of urban wages fostered manufacturing expansion by producing non-durable consumer goods and substituting durable consumer goods (at the end of the period). The levels achieved by the industry were significant (see Table 7.1). Those policies are closely linked with regional promotion as the creation of Free Trade Zone in Arica (1958) and the support of the Concepción steel industry (Gwynne 1984; Haindl Rondanelli 2006). In the copper sector, the state first favoured the "chilenization" and later the nationalization of copper production.

Nevertheless, fiscal imbalances, constant inflationary pressures, current account imbalance, reduced market dimension and problems to expand productivity (rigidities in labour market and difficulties to adopt technology) marked the performance of the economy. The model seemed to have been exhausted in the late 1960s and the early 1970s.

The coup d'état and the dictatorship prevented the continuity of some of the reforms initiated before (agrarian and labour reform), balanced public budgets and changed the economic model towards the liberalization of the economy (drop in foreign trade tariffs, reduction of public deficit through the cuts in public expenses, privatizations and elimination of market regulations). The result was a huge shock in the Chilean economy until 1976, when it started to recover and reduced inflation at the cost of a considerable increase in unemployment, a fall in real wages, a de-industrialization of those sectors oriented towards domestic demand (that could not compete with products produced abroad), the return of lands to former owners and a gradual recovery of natural resource exports.

Table 7.1 Evolution of sectorial GDP during the period 1890–2010 (%)

	1890 (%)	*1907 (%)*	*1925 (%)*	*1935 (%)*	*1950 (%)*	*1960 (%)*	*1980 (%)*	*2000 (%)*	*2010 (%)*
Agrarian GDP	5.6	6.3	5.9	6.6	5.4	4.4	3.3	3.4	3.6
Industrial GDP	15.1	11.7	11.4	11.7	20.3	21.7	21.0	17.0	14.3
Mining GDP	17.5	17.9	20.0	15.5	11.9	7.6	7.1	8.7	6.4

Source: Díaz et al. (2016)

In 1982 the Chilean economy, as other Latin American countries, suffered a new recession as a result of debt expansion (mostly private), a slowing down of export performance due to a slump in world demand (second oil shock crisis) and the increase of international interest rates. The state intervened in the banking system to avoid financial collapse and the IMF provided credit to stabilize the economy. Moreover, some import tariffs were imposed and the peso was devalued to reduce trade imbalances. After the crisis, liberalization policies continued to guide the country's economic performance in the 1980s.

In 1990, when the Concertation won the elections and initiated the transition to democracy, the Chilean economy showed sustained growth based on exports of natural resources, fiscal equilibrium and low inflation levels (Bértola and Ocampo 2012; Bulmer-Thomas 2003). Nevertheless, huge disparities in income and wealth placed the country among the most unequal in the region. In addition, the Chilean economy was characterized by the existence of informal jobs, low wages and the re-primarization of its export basket (Hausmann et al. 2014).

3 Estimation of the Chilean Provincial GDP for the Period 1890–1973

One of the aims of this study is to fill in the gaps of the regional GDP per capita data between the War of the Pacific, when Chile established its present-day borders, and the 1960s when official figures started being issued. In order to do this, I have combined several strategies to distribute the sectorial GDP among the different provinces. The national data used comes from Díaz et al. (2016), by correcting his industrial data with new estimations offered by Ducoing and Badia-Miró (2013).[5] I split the national GDP considering:

$$\mathrm{GDP} = \sum_i \mathrm{GDP}_i, \tag{7.1}$$

where GDP_i is the GDP of region i and the sum of all the regional GDPs is the national GDP. Considering Eq. (7.1), I have also split each sectorial GDP for each region. To obtain each GDP for every sector and region, we

[5] A detailed description of the reconstruction of the regional GDP of Chile can be found in Badia-Miró (2008).

have adopted different strategies. I define the regional GDP for the agricultural sector and for the industrial sector according to the methodology proposed by Geary and Stark (2002, 2016). For the mining sector, I have considered the production approach. For the other sectors, I have approximated the regional value added by a set of representative variables.

The integration of the labour market in the agricultural sector was low and agricultural wages could not be representative for each province. To solve this, I have approximated the economically active population to the gross production of these representative products and I have used production per unit area (as a proxy for productivity) for these same years.[6] For the provincial GDP of the industrial sector we do have wage data to obtain the differentials of productivity among the provinces, as well as the data of the sectorial labour force for each industrial sector, so we applied the Geary Stark Methodology.

For the mining sector, the estimation was carried out using two types of data: on the one hand, and with the intention of reflecting export-oriented mining, I have considered total provincial exports. In parallel, I have considered mining production for domestic consumption (particularly coal and oil), not considered in export statistics. In order to obtain the contribution of the foreign sector, we have taken exports for mining provinces (Tarapacá, Antofagasta, Atacama, Coquimbo, Valparaíso, Aconcagua, Santiago, O'Higgins and Aysén), and I have calculated the percentage that the sum of these represent over the total of the country.[7]

The relative value obtained through exports was applied to the total mining GDP in order to obtain the provincial mining GDP. Bearing in mind that I have not considered coal, I have corrected the GDP value, deducting the percentage represented by coal in total production. I did

[6]We have considered those products with which we can explain almost 80% of the total product, which were cereals, vines, potatoes and cattle. For more information, see Badia-Miró (2008).

[7]In the mining provinces of the North we have confirmed that most of mining production destined for exports were produced in the same province (Badia-Miró 2007, 2008, 2015). This is also valid for the province of Aysén. Difficulties appeared assigning exports in the *Zona Central*. In these provinces it is difficult to link the production province with the export province. Though it was clear that the production of Aconcagua and Valparaíso would leave the country via Valparaíso, we do not know what part of the production of Santiago would leave the country via the neighbouring provinces. The same occurred with the O'Higgins (*San Antonio* started to be important after the 1960s and 1970s). To solve this, we have adjusted the export values by mining production per provinces, easily available from 1930 onwards, and estimated before the 1930s.

the same for oil, but in this case, only the data post-1960 was affected. Throughout most of the period analysed, coal production was around 10% of the total. Thus, with exportation data I can assign the provincial weight for approximately 90% of the mining GDP, until 1960.

Coal has a significant contribution in regional GDP, not so much for its total weight in total national mining, but rather because it is concentrated in a few provinces, and thus its impact on these provinces is striking. Only four provinces have coalmines and in two of these the production is almost token. The main productive provinces are Concepción and Arauco, with more than 95% of total production. The provinces of Valdivia and Magallanes follow at a considerable distance. In order to distribute the value of coal production per province, I have considered gross coal production per province against some benchmarks. With these data, I have constructed series of percentages of participation of these provinces over the total and I have applied these values to the aggregated series of coal production. The percentages applied prior to 1900 are those of that year.

Between the years for which we do have data I consider constant growth of the percentages and, from 1949 onwards, I use the percentages obtained for 1949 for that year. The coal production data was obtained from Díaz et al. (1998, 2016), although they provide data only for the period 1860–1940. For the rest of the period I have applied the prices used by Díaz in 1940 and gross mining production data (in weight) from Braun et al. (2000) for the period 1941–1973.

Finally, something like what occurs with coal also occurs with oil, and therefore, not counting it may generate important imbalances in the province of Magallanes, given that oil production is concentrated there. The main problem lies in the fact that in Díaz et al. (1998), they do not count the contribution of oil in the total products used to obtain the mining GDP. Thus, the methodology used for coal cannot be applied. Oil production in Magallanes started at the end of the 1950s and beginning of the 1960s. I have used the sectorial GDP data generated by ODEPLAN (National Planning Office) of 1960, to obtain the percentage that Magallanes represents over the total mining GDP. Using this data, the rest of the mining product of 1960 has been redistributed, according to the percentages obtained without considering oil. Between 1960 and 1973 coastal shipping departures in this province are very important and quite steady, clearly responding to the beginning of oil exploitation. Based on these data I consider that the percentage of provincial over national mining production remains steady until the end and hereby I recalculate the values for the remaining provinces. To this end, it has been assumed that the volume of total mining production without oil does not change during the period 1960–1973.

In order to construct the regional GDP figures for the other sectors of the economy we have to deal with some problems. First, Díaz et al. (2016) do not provide information for sectorial desegregation of the GDP before 1940 (nearly of 40–50% of total GDP is not assigned). In addition to this problem, nearly 20% of the total GDP came from the service sector. Unlike what happens with mining, agriculture or industry, we have scarce information by region. To overcome this problem, we propose a shortcut based on the Geary and Stark (2002) methodology: we consider economic active population at a regional level for those sectors not included in manufacturing, industry or mining and we correct it considering the average productivity of mining, agriculture and manufacturing (a similar assumption is considered by Geary and Stark [2002, 2016] to obtain regional GDP figures for the UK).

In 1973, Chile modified the administrative division and what were 25 provinces became 13 regions.[8] Since 1960, official estimations are provided by ODEPLAN and the Central Bank of Chile. I have reconstructed historical data for the provinces, which I have subsequently transformed into regions to permit comparability for the entire period.[9] Although the different regional price levels distort regional GDP figures in real terms, it goes beyond the scope of this work. In that sense, it is assumed that the GDP per capita figures are in nominal prices and therefore regional inequality has been overestimated.

4 Regional GDP Evolution in Chile in the Long Run: 1890–2010

In the mid-nineteenth century, before the expansion of Chile towards the mining regions of the North and the settlement of the southern regions, the country was divided into three big regions. The *Norte Chico*

[8] That is assuming that the GDP per capita of Santiago is the same as that observed for the Metropolitan Region of Santiago, despite the differences that exist between the two administrative divisions.

[9] The results of the robustness test between own figures and official sources was very good. Rank analysis confirmed the same analysis and we could identify the main differences obtained in Santiago, due to the impact of being the administrative capital of a country.

specialized in mining and agriculture boosted by the expansion of Peruvian, Californian, Australian and European demand. In the centre of the country, around Santiago and the *Valle Central*, there was also agricultural production and mining. The third region, in the South, around Concepción, was a region that specialized in agricultural production and livestock. This distribution already showed the existence of high levels of spatial inequality. Its roots were at the end of the colonial period, with the expansion of the agricultural sector in the *Valle Central*, particularly based on flour production, driven by foreign demand.[10] At the same time, much of the country's mining exportation was concentrated in the port of Valparaíso, in addition to most of the commercial and financial activity of the country.[11] In the North, the export boom also lay behind the emergence and expansion of an important number of metal smelting plants and forges, which transformed the minerals for subsequent exportation, propelling economic and demographic growth. This expansion lasted until the end of the nineteenth century, when the richest veins of minerals came to an end, and new competitors emerged in international markets. At the time, coal mining emerged strongly in the South around Concepción, parallel to the region's manufacturing specialization in the textile sector, particularly wool. Together with these changes, Santiago grew as a trade hub and reinforced its role as the capital of the country, taking advantage of the benefits of the export cycle, which covered the costs of urban expansion and the development of the service industry (Hurtado Ruíz-Tagle 1966). In the 1860s, there was a point of inflection in the location of economic activity. Growth based on the expansion of exports ended. Simultaneously, the country began to expand in the *Araucanía*, occupying vast fertile expanses of the South. Towards 1880, Chile also occupied the Bolivian and Peruvian mining provinces in the Atacama Desert, in the *Norte Grande*, an area with vast nitrate deposits. The economic expansion along the "new" Chilean regions and the expansion of the railway network propelled the expansion of the manufacturing sector, particularly in relation to the intensive mining activities in the North, favouring the integration of the domestic market.

[10] Carmagnani (1998) and Palma (1979) state that this expansion was driven by the growth of the demand from the United States East Coast and ended with the emergence of Australia as the main wheat producer of the Pacific.

[11] Valparaíso had become the headquarters of the main trading companies, while simultaneously it was the point where most of the products entered and left the country (Carmagnani 2001; Cavieres Figueroa 1988; Coudyoumdjan 2000; Pinto Vallejos 1987).

From this time onwards, the new quantitative evidence provided enables us to understand the behaviour of location of economic activity throughout most of the twentieth century (see Table 7.2).

Table 7.2 shows the impact of the localization of natural resources in the levels of income per capita. The highly spatially concentrated nitrate cycle fostered regional GDP per capita in northern regions (I and II) until 1920, and the more spatially diversified copper cycle pushed the regional GDP per capita of other regions (II, III, V and RM) since then. Oil also fostered region XII during the 1960s and the 1970s, a region with persistently higher incomes per capita due to its role as a transport hub at the turn of the twentieth century and its low population density levels during the period.[12] We also observe the long-run stagnation of southern agrarian regions, which in the mid-nineteenth century had been the main driver of the Chilean export economy.

Going deeper into the analysis, Fig. 7.1 shows a clear σ-convergence in the GDP per capita dispersion, accompanied by a reduction in the levels of inequality of GDP per capita, until the 1980s, before the debt crisis and the liberalization. After that turning point, we observe a slight expansion of inequality as a result of the income growth in mining regions driven by the commodities boom. As a measurement of dispersion, their evolution enables to confirm the reduction of the differences between the levels of income in the provinces in the long run. This result confirms the hypothesis proposed by Sala-i-Martin (1996) and would contradict NEG's postulates. One plausible reason for this result, and therefore the convergence observed, lies in the existence of great differences in the starting point around 1890 and 1900. These differences appeared with the emergence of the nitrate cycle and the extreme concentration of mining exports in few provinces, whereas others continued to have traditionally based economies, with a subsistence agricultural sector, which retained an important weight.[13] The differences in levels between weighed and non-weighted figures were related to the low population located in this northern mining region, and the stagnation of the other regions, but the evolution is quite similar. The collapse of nitrate exports after World War I, along with the appearance of the copper cycle, which was much more spatially dispersed,

[12] This high level of income per capita is also observed in the Patagonian and southern regions in Argentina, which were also characterized by low population density levels.

[13] Mainly in Tarapacá, province in the North of the country which was recently incorporated into Chile because of the War of the Pacific.

Table 7.2 Regional GDP per capita in Chile, 1895–2010 (average = 1)

	1895	*1907*	*1920*	*1930*	*1940*	*1950*	*1960*	*1970*	*1980*	*1990*	*2000*	*2010*
Tarapacá (I)	8.1	3.6	3.8	2.4	0.5	0.7	1.9	1.3	1.3	1.2	1.4	1.8
Antofagasta (II)	2.7	4.1	4.4	4.3	2.0	2.0	1.5	1.7	1.9	2.0	2.4	3.4
Atacama (III)	0.6	0.3	0.5	2.4	1.7	1.2	1.0	1.0	0.9	0.9	1.1	1.5
Coquimbo (IV)	0.2	0.4	0.3	0.6	0.3	0.3	0.5	0.5	0.5	0.6	0.7	0.8
Valparaíso (V)	1.1	0.9	0.9	1.0	1.2	1.5	1.2	1.1	1.1	1.0	0.9	0.8
O'Higgins (VI)	1.0	0.8	1.0	1.1	0.9	1.0	0.8	0.9	0.9	0.9	0.9	0.9
Maule (VII)	0.5	0.7	0.7	0.5	0.6	0.6	0.5	0.5	0.5	0.6	0.6	0.6
Bío (VIII)	0.8	0.8	0.8	0.7	1.0	0.8	0.8	0.8	0.9	0.9	0.7	0.7
Araucanía (IX)	0.4	0.5	0.3	0.3	0.4	0.5	0.4	0.4	0.4	0.5	0.5	0.4
Los Lagos (X)	0.6	0.7	0.6	0.6	0.5	0.5	0.5	0.5	0.6	0.7	0.7	0.5
Aysén (XI)	0.0	0.0	0.0	0.0	0.2	0.2	0.7	1.1	1.0	0.9	0.9	0.5
Magallanes (XII)	12.6	15.7	8.1	2.0	0.5	1.1	2.5	2.1	1.9	1.8	1.3	0.7
Región Metropolitana	1.2	1.0	0.8	1.0	1.6	1.3	1.4	1.3	1.3	1.2	1.2	1.2

Source: Own elaboration. See text

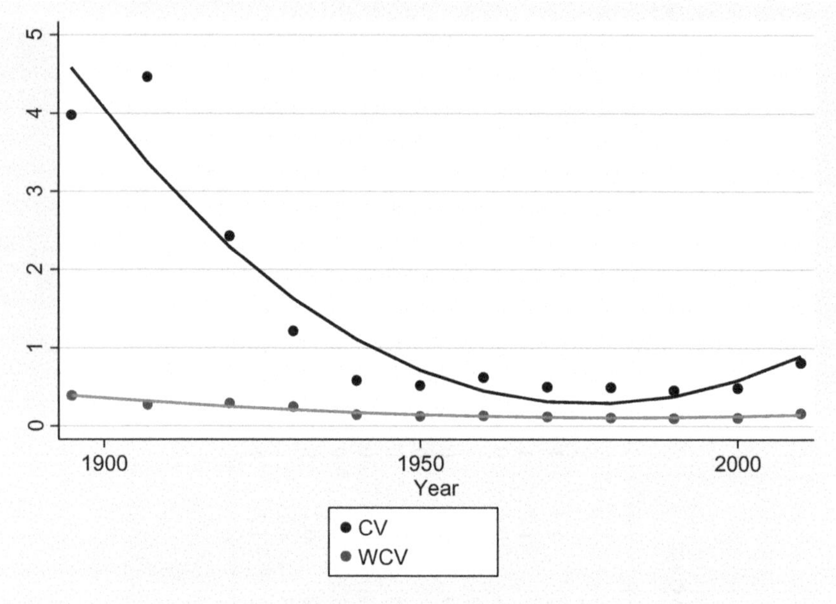

Fig. 7.1 Standard deviation (weighted by population and non-weighted) for regions in Chile, 1895–2010. (Source: Own elaboration. See text)

propelled the reduction in dispersion until the 1990s when this indicator stagnated. The discovery of oil deposits in *Magallanes* during the 1960s changed this story slightly, although only in a temporary manner. The later commodity price boom, since 2000, also boosted dispersion (both weighted and non-weighted figures). The reason behind that is the expansion of the copper regions (mainly II, III and RM which also had concentrated large copper mines), but also the decline in relative terms of income per capita of the southern agrarian regions, expanding the difference between rich and poor regions. What is clear is that, unlike what had been observed for other countries, the exploitation of natural resources would explain a significant part of the regional differences in terms of GDP per capita among the Chilean provinces, during the twentieth century.

In addition to the key role that natural resources played, it is also important to understand what happened to other sectors of the economy, such as industry. To do a more detailed analysis of this sector, I follow the seminal work of Gwynne (1984), which analyses the evolution of the location of industry during the twentieth century, and Gómez (1974), which delves deep into the evolution of industry from 1957 to 1970, focusing his work on the regional impact of regional development policies. Subsequently, during the 1980s, new studies emerged, focusing on the study of the impact of policies of trade deregulation that were applied after the 1973 Coup.[14]

Industrial GDP figures in the long run witnessed a process of intense concentration since the first third of the twentieth century, related with the industrial expansion located close of saltpetre mining centres (mainly non-durable consumer goods), and ended in the 1960s as a result of regional development policies during the ISI (more oriented towards intermediate and capital goods near the coal mines in Concepción) and the expansion of those industries better connected to the main markets (Metropolitana region). The main driver of this concentration, as it happened with the whole economy, was the expansion of industry in Santiago and a decline in Valparaíso (region V). Lastly, liberalization economies and de-industrialization favoured manufacturing dispersion in those regions where the sector has competitive advantages (this will be examined in greater detail further on).

The following step is the observation of the behaviour of certain indicators. Following Sala-i-Martin (1996), the reduction of the differences between regions in the long run can be observed through the behaviour of β-convergence and σ-convergence due to the impact of technological diffusion and diminishing capital returns. For the period 1890–1970, Badia-Miró (2008) found β-convergence although at levels below the world average, mostly driven by the location of natural resources. Furthermore, the author found marked differences between what occurred before 1930 and after. For the first period, β-convergence is significantly greater. In parallel, Duncan and Fuentes (2006) found the existence of β-convergence for the period 1960–2000, although at lower levels than those by Badia-Miró (2008).

Figure 7.2 shows a high degree of convergence of the Chilean regions, although the low number of observations and the figures in the extremes mostly dependent on natural resource cycles and low density could bias

[14] Gwynne's initial articles analyse the economic impact of the de-industrialization after 1973 (Gwynne 1984, 1986). His subsequent articles focus on the economic development of specific sectors such as forestry or viticulture, and their industrialization process (Gwynne 1999, 2003, 2006).

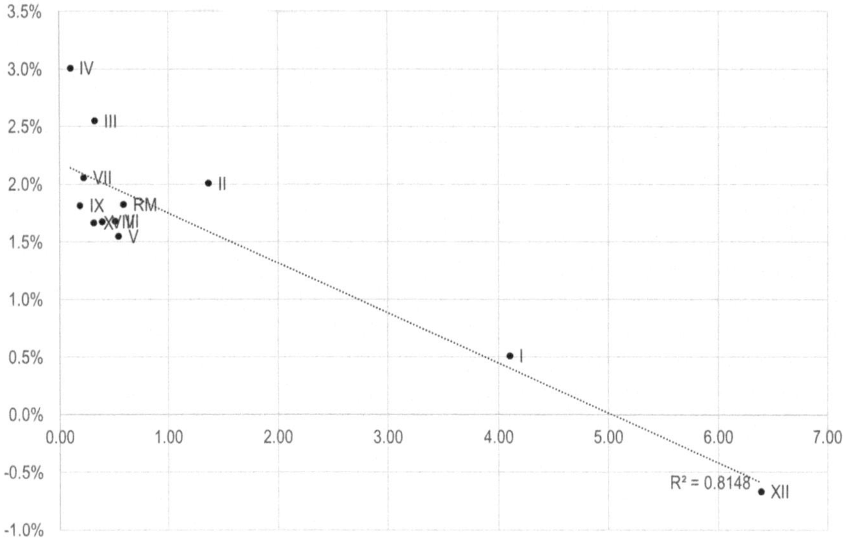

Fig. 7.2 Beta-convergence for Chilean regions, 1895–2010. (Source: Own elaboration. See text)

the interpretation of the results. We have to keep in mind that most of the results are driven by the initial levels of regions I and XII while the higher rate figures are also observed in copper regions in the North (regions II, III and IV).[15]

A third set of studies concentrated on analysing concrete areas of the country, especially in studies of the capital, such as Daher (1993) and Odeplan (1978) and the official estimations published by the Central Bank of Chile from 1980 onwards,[16] in order to check the possible existence of long-term convergence.[17] In this sense Echeverria (2006) did

[15] The high level of income in region I is devoted to the nitrate cycle, at the beginning of the period, and the high level of income in region XII is related with its low density. High rates for region II, III and IV are related with the copper cycle from the beginning of the twentieth century. To obtain real figures we have considered real GDP per capita by Díaz et al. (2016).

[16] The Central Bank of Chile offers annuals data for the regions from 1985: http://www.bcentral.cl/publicaciones/estadisticas/actividad-economica-gasto/aeg07.htm.

[17] An example of this are the works of Atienza and Aroca (2012), Aroca and Bosch (2000) and Duncan and Fuentes (2006).

some remarkable work on the evolution of the economic concentration of industry, and he relates it with the production of primary products and their competitiveness in domestic and international markets. He also offers an analysis of the economic convergence of the regions in the second half of the twentieth century.

Although inequality data enable us to offer an initial perspective on the economic behaviour of the provinces, it is also true that they have some limitations. A way of refining the analysis and deepening our understanding would involve observing the detailed evolution of the regional GDP per capita. As we have said, we observe the existence of regions with extreme values at the start of the period (around 8–12 times the national average GDP per capita).[18] This was the consequence of the unequal spatial distribution of natural resources and specifically the consequence of the nitrate cycle, which affected the regions of the *Norte Grande*. The figure also shows that the great majority of provinces, which have a far more traditional economic structure, are situated significantly below the average (around 0.5 times this value). Later, the dispersion in the location of copper exploitations prevents this extreme concentration and shows a greater dispersion and a uniform distribution around the average. Despite this, most provinces remain below the average.

Together with a greater or smaller concentration, what also appears relevant for the mining cycles is the capacity to generate forward and backward linkages, in the sense of Hirschman (1958, 1968), of greater or lesser intensity. Both the copper and the nitrate cycle boosted the economic growth of other regions, due to the demand for non-durable consumer goods in the leading regions. What differentiates the two is the magnitude of this impact. Whereas nitrate mining was labour-intensive (and therefore boosted consumption which was largely not satisfied by local production), the copper cycles were far more capital-intensive. For copper mining, the most intense linkages functioned in terms of the demand for intermediate goods on the part of the mining industry itself. In parallel, as Hurtado Ruíz-Tagle (1966) and Raczynski (1978) point out, migratory movements went in the opposite direction and tended to reduce the difference between levels of GDP per capita since people abandoned the poor regions

[18] Part of these higher values comes from an overvaluation of the figures, because I have not corrected it with the differences in regional prices. Natural resource regions have higher prices than the other parts of the country.

(increasing their GDP per capita) towards the rich regions (decreasing those levels of GDP per capita).

Despite the importance of mining in describing the spatial distribution of the Chilean economy, there were great differences within this sector, especially between export mining and mining oriented towards the domestic market. Polarization in Chile was not explained by the regional GDP per capita performance between mining and non-mining regions. On the one hand, there are very productive regions oriented towards exportation and, on the other hand, there are low-productivity regions where most of the population is involved in subsistence economy or production is oriented towards the domestic market. The list of members of the select group of rich provinces confirms this point: the mining regions of I, II and RM, but not region VIII (specialized in coal production and low-productivity coal mining), together with the regions IV and V (where the mining sector is somewhat important, but the economic structure was much more diversified). The differences between these two groups of regions increased from the 1930s onwards, coinciding with the ISI` period and the protectionist shift. These levels remained high until the 1970s, showing the maintenance of the differences between rich provinces and poor ones, in a context of the reduction of levels of aggregated inequality and in spite of the existence of intense regional development policies. However, we observe a relative backwardness of Santiago due to the specialization in low-productivity sectors, which, in turn, show productivity levels below the sector average. As a result, these sectors were unable to generate agglomeration economies. Lastly, a third group of provinces, mainly agrarian (regions VI, VII, IX and X), stagnated below the average throughout the period, except for a slight decrease during the ISI period. This is an expected result due to the preponderant role of industry in mobilizing resources to the detriment of the agricultural sector (and of those agrarian regions).

Up to this point, I have focused on understanding the evolution of the income levels per inhabitant in the regions of Chile. The next step aims to understand the behaviour of the spatial distribution of the economy in absolute terms. What first draws our attention is the role that Santiago gradually acquires within the Chilean economy. As can be seen from Fig. 7.3, the weight of the economy of Santiago over the entire country went from 20% at the end of World War I to 40–50% of the total towards the end of the twentieth century (see Table 7.3).

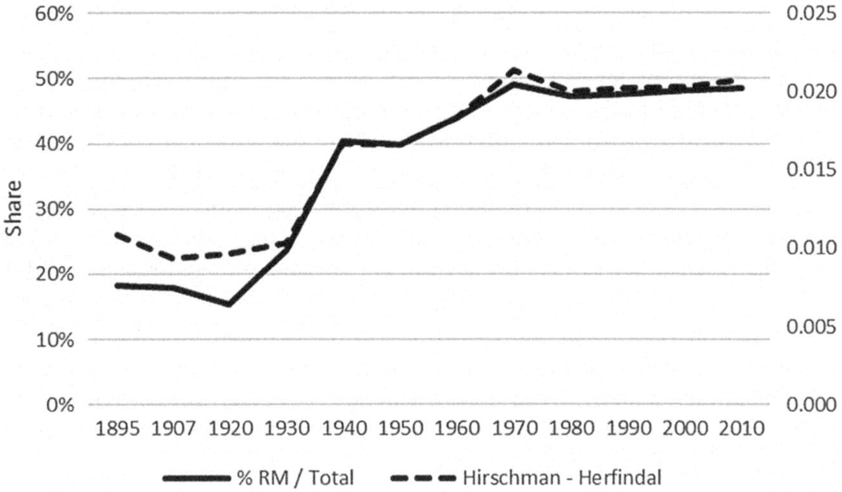

Fig. 7.3 Concentration of economic activity in Chile, 1895–2010. (Source: GDP data comes from own elaboration from 1890 to 1973 and official sources from 1960 to 2010)

Table 7.3 Share of regional GDP in Chile, 1895–2010 (%)

	1895	*1907*	*1920*	*1930*	*1940*	*1950*	*1960*	*1970*	*1980*	*1990*	*2000*	*2010*
I	22.6	13.7	11.9	6.3	1.1	1.3	3.1	2.5	3.2	3.0	3.5	3.4
II	4.5	14.7	20.5	18.4	5.8	6.4	4.5	4.6	5.9	6.2	7.4	11.5
III	1.5	0.7	0.6	3.4	2.8	1.7	1.6	1.6	1.5	1.5	2.0	2.5
IV	1.3	2.6	1.5	2.9	1.6	1.5	1.9	1.8	1.9	2.1	2.5	3.2
V	13.0	10.6	10.5	11.2	13.1	16.1	13.9	11.9	11.3	10.0	9.1	8.3
VI	9.3	6.5	8.1	7.9	6.1	6.4	4.6	4.5	4.6	4.6	4.4	4.6
VII	7.6	7.9	9.0	4.6	5.1	5.1	3.5	3.3	3.2	3.6	3.8	3.5
VIII	14.4	14.7	12.5	11.6	15.2	12.2	12.4	11.5	11.6	11.4	9.4	8.0
IX	2.5	4.3	3.2	3.5	3.9	4.4	3.0	2.6	2.7	2.8	2.8	2.2
X	4.6	5.4	5.7	5.7	4.7	4.5	4.7	4.2	4.2	4.7	4.9	1.2
XI	0.0	0.0	0.0	0.0	0.0	0.0	0.4	0.5	0.5	0.5	0.6	2.5
XII	0.5	1.0	1.1	0.8	0.3	0.7	2.5	2.0	2.2	1.9	1.4	0.5
RM	18.2	17.9	15.3	23.7	40.3	39.9	43.9	49.0	47.2	47.7	48.2	48.5

Source: Own elaboration. See text

Contrary to our expectations, given the NEG predictions and the positive impact of the agglomeration economies, this did not result in an increase in income levels of the province, nor in the improvement of productivity levels. On the contrary, the evolution of the GDP per capita during the period studied remained quite steady, around 1.2–1.3 times the country average. Although the ISI policies coincided with the reinforcement of the concentration of the economy in the centre of the country, this did not affect taking advantage of positive externalities of the market potential or of scale economies in industry or services. As a result, we did not observe any improvements in the productivity levels of these sectors, in the central regions of the country. The Hirschman-Herfindal (H-H) index enables us to observe in more detail how this process of extreme concentration behaved, from a global perspective, beyond that of simple observation of the percentages represented by each of the provinces over the total. The index is defined by:

$$H_j^C = \sum_{i=1}^{N} \frac{\text{GDP}_{i,j}}{\sum_{i=1}^{n} \text{GDP}_{i,j}} \tag{7.2}$$

The index is limited between 1 when all the activity is concentrated in one region and $1/N$ when the economy is equidistributed among all the regions. From Fig. 7.3 it can be deduced that much of the extreme concentration experienced by the Chilean economy is related to the boost of the country's capital from 1920 onwards. Only the stagnation of this growth towards the 1970s stopped this trend, turning it into a stable trend.

A more detailed observation confirms that Santiago started to assume importance in the whole of the economy some 40 years previously. The reason is related with the fact that in the decades of the 1920s the nitrate and copper cycles coexisted, which maintained the dynamism of several of the mining provinces, and therefore delayed the growth of the H-H index. What appears clear is the importance that the ISI period had in reinforcing these trends. The import substitution policies, due to the increase in protectionism in these years, ended up propelling these indicators and only with the end of protectionism was this rising trend curtailed. Furthermore, the failuler of regional development policies (...) were possible drivers of a spatial redistribution of economic activity. These policies, which in most of the cases relied on manufacturing production, did not generate enough sustained linkages towards the rest of the regional economy, for these to initiate a process of lasting self-sustained economic growth. Once the period of intervention was over, the effects faded and the concentration of economic activity around the capital continued. Later, it was the change of economic model in 1973 and the subsequent liberalization of the economy that altered this trend. This is when the H-H index stagnates, principally because of the process of de-industrialization which the country went through in the context of drastic liberalization of the economy. This did great damage to the evolution of the capital and allowed those regions which could take advantage of better natural resource endowment to experience some recovery, based on the boost from exportations of natural products and semi-manufactured goods.

In summary, this set of indicators of the spatial distribution of economic activity in Chile, in the long run, points out that, first, there is a clear reduction in GDP per capita inequality among the regions and the provinces, disrupted only by the punctual expansion of some mining booms (nitrate and oil). This disruption is only circumstantial, and resumes the long-term path described above. In this sense, the non-existence of an inverted-U curve makes it necessary to find a different explanation to what can be observed for most industrialized countries.

Second, differences between mining and non-mining provinces do not generate conclusive results to explain the regional differences of spatial distribution in income. The explanation seems to lie in the diversity of economic structures related with whether they are export-oriented mining provinces or domestic market-oriented. On the other hand, differences appeared between regions specializing in manufactured and semi-manufactured products, together with the provinces with an important agricultural sector coexisting with manufacturing industry, mining and low-productivity services, oriented mainly towards the domestic market.

Furthermore, we must not lose sight of the fact that the concentration of economic activity was accentuated during the central period of our study, particularly in the 1930s and 1960s. However, this process does indeed coincide with one period, that of the ISI, when industry came to acquire a relevant role. It is also certain that it never reaches levels high enough to be capable of generating linkages, which pull along the whole of the economy towards higher levels of development. This is what occurs in many of the studies on industrializing countries, and it is related to the process of increasing spatial inequalities. As has been pointed out, we do not observe signs of the increase in the spatial dispersion of the economy in the period, and neither do we observe increase in the GDP per employed worker in the industrial sector. The levels of GDP per capita in the region where much of the economic activity is concentrated do not grow either. In the face of these results, it becomes necessary to look at the factors that reinforce this process of concentration of economic activity.

5 Conclusions

A detailed analysis of the evolution of the spatial location of the economic activity in Chile enables us to understand a good deal of the processes that have reinforced the emergence of an extreme concentration of economic activity around the capital. The natural resource endowment and the dynamics that emerge around the administrative capital, linked to its political role, as well as it being a centre of high demand, predominate over agglomeration economies, which could have emerged around the more dynamic sectors of the economy. This pattern contrasts head on with what has been found in several similar studies for industrialized countries. In these, the agglomeration economies and the impact of the market potential are determinants during the process of industrialization. It appears that this is not the norm in un-industrialized countries.

Bearing these factors in mind, we need to consider that mining does not always have the same impact on the location of economic activity. What does have an impact in this sense is the location of this sector in space and the level of modernization of the sector in different periods. On the one hand, nitrate mining had a specific impact which generated dynamics of dispersion of the economic activity due to the impact of the dimension of the market potential. In contrast, copper mining, much more disperse in space, had a lower demand potential although it generates greater linkages towards the rest of the economy. Finally, coal mining, linked to less-modern sectors, although concentrated in space, was not capable of boosting demand or dragging along the other sectors of the economy. The analysis of the differences in productivity among the provinces reinforces this last argument.

In parallel, the impact of "modern" mining on the level of productivity of the province (and, therefore, also on the income level) has been identified, which drives to understand what lies behind the low-income levels of the capital. In this case, the reason is twofold. On the one hand, the economic structure of Santiago shows a greater level of specialization in low-productivity sectors, and, on the other hand, these sectors show productivity levels below the sector average. Behind these factors lie the causes of the incapacity of these sectors to generate agglomeration economies, which drive sustained growth in the long run.

References

Aroca, P. and Bosch, M. (2000). Crecimiento, convergencia y espacio en las regiones chilenas: 1960–1998. *Estudios de Economía*, 27, 199–224.

Atienza, M. and Aroca, P. (2012). Concentración y crecimiento en Chile: una relación negativa ignorada. *EURE (Santiago)*, *38*(114), 257–277.

Badia-Miró, M. (2007). The Ports of Northern Chile: A mining history in a Long-run Perspective. In T. Bergholm, L. R. Fischer, and M. E. Tonizzi (eds.), *Making Global and Local Connections: Historical Perspectives on Ports* (Vol. 35, pp. 153–170). Country: St. John's. Newfoundland: International Maritime Economic History Association.

———. (2008). *La localización de la actividad económica en Chile, 1890–1973. Su impacto de largo plazo.* PhD Thesis dissertation. Universitat de Barcelona.

———. (2015). The evolution of the location of economic activity in Chile in the long run: a paradox of extreme concentration in absence of agglomeration economies. *Estudios de Economía*, *42*(2), 143–167.

Badia-Miró, M. and Ducoing, C. A. (2015). The long run development of Chile and the Natural Resources curse. Linkages, policy and growth, 1850–1950. In M. Badia-Miró, V. Pinilla and H. Willebald (eds.), *Natural Resources and Economic Growth: Learning from history* (pp. 204–225). London, United Kingdom: Routledge, London.

Badia-Miró, M., Guilera, J. and Lains, P. (2012). Regional Incomes in Portugal: Industrialisation, Integration and Inequality, 1890–1980. *Revista de Historia Económica*, *30*(02), 225–244.

Barro, R. J. and Sala-i-Martin, X. (1992). Convergence. *Journal of Political Economy*, 100, 223–251.

Bértola, L. and Ocampo, J. A. (2012). *The Economic Development of Latin America since Independence.* Oxford, United Kingdom: Oxford University Press.

Braun, J., Braun, M., Briones, I., Díaz, J., Lüders, R. J. and Wagner, G. (2000). Economía chilena 1810–1995: Estadisticas históricas. *Documentos de Trabajo—PUC*, (187).

Bulmer-Thomas, V. (2003). *The Economic History of Latin America since independence.* Cambridge, UK: Cambridge University Press,.

Cariola Sutter, C. and Sunkel, O. (1983). *Un Siglo de historia económica de Chile 1830–1930: dos ensayos y una bibliografía.* Madrid: Cultura Hispánica.

Carmagnani, M. (1998). *Desarrollo industrial y subdesarrollo económico: El caso chileno (1860–1920)* (Vol. 16). Santiago de Chile, Chile: Ediciones de la Dirección de Bibliotecas, Archivos y Museos.

———. (2001). *Los mecanismos de la vida económica en una sociedad colonial. Chile 1680–1830*. Dirección de Bibliotecas, Archivos y Museos. Chile.

Cavieres Figueroa, E. (1988). *Comercio chileno y comerciantes ingleses 1820–1880: (un ciclo de historia económica)*. Valparaíso, Chile: Universidad Católica de Valparaíso, Instituto de Historia.

Collier, S. and Sater, W. F. (2004). *A history of Chile, 1808–2002*. New York, USA: Cambridge University Press.

Combes, P. P., Mayer, T. and Thiesse, J. F. (2008). *Economic Geography: The Integration of Regions and Nations*. New York, USA: Princeton University Press.

Coudyoumdjan, J. R. (2000). El alto comercio de Valparaíso y las grandes casas extrangeras: 1880–1930, una aproximación. *Historia*, *33*, 63–99.

Crafts, N. (2005). Regional GDP in Britain, 1871–1911: Some estimates. *Scottish Journal of Political Economy*, *52*(1), 54–64.

Daher, A. (1993). Santiago estatal, Chile liberal. *Revista Interamericana de Planificación*, *101/1002*, 43–62.

Díaz, J., Lüders, R. J. and Wagner, G. (1998). Economía chilena 1810–1995: evolución cuantitativa del producto total i sectorial. *Documentos de Trabajo-PUC*, (186).

———. (2016). *Chile, 1810–2010. La República en Cifras. Historical Statistics*. Santiago de Chile, Chile.: Ediciones Universidad Católica de Chile.

Díaz, J. and Wagner, G. (2004). Política Comercial: Instrumentos y Antecedentes. Chile en los Siglos XIX y XX. *PUC Economics Institute Working Paper*, *223*.

Diez-Minguela, A., Rosés, J. R. and Sanchis-Llopis, M. T. (2018). France. In *The Economic Development of Europe's Regions. A Quantitative History since 1900*.

Ducoing, C. and Badia-Miró, M. (2013). El PIB industrial de Chile durante el ciclo del salitre, 1880–1938. *Revista Uruguaya de Historia Económica*, III(3), 11–32.

Duncan, R. and Fuentes, R. (2006). Regional Convergence in Chile: New Tests, Old Results. *Cuadernos de Economía*, *43*(127), 81–112.

Echeverria, R. A. (2006). *Essays on productivity, economic geography and trade: the case of Chile*. PhD. Thesis dissertation. Oregon State University.

Fujita, M. and Krugman, P. (2004). The new economic geography: Past, present and the future. *Papers in Regional Science*, *83*, 139–164.

Fujita, M., Krugman, P. R. and Venables, A. J. (1999). *The Spatial Economy: Cities, Regions and International Trade* (Vol. 18). MIT Press.

Gallo, C. (2008). Tax bargaining and nitrate exports: Chile 1880–1930. In D. A. Bräutigam, O. H. Fjeldstad, and M. Moore (eds.), *Taxation and State-*

Building in Developing Countries (pp. 160–182). The Edinburgh Building, Cambridge CB2 8RU: Cambridge University Press.

Geary, F. and Stark, T. (2002). Examining Ireland's Post-Famine Economic Growth Performance. *The Economic Journal*, *112*(482), 919–935.

———. (2016). What happened to regional inequality in Britain in the twentieth century? *The Economic History Review*, 69(1), 215–228.

Gómez, A. (1974). El proceso de localización industrial en chile: Análisis y políticas. *Eure : Revista Latinoamericana de Estudios Urbano Regionales*, 3, 9–56.

Gwynne, R. N. (1984). Geografía Industrial. In *Geografía de Chile*. Santiago de Chile, Chile: Instituto Geográfico Militar.

———. (1986). The Deindustrialization of Chile, 1974–1984. *Bulletin of Latin American Research*, 5(1), 1–23.

———. (1999). Globalisation, Commodity Chains and Fruit Exporting Regions in Chile. *Tijdschrift Voor Economische En Sociale Geografie*, 90(2), 211–225.

———. (2006). Export-orientation and enterprise development: a comparison of New Zealand and Chilean wine production. *Tijdschrift Voor Economische En Sociale Geografie*, 97(2), 138–156.

———. (2003). Transnational capitalism and local transformation in Chile. *Tijdschrift voor Economische en Sociale Geografie*, 94(3), 310–321.

Haindl Rondanelli, E. (2006). *Chile y su desarrollo económico en el siglo XX*. Editorial Andrés Bello, Universidad Católica de Chile.

Hausmann, R., Hidalgo, C. A., Bustos, S., Coscia, M., Simoes, A. and Yildirim, M. A. (2014). *The Atlas of Economic Complexity. The Atlas of Economic Complexity*. The MIT Press.

Hirschman, A. O. (1958). *The Strategy of economic development*. New Haven: Yale University Press.

———. (1968). The Political Economy of Import-Substituting Industrialization in Latin America. *The Quarterly Journal of Economics*, 82(1), 1–32.

Hurtado Ruíz-Tagle, C. (1966). Concentración de población y desarrollo económico—el caso de Chile. *Documentos de Trabajo—PUC*, 89, 195.

Krugman, P. R. (1991). *Geography and trade*. Cambridge, MA: The MIT Press.

Odeplan. (1978). *Regionalización gasto del producto geográfico bruto a precios constantes del año 1965. 1960–1976*. Santiago de Chile: ODEPLAN.

Palma, J. G. (1979). *Growth and structure of Chilean manufacturing industry from 1830 to 1935*. PhD Dissertation. University of Oxford.

———. (1984). Chile 1914–1935: De economía exportadora a sustitutiva de importaciones. *Colección de Estudios del CIEPLAN*, 12(81), 61–88.

Pinto Vallejos, J. (1987). Valparaíso. metrópoli financiera del boom del salitre. In Pinto Vallejos, J. (ed). *Valparaíso 1536–1986: Primera Jornada de Historia Urbana* (pp. 119–134). Valparaíso, Chile: Instituto de Historia Universidad Católica de Valparaíso. Valparaíso: Ediciones Altazo.

Raczynski, D. (1978). Migraciones internas en Chile: metodología e información estadística. *Apuntes del CIEPLAN, 11*.

Rosés, J. R., Martinez-Galarraga, J. and Tirado-Fabregat, D. A. (2010). The upswing of regional income inequality in Spain (1860–1930). *Explorations in Economic History*, 47(2), 244–257.

Sala-i-Martin, X. (1996). Regional cohesion: evidence and theories of regional growth and convergence. *European Economic Review*, 40(6), 1325–1352.

Williamson, J. G. (1965). Regional inequality and the process of national development: a description of the patterns. *Economic Development and Cultural Change*, 13(4), 1–84.

CHAPTER 8

Regional Economic Inequality in Colombia, 1926–2018

Adolfo Meisel Roca and Lucas Hahn

1 Introduction

Colombia is a developing country with a GDP of US$330 billion in 2018 (World Bank n.d.). According to the 2018 census, the country has a population of about 48 million, the second largest in South America. Its GDP per capita, US$6700, is below the continental average. Colombia also has high income inequality, with a Gini coefficient of 0.5 in 2017 according to

We are very grateful to Marc Badia-Miró, Daniel A. Tirado-Fabregat and Julio Romero for their insightful comments and for generously supplying historical data. We also thank Haroldo Calvo for his comments and the participants at seminars organized by *Banco de la República* and the Latin American Congress of Economic History.

A. Meisel Roca (✉)
Universidad del Norte, Barranquilla, Colombia
e-mail: ameisel@uninorte.edu.co

L. Hahn
Banco de la República, Cartagena, Colombia
e-mail: lhahndec@banrep.gov.co

D. A. Tirado-Fabregat et al. (eds.), *Time and Space*,
Palgrave Studies in Economic History,
https://doi.org/10.1007/978-3-030-47553-6_8

the World Bank Gini Index. It is one of the highest in Latin America, after Brazil, Panamá and Honduras. This inequality is present not only in the distribution of income but also in the country's regional development. Bogotá, its capital city, produces more than 25% of the total GDP.

A major characteristic of Colombia is its abrupt geography. Located in the northwestern corner of South America, its territory has the last ramifications of the Andes, a mountain range that runs through the western part of the continent. In the south of Colombia, the Andes Mountains split into three separate ranges, the Western, Central and Eastern *cordilleras*, which constitute the most conspicuous feature of the country's geography. Map 8.1 shows the three subdivisions of the Andes Mountains in Colombia.

This geographical feature naturally divided the territory into six different regions. The territories located to the east of the Andes constitute two of these natural regions: Amazonía and Orinoquía. The first owes its name to the Amazon rainforest that covers most of the southern territories, while the second corresponds to an extensive savannah in the northern part of the first region. Both contain only a small fraction of the total population, about 5%, though they represent almost 60% of Colombia's territory. A third natural region is the Andean region, which comprises the territories located in the Andean mountains. There are also two coastal regions, the Caribbean and Pacific coasts. Finally, another natural region are the islands located in both the Caribbean Sea and the Pacific Ocean.

Because of its abrupt geography and the existence of large regional differences in economic performance, there is a large volume of research on regional development and convergence in Colombia. The first study that worked on the hypothesis of regional convergence in Colombia was Cárdenas et al. (1993). The authors argued that the country experienced a regional convergence process during the second half of the twentieth century, with its poorest regions catching up with the richest ones. However, their results were quickly questioned. For instance, Meisel (1993) showed that the regional dispersion of income per capita did not decrease during the same period. The difference between the two studies lies in their methodology. While Cárdenas et al. (1993) used the standard deviation as a measure of σ-convergence, Meisel (1993) argued in favor of the coefficient of variation, a measure that was more commonly used in the literature.

After these two studies, many other authors have contributed to the academic debate on regional economic development in Colombia. Some

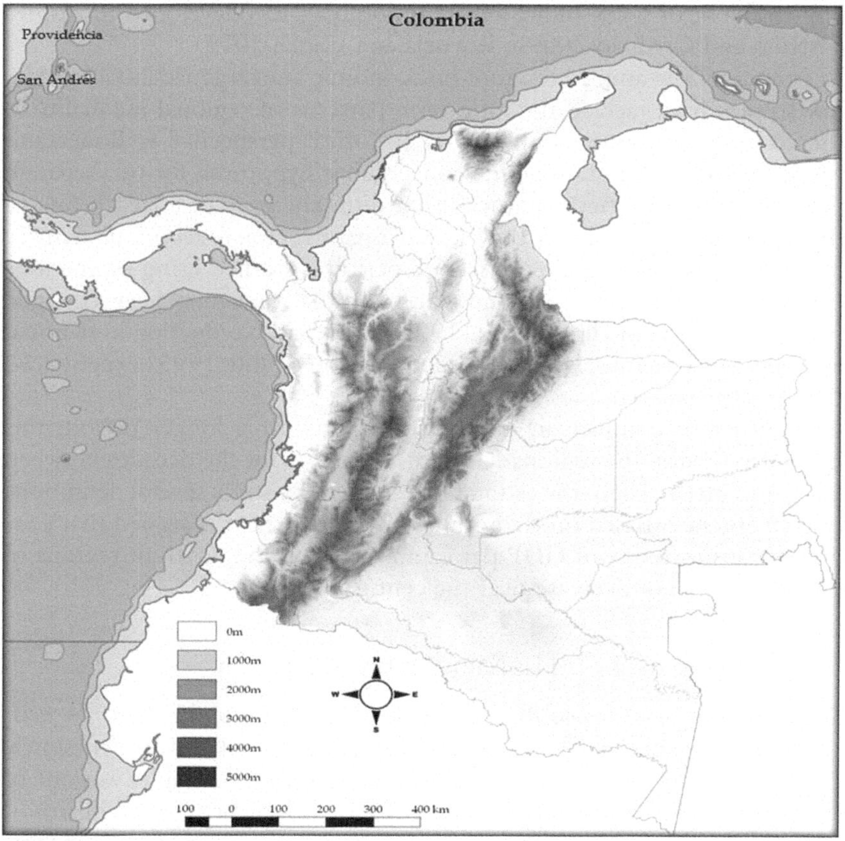

Map 8.1 Relief map of Colombia and the Andes Mountains. (Source: Geographical information provided by official institutions in Colombia [DANE, IGAC] and Natural Earth [http://www.naturalearthdata.com/])

have argued that less developed regions have grown faster than developed ones (Gómez 2006; León and Benavides 2015; Royuela and García 2015), while others have argued the opposite (Rocha and Vivas 1998; Bonet and Meisel 2001; Branisa and Cardozo 2009a; Galvis and Meisel 2013; Galvis and Hahn 2016). These mixed results are due not only to the ample range of methodologies applied to the study of regional convergence, but also to the increasing availability of new data sources in recent years. On the other hand, there exists more consensus in the academic literature on the improvement of social indicators in Colombia's less developed territories (Branisa and Cardozo 2009b; Royuela and García 2015).

In spite of the ample literature on economic convergence in Colombia, few studies have tackled the long-term patterns of regional inequality in the country. The only study with a historical perspective is Bonet and Meisel (2001), who examine the convergence hypothesis for two separate periods of the twentieth century using different sources for each one of them. For the first period they approximate regional economic activity using bank deposits, while the second period is studied using estimations of regional GDP. They conclude that regional dynamics have changed over the century: the first period (1926–1960) saw a reduction in regional economic inequalities, while the second period (1960–1995) experienced the opposite pattern.

In order to conduct an integrated analysis for a longer period, this chapter estimates the regional GDP of Colombia for the decades between 1926 and 2018. Then, the estimations are used to study several definitions of convergence. Based on the results of the analysis, it is argued that economic gaps in terms of GDP per capita between the different regions of Colombia did not decrease over the century.

2 Historical Background

Until the first decades of the twentieth century, Colombia had few economic ties to the rest of the world. Its total exports had grown slowly during the nineteenth century and, in 1915, its trade per capita was one of the lowest in the continent (Ocampo 2013). Coatsworth and Williamson (2004) argue that at the beginning of the twentieth century Colombia was among the most protectionist countries in Latin America, with tariffs that were several times higher than those of China or India. The high tariffs and costs of transportation, as a result of the geographical characteristics of the country, were a main obstacle for the integration of Colombia with international markets. Despite these difficulties, Colombian exports grew intermittently during the century, with temporal and cyclical expansions, given that they responded more to international price movements than to advances in productivity. Some examples of products that underwent temporal export booms during the second half of the nineteenth century were tobacco, chinchona bark (quinine) and cattle (Ocampo 2013).

The first years of the twentieth century were particularly turbulent and of great political instability. At that time, two events profoundly shaped the economic and political history of the country. The first was the *Guerra de los Mil Días* (the War of the Thousand Days), 1899–1902, fought between the Conservative government and a group of Liberal Party rebels. Recent research shows that approximately 39,000 people probably perished during the conflict (Meisel and Romero-Prieto 2017). The second event was the separation of Panamá from Colombia in 1903, immediately after the war. Kalmanovitz (2012) argues that the separation resulted from several factors, among them the adoption of a centralist and protectionist constitution in 1886, which affected the economic interests of Panamanians, and the rejection by the Colombian Congress of the Hay-Herrán treaty, by which the United States established a set of conditions to undertake the construction of the Panama Canal.

Colombia's population at the beginning of the twentieth century was barely above 4 million inhabitants and its GDP per capita was about 18% of the GDP of the United States (Coatsworth 1998). The economic conditions of the country during the first years of the century were not good, in part because of the consequences of the civil war. Fiscal constraints pushed the government to finance public expenditures with monetary emissions, which accelerated inflation to more than 100% by 1901 (Ocampo 1994). The war also affected agricultural production, where exports decreased substantially (Ocampo 1979). For instance, coffee exports dropped from 531,000 bags in 1898 to 300,000 in 1901 (GRECO 2000). Moreover, Kalmanovitz and López (2006) argue that livestock productivity at the beginning of the century was very low because of the lack of technical knowledge about efficient farming practices. Industrial activities were also very limited at that time, with only eight modern factories created between 1901 and 1909 (Echavarría and Villamizar 2006).

The 1920s were of particular economic importance for Colombia. The country became more attractive for international markets because of two different factors. The first was a coffee boom, in which both the international price of coffee and the volume of the country's exports grew substantially. At the end of the nineteenth century, the price of a pound of coffee in New York varied between 7 and 15 cents of a dollar, and Colombia exported approximately 500,000 bags of coffee. By 1925, the price was 27 cents and Colombia exported 1.9 million bags (Junguito 1996). This increase in both prices and volume made coffee the most important export, accounting for 78% of total exports and boosting foreign interest in Colombia (Meisel et al. 2016). Coffee had already benefited from export booms during the last decades of the nineteenth century, so regions that specialized in its production were able to profit the most from these expansions.

The production of crops that benefited from export booms, such as coffee, tobacco and chinchona, was not evenly distributed across the country. Hence, their prosperity did not necessarily have an impact on the other territories of Colombia. For instance, Antioquia and the previous Viejo Caldas benefited the most from the boom in coffee exports. Both regions specialized in the production of coffee, and in 1932 produced 47% of the total in Colombia (Kalmanovitz et al. 1999). Although the coffee boom increased the availability of capital resources for the country and made Colombia attractive to foreign investors, it promoted the development of particular regions in or near the center of the country, where coffee production was concentrated.

The second factor during the 1920s that contributed to broaden Colombia's access to international markets and, consequently, improved its economic conditions was institutional change. Edwin Kemmerer, a professor at Princeton University and well-known economic advisor to developing countries, defined a series of institutional reforms in 1923 that were well received by foreign investors. Several Latin American countries, such as Colombia, Perú, Bolivia and Ecuador, accepted his recommendations, in particular the establishment of independent monetary authorities (Kemmerer 1927). The reforms in Colombia included the creation of an independent central bank, the adoption of the gold standard and the establishment of an institution that regulated private banking (Meisel et al. 2016). These changes gave confidence to the international markets and improved Colombia's access to foreign capital. Therefore, during that period private and public foreign debt increased substantially. The percentage of total debt to GDP tripled between 1925 and 1933, from 12.92% to 36.81% (Echavarría 1982).

In addition to the coffee boom and the higher integration to financial markets, a third factor that improved public finances in the 1920s was the indemnity of US$25 million that the United States paid to the Colombian government for its role in the secession of Panamá. The funds were spent mostly in the construction of transportation infrastructure, with approximately 65% on railroads (Pachón and Ramírez 2006). New railroads were built mostly in the central regions to link Bogotá and its hinterland with other important markets of the region. This period is known in Colombian history as *La Danza de los Millones* (The Dance of the Millions), given the sudden increase in public expenditures by the central government.

Kemmerer (1923) argued that the lack of adequate transportation was one of the most important obstacles to the development of Colombia. The construction of the transportation system began relatively late in the century, in part because of the scarcity of funds. As Safford (2010) has argued, there were no incentives for foreign investment in transportation infrastructure, such as railroads. The lack of resources and the geographical conditions made Colombia one of the countries in Latin America that built fewer railroads during the nineteenth century. In 1900, the country had only 0.15 kilometers of railroad per 1000 inhabitants, surpassing only three other countries in the region: Nicaragua, Ecuador and Haiti (Meisel et al. 2016).

The abundance of funds derived from the coffee boom, the increased access to foreign capitals and the Panamá indemnity by the United States enabled Colombia to make unprecedented investments in transportation after 1920. Railroad lines increased from 500 kilometers at the beginning of the twentieth century to 3000 kilometers in 1940 (Pachón and Ramírez 2006). They were mostly built in the Central-West and Central-East areas of the country, in order to reduce the transportation costs for the markets located in these regions. Highways were also constructed, but their greater expansion occurred later in the century (Pachón and Ramírez 2006).

The improvements in transportation infrastructure reduced the regional price differences of agricultural products. Pachón and Ramírez (2006) show evidence of regional convergence in the prices of six different agricultural products between the 12 largest cities in Colombia. They argue that the reduction in transport costs contributed to lower market prices for goods such as potatoes, rice, sugar, salt, corn and cane sugar during the first half of the century.

This finding points to a better integration of distant markets across the country. However, production became more concentrated in a few regions during the second half of the century (Bonet and Meisel 2001). As Krugman (1991) points out, industrial production tends to concentrate in regions where higher demand is already present in order to minimize transport costs and exploit economies of scale, so long as transport costs are decreasing and congestion costs are limited. Hence, the improvement in transportation infrastructure and the consequent integration of markets spurred economic growth in the largest cities, while regions located in the periphery remained with limited economic conditions and a restricted access to international markets.

Bonet and Meisel (2001) argue that two other factors contributed to the regional concentration of economic activity during the second half of the century. The first was a substantial increase in the size of the national government. During the first half of the century, public expenditure remained close to 5% of GDP (Junguito and Rincón 2004). However, this proportion increased steadily during the second half, and in 1990 reached about 10% of GDP. Since the Colombian government is highly centralized, the increase in public expenditures had a larger impact on the economy of Bogotá, where many of the administrative offices are located.

The second factor was the introduction of policies of import substitution to promote industrialization. These policies protected national production from their foreign competitors during a time when transport costs were decreasing, and therefore regional concentration accelerated. Some of these measures were adopted between 1956 and 1967, and in general corresponded to the implementation of tariffs to industrial imports or quantitative restrictions to imports (Villar and Esguerra 2005). The strategy of Import Substitution Industrialization (ISI) promoted industrial activities located in the central region of the country, because the size of the market made it more profitable for industrial activities. The regions with the strongest industrial sectors at the time were Antioquia, Cundinamarca and Valle del Cauca (Echavarría and Villamizar 2006). In contrast, between 1975 and 1989 industrial incentives were weakened, given the fiscal constraints generated by the debt crisis and the increased external debt service during the 1980s (Pombo 2002). Finally, with the economic liberalization strategy of the 1990s, several sectorial policies were abolished, such as export subsidies and non-trade barriers (Pombo 2002).

As Krugman and Livas Elizondo (1996) point out, the increase in the size of cities in the developing world was stimulated by strong domestic linkages produced by a growing industrial sector, which tends to grow inwards in regions with large markets given the lack of economic ties to the rest of the world. During the ISI period in Colombia, regions that lacked an industrial sector but required its products as inputs for their economic activities assumed higher costs of production. Hence, less industrialized regions paid part of the costs of ISI policies.

3 New Data: Descriptive Analysis

The study of long-term regional patterns in Colombia requires a discussion of economic dynamics that goes back to the first half of the twentieth century, a period rarely discussed by the literature on regional convergence. The reason is that data on the economic performance for this period is scarce. In this chapter we present a quantitative approach using several historical data sources to study regional economic inequalities throughout the century. The institution in charge of producing the official statistics in Colombia is the Administrative Office for National Statistics (DANE). Regional GDP is currently available from 1980 to 2018. The base year of the official estimations has changed three times during that period, which means that the annual series is divided into four different segments. The segments cover the periods 1980–1995, 1990–2005, 2000–2016 and 2005–2018. These four series are available in both current and constant prices on the official webpage of DANE.[1]

DANE has no estimates of regional GDP for the years before 1980. For this reason, some institutions have published independent estimates of regional GDP. Most estimations have the same regional configuration and are estimated at constant prices, but cover different periods. Three of these are of particular interest. The first is the series of regional GDP produced by the former Center for Agricultural Studies (CEGA). It consists of an annual estimate between 1975 and 2000 (CEGA 2004). The second is a series produced by the Pontificia Javeriana University (PUJ), which covers the period between 1970 and 1990 (PUJ 1992). The third is an estimation by the National Planning Office (DNP) for the year 1950 and the period between 1960 and 1975 (DNP 1977).

Another indicator of regional economic activity is bank deposits. Bank deposits have been used in Colombia as a proxy for GDP to study regional convergence (Bonet and Meisel 2001) and are available for 15 regions between 1926 and 1960. Their source is the *Revista del Banco de la República*, a journal edited by the Central Bank of Colombia. It contains information on short-term and savings deposits in current prices. These were initially reported by the *Superintendencia Bancaria*, the institution that regulated private banking in the country. Bank deposits in current prices for the period between 1926 and 1960 were converted to constant prices using the consumer price index estimated by Meisel (1990).

[1] Volume series are produced by DANE using regional prices for a base year.

Before 1950 there are no official or independent estimates of regional GDP that include all regions of Colombia. Hence, to study regional disparities in economic activity for the first half of the century it is necessary to estimate regional GDP with an indirect approach that uses other available sources of information. We will use the average of bank deposits observed during two time periods, 1926–1928 and 1937–1939, as a proxy for regional GDP. Averages over three years are selected to smooth temporal annual changes in bank deposits. The reason for selecting those specific years are the following: the first period consists of the first three years of bank deposits, which means that these years will be the farthest we can approximate regional economic activity; the second period is selected to compare the data of bank deposits with estimations of regional GDP for 1938 produced by Tirado-Fabregat et al. (2014). These authors used the methodology proposed by Geary and Stark (2002, 2015), which estimates regional GDP shares by sector (agriculture, industry and services) using the regional and sectorial labor supply and their corresponding estimated productivities.

The correlations and Spearman correlations between the different historical sources for available years are shown in Fig. 8.1. Estimates of regional GDP are available for the years 1950, 1960, 1970, 1980, 1990, 2000, 2010 and 2018. We use the three-year average of bank deposits as a proxy for regional GDP in 1926–1928 and also in 1937–1939. The correlation between bank deposits and regional GDP for different years and sources is at least 78.9%, which shows a strong relationship between both variables. Also, the Spearman correlation for the same data is 0.807, which shows that ranks were relatively similar between both sets.

However, approximating regional GDP using bank deposits has a few drawbacks. The higher concentration of bank deposits in certain regions of the country leads to an overestimation of their regional share of national GDP, especially in urban areas and Bogotá.[2] Moreover, bank deposits may not comprehensively account for agricultural activity, which was an important source of GDP during the first half of the century. Other economic

[2] Two regions, Bogotá and the department of Atlántico, show this particular bias. Bogotá has the largest share of bank deposits in the country, given the high concentration of financial activities in the capital. This is especially the case during the early stages of economic development because of a shortage of financial institutions in peripheral regions. Atlántico, on the Caribbean coast, whose capital, Barranquilla, was the most important port in Colombia during the first decades of the twentieth century, benefited from trade and financial transactions that emerged from those operations.

		Geary Stark		DNP		PUJ		
		1938	1951	1950	1960	1970	1980	1990
Bank deposits	1938	0,789\0,807						
	1950		0,922\0,917	0,866\0,929				
	1960				0,910\0,836			
DNP	1950		0,968\0,946					
	1970					0.997		
DANE	1980						0.999	
	1990							0.998

Fig. 8.1 Colombia: Correlations and Spearman correlations between bank deposits and regional GDP by sources (selected years, 1938–1990). (Source: Authors' calculations based on DNP, PUJ, CEGA and DANE. Numbers in the table are in the format correlation/Spearman correlation)

activities may also be misrepresented, such as those that are highly intensive in capital. Therefore, regions with these economic characteristics may differ considerably in their true economic production from their observed bank deposits. Due to the lack of other historical sources on regional economic activity during the first decades of the century, we will use the average bank deposits for 1926–1928 and 1937–1939 as a proxy, recognizing the potential shortcomings of such an approach.

Colombia is currently divided into 32 departments and Bogotá. However, to examine regional inequalities in the whole twentieth century, we have disaggregated the country into 16 different regions. This configuration was the most detailed possible considering the regional aggregation already present in the original data sources, but also given the fact that the administrative organization of Colombia underwent multiple changes during the twentieth century. Several new departments were created during this period, which makes it difficult to work with a more detailed disaggregation. The different regions are presented in Table 8.1 and Map 8.2.

Some general results of the data collection are the following. Table 8.2 shows the regional shares of GDP by decades since 1950. Besides, we have also used the regional share of the average bank deposits of 1926–1928 and 1937–1939 for the first two benchmark years in the century. It is clear that some regions concentrated a higher share of bank deposits in those years, in particular Cundinamarca, which includes Bogotá. After 1950 there are some clear patterns in the evolution of regional shares of GDP. One of the main results is that the production share of Cundinamarca

Table 8.1 Departments in the 16 regions of this study

Region	*Current* Departamentos
Antioquia	Antioquia
Atlántico	Atlántico
Bolívar	Bolívar, Sucre, Córdoba
Boyacá	Boyacá, Casanare
Caldas	Caldas, Quindío, Risaralda
Cauca	Cauca
Chocó	Chocó
Cundinamarca	Bogotá D.C., Cundinamarca, Meta
Huila	Huila
Magdalena	Cesar, La Guajira, Magdalena
Nariño	Nariño
Norte de Santander	Norte de Santander
Santander	Santander
Tolima	Tolima
Valle	Valle del Cauca
Resto	Amazonas, Arauca, Caquetá, Guainía, Guaviare, Putumayo, San Andrés y Providencia, Vaupés, Vichada

Note: The departments of Boyacá and Casanare are put together given that they belonged to the same region for a long period of time during the twentieth century. However, Casanare's GDP in 1980 is accounted into the category Resto by DANE. We do not expect this discrepancy to be of significant importance for our analysis of that year, given that Casanare contributed with 1% of the country's GDP in 1990 and only started to grow significantly during that decade because of the discovery of oil deposits

increased consistently. It grew from 19.8% in 1950 to 35.4% in 2018. Antioquia and Valle, the next two regions in size, maintained similar shares of approximately 14% and 10% along the whole period. The sustained increase of Cundinamarca's share throughout the century was not offset by any systematic reduction of the share of one territory in particular. Instead, several regions experienced modest decreases in their share of GDP during the second half of the century, such as Caldas, Cauca and Tolima.

To produce regional estimations of GDP per capita, we have divided the GDP by the regional population in each period. In Colombia, DANE is the institution that produces the official estimations of regional population, but such data is currently available only after 1985. There are no annual official estimations of regional population in Colombia before that year. However, there were several censuses before 1985, which were taken

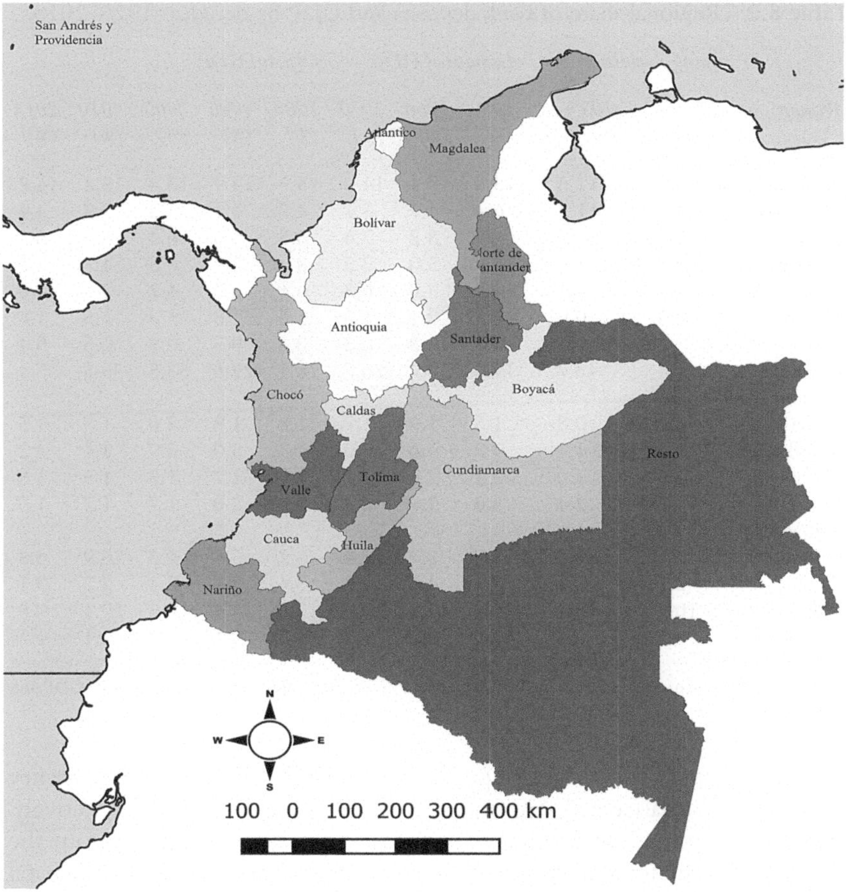

Map 8.2 Colombia: Aggregation of departments into 16 regions. (Source: Elaboration by the authors based on geographical information produced by DANE and Natural Earth [http://www.naturalearthdata.com/])

in 1905, 1912, 1918, 1928, 1938, 1951, 1964 and 1973.[3] We have approximated annual regional population for periods between censuses by using their average annual growth rate. The estimates of regional population are presented in Table 8.3.

[3] There are concerns regarding the accuracy of the 1928 census (Estrada 2017).

Table 8.2 Regional share of bank deposits and GDP by decades (1926–2018)

	Bank deposits		*Estimated GDP*			*Official GDP*				
Region	*1926–1928 (%)*	*1937–1939 (%)*	*1950 (%)*	*1960 (%)*	*1970 (%)*	*1980 (%)*	*1990 (%)*	*2000 (%)*	*2010 (%)*	*2018 (%)*
Antioquia	12.9	11.5	15.5	13.4	14.3	15.5	14.9	13.4	13.4	14.7
Atlántico	8.8	11.2	6.4	4.9	5.1	4.7	4.1	4.2	3.9	4.4
Bolívar	5.2	4.1	6.4	8.2	7.6	6.5	6.0	6.4	6.5	6.1
Boyacá	0.8	1.1	3.9	5.0	3.5	3.4	2.9	6.8	4.3	4.3
Caldas	7.9	6.1	11.8	8.0	6.3	6.6	6.2	4.2	3.8	4.0
Cauca	0.8	0.9	3.5	2.1	1.5	1.8	1.8	1.3	1.5	1.8
Chocó			0.3	0.3	0.3	0.4	0.5	0.3	0.5	0.4
Cundinamarca	44.4	43.7	19.8	22.7	26.7	28.1	29.6	32.5	35.5	35.4
Huila	0.4	0.8	1.5	1.9	1.7	1.8	1.9	2.0	1.7	1.5
Magdalena	1.2	1.4	4.3	4.6	5.0	4.1	5.0	3.9	4.4	4.2
Nariño	0.6	1.0	2.1	2.5	2.1	1.8	1.7	1.5	1.5	1.5
Norte de Santander	1.5	2.4	3.0	2.9	2.3	2.2	2.0	1.7	1.7	1.6
Santander	3.0	3.3	5.7	5.7	5.4	5.2	5.5	6.3	6.9	6.5
Tolima	2.1	2.1	4.5	4.6	4.2	3.4	3.1	2.4	2.2	2.1
Valle	10.3	10.2	10.9	12.5	12.5	12.2	11.4	10.5	10.1	9.8
Resto		0.3	0.6	0.7	1.7	2.2	3.4	2.5	2.1	1.7

Source: Authors' own elaboration based on official data by DANE, independent estimations of GDP and bank deposits

The regions with the largest population at the beginning of the century were Cundinamarca and Antioquia, with 14.3% and 14.1%, respectively. While Antioquia underwent a small reduction in its share throughout the century, Cundinamarca's grew to 24.7% in 2018. Today 38.2% of the total Colombian population is concentrated in these two regions. Regions that increased their share of population were Atlántico, Magdalena and Resto, while those that experienced the largest reductions were Boyacá, Caldas and Valle. Patterns of regional migration in Colombia during the twentieth century have been studied by several authors, such as Fields (1979), Flórez (2003), Schultz (1971) and Simmons and Cardona (1972).[4] In general, rural-urban migration was particularly important during the 1950s and 1960s, as well as during the last decades of the twentieth

[4]For a review of the literature on internal migration in Colombia, see Romero-Prieto (2010).

Table 8.3 Regional share of population by decades (1926–2018)

	Bank deposits		*Estimated GDP*			*Official GDP*				
Region	*1926–1928 (%)*	*1937–1939 (%)*	*1950 (%)*	*1960 (%)*	*1970 (%)*	*1980 (%)*	*1990 (%)*	*2000 (%)*	*2010 (%)*	*2018 (%)*
Antioquia	14.1	13.7	13.6	14.0	14.0	13.9	13.4	13.2	13.3	13.5
Atlántico	2.6	3.1	3.7	4.0	4.4	4.9	5.1	5.0	5.1	5.3
Bolívar	8.3	8.8	8.6	8.9	9.3	9.4	9.5	9.6	9.6	9.8
Boyacá	10.2	8.5	6.9	6.3	5.3	4.3	4.0	3.8	3.5	3.4
Caldas	8.0	8.8	9.2	8.6	7.4	6.7	6.4	5.9	5.4	5.1
Cauca	4.1	4.1	3.9	3.6	3.2	3.0	2.9	3.0	2.9	2.8
Chocó	1.3	1.3	1.1	1.1	1.1	0.9	1.0	1.1	1.0	1.0
Cundina marca	14.3	14.1	14.1	16.1	18.2	20.0	21.3	22.5	23.5	24.7
Huila	2.9	2.5	2.5	2.4	2.2	2.2	2.3	2.3	2.4	2.3
Magdalena	4.0	3.9	4.0	4.9	6.0	6.0	6.0	6.2	6.6	7.2
Nariño	5.7	5.4	4.8	4.2	3.9	3.7	3.8	3.7	3.6	3.0
Norte de Santander	4.1	4.0	3.4	3.1	3.2	3.2	3.2	3.0	2.9	3.0
Santander	0.7	1.5	2.2	1.6	1.5	2.1	2.5	2.9	3.1	2.8
Tolima	7.4	7.1	6.5	5.9	5.5	5.2	4.9	4.7	4.4	4.5
Valle	6.0	6.3	6.2	5.2	4.4	3.9	3.6	3.3	3.0	2.8
Resto	5.6	7.0	9.4	9.8	10.3	10.3	10.1	9.8	9.6	8.6

Source: Before 1985, authors' estimates of regional population using the population censuses since 1918; between 1985 and 2018, DANE

century. This last wave was due to an intensification of the armed conflict in the country (Flórez 2003). Moreover, some cities were particularly receptive to migratory flows, in particular Bogotá: in 1964, 70% of its population aged 15 to 64 had been born outside of the city (Simmons and Cardona 1972).

Using the estimations of regional GDP and population, we calculate regional GDP per capita. Table 8.4 presents the standardized GDP per capita by decades since 1926 for the 16 regions under analysis. The standardization of the series was conducted by dividing the regional value by the national GDP per capita for the same year. For instance, a standardized indicator for a particular region that has a value of 1.0 means that the region had the same GDP per capita as the country as a whole. Again, for the first two periods we present the results using bank deposits as a proxy for regional GDP per capita.

Table 8.4 Standardized regional GDP per capita by decades (1926–2018)

	Bank deposits		*Estimated GDP*			*Official GDP*				
Region	*1926–1928*	*1937–1939*	*1950*	*1960*	*1970*	*1980*	*1990*	*2000*	*2010*	*2018*
Antioquia	1.0	1.0	1.1	1.0	1.0	1.1	1.1	1.0	1.0	1.1
Atlántico	3.6	4.2	1.7	1.2	1.2	1.0	0.8	0.8	0.8	0.8
Bolívar	0.7	0.5	0.7	0.9	0.8	0.7	0.6	0.7	0.7	0.6
Boyacá	0.1	0.1	0.6	0.8	0.7	0.8	0.7	1.8	1.2	1.2
Caldas	1.1	0.8	1.3	0.9	0.9	1.0	1.0	0.7	0.7	0.8
Cauca	0.2	0.3	0.9	0.6	0.5	0.6	0.6	0.4	0.5	0.6
Chocó			0.2	0.3	0.2	0.4	0.6	0.3	0.4	0.4
Cundina marca	3.4	3.6	1.4	1.4	1.5	1.4	1.4	1.4	1.5	1.4
Huila	0.2	0.4	0.6	0.8	0.8	0.8	0.8	0.9	0.7	0.7
Magdalena	0.3	0.4	1.1	1.0	0.8	0.7	0.8	0.6	0.7	0.6
Nariño	0.1	0.2	0.4	0.6	0.5	0.5	0.5	0.4	0.4	0.5
Norte de Santander	0.4	0.7	0.9	0.9	0.7	0.7	0.6	0.6	0.6	0.5
Santander	0.4	0.5	0.9	1.0	1.0	1.0	1.1	1.3	1.6	1.4
Tolima	0.4	0.4	0.7	0.9	0.9	0.9	0.9	0.7	0.7	0.8
Valle	2.0	1.7	1.2	1.3	1.2	1.2	1.1	1.1	1.0	1.1
Resto		0.2	0.3	0.4	1.1	1.0	1.4	0.8	0.7	0.6

Source: Authors' calculations based on the estimates of population and regional GDP

The results show several regional patterns. For instance, Boyacá and Santander increased their relative GDP per capita substantially between 1950 and 2018. Boyacá was an important source of migration to Bogotá (Simmons and Cardona 1972), which may explain the decrease in its share of total population. Santander benefited from having an oil refinery in its territory, an activity that produces high value added using low labor requirements. Cundinamarca remained with a GDP per capita above the average, starting at 1.4 in 1950 and finishing at the same value in 2018. Resto experienced a large temporal increase in its production due to the exploitation of oil and gas in its territory, especially during the second half of the century. Given its low demographic density, the high value added from the exploitation of natural resources gave an impulse to the region's GDP per capita. However, such a trend has been slowing down during the last decades, given the fewer discoveries of oil in the region and a reduction in oil prices. It should also be noted that some regions—Chocó, Cauca, Nariño and Bolívar—had a lower GDP per capita than the country as a whole for most of the century. These territories are located in the coastal regions of Colombia.

In the following pages we present the spatial concentration of economic activity in Colombia during three different periods of time. Maps 8.3, 8.4 and 8.5 show the regional GDP per capita in the country for the

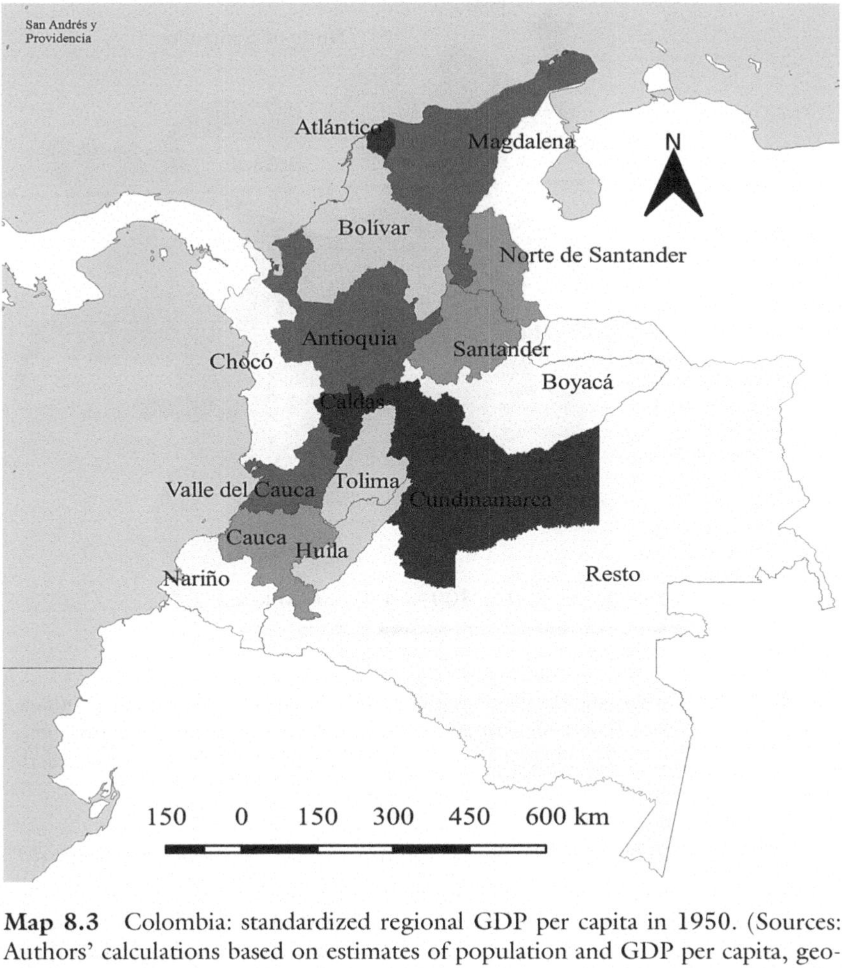

Map 8.3 Colombia: standardized regional GDP per capita in 1950. (Sources: Authors' calculations based on estimates of population and GDP per capita, geographical information by DANE and Natural Earth [http://www.naturalearthdata.com/])

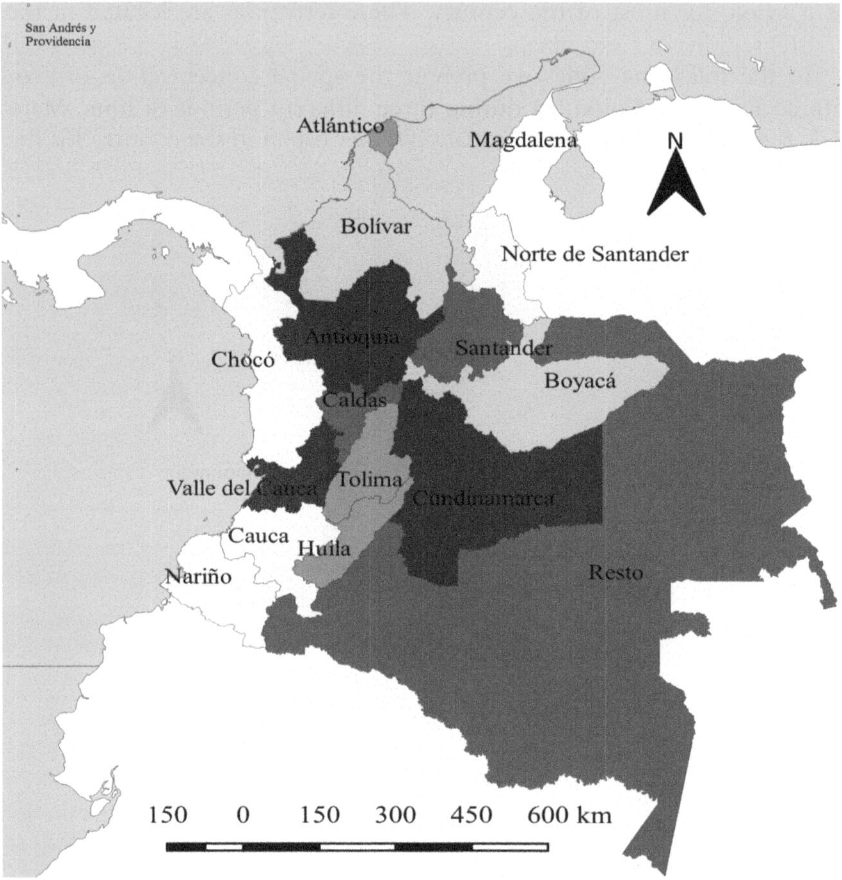

Map 8.4 Colombia: standardized regional GDP per capita in 1980. (Sources: Authors' calculations based on estimates of population and GDP per capita, geographical information by DANE and Natural Earth [http://www.naturalearthdata.com/])

years 1950, 1980 and 2018. The following maps categorize, for three different benchmark years, the 16 regions according to their GDP per capita in quintiles. The regions that belong to higher quintiles of GDP per capita are shown in the maps with darker colors, while those with lower GDP per capita appear colored in lighter tones. We can see in Map 8.3 that the richest regions of the country were already concentrated in 1950 in central

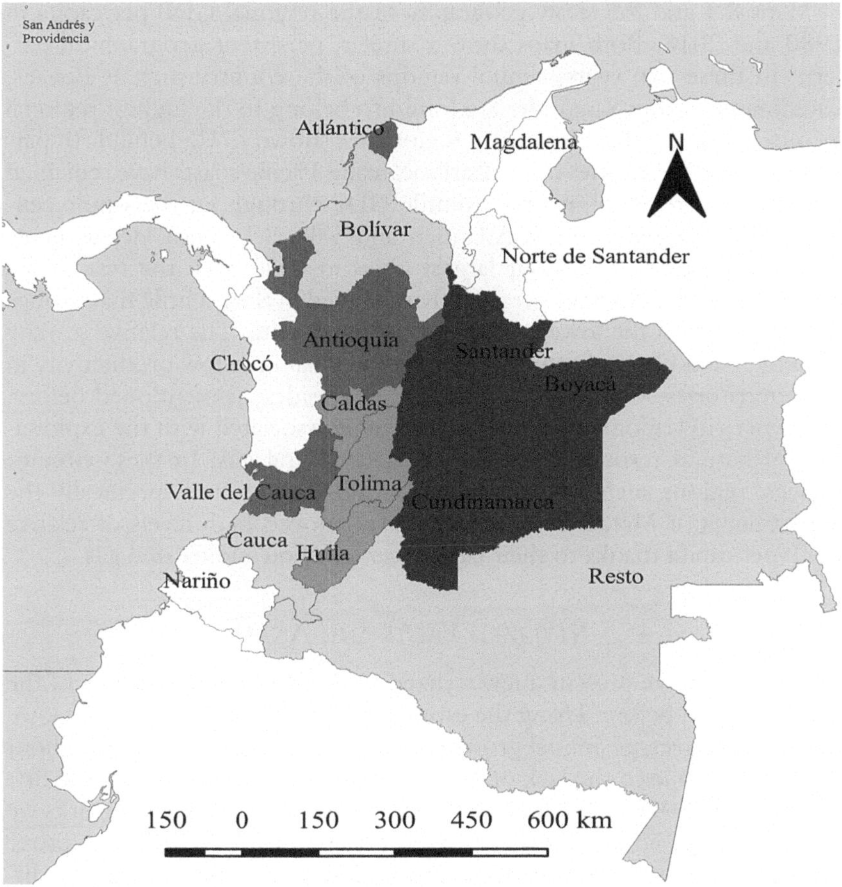

Map 8.5 Colombia: standardized regional GDP per capita in 2018. (Sources: Authors' calculations based on estimates of population and GDP per capita, geographical information by DANE and Natural Earth [http://www.naturalearthdata.com/])

regions such as Cundinamarca and Caldas. However, there were territories in the periphery, particularly on the Caribbean and Pacific coasts, that also had a relatively high GDP per capita. Besides, some other central regions such as Boyacá and Santander were not among the richest regions on this date.

Maps 8.4 and 8.5 show geography of the regional GDP per capita in 1980 and 2018. Both maps show a similar, persistent geographical pattern. In these two years, central regions of the country such as Boyacá, Cundinamarca and Santander are found to belong to the highest regional income quintile, while peripheral regions are shown to lag behind. In particular, several territories in the Caribbean and Pacific coasts have remained in the lowest regional income quintile GDP throughout the whole century. With the exception of Atlántico and Valle del Cauca, departments that contain two of the four largest cities in Colombia, the rest of the peripheral territories have persistently remained in the quintile that groups the regions with the lowest relative GDP per capita. The relative scarcity of human and physical capital may help to explain the low productivity in these territories (Galvis and Meisel 2013). Besides, as mentioned before, differences in regional performances are also associated with the exploitation of natural resources, such as oil and natural gas. In these circumstances, regions such as Cundinamarca and Boyacá, and specifically the departments of Meta and Casanare, have enjoyed high levels of relative GDP per capita thanks to their large reserves of oil and natural gas.

4 Stylized Facts and Analysis

In this section we present a few stylized facts, as well as an analysis of the data described before. Using the estimates of regional GDP per capita, we calculate the average annual growth rates for different periods throughout the century. Due to the lack of direct regional GDP estimates for the first two periods (1926–1937 and 1938–1950), for these two benchmarks we use the average annual growth rate of per capita bank deposits as a proxy for regional economic growth. For the periods that follow, we use the different direct estimates of regional GDP per capita to calculate economic growth rates. Particularly, in order to maintain methodological homogeneity, for each period considered we have used the existing estimation that covers the beginning and the end of each time span. For instance, the average annual growth rate between 1950 and 1960 has been calculated using the regional GDP estimation offered by the National Planning Office (DNP).

The exploitation of natural resources, such as oil, natural gas and coal has been a significant driver of regional growth during the last decades. Departments such as Arauca, Casanare, Meta and Huila are known for their exploitation of oil and natural gas. Arauca is currently grouped with the region *Resto* and it was the most important producer of oil in 1990 as measured by value added. However, the biggest oil field in Colombia was discovered in the early 1990s in Casanare, a department grouped in the region of Boyacá. This discovery sparked an enormous, ten-fold growth in its GDP from 1990 to 1999. Currently the biggest oil producer is Meta, a department in the region of Cundinamarca. It produces half the country's GDP that comes from oil and natural gas. Moreover, coal has also been an important natural resource in Colombia for its large value added. The departments of Cesar and La Guajira (Magdalena region) are its largest producers.

The financial crisis of 1999 was a setback for regional economic growth. In the early 1990s, Colombia adopted a set of reforms that deregulated the financial system, which produced an expansion of financial services. The expansion went hand in hand with a decrease in the quality of loans and an increase in the fragility of the system. In consequence, capital flows reversed during the last years of the decade and the terms of trade deteriorated, giving way to a reduction in aggregate demand (Gomez-Gonzalez and Kiefer 2009). As a result, at the end of the decade economic growth plummeted: Colombian GDP decreased 4.2% between 1998 and 1999, with most of its impact felt in Bogotá, the center of financial activity. Many other departments were also affected, especially those with the largest economies and strongest ties to the financial sector.

Another important factor in the development of particular urban regions was the adoption of policies to promote industrial growth through import substitution (ISI). According to Pombo (2002), the industrialization process in Colombia underwent several phases. The first occurred from 1900 to 1930, when the bases for modern industrial activities were established. Several factors boosted industrialization during this stage, such as the electrification of large cities, railroad construction and the boom in coffee exports. The second stage, between 1930 and 1945, was characterized by the early implementation of import substitution policies, particularly in manufactured raw materials. Industrial activities grew at a fast pace during this time, not only because of favorable economic policies but also because of an increase in the domestic consumption of manufactured goods. In a third stage, between 1945 and 1967, ISI policies focused on the establishment of capital-intensive industries. Quantitative restrictions to imports, such as import licenses and prior deposits, were important measures to protect domestic industries from external competition.

The adoption of ISI policies contributed to the development of local industries in Colombia, which were particularly clustered around the biggest cities of the country. By 1930, the three largest cities specializing in industrial activities related to textiles (Medellín), sugar refineries (Cali) and brewery and cement industries (Bogotá) (Pombo 2002). These early industrial sectors benefited from state-promoted industrialization through policies such as quantitative restrictions to imports and higher nominal tariffs. In some cases, ISI policies were not successful. The economic viability of particular industrial enterprises was artificially sustained by government subsidies and protection (Pombo 2002). Public resources were used to promote and protect nascent industries, which were mainly located in urban areas. In contrast, rural territories lacked an adequate provision of public goods, such as infrastructure and human capital, a condition that limited their economic development throughout the century.

To study the magnitude of regional inequalities in Colombia, in this chapter we apply some of the traditional approaches in the literature. The first is β-convergence, which compares economic growth to the initial GDP per capita for each region. This type of convergence exists when the poorest economies exhibit the highest long-term growth rates and therefore they eventually catch up with richest regions.

In Fig. 8.2 we present the average growth rate per decade and the initial standardized GDP per capita in 1950 for the 16 regions. We observe that the poorest regions at the beginning of the century had higher growth rates than the richest. Nevertheless, the correlation between the two variables is barely significant at the 5% level. This means that there is only weak evidence in favor of the hypothesis of regional convergence. Besides, as mentioned before, economic growth in some regions of the country originated from the sudden discovery of natural resources such as oil, gas and coal. Under these conditions it could be said that convergence was not the result of fundamental economic factors such as migration or capital movements across regions.

In any circumstance, the absolute β-convergence approach does not take into account other variables that could improve the economic performance of territories. In this regard, Mankiw et al. (1992) argued that international differences in investment on physical and human capital account for a large part of the observed difference in growth rates between countries. Moreover, the presence of β-convergence does not guarantee that the dispersion of income diminishes over time (Quah 1993). Because of these arguments, and given the different sizes in economic activity and

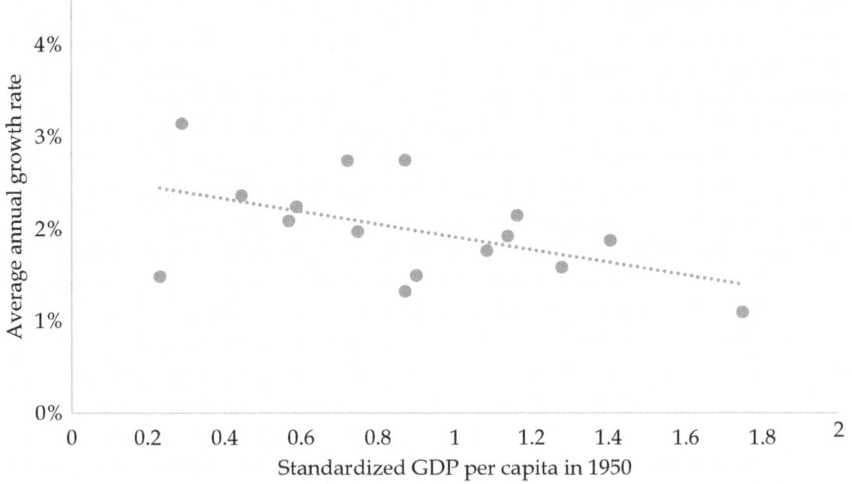

Fig. 8.2 Absolute β-convergence (1950–2018)

population of the regions under study, additional definitions of convergence are required for a better understanding of the dynamics of regional inequalities.

A different approach to convergence in the literature is that of σ-convergence, which studies the evolution over time of the dispersion of income per capita across regions. In relation to this approach, Table 8.5 shows the evolution of the population-weighted coefficient of variation (WCV), which measures the dispersion of regional GDP per capita by taking into account the differences in regional population.[5] As can be seen, the WCV remains relatively stable throughout the century, with a minor increase after 1990. This evidence points to neither a convergence nor a divergence process across Colombian regions, as opposed to previous results suggesting the existence of a regional convergence process. In this chapter we have argued that regional economic disparities have remained and that central regions of the country have kept the largest shares of economic production in Colombia.

[5] The population-weighted coefficient of variation (WCV) is calculated dividing the weighted standard deviation (σ_w) by the weighted average (μ_w): WCV = σ_w/μ_w. In this case, μ_w is the average GDP per capita (x_i), calculated using the regional share of the population as weight (w_i).

Table 8.5 Colombia: population-weighted coefficient of variation of regional GDP per capita (1950–2018)

Year	*Population-weighted CV*
1950	0.343
1960	0.258
1970	0.293
1980	0.277
1990	0.284
2000	0.368
2010	0.370
2018	0.348

Source: Authors' calculations based on the estimates of population and GDP per capita

5 Conclusions

This chapter analyzed regional economic inequalities in Colombia during the twentieth century. Given the lack of historical information for regional economic performance, the literature on this subject is scarce. For this reason we have presented a unified analysis of regional economic growth in Colombia that covers the period between 1926 and 2018. We collected the data to study long-term patterns of regional inequality and used several definitions of regional convergence found in the literature. Some of the factors behind these inequalities such as the exploitation of natural resources and the implementation of industrial policies are also discussed. We argue that the geographic conditions of Colombia led to the development of isolated markets that concentrated in particular areas of the country, especially in the Andes Mountains. The integration of regional markets in Colombia occurred quite late in comparison to other South American countries, and was undertaken through the construction of railroads and highways during the first half of the twentieth century.

However, the expansion of the transportation system might have reinforced the patterns of regional economic inequality observed during the second half of the century. As has been identified in the literature, the reduction of transport costs can interact with the presence of economies of scale and as a result produce a larger concentration of particular economic sectors, such as manufacturing. In Colombia, the largest industrial economies in the mid-twentieth century were located in its three largest cities: Bogotá, Medellín and Cali. These regions are located near the geographic center of the country and were the locus of most of Colombia's economic growth during the second half of the century. During this period the economic significance of both coastal regions declined. The reduction of transportation costs and the integration of national markets may have influenced this result given the presence of scale economies and the existence of a large demand for goods and services already being produced in the central regions of the country.

The adoption of ISI policies in the mid-twentieth century is another factor that could have influenced the development of a core-periphery pattern in Colombia. While industrial sectors that were located in the central regions benefited from these policies, peripheral regions did not due to the absence of manufacturing activities in their territories. They also had to assume the costs of higher prices for industrial products given the protection against foreign competition that national manufacturers received. The lack of attention to local realities, especially those of the territories located in the periphery of Colombia, and the consequent lack of policies to foster economic development in the poorest regions of the country are two pending challenges for Colombia at the beginning of the twenty-first century.

The main conclusion of this study is that Colombian regions did not converge during this period. Though poorer regions show higher growth rates, the dispersion of regional GDP per capita has not decreased. It remained relatively stable with minor changes during the century. This lack of regional convergence has its origin in the uneven economic performance across the country. The data shows that the central regions concentrate a larger proportion of national production, while the periphery lags behind. In particular, the coastal regions have remained the poorest. The reasons for the underdevelopment of the peripheral territories of Colombia need to be further studied, in order to design strategies for improving their economic and social conditions in the future.

References

Bonet, J. A. and Meisel, A. (2001). La convergencia regional en Colombia: una visión de largo plazo 1926–1995, in A. Meisel (ed.) *Regiones, Ciudades y Crecimiento Económico en Colombia*. Colección de Economía Regional del Banco de la República: Bogotá.

Branisa, B. and Cardozo, A. (2009a). Revisiting the Regional Growth Convergence Debate in Colombia using Income Indicators. Discussion Paper 194, Ibero American Institute for Economic Research.

———. (2009b). Regional Growth Convergence in Colombia using Social Indicators, Discussion Paper 195, Ibero America Institute for Economic Research.

Cárdenas, M., Pontón, A. and Trujillo, J. P. (1993). Convergencia y migraciones inter-departamentales en Colombia: 1950–1983. *Coyuntura Económica* 23, 1.

Centro de Estudios Ganaderos y Agrícolas. (2004). *Sistema simplificado de cuentas departamentales de Colombia 1975–2000*. CEGA: Bogotá.

Coatsworth, J. H. (1998). Economic and Institutional Trajectories in Nineteenth Century Latin America, in Coatsworth, J. H. and A. M. Taylor (eds.) *Latin America and the World Economy since 1800*. David Rockefeller Center for Latin American Studies, Harvard University Press.

Coatsworth, J. H. and Williamson, J. G. (2004). Always Protectionist? Latin American Tariffs from Independence to Great Depression. *Journal of Latin American Studies* 36, 2.

Departamento Nacional de Planeación. (1977). *Cuentas regionales de Colombia 1960–1975*. DNP: Bogotá.

Echavarría, J. J. (1982). La deuda externa colombiana durante los 20s y los 30s: Algunas enseñanzas para el presente. *Coyuntura Económica* 12, 2.

Echavarría, J. J. and Villamizar, M. (2006). El proceso colombiano de desindustrialización. *Borradores de Economía*, Banco de la República.

Estrada, V. (2017). ¿Cuántos somos? Una historia de los censos civiles y de la organización estadística en Colombia en la primera mitad del siglo XX. *Historia Crítica*, 64.

Fields, G. S. (1979). Lifetime Migration in Colombia: Tests of the Expected Income Hypothesis. *Population and Development Review* 5, 2.

Flórez, C. E. (2003). Migration and the Urban Informal Sector in Colombia. Conference on African Migration in Comparative Perspective, Johannesburg, June 4–7, 2003.

Galvis, L. A. and Meisel, A. (2013). Regional Inequalities and Regional Policies in Colombia: the Experience of the Last Two Decades, in Cuadrado-Roura, J. R. and P. Aroca (eds.) *Regional Problems and Policies in Latin America*. Berlin: Springer.

Galvis, L. A. and Hahn, L. (2016). Crecimiento municipal en Colombia: el papel de las externalidades espaciales, el capital humano y el capital físico. *Sociedad y Economía*, 31, 149–174.

Geary, F. and Stark, T. (2002). Examining Ireland's Post-Famine Economic Growth Performance. *The Economic Journal* 112, 482.

———. (2015). Regional GDP in the UK, 1861–1911: new estimates. *The Economic History Review*, 68, 1.

Gómez, C. (2006). Convergencia regional en Colombia: un enfoque en los Agregados Monetarios y en el Sector Exportador. *Ensayos sobre Economía Regional*, 45. https://repositorio.banrep.gov.co/bitstream/handle/20.500.12134/2034/eser_45.pdf?sequence=1&isAllowed=y

Gomez-Gonzalez, J. E. and Kiefer, N. (2009). Bank Failure: Evidence from the Colombian Financial Crisis. *The International Journal of Business and Finance Research* 3, 2.

GRECO. (2000). Comercio exterior y actividad económica de Colombia en el siglo XX: exportaciones totales y tradicionales. *Borradores de Economía*, Banco de la República: Bogotá.

Junguito, R. (1996). The Management of Coffee Bonanzas and Crisis: Political Economy Issues. *Borradores Semanales de Economía*, Banco de la República: Bogotá.

Junguito, R. and Rincón, H. (2004). La política fiscal en el siglo XX en Colombia. *Borradores de Economía*, Banco de la República: Bogotá.

Kalmanovitz, S. (2012). Por qué se fue Panamá. *El Espectador*, March 19, 2012. https://www.elespectador.com/opinion/por-que-se-fue-panama-columna-333102.

Kalmanovitz, S. and López, E. (2006). *La agricultura colombiana en el siglo XX*. Fondo de Cultura Económica, Banco de la República: Bogotá.

Kalmanovitz, S., López, E. and Romero, C. A. (1999). La producción agropecuaria colombiana 1915–1950. *Borradores de Economía*, Banco de la República: Bogotá.

Kemmerer, E. W. (1923). *Address at a Luncheon Given by the Pan American Society at the Bankers Club*, Edwin Walter Kemmerer Papers, Box. 488, Princeton University, Manuscript Library: New York.

———. (1927). Economic Advisory Work for Governments. *American Economic Review* 17, 1.

Krugman, P. and Livas Elizondo, R. (1996). Trade Policy and the Third World Metropolis. *Journal of Development Economics*, 49, 1.

Krugman, P. (1991). Increasing Returns and Economic Geography. *Journal of Political Economy*, 99, 3.

León, G. and Benavides, H. (2015). Inversión pública en Colombia y sus efectos sobre el crecimiento y la convergencia departamentales. *Dimensión Empresarial*, 13, 1.

Mankiw, N. G., Romer, D. and Weil, D. N. (1992). A Contribution to the Empirics of Economic Growth. *Quarterly Journal of Economics*, 107, 2.

Meisel, A. (1993). ¿Polarización o Convergencia? A Propósito de Cárdenas, Pontón y Trujillo. *Coyuntura Económica*, 23, 2.

———. (1990). El Banco de la República, 1946–1954 y la reforma de 1951, in Ortega, F., Meisel, A., Ibáñez, J., López, A., Gómez, H. and M. Lombo (eds.). *El Banco de la República, antecedentes, evolución y estructura*, Banco de la República: Bogotá.

Meisel, A., Ramírez, M. T. and Jaramillo, J. (2016). Too Late but Profitable: Railroads in Colombia during 1920–1950. *Economic History Research*, 12, 3.

Meisel, A. and Romero-Prieto, J. E. (2017). La mortalidad de la Guerra de los Mil Días, 1899–1902. *Cuadernos de Historia Económica*, Banco de la República: Bogotá.
Ocampo, J. A. (2013). *Colombia y la economía mundial 1830–1910*. Ediciones Uniandes: Bogotá.
———. (1994). Regímenes monetarios variables en una economía preindustrial: Colombia, 1850–1933, in Sánchez, F. (ed.) *Ensayos de historia monetaria y bancaria de Colombia*, Tercer Munda: Bogotá.
———. (1979). Desarrollo exportador y desarrollo capitalista colombiano en el siglo XIX (una hipótesis). *Desarrollo y Sociedad*, 1.
Pachón, A. and Ramírez, M. T. (2006). *La infraestructura de transporte en Colombia durante el siglo XX*. Banco de la República and Tercer Mundo Editores: Bogotá.
Pombo, C. (2002). Industrialization and industrial policy in Colombia: a tale of economic development. *Borradores de Investigación*, 31, Universidad del Rosario.
Pontificia Universidad Javeriana. (1992). *Evolución de PIB por departamentos, 1970–1990*. Final Report.
Quah, D. (1993). Galton's Fallacy and Tests of the Convergence Hypothesis. *Scandinavian Journal of Economics*, 95, 4.
Rocha, R. and Vivas, A. (1998). Crecimiento regional en Colombia: ¿persiste la desigualdad? *Revista de Economía del Rosario*, 1, 67–108.
Romero-Prieto, J. E. (2010). El éxito económico de los costeños en Bogotá: migración interna y capital humano. *Revista del Banco de la República*, 83, 992.
Royuela, V. and García, G. (2015). Economic and Social Convergence in Colombia. *Regional Studies*, 49, 2.
Safford, F. (2010). El problema de los transportes en Colombia en el siglo XIX, in Meisel and M. T. Ramirez (eds.) *Economía colombiana del siglo XIX*. Banco de la República and Fondo de Cultura Económica: Bogotá.
Schultz, T. P. (1971). Rural-Urban Migration in Colombia. *Review of Economics and Statistics*, 53, 2.
Simmons, A. and Cardona, R. (1972). Rural-Urban Migration: Who Comes, Who Stays, Who Returns? The Case of Bogota, Colombia, 1929–1968. *International Migration Review*, 6, 2.
Tirado-Fabregat, D. A., Romero, C. A. and Badia-Miró, M. (2014). Evolución del PIB regional de Colombia (1938–2010). Paper presented in "PIBs regionales en América Latina, una perspectiva de largo plazo (1870–2010)", Fourth Latin American Congress of Economic History (CLADHE-IV), July 23, 24 and 25 2014, Bogotá, Colombia. http://www.utadeo.edu.co/es/micrositio/cuarto-congreso-latinoamericano-de-historia-economica.
Villar, L. and Esguerra, P. (2005). El comercio exterior colombiano en el siglo XX. *Borradores de Economía*, Banco de la República: Bogotá.
World Bank. (n.d.). *World Bank Open Data, Colombia*. Accessed December 12, 2019. https://data.worldbank.org/country/colombia?view=chart.

CHAPTER 9

Regional GDP in Mexico, 1895–2010

José Aguilar Retureta, Marc Badia-Miró, and Alfonso Herranz-Loncán

1 Introduction

Economic differences among Mexican regions are substantial and have been increasing for a long time, according to different indicators. Although this problem has been object of serious public concern since the mid-twentieth century, there has been no significant progress towards its

Previous versions of this chapter have been published in Aguilar-Retureta (2015, 2016a, b). We appreciate the comments received by D. A. Tirado-Fabregat and H. Willebald. We also acknowledge the financial support offered by the project PGC2018-095821-B-I00 and ECO2015-65049-C12-1-P, funded by the Ministerio de Ciencia, Innovación y Universidades (MCIU), to the Agencia Estatal de Investigación (AEI) and the Fondo Europeo de Desarrollo Regional (FEDER). We also thank the financial support of the Catalan government (2017SGR1466).

J. Aguilar Retureta
Independent Scholar, Mexico City, Mexico

M. Badia-Miró • A. Herranz-Loncán (✉)
Departament d'Història, Institucions, Política i Econòmica Mundial
Universitat de Barcelona, Barcelona, Spain
e-mail: mbadia@ub.edu; alfonso.herranz@ub.edu

D. A. Tirado-Fabregat et al. (eds.), *Time and Space*,
Palgrave Studies in Economic History,
https://doi.org/10.1007/978-3-030-47553-6_9

mitigation. According to the National Institute of Statistics and Geography (INEGI), in 2016 gross domestic product (GDP) per capita in the richest state was 14.3 times as high as in the poorest state, whereas the National Council for Evaluation of Social Development Policy (CONEVAL) estimates that 54% of the total population suffering extreme poverty in 2018 were living in just four southern states (INEGI 2019). These figures stand out globally, not only in comparison to high-income countries but also to most middle- and low-income economies. In fact, the Economic Commission for Latin America and the Caribbean (ECLAC) has pointed out that Mexico has the second highest income ratio between the richest and the poorest regions among Latin American countries, only surpassed by Ecuador (ECLAC 2014, p. 73).

In this research, we provide evidence on the evolution of Mexican regional inequality since the late nineteenth century. Despite the deep-rooted and historically persistent large economic differences among Mexican regions, so far the country's literature on regional disparities has focused on the period from the 1980s onwards. By contrast, there is very little research on the State-led industrialization period (1930–1980) or the First Globalization. Here we aim at filling this gap by providing a comprehensive approach to the long-term evolution of regional inequality in Mexico.

In addition to the huge size of the current regional divide, there are other reasons that make the long-term analysis of Mexican spatial inequalities interesting. First, this is (together with other chapters of this volume) one of the few available studies of the long-term evolution of regional inequality in a middle-income economy, where the spatial dynamics of development is very different from the much better known cases of industrialized countries. In addition, Mexico has some characteristics that make it a particularly interesting case study. While the northern regions of the country share a long border with the biggest world market, the US, the southern one's limit with one of the poorest regions in the world, Central America. In addition, Mexico provides an interesting case in which regional income inequality has been affected over time by a large range of different elements, such as factor endowments, factor mobility, natural resources, structural change, market potential and regional and development policies.

Our research describes the evolution of regional inequality from 1895 to the present. This has been a period of intense transformation of the Mexican economy, which accelerated in the late nineteenth century after

Table 9.1 Composition of Mexican GDP by sector, 1895–1929 (%)

	1895	*1910*	*1921*	*1929*
Agriculture	23.8	19.9	17.9	13.9
Livestock	9.6	7.5	7.4	6.7
Mining	4.9	7.5	4.2	9.5
Oil	–	0.1	6.9	2.0
Manufacturing	9.1	12.3	10.4	13.2
Transport	2.3	2.2	2.8	4.3
Others	50.3	50.5	50.4	50.4

Source: Pérez López (1960: 585)

decades of stagnation and political turmoil. In the few decades before 1910, Mexico started a process of economic growth and structural change (see Table 9.1), which was initially led by primary exports. Several changes boosted the country's gradual transition to a modern capitalist economy. To start with, the government introduced extensive institutional reforms, which allowed, for instance, the establishment of limited liability companies in the mining sector since 1884. Moreover, important measures of protection of private property were established in 1892 (Kuntz-Ficker 2010: 314), and, what is more relevant from the viewpoint of the economic integration of the different regional spaces, taxes on domestic trade (*alcabalas*) were abolished at the end of the nineteenth century.[1] This largely encouraged the integration of national markets by simplifying (in terms of costs and safety) the domestic movement of goods across the national territory.[2] All these transformations encouraged the incorporation of traditional sectors into the market economy, contributing therefore to their modernization. At the regional level, those changes had an uneven impact, boosting the performance of some regions, especially those with comparative advantages in primary exports.

Together with institutional changes, the revolution in the transport system, and particularly the expansion of the railway network, played a

[1] Even though this reform was formally approved in the middle of the nineteenth century, it was only applied at the end of the century.

[2] There is some debate on the actual effects of institutional change. For instance, Haber et al. (2003) argue that it was biased in favour of national elites (businessmen and politicians), which used the new institutions to preserve the late nineteenth-century authoritarian regime.

central role in the modernization of the Mexican economy, increasing market integration and boosting regional specialization, which was largely determined by the location of natural resources.[3] Coatsworth (1979) estimated that the social savings of the Mexican railways represented 24.6 to 38.5% of total GDP by 1910. This is a very high figure, compared with both the developed countries and other Latin American economies (Herranz-Loncán 2014; Leunig 2010: 791), and can be explained by the precarious condition of the transport system in Mexico before the introduction of the railroad.

As mentioned before, economic growth during the late nineteenth and early twentieth centuries was largely led by primary exports (mostly agricultural and mining products).[4] The value of Mexican exports grew at a yearly 7% on average from 1870 to 1925 (Kuntz-Ficker 2010: 324). Haber (2010) considers that the first wave of Mexican industrialization, which took place during the late nineteenth and early twentieth century, was mainly a consequence of export activity, since a large share of export revenues were used to import inputs (such as machinery) necessary for industrialization advance. Foreign investment was also crucial in this period, directly contributing to the extension of the railroad network and the modernization of the mining sector.[5]

Due to the central role of primary exports in economic growth, natural resource endowments were among the main determinants behind the location of economic activity. Thanks to the export boom, some regions could substantially increase their capital-labour ratio, while others stagnated and lagged behind. The result was a process of spatially uneven structural change and, therefore, regional divergence, with a few regions being able to reassign their labour force towards high productivity sectors and grow faster than the rest.

The 1910 Revolution and the subsequent civil war did not cause a general collapse in the economy nor moved it out of the growth trend initiated during the First Globalization. The most important effects of the war were concentrated between 1913 and 1916 and were different across

[3] See Dobado-González and Marrero (2005) for commodity market integration and Kuntz-Ficker and Speckman (2011) for labour market integration.

[4] The main Mexican exports during the first globalization were silver bars, rubber, copper and fibres (Kuntz-Ficker 2017).

[5] The financial system was also modernized in this period thanks to its integration in the international capital markets and the presence in Mexico of the Guggenheim, Rothschild and Mirabaud banks, among others.

regions and sectors, with some areas and activities remaining barely unaffected. At the same time, the transformation of the economy did not stop, with some activities keeping a high dynamism. This happened, for instance, with oil production, which grew at a yearly rate of 36% from 1910 to 1921.

By contrast, the 1929 Great Depression had a great impact on the Mexican economy. The international context forced a move towards an inward-looking strategy of economic growth largely based on domestic industrialization. This shift was widespread in many Latin American economies from the 1930s to the 1980s, during the so-called state-led industrialization or Import Substitution Industrialization (ISI) period. According to Bértola and Ocampo (2012) this model had two main features: industrialization and the increasing participation of the state in the economy and society. Taking Latin American as a whole, these authors identify two phases within the model. The first one, corresponding to the period between the Great Depression and World War II, was a transition phase of slow growth, whereas the second one, from 1945 to the 1980s, was the period in which Latin America achieved its highest growth rates ever.

During the state-led industrialization period, Mexico had the highest economic growth in its history, and the second highest growth rate in Latin America, only after Brazil. From 1950 to 1980, Mexican GDP per capita grew at a yearly rate of 6.6%. The growth rate of labour productivity (3.4%) was also remarkable, not only compared to Latin America but also to the US (2.8%), being quite close to the equivalent figure in the industrialized European economies (3.9%) (Bértola and Ocampo 2012). Economic growth was closely associated to the government's strategy of national development, in which trade policy played a central role. Even though protectionist policies started to be implemented in the late nineteenth century in order to promote industrial activity and import substitution, they were substantially reinforced after World War II.[6] In 1947, ad valorem rates and quantitative controls were introduced as key instruments for the promotion of industrialization. With this policy, the Mexican economy became much more closed than before (Esquivel and Márquez 2007: 344). In addition, from the 1950s onwards, industrial activity was promoted not only by trade policy, but also by fiscal stimuli, such as sub-

[6] World War II was an exceptional period in which industrial growth was not based on protection but on external demand (which explains 79% of manufacturing expansion), especially from the US (Cardenas 2010, p. 515).

sidies and tax exemptions, aimed at encouraging the reinvestment of the available surplus. Thanks to this policy, industrial sectors producing consumption goods could grow at high rates based on domestic demand, and industry accounted for 40% of total GDP growth from 1962 to 1970 (Cardenas 2010: 517).

Mexican growth was strongly affected by the discovery of very rich oil fields in the country in the late 1970s. Public and private investment in the sector boomed, and this accelerated GDP growth, which reached an average yearly rate of 7.8% between 1977 and 1981. Although, due to the specific locations of the fields, the effects of the expansion of the oil sector were unevenly distributed between regions, the government partially made up for this concentration by using oil revenues to finance many public investment projects across the entire country, although many of those projects had very low levels of efficiency.

By the late 1970s, the economy was totally oil dependent. Around 75% of exports and 38% of fiscal revenues came from oil activity (Cardenas 2010: 525). Therefore, the Mexican economy was seriously affected by the drop of oil prices in 1981. The simultaneous increase in international interest rates gave rise to the so-called debt crisis. By 1982, the country had to pay around $14 billion in debt interests, which represented almost half of the total value of Mexican exports at the time. This triggered a drastic change in the model of economic development, as state-led industrialization was rapidly replaced by a much more market-oriented policy complex. The government carried out massive privatization and public budget cuts and liberalized the financial sector, and public investment sank as a consequence of macroeconomic adjustments (Moreno-Brid and Ros 2009).

The last decades of the twentieth century were characterized by trade liberalization and increasing integration in the international economy. In 1986, Mexico joined the General Agreement on Tariffs and Trade (GATT), and by 1994 the North American Free Trade Agreement (NAFTA) came into effect, which had dramatic effects on Mexican international trade. According to INEGI, 76.3% of the total exports of the country went to the US market in 2018. On the other hand, despite the economic stability that was gradually achieved during this period (controlled inflation rates and healthy public finances), economic growth has been, to say the least, disappointing. The average GDP growth rate from 1981 to 2017 was 2.4%, representing the lowest rate in the entire twentieth century (Márquez 2010: 553), and the country fell behind other economies of the region.

As indicated above, Mexican regional imbalances have been a reason of constant concern, at least since World War II. Firstly, the available literature tends to blame the ISI 'miracle' years for the concentration of economic activity in certain regions, especially Mexico City and the surrounding areas. Indeed, by 1980 Mexico City and the State of Mexico represented 36.1% of the country's total GDP (German-Soto 2005). Secondly, recent research has highlighted the impact on regional inequality of the economic opening of the country since the 1990s, which has brought about the agglomeration of industrial activity in the high-income northern states (Hanson 1998; Sánchez-Reaza and Rodríguez-Pose 2002; Chiquiar 2005). However, given the lack of information on the late nineteenth and early twentieth century, so far it has not been possible to know to what extent the current imbalances are really a legacy of the state-led growth model and the NAFTA period, or have more remote origins. Here, thanks to the newly available evidence, we argue that the actual take-off of Mexican regional inequality can be traced back to the early twentieth century, and that Mexico was already a rather unequal country in the 1930s, due to the combination of market integration and regional specialization in the previous decades. In this regard, as is shown below, in the evolution of Mexican regional inequality market forces might have been much more critical than state policies.

2 Data and Sources

The *Instituto Nacional de Estadística y Geografía* (INEGI), the Mexican official national institute of statistics, does not have any estimates of the states' GDP for the years before 1970 (INEGI 1985). For previous years, scholars have commonly used the estimations made by Appendini (1976), either directly or as a basis for new estimations (Esquivel 1999; German-Soto 2005; Ruiz 2006, 2007, 2010). Appendini (1976) estimated regional GDPs for 1900, 1940, 1950 and 1960 using a homogenous methodology (Unikel et al. 1978).[7] The method used by Appendini (1976) consists of

[7]The regional GDPs presented in Appendini (1976) for 1900 and 1960 had been previously published in Appendini et al. (1972). Moreover, the methodology applied in Appendini (1976) for the years 1940 and 1950 is the same that had been previously applied in Appendini et al. (1972) for 1900 and 1960.

disaggregating the national output of each sector across states according to the relative participation of each state in certain output indicators, measured at the state level. More recently, Ruiz (2007) has offered alternative estimations of regional GDP per capita at the state level for the years 1930, 1940, 1950, 1960 and 1965. This author uses the series provided by Appendini (1976) as a basis for his estimates and applies a very similar estimation methodology (Ruiz 2006).[8]

As mentioned before, this chapter aims at estimating regional GDP per capita figures from 1895 to 1930.[9] As in previous studies, we disaggregate, for each sector, national GDP across states based on several indicators. This implies that, for each sector, the sum of all states' GDP is equal to national GDP. As mentioned before, priority is given to direct production sources. Only in those sectors for which there is no direct information, such as industry for the early years and most services for all the period, we apply the indirect methodology developed by Geary and Stark (2002). There is a potential problem to apply the latter method to the Mexican case, associated to the Mexican labour market structure and its insufficient level of integration (Kuntz-Ficker 2010: 327). This could distort the results due to the underestimation of labour productivity in certain regions and sectors, which might introduce biases in the distribution of national GDP among regions. However, this problem seems to affect essentially the primary sector, which is precisely the sector for which direct output information is more abundant and, therefore, where we do not need to apply the Geary and Stark methodology. In the case of the secondary and tertiary sectors, there is abundant evidence of labour market mobility across regions and sectors, responding to economic incentives such as higher relative wages (Kuntz-Ficker and Speckman 2011: 517).

Another estimation problem is related with the changes in the Mexican administrative division. During the period under study (1895–1930), the current State of Quintana Roo (which was only established as an autonomous state in 1974) changed its status several times, being considered

[8] This author has recently published new estimates of industrial GDP at the state level from 1930 to 1965 (Ruiz 2014).

[9] In 1893, the *Dirección General de Estadística* published, for the first time, the *Anuario Estadístico de la República* (Mexican Statistical Yearbook), which involved a substantial quality improvement in national statistics. Moreover, the first national Population Census (*Censo Nacional de Población*) was published, also by the *Dirección General de Estadística*, in 1895. By contrast, the available information for previous years is much scarcer and makes much more difficult to estimate regional GDP figures.

either as a federal territory or as a part of the Yucatán State. To allow comparability of the estimates over time, we had therefore to include Quintana Roo within the State of Yucatán for the entire period, even in those cases in which data is available for Quintana Roo as an independent state. Furthermore, during this period, the Baja California peninsula (nowadays divided into two autonomous states: Baja California North and Baja California South) was a single federal territory. Therefore, we consider, for the period 1895–1930, the peninsula of Baja California as a single unit of analysis.

There are two main series of Mexican aggregate GDP for the period under consideration, which were estimated by Pérez López (1960) and Gutiérrez Requenes (1969) and cover the years 1895–1959 and 1895–1967, respectively. Both estimations have been repeatedly used in other works, and the National Institute of Geography and Statistics (INEGI) reproduced Pérez's estimation in INEGI (2009). This, in turn, was also incorporated to Maddison's (1992) and Barro and Ursúa's (2008) databases. On the other hand, Leopoldo Solís used Gutiérrez Requenes' series in his work *La realidad económica mexicana: retrovisión y perspectivas*, which has been widely used by Mexican and international scholars (Solís 1970). Finally, the Bank of Mexico has also included this series in its database.

As in the case of Appendini et al. (1972), we use Gutiérrez Requenes' (1969) national GDP series for our estimates, for two main reasons. First, Gutiérrez Requenes, unlike Pérez, was explicit on both the methodology that he applied and the sources he used for his aggregate GDP estimation. Secondly, Gutiérrez Requenes' GDP is disaggregated into 13 sectors (agriculture, livestock, forestry, fishing, mining, oil, manufacturing, construction, electric energy, transport, government, commerce and others), while Enrique Pérez's GDP is only disaggregated in seven subsectors (agriculture, livestock, mining, oil, manufacturing, transport and other activities). Both reasons are important for this research since, whereas knowing the data and the method used by Gutiérrez Requenes to reconstruct the national GDP allows a more consistent estimation of regional figures, its higher disaggregation also allows a more precise distribution of national output. Nevertheless, it is important to stress that both series present very similar trends and fluctuations over the period analysed.

As mentioned before, we distribute Gutiérrez Requenes' national output figures (in pesos of 1950) for each sector among states following different procedures.[10] Firstly, we distribute sectoral production directly, on the basis of output indicators, in the cases of the primary sector (which includes agriculture, livestock, forestry, fishing, mining and oil) and commerce. By contrast, estimates for the secondary sector (i.e. manufacturing—except for 1930-, construction and electric energy) and services, with the exception of commerce (i.e. Transport, Government and Others), are obtained by applying the Geary and Stark's (2002) method.

For those sectors in which the estimates are based on production values, depending on the availability of data we use information in current or in constant prices to obtain regional output shares. Thus, while for agriculture and livestock we use data in current prices for the entire period, for mining and forestry (apart from 1930) information is available in constant prices (gold *pesos*). The estimates for the commerce sector are also based on data in constant prices (with the exceptions of 1921 and 1930). When current prices are used, inflation differentials across states might have affected the relative participation of each state in national output. Unfortunately, there are no price indices available at the state level for the entire period to account for this problem. This potential distortion does not affect estimates based on data in constant (national) prices, or in the case of the oil sector, for which we use units of production (barrels produced). Finally, it is also absent from those sectors in which the estimates are based on the Geary and Stark's methodology (i.e. the secondary sector, with the exception of manufacturing in 1930, and the services sector, with the exception of commerce), although in these cases the reliability of the estimates depends on the assumption that differences in wage levels across states reflect productivity differentials. Thus, although it seems unlikely that inflation differentials across states may change the global picture, for some sectors the estimates may include small biases associated to our inability to account for those differences.[11]

[10] It is not clear if Gutiérrez Requenes' (1969) national output figures were estimated using a constant structure of prices, taken from one benchmark year for all different sectors, or whether the structure of prices used varied over time.

[11] To overcome the bias produced by the concentration of the oil sector, we have estimated regional GDP figures without this sector for 1950 onwards.

3 Regional Growth in Mexico

Table 9.2 presents estimates of GDP per capita of the Mexican regions between 1895 and 2010, expressed as a ratio of the national average of each year, combining our figures until 1930, German-Soto (2005) for 1940–1990 and INEGI (2019) for the most recent years. Those figures show that Mexican regional inequality was very high since the take-off of modern economic growth in the late nineteenth century. Regional disparities appear even clearer when the states are grouped in macro-regions, showing the long-term differences between the north and the south of the country. Only a few states scape from this picture of persistence, showing wide fluctuations over time in their relative levels of GDP per capita. This is the case, for instance, of Aguascalientes' GDP per capita, which amounted to 106% of the national average in 1895, increased up to 265% in 1900, and decreased again to 88% in 1930. Although such processes will be analysed and explained in detail in further research, quick structural change in certain regions—such as the mining production areas—and some external shocks (such as international demand fluctuations, or movements in the prices of some exportable agrarian and mining commodities)—could largely explain those cases of high instability.

Moving to the sector level, while the centre region was characterized by sustained deindustrialization, the north and the capital became more industrialized over time. Those changes in the spatial distribution of industry started at least in the 1910s, which would partially contradict the widespread idea that the process of concentration of industry in Mexico City started with the ISI policies. Our estimates suggest instead that this process of manufacturing concentration began well before the state-led industrialization period (although it substantially accelerated after 1930).

The standard deviation of regional GDP per capita figures (with and without oil production), which can be taken as an indicator of σ-divergence, has followed a 'W' trend in the long term. After 15 years of very mild decrease in regional inequality, differences across regions widened rapidly between 1910 and 1940. The reasons for that inequality increase, which was especially intense during the 1920s, can be understood by looking at the income per capita estimates.

Between 1910 and 1930, the North region and Mexico City had an extraordinarily good performance relative to the national average. Mexico City started with a GDP per capita 2.46 times as large as the national one in 1910 and increased up to 2.83 in 1930. In the North region, the

Table 9.2 Regional GDP per capita in Mexico, 1895–2010 (Mexico = 1)

	1895	*1900*	*1910*	*1921*	*1930*	*1930*[a]	*1950*	*1950*[a]	*1980*	*2010*	*2010*[a]
Mexico City	2.68	2.61	2.46	2.53	2.71	*2.83*	*2.63*	*2.71*	*1.91*	*2.27*	*2.39*
North	*1.94*	*1.71*	*1.53*	*1.45*	*2.21*	*2.27*	*1.59*	*1.64*	*1.19*	*1.22*	*1.27*
Baja C. North*	3.63	3.11	2.28	2.62	4.40	4.54	2.87	2.96	1.28	1.03	1.08
Baja C. South	n.d.	n.d.	n.d.	n.d.	n.d.	n.d.	1.18	1.22	1.27	1.11	1.16
Chihuahua	1.93	1.29	1.39	1.02	1.82	1.89	1.41	1.45	0.94	1.04	1.09
Coahuila	1.64	1.46	1.40	1.05	1.72	1.78	1.28	1.33	1.15	1.31	1.37
Nuevo León	1.25	1.60	1.28	1.28	1.66	1.71	1.57	1.62	1.58	1.90	1.97
Sonora	2.11	1.79	1.93	1.26	1.77	1.82	1.56	1.61	1.08	1.05	1.11
Tamaulipas	1.06	1.03	0.91	1.50	1.90	1.85	1.28	1.31	1.03	1.12	1.08
Pacific-North	*1.3*	*1.22*	*1.19*	*0.78*	*0.77*	*0.79*	*0.81*	*0.84*	*0.85*	*0.88*	*0.93*
Colima	1.02	0.91	1.52	0.89	0.80	0.82	0.83	0.85	0.91	1.01	1.06
Jalisco	0.95	0.98	0.71	0.61	0.55	0.57	0.71	0.74	1.01	1.01	1.06
Nayarit	1.38	1.51	1.42	0.84	0.78	0.8	0.74	0.77	0.71	0.65	0.69
Sinaloa	1.85	1.46	1.11	0.79	0.93	0.96	0.95	0.98	0.76	0.85	0.90
Centre-North	*1.13*	*1.25*	*1.23*	*0.83*	*0.89*	*0.91*	*0.62*	*0.64*	*0.64*	*0.85*	*0.89*
Aguascalientes	1.17	2.13	2.62	1.22	0.88	0.91	0.46	0.48	0.79	1.10	1.16
Durango	1.78	1.32	0.86	0.69	0.97	1.00	0.75	0.78	0.72	0.86	0.90
San Luis Potosí	0.65	0.68	0.71	0.73	0.84	0.83	0.70	0.71	0.58	0.79	0.83
Zacatecas	0.92	0.86	0.71	0.67	0.85	0.88	0.55	0.57	0.47	0.63	0.66
Gulf of Mexico	*1.04*	*1.14*	*1.31*	*1.55*	*1.03*	*0.97*	*1.10*	*1.06*	*1.18*	*1.72*	*0.96*
Campeche	1.41	0.98	1.11	1.21	0.88	0.91	0.84	0.87	0.76	4.39	1.17
Tabasco	0.91	0.83	0.62	0.46	0.68	0.70	0.57	0.59	2.51	1.41	0.71
Quintana Roo	n.d.	n.d.	n.d.	n.d.	n.d.	n.d.	1.93	1.99	1.20	1.28	1.35
Veracruz	0.71	0.97	1.03	2.66	1.26	0.91	1.28	0.97	0.72	0.68	0.67
Yucatán	1.11	1.77	2.47	1.85	1.30	1.34	0.87	0.90	0.72	0.84	0.88
Centre	*0.87*	*0.86*	*0.82*	*0.62*	*0.65*	*0.68*	*0.5*	*0.52*	*0.73*	*0.76*	*0.8*
Guanajuato	0.78	0.82	0.83	0.57	0.62	0.65	0.46	0.48	0.65	0.84	0.88
Hidalgo	0.78	0.79	0.68	0.68	0.79	0.83	0.43	0.45	0.66	0.61	0.64
Morelos	1.27	1.28	1.04	0.54	0.72	0.74	0.79	0.81	0.77	0.77	0.81
Puebla	0.66	0.87	0.73	0.68	0.70	0.72	0.53	0.55	0.65	0.69	0.73
Querétaro	0.78	0.76	0.76	0.66	0.51	0.53	0.41	0.43	0.86	1.14	1.20
State of Mexico	0.71	0.64	0.9	0.6	0.54	0.56	0.51	0.53	0.97	0.72	0.76
Tlaxcala	1.13	0.84	0.79	0.61	0.68	0.70	0.37	0.38	0.55	0.53	0.55
South	*0.75*	*0.60*	*0.70*	*0.42*	*0.40*	*0.41*	*0.40*	*0.41*	*0.59*	*0.51*	*0.53*
Chiapas	0.85	0.74	0.86	0.54	0.50	0.52	0.40	0.42	0.87	0.44	0.44
Guerrero	0.82	0.41	0.56	0.26	0.28	0.29	0.40	0.41	0.53	0.52	0.55
Michoacán	0.83	0.77	0.87	0.56	0.49	0.51	0.42	0.44	0.55	0.63	0.66
Oaxaca	0.48	0.46	0.51	0.32	0.31	0.32	0.36	0.37	0.4	0.45	0.48

Sources: Aguilar-Retureta (2015), German-Soto (2005) and INEGI (2019)

[a]Excluding oil * Baja C. North and Baja C. South until 1930

equivalent figures were 1.53 and 2.27. At the same time, other regions lost positions relative to the national average. This was the period in which the North/South income division was consolidated, since the South region lagged behind and would never significantly converge again with the national average (see Map 9.1).

From the 1940s onwards (see Map 9.1), coinciding with the consolidation of the ISI model, an accelerated process of regional income convergence took place, which lasted until the economic liberalization of the 1980s. From then on, regional divergence has been a constant—except for the 2000s. This recent divergence can be explained because, while the poorest states (mainly the south) have remained far below the national average income, the north-border region has kept its income advantage and some particular states, such as Guanajuato (centre-north region), Querétaro (centre region) and Quintana Roo (Gulf of Mexico region), have improved their performance (Rodríguez-Oreggia 2005). In addition, Mexico City's GDP per capita has also experienced an upswing trend during this period (from 2.00 to 2.54 times the national average between 1980 and 2000).

The oil sector did not have any significant impact on regional disparities before the 1970s first oil boom. As Fig. 9.1 shows, when oil production is considered, the reversal of the convergence process begins around 1970, only a few years before the breakpoint of the series without oil. The highest impact of the oil industry took place during the oil production boom of the last decade of the analysis (2000–2010). As a consequence, the inequality trend is totally different between both series during this decade. If oil production is included, the series shows a strong process of regional divergence (up to a level close to that of 1950). However, when oil is excluded, this was a period of slight income convergence among states. From now on, the analysis will be limited to the series without oil.[12]

These results are consistent with interpretations suggested in previous studies, with the only difference that, due to the scarcity of data, previous research had completely overlooked the earliest regional income disparity upswing (1910–1940). Rather, most analyses have so far focused either on

[12] The literature on Mexican regional disparities has often warned against the bias associated to oil production. See, for instance, Esquivel (1999), Sánchez-Reaza and Rodríguez-Pose (2002) or Aroca et al. (2005). Due to its extremely high spatial concentration, the oil industry production could cause a distorted picture of some regions' income per capita, given that those regions may not really benefit from oil revenues.

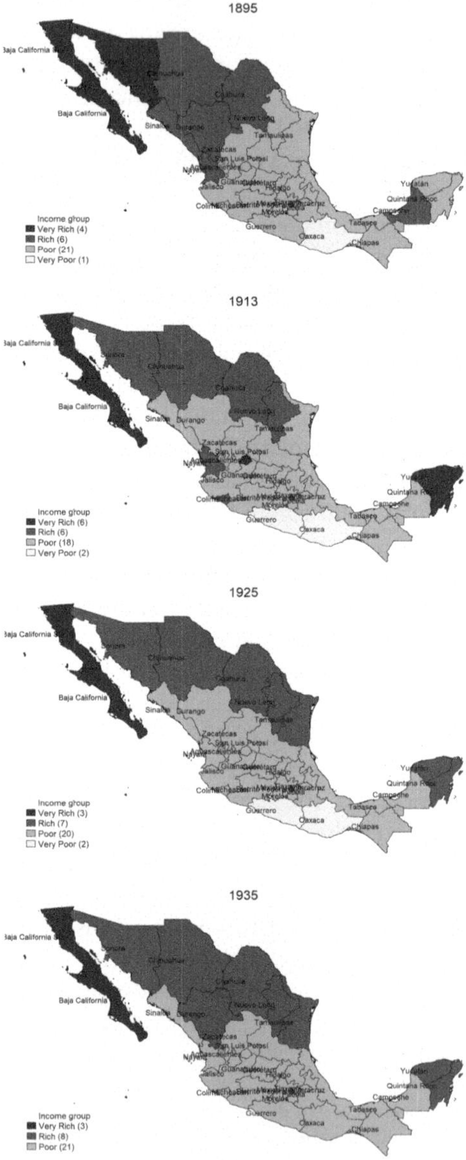

Map 9.1 Regional GDP per capita of the Mexican states, 1895–2010. (Source: Main text)

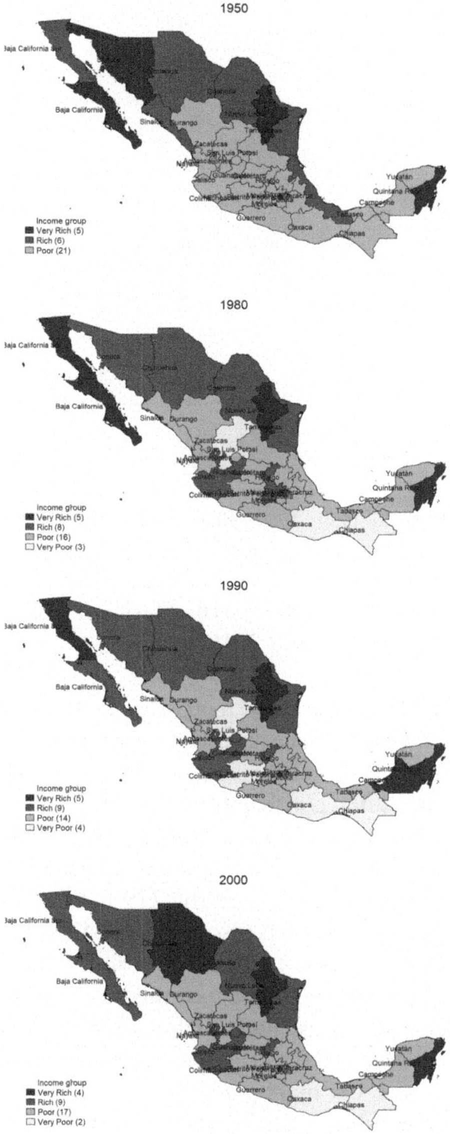

Map 9.1 (continued)

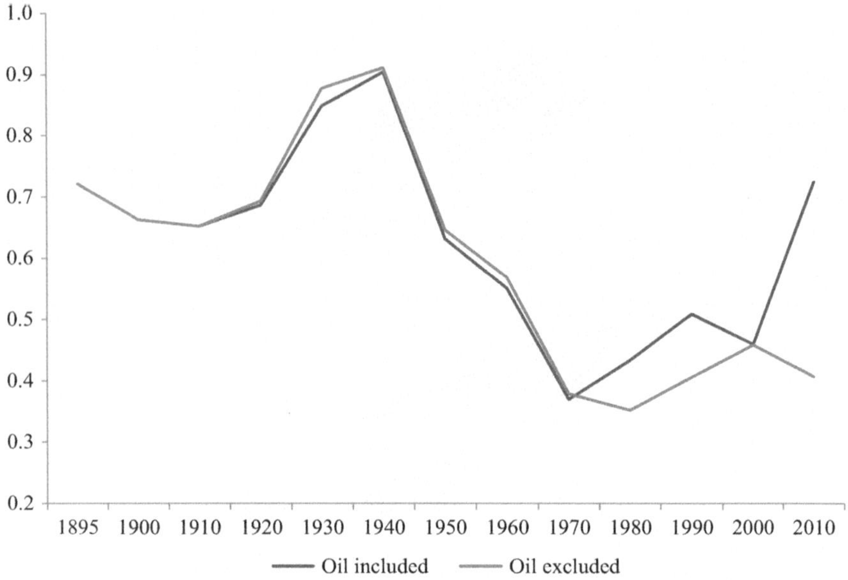

Fig. 9.1 Standard Deviation, 1895–2010. Mexico=1. (Source: German-Soto 2005; Aguilar-Retureta 2015; INEGI 2019)

the convergence period under way from the 1940s onwards or on the inequality increase that took place after the economic liberalization, which started in the 1980s. Sánchez-Reaza and Rodríguez-Pose (2002), for instance, observe that, after controlling for possible biases related to the inclusion of oil-producing and *maquiladora*-based states, the economic openness period that started in 1985 appears to have led to a divergence process, in which the states closest to the US market have obtained the highest benefits. This hypothesis is also supported by other authors, such as Hanson (1998) or Chiquiar (2005), who focus on the post-NAFTA period. They highlight that the winners of the divergence process that was triggered by liberalization were the northern states, which had a higher initial endowment of human and physical capital, and that could benefit from its proximity to the US market.

While σ-convergence shows the evolution of the dispersion of regional income, β-convergence indicates if low-income regions have grown faster over time. Figure 9.2 confirms the existence of intense β-convergence for Mexico between 1895 and 2010.

Nevertheless, if we focus our analysis on what happened between 1895 and 1950 (see Fig. 9.3), β-convergence is much weaker due to the low rates of economic growth of a high number of Mexican states.

By contrast, strong convergence is observed when we consider the period 1950–2010, both including and excluding the oil sector in the analysis (see Fig. 9.4).

Figure 9.5 presents several income inequality measures as an alternative to the standard convergence analysis, such as the Williamson Index, the Gini coefficient, the Theil index and the Coefficient of Variation. The first one is especially useful, since it considers the effect of each state's population on regional income disparities by weighting deviations with population shares. Thus, less-populated regions have a minor impact on the index and vice versa.[13] Although the general trend is still the same as in the standard deviation (see Fig. 9.1), this index would suggest a slight interruption of the convergence process during the 1950s. This may be explained for two main reasons. The first one is the comparatively good performance of Mexico City, by far the most populated region of the country (it concentrated 11.8% and 14.0% of national population in 1950 and 1960, respectively), and whose GDP per capita, relative to the national average, increased from 2.71 in 1950 to 2.76 in 1960. The second reason is the low population density of some of the rich states that were performing worse than the national average, such as Baja California North (with 0.8% and 1.4% of the national population in 1950 and 1960, respectively), Baja California South (0.2% in both years), and Quintana Roo (with 0.10% and 0.14% of the national population in 1950 and 1960, respectively). These states went from having a relative GDP per capita of 2.96, 1.22 and 1.99 in 1950 to 1.89, 0.96 and 0.50 in 1960, respectively. By contrast, during the 1960s Mexico City's GDP per capita converged with the

[13] The Williamson index, proposed in Williamson (1965), is calculated as follows:

$$WI = \sqrt{\sum_{i=1}^{n}\left(\frac{y_i}{y_m}-1\right)^2 \frac{p_i}{p_m}},$$

where y is income per capita, p is population, and i and m refer to the i-region and the national total, respectively.

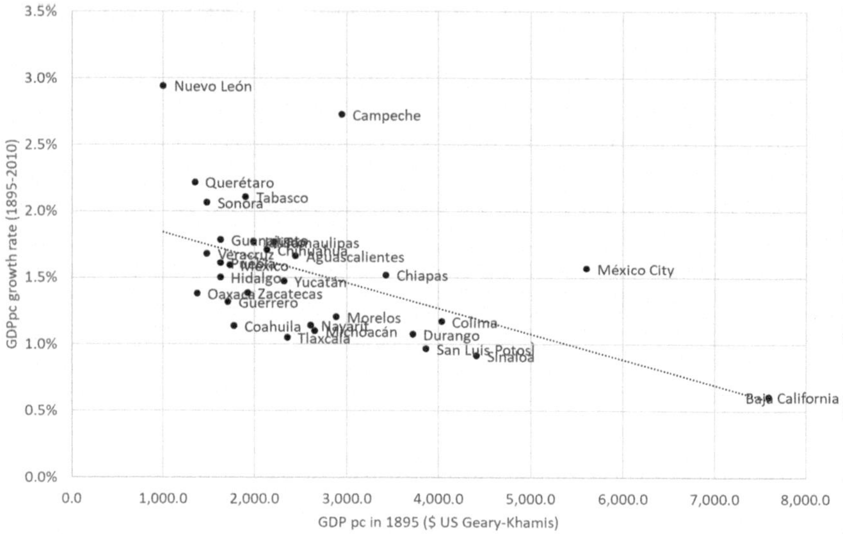

Fig. 9.2 Beta convergence, regional GDP per capita of the Mexican states (1895–2010). (Sources: Aguilar-Retureta 2015; German-Soto 2005; INEGI 2019)

national average (from 2.76 in 1960 to 1.95 in 1970), as did other highly populated rich states, such as Nuevo León, which had a relative GDP per capita of 2.13 in 1960 and 1.69 in 1970.

Both the Gini coefficient and the Theil index increase with income inequality. Once again, a W-shape pattern emerges in the long run. In fact, the trend shown by both indices is very similar, and follows closely the evolution of the Williamson Index. The years 1910–1940 remain as the period of fastest regional income divergence, and the maximum levels of inequality were reached in 1940. The levels of the Gini and Theil indices in Mexico are relatively high in comparison with those estimated for the European periphery. For instance, the maximum value of the Gini index in Italy, Spain and Portugal in the long term was around 0.21, that is, half of the maximum Mexican value. The Theil index offers similar results: while in the Mexican case the maximum value was close to 0.25, the Spanish and Portuguese maximum values were 0.17 and 0.04 respectively (Badia-Miró

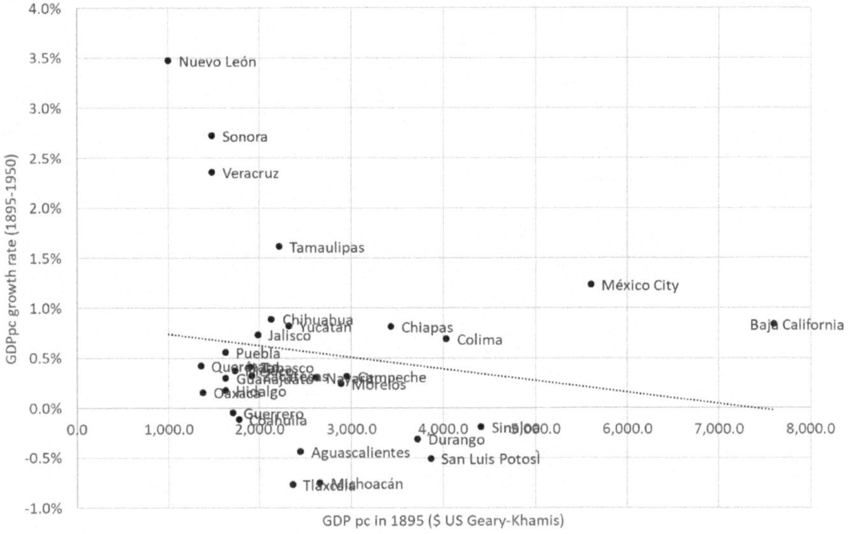

Fig. 9.3 Beta convergence, regional GDP per capita of the Mexican states (1895–1950). (Sources: Aguilar-Retureta 2015; German-Soto 2005; INEGI 2019)

et al. 2012; Rosés et al. 2010).[14] Finally, the trend followed by the Coefficient of Variation (CV) is also the same as in the other indicators. An international comparison of CV levels reinforces the idea that Mexico had relatively high levels of regional income inequality. According to Crafts (2005), Britain's CV values, which have been regularly used as a reference for the core economies, ranged between 0.10 and 0.25 in the long term (1871–2001). Meanwhile, in Mexico, CV values ranged from 0.39 to 0.83.

In order to obtain a more complete picture of the distribution of activity across Mexican regions, Table 9.3 shows the evolution of the economic size of each region during our period of analysis. Figures in the table confirm the concentration of economic activity in the traditional industrial poles (Mexico City and Veracruz), especially during the ISI period, as well as a process of gradual diffusion from Mexico City to its neighbouring

[14] This comparison may be affected by differences in the number and scale of the spatial units among countries. However, the number of Mexican states (36) lies in between the number of Spanish provinces (50) and the number of Portuguese districts (18) and Italian regions (19).

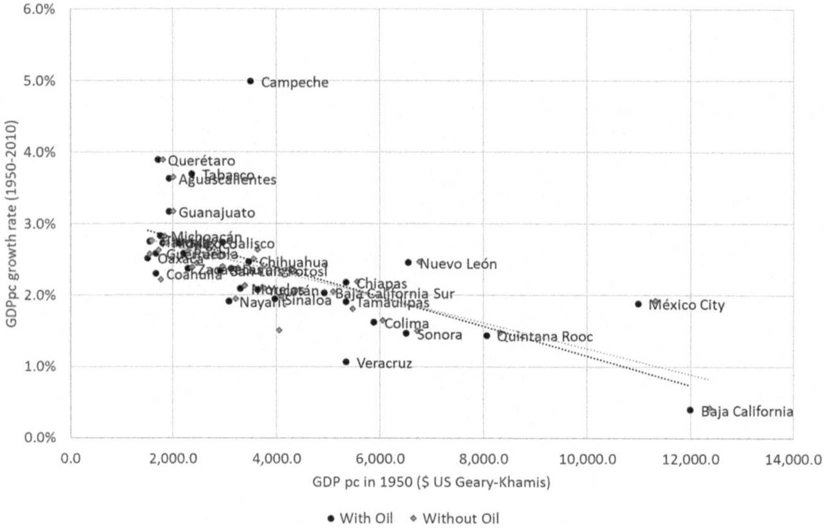

Fig. 9.4 Beta convergence, regional GDP per capita of the Mexican states (1950–2010). (Sources: Aguilar-Retureta 2015; German-Soto 2005; INEGI 2019)

states (Mexico) since the mid-twentieth century. On the other hand, we do not observe significant changes in the economic share of the northern regions in the long run, except for Nuevo León, which increased its share from 1950 to 2010.[15]

A synthetic instrument to analyse the evolution of size disparities across regions in the long run is provided by the Herfindahl-Hirschman Index (HHI) of Mexican regional incomes, which can be complemented with the share of Mexico City within the national total GDP (Fig. 9.6). The HHI offers an alternative approach to regional income disparities, since it does not consider each state's relative GDP per capita, but the share of each state within national GDP, measuring therefore the level of spatial concentration of national income. The HHI is defined as:

[15] Sonora, Chihuahua, Coahuila and Tamaulipas represent around 11% in 1930 and 10% in 2010 of the total Mexican output.

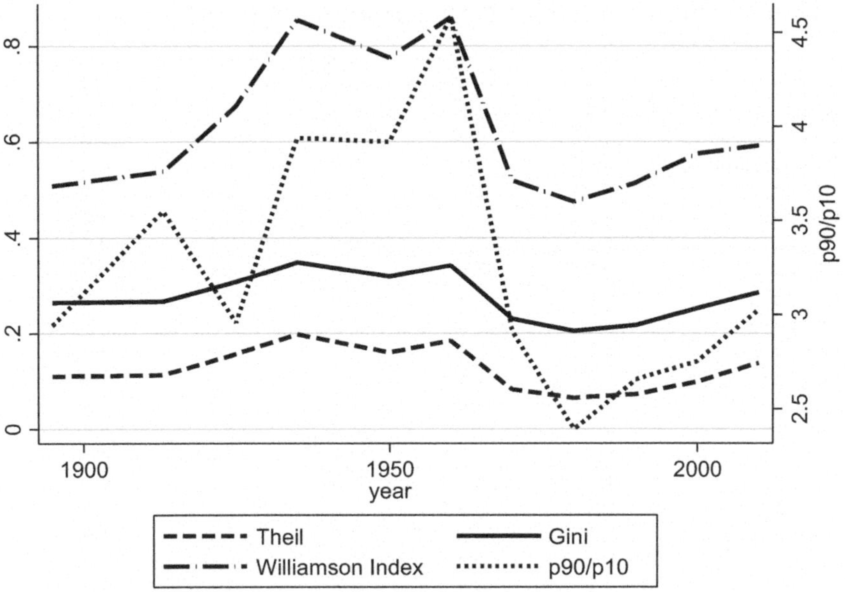

Fig. 9.5 Inequality indices: Theil, Gini, Williamson and coefficient of variation (1895–2010). (Sources: Aguilar-Retureta 2015; German-Soto 2005; INEGI 2019)

$$H_j^C = \sum_{i=1}^{N} \left(\frac{X_{ij}}{\sum_{i=1}^{n} X_{ij}} \right)^2 ,$$

where X_{ij} is GDP in region i and sector j.

This index ranges from 1 (when all activity is concentrated in one region) to 1/n (when the activity is equally distributed among the n regions of a country). In Mexico, the index follows an inverted-U pattern, in which the divergence process of the period 1980–2010 is missing. In addition, the initial process of increasing concentration lasts until the 1960s, and not until the 1940s. These differences between the evolution of concentration of economic activity and the trends in income inequality respond to one fact: the economic importance of Mexico City, the biggest

Table 9.3 Share of regional GDP, Mexican states (1895–2010)

	1895 (%)	*1930 (%)*	*1950 (%)*	*1980 (%)*	*2010 (%)*
Aguascalientes	0.9	0.7	0.3	0.6	1.0
Baja California	1.3	2.6	2.6*	2.3*	2.6*
Baja California Sur	n.d.	n.d.	0.3	0.4	0.5
Campeche	0.9	0.5	0.4	0.5	3.1
Coahuila	3.5	1.3	1.1	2.0	1.0
Colima	0.5	0.7	0.6	0.5	0.6
Chiapas	2.2	5.6	4.6	3.6	5.2
Chihuahua	4.6	2.4	2.8	2.7	3.1
Durango	4.8	2.4	1.9	1.3	1.3
Guanajuato	6.0	3.3	2.4	2.9	3.9
Guerrero	2.8	1.1	1.4	1.7	1.6
Hidalgo	3.4	2.6	1.4	1.5	1.4
Jalisco	7.9	4.3	4.9	6.6	6.4
México	4.8	4.2	2.8	11.0	9.5
Mexico City	10.5	20.6	31.6	25.2	19.7
Michoacán	5.6	3.2	2.4	2.4	2.5
Morelos	1.5	0.6	0.8	1.1	1.2
Nayarit	1.5	0.8	0.8	0.8	0.6
Nuevo León	3.0	4.3	4.6	5.9	7.3
Oaxaca	3.3	2.1	2.0	1.4	1.6
Puebla	4.9	5.0	3.4	3.3	3.5
Querétaro	1.3	0.7	0.5	1.0	1.6
Quintana Roo	n.d.	n.d.	0.2	0.4	1.1
San Luis Potosí	2.7	3.0	2.4	1.5	1.8
Sinaloa	4.0	2.3	2.4	2.1	2.2
Sonora	3.4	3.5	3.1	2.4	2.3
Tabasco	1.0	0.9	0.8	4.0	2.7
Tamaulipas	1.7	4.0	3.6	3.0	3.1
Tlaxcala	1.4	0.9	0.4	0.5	0.5
Veracruz	5.0	10.7	10.3	5.8	4.7
Yucatán	2.5	3.2	1.8	1.1	1.4
Zacatecas	3.1	2.4	1.4	0.8	0.9

Sources: Aguilar-Retureta (2015), German-Soto (2005) and INEGI (2019) *Only Baja California North

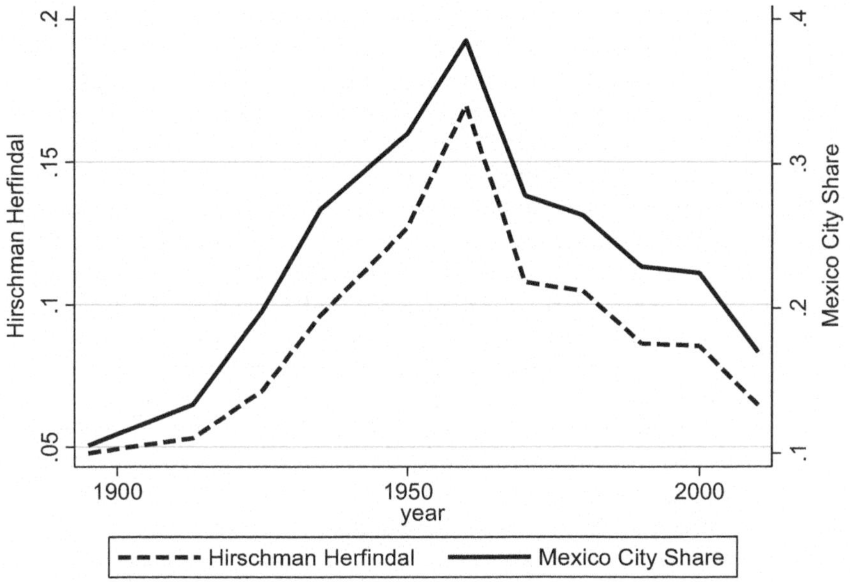

Fig. 9.6 Herfindahl-Hirschman Index (1895–2010) and share of Mexico City within national GDP. (Sources: Aguilar-Retureta 2015; German-Soto 2005; INEGI 2019)

economic centre of the country. As Fig. 9.6 shows, there is a close correlation between the importance of the capital and the HHI.[16]

Previous literature has insisted that the ISI model (1930–1980) boosted the concentration of economic activity in Mexico City. However, Fig. 9.6 shows that this process started earlier, in the 1910s, during the export-led growth period. Concentration in the capital reached its maximum in 1960, and the sudden decrease of the HHI and Mexico City's GDP share during the 1960s can be partially explained by the behaviour of the State of Mexico, which was by then becoming, to a large extent, an extension of Mexico City. So, while Mexico City lost 10.7 percentage points of participation in national GDP from 1960 to 1970, the State of Mexico won 4.8 points in the same period.

[16]This is rather usual in countries in which a single economic centre concentrates a large part of total GDP. See, for instance, the case of Chile and its capital, Santiago (Badia-Miró 2015).

This pattern changed from 1980s onwards, when both Mexico City's and the State of Mexico's GDP shares fell. From 1980 to 2010, they lost 7.6 and 1.2 percentage points of participation in national GDP, respectively. The 'winners' in this period, as mentioned before, have been those states that could benefit most from the economic openness policy. The main ones were the north border states, led by Nuevo León, which won 2 percentage points of national GDP since 1980, and also some central and southern states, such as Guanajuato, Querétaro and Quintana Roo, which won 1.2, 0.9 and 1.2 percentage points of participation in national GDP from 1980 to 2010. In Guanajuato and Querétaro, large foreign investment has contributed to the development of the capital-intensive industrial sector, whereas the Quintana Roo case has benefited from the development of tourism.

Summing up the evidence in Table 9.3 and Fig. 9.6, it is interesting to observe that the increasing concentration of economic activity in Mexico City was accompanied, at least since 1940, by a regional convergence process, which brought the southern regions close to Mexico City in terms of average productivity. There are two potential explanations for convergence during this period. Firstly, the concentration of industry in Mexico City boosted the agglomeration in the capital of other activities with low productivity levels, mainly within the service sector. Secondly, productivity in the primary sector of the southern regions increased substantially due to large migration flows to the rest of the country. By contrast, the dispersion of industrial activity in the most recent decades has not been accompanied by income convergence, as in most industrialized economies, but by a slight divergence process, especially during the 1990s. This has been associated to the movement of industry towards regions with relatively high-income per capita levels and close to the US border, thanks to a large extent to the openness of that market to the Mexican products, and also to a reduction in the concentration of economic activity around Mexico City.

4 Conclusions

This chapter aimed at contributing to the international literature on the causes of the long-term evolution of regional inequality by analysing the case of Mexico from 1895 to 2010. Even though previous research on Mexican regional disparities is very abundant, this is the first analysis to cover the period from the late nineteenth century to the present. This has allowed us to present the current Mexican regional disparities, not only as the outcome of recent institutional and economic changes (as most recent research) but as a result of a long-term historical process.

The study of the Mexican case confirms that regional inequality in low- and middle-income economies may have different trends and determinants from those of the industrialized economies. In the latter, regional inequality has often followed an inverted-U trend in the long term, mainly associated to changes in the location of the industrial activity and agglomeration effects. By contrast, in the Mexican case, as in other developing countries, other determinants, such as comparative advantages associated to natural resource location, changes in international markets, the spatial distribution of FDI and differences across regions in economic structure, agrarian productivity and institutional change, may have also played a central role. This complexity makes it difficult to explain the evolution of regional inequality in peripheral economies based on a single theoretical framework. The results of this chapter reinforce the importance of combining different theoretical approaches, and the centrality of history in the explanation of the current levels of regional inequality.

From a comparative point of view, Mexican regional inequality has always been very high. It has followed a W-form in the long term, which largely reflects the alternation of different development models in the country since the late nineteenth century. Thus, between 1910 and 1940, or in the most recent period of economic openness (from the 1980s to the present), regional inequality has tended to increase. Divergence among Mexican regions was especially intense during the last period of the First Globalization (the 1920s). It was also in this period when the regional structure that has characterized the Mexican economy during the twentieth century was established, with a strong concentration of activity in Mexico City and a clear division between the rich North and the poor South. However, the period from 1940 to 1980 was characterized by regional convergence, although it was accompanied by persistence in the geographical concentration of industry.

A deeper analysis has provided several interesting results. Firstly, the early divergence among the Mexican regions (1910–1940) was driven by the richest states becoming richer and, correspondingly, by the poorest regions becoming relatively poorer. The following period of regional convergence (1940–1980) was characterized, on the contrary, by the fall of the richest states' relative income levels towards the national average. The latest period of divergence (1980–2010) has been led by some of the northern and central states, and specially Mexico City, moving far away from the national average. Moreover, we have found a very low rank mobility among the states throughout the entire period, with the richest and poorest regions remaining mostly the same.

The main determinants of regional inequality changes have been different in each period. During the early twentieth century, a spatially uneven process of structural change explains the increase in regional inequality. Those regions that could benefit from the international integration of the country (mainly Mexico City and the northern states) achieved faster rates of structural change, higher capital/labour ratios, and, therefore, higher levels of labour productivity and income per capita. By contrast, regional convergence during the state-led industrialization period was led by an intense process of factor mobility (and, particularly, labour flows) across the Mexican states and the concentration of economic activity around the main market (Mexico City) pushed by agglomeration economies in industry. Finally, since the mid-1980s divergence has been mainly driven by labour productivity differentials within each sector. As in the early twentieth century, inequality increase was associated to differences in the states' ability to take advantage of the international integration of the country. In this period, the uneven spatial distribution of FDI (once again, largely concentrated in Mexico City and the northern states), and the spatial concentration of high value-added services in Mexico City, appear to be the main determinants behind the regional divergence.

References

Aguilar-Retureta, J. (2015). The GDP per capita of the Mexican regions (1895–1930): new estimates. *Revista de Historia Económica—Journal of Iberian and Latin American Economic History*, 33 (3), 387–423.

———. (2016a). Regional Income Distribution in Mexico: New Long-Term Evidence, 1895–2010. *Economic History of Developing Regions*, 31 (2–3), 225–252.

———. (2016b). *Regional income inequality in Mexico, 1895–2010.* PhD Dissertation, Universitat de Barcelona.

Appendini, K. A. (1976). *Producto Interno Bruto por entidades federativas 1900, 1940, 1950 y 1960.* México DF, México: Mimeo.

Appendini, K. A., Murayama, D. and Domínguez, R. (1972). Desarrollo desigual en México, 1900–1960. *Demografía y Economía*, 16, 1–40.

Aroca, P., Bosch, M. and Maloney, W. F. (2005). Spatial Dimensions of Trade Liberalization and Economic Convergence: Mexico 1985–2002. *The World Bank Economic Review*, 19 (3), 345–378.

Badia-Miró, M. (2015). The evolution of the location of economic activity in Chile in the long run: a paradox of extreme concentration in absence of agglomeration economies. *Estudios de Economía*, 42 (2), 143–167.

Badia-Miró, M., Guilera, J. and Lains, P. (2012). Regional Incomes in Portugal: Industrialisation, Integration and Inequality, 1890–1980. *Revista de Historia Económica*, 30 (2), 225–244.

Barro, R. J. and Ursúa, J. (2008). Macroeconomic crises since 1870. *National Bureau of Economic Research Working Paper Series.*

Bértola, L. and Ocampo, J. A. (2012). *The Economic Development of Latin America since Independence.* Oxford, United Kingdom: Oxford University Press.

Cardenas, E. (2010). La economía Mexicana en el dilatado siglo XIX, 1929–2009. In S. Kuntz-Ficker (Ed.), *Historia Económica General de México: de la Colonia a nuestros días.* 503–548. México DF, México: El Colegio de México.

Chiquiar, D. (2005). Why Mexico's regional income convergence broke down. *Journal of Development Economics*, 77 (1), 257–275.

Coatsworth, J. H. (1979). Indispensable Railroads in a Backward Economy: The Case of Mexico. *The Journal of Economic History*, 39 (4), 939–960.

Crafts, N. F. R. (2005). Regional GDP in Britain, 1871–1911: Some estimates. *Scottish Journal of Political Economy*, *52* (1), 54–64.

Dobado-González, R. and Marrero, G. A. (2005). Corn Market Integration in Porfirian Mexico. *The Journal of Economic History*, 65 (1), 103–128.

ECLAC. (2014). *Cambio estructural para la igualdad. Una visión integrada del desarrollo.* Santiago de Chile, Chile: CEPAL/ECLAC. Naciones Unidas.

Esquivel, G. (1999). Convergencia regional en México, 1940–1995. *Trimestre Economico*, 66 (264), 725–761.

Esquivel, G. and Márquez, G. (2007). Some Economic Effects of Closing the Economy: The Mexican Experience in the Mid-Twentieth Century. In S. Edwards, G. Esquivel and G. Márquez (Eds.), *The Decline of Latin American Economies: Growth, Institutions, and Crises.* (pp. 333–361). Chicago, Illinois: University of Chicago Press.

Geary, F. and Stark, T. (2002). Examining Ireland's Post-Famine Economic Growth Performance. *The Economic Journal*, 112 (482), 919–935.

German-Soto, V. (2005). Generación del producto interno bruto Mexicano for entidad federativa, 1940–1992. *Trimestre Economico*, 72 (287), 617–653.

Gutiérrez Requenes, M. (1969). *Producto Interno Bruto y Series Básicas 1895–1967.* México DF, México: Banco de México.

Haber, Stephen., Razo, Armando., and Maurer, Noel. (2003). *Political Instability, Credible Commitments, and Economic Growth in Mexico, 1876–1929.* Cambridge, USA: Cambridge University Press.

Hanson, Gordon H. (1998). Regional adjustment to trade liberalization. *Regional Science and Urban Economics*, 28 (4), 419–444.

Haber, Stephen H. (2010). Mercado Interno, Industrialización y Banca, 1890–1929. In S. Kuntz-Ficker (Ed.), *Historia Económica General de México: de la Colonia a nuestros días.* 411–436. México DF, México: El Colegio de México.

Herranz-Loncán, A. (2014). Transport technology and economic expansion: the growth contribution of railways in Latin America before 1914. *Revista de Historia Económica*, 32, 13–45.

INEGI. (1985). *Estadísticas Históricas de México* (Vol. 1). México DF, México: Instituto Nacional de Estadística, Geografía e Informática.

———. (2009). *Estadísticas Históricas de México.* México DF, México: Instituto nacional de estadística y geografía.

———. (2019). PIB por Entidad Federativa (PIBE). Base 2013.

Kuntz-Ficker, S. (2010). De las Reformas Liberales a la Gran Depresión, 1856–1929. In S. Kuntz-Ficker (Ed.), *Historia Económica General de México: de la Colonia a nuestros días.* 305–352, México DF, México: El Colegio de México.

———. (2017). Mexico in the Export Era (1870s–1929): Export Boom, Economic Modernization, and Industrialization. In S. Kuntz-Ficker (Ed.), *The First Export Era Revisited. Reassessing its Contribution to Latin American Economies.* 235–278, Cham, Switzerland: Palgrave Macmillan.

Kuntz-Ficker, S. and Speckman, E. (2011). El Porfiriato. In *Nueva Historia General de México* 487–536, México DF, México: El Colegio de México.

Leunig, T. (2010). Social Savings. *Journal of Economic Surveys*, *24* (5), 775–800.

Maddison, A. (1992). *Brazil and Mexico—The political economy of poverty, equity, and growth.* (Vol. 1). The World Bank.

Márquez, G. (2010). Evolución y estructura del PIB, 1921–2010. In S. Kuntz-Ficker (Ed.), *Historia Económica General de México: de la Colonia a nuestros días.* 549–572, México DF, México: El Colegio de México.

Moreno-Brid, C., and Ros, J. (2009). Development and Growth in the Mexican Economy: a Historical Perspective. New York, NY: Cambridge University Press.

Pérez López, E. (1960). El producto nacional. In *México: cincuenta años de revolución.* 571–592, México DF, México: Fondo de Cultura Económica.

Rodríguez-Oreggia, E. (2005). Regional disparities and determinants of growth in Mexico. *The Annals of Regional Science*, *39*(2), 207–220.

Rosés, J. R., Martinez-Galarraga, J. and Tirado-Fabregat, D. A. (2010). The upswing of regional income inequality in Spain (1860–1930). *Explorations in Economic History*, *47* (2), 244–257.

Ruiz, W. (2006). Alcance del método de asignación geográfica relativa del producto, para construir una visión retrospectiva del crecimiento regional en México. *Análisis Económico*, 21, 328–353.

———. (2007). *Convergencia económica interestatal en México, un enfoque de largo plazo, 1900–1940*. Universidad Autónoma de Madrid.

———. (2010). Convergencia económica interestatal en México, 1900–2004. *Análisis Económico*, 25, 7–34.

———. (2014). Estimaciones quinquenales del PIB estatal industrial en México durante 1930–1965, a partir de información censal. *Working Paper—Asociación Española de Historia Económica*.

Sánchez-Reaza, J. and Rodríguez-Pose, A. (2002). The Impact of Trade Liberalization on Regional Disparities in Mexico. *Growth and Change*, *33* (1), 72–90.

Solís, L. (1970). *La economía mexicana, retrovisión y perspectivas*. México DF, México: Fondo de Cultura Económica.

Unikel, L., Ruiz-Chiapetto, C. and Garza, G. (1978). *México: Desarrollo urbano e implicaciones futuras*. México DF, México: El Colegio de México.

Williamson, J. G. (1965). Regional inequality and the process of national development: a description of the patterns. *Economic Development and Cultural Change*, *13*(4), 1–84.

CHAPTER 10

Peruvian Regional Inequality: 1847–2017

Bruno Seminario, María Alejandra Zegarra, and Luis Palomino

1 Introduction

The goal of this chapter is to describe the evolution of regional inequality in Peru between the years 1847 and 2017 using the latest available statistics on the spatial distribution of population and economic activity. As we will see, the economic space in Peru was radically transformed. Regional inequality steadily rose throughout the nineteenth century and the early stages of the twentieth century. Likewise, when we analyse large territorial regions based on historical events, we find that the inequality process occurred at different speeds across the country. In the South, the phase of increasing inequality ended ten years earlier than in the North and, in the Centre, ten years later.

Special thanks to Nouhaila Oudija and María Amparo Cruz-Saco for valuable contributions in the revision of the final version of this chapter.

B. Seminario (✉) • L. Palomino
Universidad del Pacífico, Lima, Peru
e-mail: seminario_lb@up.edu.pe

M. A. Zegarra
Inter-American Development Bank, Washington, DC, USA

D. A. Tirado-Fabregat et al. (eds.), *Time and Space*,
Palgrave Studies in Economic History,
https://doi.org/10.1007/978-3-030-47553-6_10

In any case, as it has been posed in Seminario (2015) or Contreras et al. (2011), one of the most important processes of Peruvian history was the profound transformation of economic activity and population across the territory. Throughout the Colonial Era, the Peruvian southern region concentrated most of the economic activity, population, and infrastructure. The prominence of the South had its roots on the population decline during the Spanish conquest and the economic activity driven by the mines located in the so-called "Alto Peru", today's Bolivia.

After the independence of Peru in 1821, the country experienced a period of anarchy that ended around 1847 due to the exploitation of the Guano deposits in the Central Coast. The revenues from the export of guano and saltpetre allowed the government to finance infrastructure in the *departmentos* along the Northern Coast. The guano and saltpetre export period ended in 1878 with the beginning of the War of the Pacific. After the end of the war in 1884, the Northern Coast, Lima, and the Central Sierra benefited from the development of transportation technology. For instance, the construction of the Central Railway enabled the exploitation of non-ferrous mineral reserves located in Lima and Cerro de Pasco. Therefore, in the period 1847–1884, two historical events occurred that had significant impact on the regional Peruvian economy. The first event corresponds to the Age of Guano, which increased regional inequality. The second event corresponds to the War of the Pacific, which reduced regional inequality.

After the War of the Pacific, many structural changes took place; the modernization of Lima's manufacturing industry began, the mining of the Central Sierra was restructured, the plantation agriculture of the Northern Coast was strengthened, the development of the Amazon began with the exploitation of rubber, and the oil deposits located in Piura (Northern Coast) started being exploited. In 1914, with the opening of the Panama Canal,[1] exports of sugar and cotton to the United States and Europe was revitalized. With the construction of the Panamericana Highway,[2] in the 1930s and 1940s, the coastal economic space was integrated into a single

[1] The Panama Canal improved the connectivity of Peru with Europe and the east Coast of the United States. Even before its construction, it was necessary to use the *Cabo de Hornos* route, which made it difficult to export agro-industrial products.

[2] In the twentieth century, the Peruvian railways failed to connect Lima with the cities of the northern Coast. For this reason, the construction of the Panamericana Highway north affected the connectivity of this area. Until before its construction, the cities of the Coast were united with Lima through maritime transport.

market. This dynamism promoted the migration to these regions and consolidated a new regional distribution of economic activity. In the period 1895–1934, regional inequality increased steadily. This increase in regional inequality may be a consequence of the unequal modernization of the Peruvian economy.

In 1950, regional inequality started a downward trend. After 1950, the Peruvian economy grew at an average annual rate of 3.9%, with periods of expansion and recession, both in contexts of greater market share and private activity and in those where the role of the state in economic activity had greater preponderance. Several of the recessions registered in the Peruvian economy coincided with or were preceded by international crises, such as the cases of the recession of 1958, the recession from 1976 to 1978, the recession of 1982 and 1983, the recession of the years 1998 and 1999, and the recession in the year 2009. In all these recessions, the external factors derived from the international crises affected economic activity. These recessions were in some cases attenuated by macroeconomic policies or worsened by the impact of climate events ("El Niño"), such as those recorded in the years 1982–1983 and 1998–1999. Peru has experienced several types of policies, from laissez-faire models in the 1950s to policies of greater state intervention in the 1970s. The expansive fiscal policies of the 1960s were the subject of a policy experiment that perhaps had good intentions but generated productive stagnation towards the end of the decade (Seminario 2015; Contreras et al. 2011). Also, in this period, regional inequality showed a sustained decline until 1999 and begun to increase steadily since 2003, the year in which the boom in mineral prices began.

The chapter is organized as follows. In the second section, we briefly review the history of the Republic of Peru in political, institutional, and economic terms with the objective of establishing the great development phases of the Peruvian economy. In the third section, we present the methodology used for the estimation of regional gross domestic product (GDP). In the fourth section, we analyse the historical evolution of regional inequality based on new regional statistics. Finally, in the fifth section, we discuss the potential determinants of long-term inequality phases in Peru.

2 Historical Background

Currently, the Peruvian economy is the sixth largest in Latin America in terms of real GDP. The size of the economy has gone from \$1560 million (PPP, 1990 international \$) in 1847 to \$226,639 (PPP, 1990

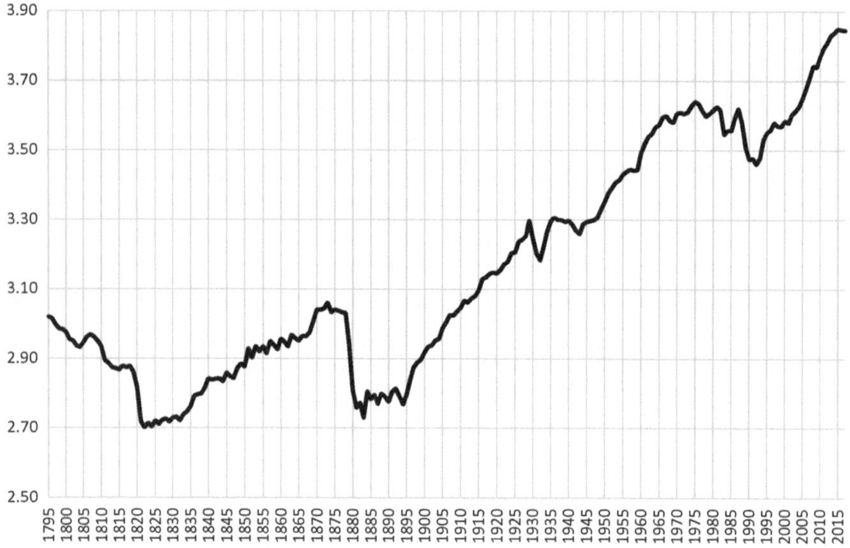

Fig. 10.1 GDP per capita of Peru, 1795–2017 (PPP, 1990 international $). (Source: Seminario (2015). Own elaboration)

international $) in 2017. When dividing this product by the total population, Peru has gone from having a GDP per capita of $698 (PPP, 1990 international $) in 1847 to $7003 (PPP, 1990 international $) in 2017. According to Fig. 10.1, we identify four cycles in the evolution of GDP per capita: (1) 1821–1883, (2) 1883–1932, (3) 1932–1991, and (4) 1992 until today.

The first cycle, 1821–1883, lasted 62 years and was characterized by three historical events that changed the structure of the economy (Bonilla 1981; Contreras and Cueto 2013; Hunt 2011; Seminario 2015): (1) the Wars of Independence, 1804–1824; (2) the Guano Era and saltpetre exports, 1847–1878; and (3) the War of the Pacific, 1878–1883.

The Guano Era began with the guano deposits exploitation located in the guano islands of the Peruvian Central Coast. The revenues that came from the guano exports funded government consumption and investment of railroads in the Central Coast and southern regions. There were two economic phases during the Guano Era. The first one started in 1847 and finished in 1866, when the guano islands began to run out of guano. The second phase lasted between 1873 and 1879, when new export products began to be exploited. These included sugar and cotton in the Northern Coast of the country and saltpetre in the department of Tarapacá. During this phase, the government implemented an expansive fiscal policy funded with external debt. The Guano Era ended with the outbreak of the War of the Pacific in 1879. As a result of the war, Peru lost the department of Tarapacá and faced the economic costs of the conflict, such as the destruction of infrastructure in the Northern Coastal areas of the country. Moreover, the war reduced the tax revenues and limited Peruvian access to the international capital market, which paralysed the construction of infrastructure and forced the government to reorganize the economy.

The second cycle, 1883–1932, lasted 50 years. During this period, Peru suffered the consequence of government management instability and international events (World War I, 1914–1919, and the international financial crisis of 1929).

The second cycle is crucial to understand the dynamics of regional inequality because the Peruvian economy experienced profound transformations (Seminario 2015; Thorp and Bertram 2013). The economic recovery that came after the War of the Pacific produced a new economy based on a fairly diversified export sector that clearly differs from other similar developments in Latin America (Contreras et al. 2011; Seminario 2015). During this period, the modernization of Lima began, the manufacturing industry grew substantially, the mining of the Central Coast was restructured, the oil deposits located in Piura began to be exploited, and the cotton plantations of the North Coast strengthened, while the exploitation of rubber in the Amazon River began. All this produced a substantial diversification of the Peruvian economy that produced substantial differences among the regions. As a consequence, the southern region tended to lag behind because it was not able to develop a successful export product in the world market. The GDP per capita of the South went from 0.89 times the national average in 1883 to 0.55 times in 1929.

After signing the Grace Contract[3] in 1888, the Peruvian government managed to complete the railroad in Central Peru and this work allowed restructuring the composition of mining production in Cerro de Pasco located in the Central Sierra. The opening of the Panama Canal, in 1914, substantially reduced the ocean freight rates to Peru. This reduction

[3] The Grace Contract was an agreement signed between an English company (Grace) and the Peruvian government. The Republic of Peru settled its debt through the transfer of the railways' ownership to the Peruvian Corporation (British bondholders).

boosted the export of agriculture products, such as cotton and sugar cane mostly located in Lima and the Northern Coast. Although the Southern Railway was completed in 1871, its impact was limited by the competition in the export of wool and textiles by the British colonies of Australia and New Zealand. Another factor that could explain the economic backwardness of the South after the War of the Pacific was the territorial losses of Arica and Tarapacá that contained the deposits of saltpetre, the main export product of the South.

Significant changes in the labour force occupations and levels of urbanization started occurring in 1920 due to increasing population growth. The rapid population growth promoted internal migration to Lima, the capital and biggest city in Peru. As a result, Lima and the nearby cities located in the north experienced an economic development based on the growth of the manufacturing industry and services. During this period, there was also a strong expansion of public spending driven mainly by the need to serve the migrant population.

The third cycle, 1932–1991, endured 61 years and is mainly characterized by the consequences of the World War II (1939–1945), the Cold War (1945–1990), and the import substitution industrialization (ISI) policy (1950–1960).

The Great Depression of 1929 produced a sharp drop in manufactured products whose production was concentrated in Lima (Contreras 2009; Seminario 2015; Thorp and Bertram 2013). The crisis lowered the growth rate of population expansion in Lima and boosted migration to the Amazon that grew substantially due to oil exploitation, agricultural growth, and the strong expansion of coca cultivation. The crisis also generated a sharp increase in export volumes and the opening of new mines in the northern and southern regions. As a result, in 1932, the increase in regional inequality that characterized the preceding period was interrupted.

In the first years of industrialization by import substitution, simple consumer goods were produced, generally with elementary production techniques (Dancourt et al. 1997). However, when the production of more sophisticated goods began and given the technological components, the import of capital and intermediate inputs from developed (or central) economies was required. This process showed the limits of the substitution process: it was easier to produce the final product locally, but it was beyond possibilities of local entrepreneurs to extend production vertically to technically complex intermediate and capital goods due to the lack of capital and of technological resources. In other words, the "easy" import substitution was destined to end quickly due to the nature of the substituted products (Contreras 2014).

With the crisis of the import substitution model, the decrease in inequality intensified due to the following reasons: (1) the decrease in the demand for manufactured goods, whose production was concentrated in Lima; (2) the development of new export products such as fishmeal; (3) the metal mining public investment projects in the northern and southern regions partially compensated the reduction in the global demand; (4) the strong migration to the Amazon due to the increased cultivation of coca and drug production. After the crisis of the import substitution model, during the period 1975–1992, the GDP of Lima decreased at a rate of −1.1%, the South region grew at a rate of 14.3%, and the northern region grew at a rate of 0.09%.

The fourth cycle began in 1992 and lasts until today. The main characteristic of this new stage is the new increase in regional inequality. In the first stage, between 1992 and 2000, there were substantial changes in economic policy: a notable opening up of the economy, the privatization of several public companies, and the restructuring of the main characteristics of the public investment system (Gonzales de Olarte 1998; Mendoza 2013; Seminario 2015). In the first phase, new gold and copper mines began exploitation in all regions. At a second phase, the sharp increase in mineral prices increased exports, public investment, and foreign investment. The substantial increase in international mineral prices made it possible to carry out large public investment projects: the Transoceanic Highway and the South-Peruvian Gas Pipeline. During this phase, Peru signed bilateral Free Trade Agreements (FTA) with the United States (2006), Chile (2006), Canada (2008), Singapore (2008), China (2009), and the European Union (2010), which allowed the entry of foreign investment and created a trade balance surplus. These FTA allowed the emergence of a new export agriculture located in the coastal region. During this period, climate events ("El Niño" of 1998) and international financial crises (i.e. the Asian and Russian crises of 1998 and the financial crisis of 2008) also affected the economy and produced inequality in the growth of the different regions of Peru.

Based on what has been described above, we can say that the Republican Era had four economic cycles between 1847 and 2017. The first cycle, from 1847 to 1878, focused on the export of guano and saltpetre. The second cycle, from 1895 to 1929, focused on the export of metal mining and agricultural products. The third cycle, from 1945 to 1976, is associated with the impulse of the export of mining and fishing products. Finally, the fourth cycle that began in 1992 corresponds to the period of neoliberalism. The latter is based on the rapid increase in mining and agricultural products. The following sections focus on the analysis of the evolution of regional inequality during the period 1847–2017.

3 Long-Term Patterns of Regional Income Inequality: Sources and Methods

We estimated the components of the departmental GDP for the period 1847–2017 using the GDP and population series derived by Seminario and Zegarra (2014), Seminario (2015), and Seminario et al. (2019). Our contribution in this chapter is to update the Peruvian GDP figures. We are also updating the population series by incorporating the population that was not considered in the nineteenth- and twentieth-century censuses.

Table 10.1 summarizes the sources and methodology used to estimate the GDP for the Peruvian departments (see Seminario et al. 2019, for a

Table 10.1 Sources and methods used to estimate the real GDP by department

Period	*Sources*	*Methodology*
1847–1876	• Population and Agrarian Censuses of 1795, 1827, and 1876 (CEPD 1972; Contreras et al. 2011; Hunt 1984; Kubler 1952) • Urban population (Hunt 2011; Maletta 1985) • Tithes of the Archbishopric (*Diezmos del Arzobispado*) of Lima, Cusco, Trujillo, and Ayacucho (Contreras et al. 2011) • Government revenues (Contreras et al. 2011) • Mining production in 1929 (INEI 1995) • Production of export products (Hunt 2011)	• Domestic agriculture was distributed among regions considering the regional distribution of tithes. • Export agriculture considers the regional production of cotton and sugar. • Metallic mining by department was obtained from the regional production of silver. Saltpeter production is assigned to the department of Tarapacá. • Non-metallic mining was assigned according to the surface of the islands where the *guano* was located because the islands belong to different departments. • Government services were distributed according to the population of each department. • Manufacturing and services were assigned according to the distribution of the urban population.

(*continued*)

Table 10.1 (continued)

Period	*Sources*	*Methodology*
1876–1970	• Population Censuses of 1876, 1940, 1961, and 1972 (CEPD 1972; INEI 1995; Maletta 1985) • Agrarian Censuses of 1926, 1944, 1961, and 1972 (Contreras et al. 2011; INEI 1995) • Production of export products (Maletta 1985; Portocarrero et al. 1992; Seminario 2015)	• Domestic agriculture was assigned using the production of crops by department. • Export agriculture was estimated using the departmental allocation of the production of coffee, sugar, and cotton. For fishing, we used the population of the cities in the Coast with more than 2000 people. • Metal mining takes as a criterion the departmental production in 1970. • Non-metallic mining is assigned to the departments of Tumbes and Piura, the most important producers of petroleum. • Government services were assigned using the population by departments. • Other industries were distributed using the urban population of 1876, 1940, 1961, and 1972.
1970–2017	Estimation of departmental GDP made by the INEI (Bureau of Statistics in Peru) (INEI 1995, 1996, 2001)	The series were transformed to prices of 1979. Fisher indexes were used to construct the departmental series.

Source: Seminario et al. (2019). Own elaboration

detailed explanation of the procedure and the sources). Given the available information, Seminario et al. (2019) divided the period in the following phases: (1) 1847–1876, (2) 1876–1970, (3) 1970–2017. Also, we distinguish four components in the GDP: (1) agriculture (domestic and export), (2) mining, (3) government services, and (4) other sectors (including manufacture).

The omitted population was estimated using the population densities of Denevan (1980) and assuming that the omitted population had a GDP per capita close to a subsistence income (400 PPP, 1990 international $). The omitted population was distributed by departments using the population densities of the three natural regions of Peru formulated by Javier

Pulgar Vidal[4] and based on altitudinal floors, flora and fauna (i.e. Yunga River, High Jungle, and Low Jungle). The corrected GDP followed:

$$Y_i^C = Y_i^{PC} + Y_i^{PO} \tag{10.1}$$

where Y_i^C indicates the corrected GDP for the region i, Y_i^{PC} represents the GDP of the surveyed population in the region i obtained by Seminario et al. (2019), and Y_i^{PO} corresponds to the GDP of the omitted population, estimated using the following formula:

$$Y_i^{PO} = \left(\sum_{r=1}^{N} AP_{r,t_0} * DP_{r,t_0} \right) * X \tag{10.2}$$

where AP_{r,t_0} represents the populated area of the natural region r in the period t_0, DP_{r,t_0} refers to the population density of the natural region r in the period t_0, and X indicates the lowest GDP per capita among the departments.

The territorial organization of Peru today has its origin in the administrative reforms of Viceroy de Croix.[5] By the time that Viceroy de Croix arrived in Peru, in 1784, Visitor General Jorge de Escobedo y Alarcón had completed the demarcation work required to establish a new administrative system. Viceroy de Croix divided Peru into seven administrative regions called *intendencias*: Lima, Trujillo, Tarma, Huancavelica, Huamanga, Arequipa, and Cusco. In 1796, the *intendencia* of Puno,[6]

[4] According to Javier Pulgar Vidal, a Peruvian geographer, Peru has eight natural regions identified (Chala, Yunga—*Marítima and Fluvial*, Quechua, Suni, Puna, Janca, *Selva Alta*, and *Selva Baja*) in accordance with their altitude, climatic conditions, flora, fauna, and natural resources.

[5] Viceroy Theodore de Croix ruled Peru between 1784 and 1790 and was the successor of the Viceroy Francisco de Taboada. Before being named viceroy in 1783, he was responsible of the internal provinces of northern New Spain, a command established in 1778 in whose territory were included Nueva Vizcaya, Santa Fe of Nuevo Mexico, Nuevo Leon, Coahuila, Sonora and Sinaloa, the Californias, and Texas. All these territories had been included in the intendancy of La Paz.

[6] The *intendencia* of Puno was established in 1783 after the Rebellion of Túpac Amaru II. Its territory included the parties of Chucuito, Lampa, Azángaro, Carabaya, and Paucarcolla. The parties of Lampa, Azángaro, and Carabaya belonged to the bishopric of La Paz (*obispado de la Paz*), while those of Chucuito and Paucarcolla belonged to the bishopric of Cusco.

previously part of the Viceroyalty of the Río de la Plata, was added to the Viceroyalty of Peru due to the intervention of the General Commandery of Maynas in 1802.[7]

The *intendencias* were organized to encompass the main economic circuits of the Viceroyalty. Tarma covered the main mining centers, and Lima, the agricultural production of the coast and the largest cities; in Huamanga, the *obrajes* were dedicated to the production of textiles and the main grazing areas. A large fraction of Trujillo´s population worked in the agricultural sector of the coastal valleys and in the cattle ranches of Piura and Cajamarca. The *intendencias* of Arequipa, Cusco, Huamanga, and Huancavelica provided the logistical support required in the mining centres of "Alto Perú". Cusco was also dedicated to the *obrajes*, and Arequipa to export beverages to "Alto Perú". The connection of these regions with Bolivia did not disappear after the Peruvian War of Independence. The territorial organization implemented by the Bourbon Monarchy tried to maintain a close correspondence between the territory and the existing economic circuits in Peru.

During the republic, the *intendencias* were transformed into departments, and these were subdivided into provinces and districts. The current administrative division of Peru includes 24 departments, 196 provinces, and 1874 districts. Likewise, we can understand the economic and social characteristics of the Peruvian territory if we divide it into three large transversal regions: the North, the Centre, and the South. Thus, in this document we are dividing the Peruvian territory into three large cross regions: North, Centre, and South. We have included in the northern region the departments of Tumbes, Piura, Lambayeque, Cajamarca, La Libertad, Amazonas, San Martin, and Loreto. The central region includes the departments of Ancash, Lima, Ica, Huanuco, Pasco, Junin, and Ucayali. Finally, the southern region includes the departments of Huancavelica, Ayacucho, Arequipa, Moquegua, Tacna, Apurimac, Cusco, Madre de Dios, and Puno. Map 10.1 shows the division of the departments and these three regions.

[7]The General Commandery of Maynas belonged to the Viceroyalty of New Granada. Its territory was transferred to Peru in 1802 and included the missions that had established the Jesuits, who were expelled in 1768. In 1802, the king created the bishopric and the General Commandery of Maynas in order to stop the progress of the Portuguese Bandeirantes. The border was demarcated in 1777 when the San Idelfonso Treaty was signed.

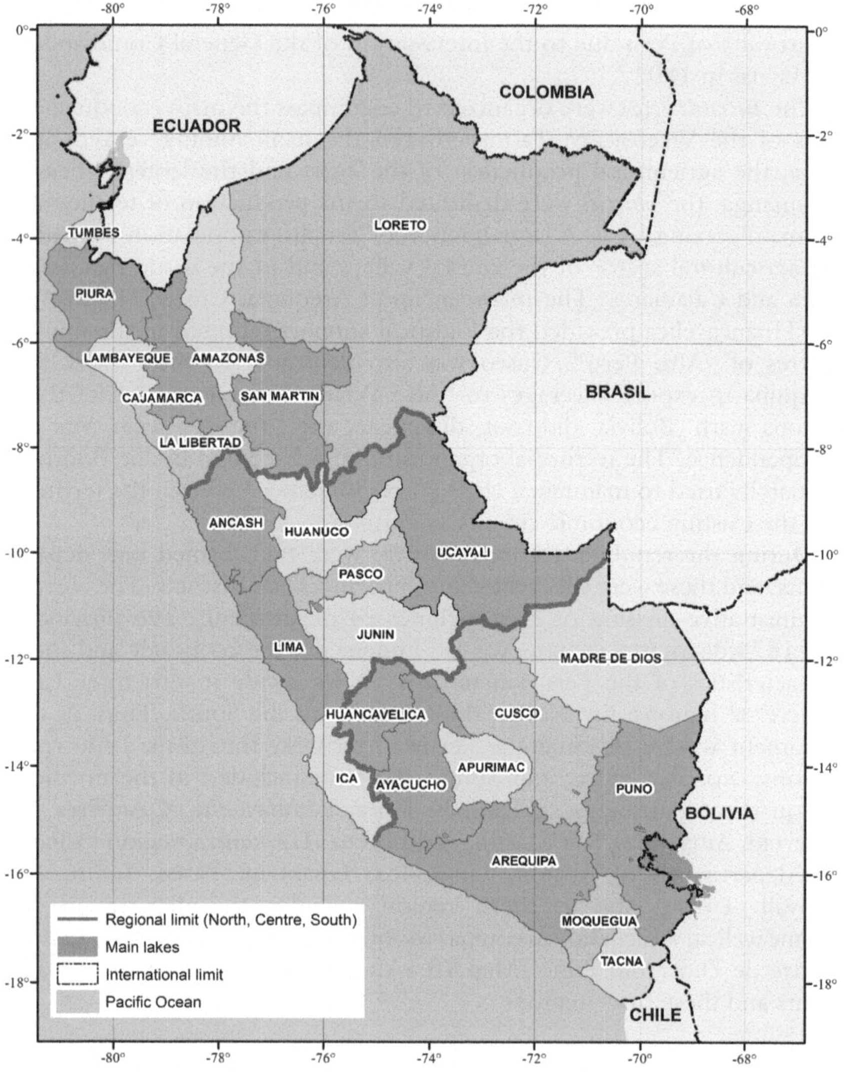

Map 10.1 Territorial administrative division of Peru (Regions and *Departmentos*). (Source: GEO GPS PERÚ. Own elaboration. Online: https://www.geogpsperu.com/p/descargas.html)

4 Long-Term Patterns of Regional Income Inequality: New Data and Stylized Facts

The data build by Seminario et al. (2019) analyses the distribution of economic activity among Peruvian regions. Table 10.2 shows the distribution of the GDP across the regions for some years between 1847 and 2017.

Table 10.2 Regional GDP as a share of the total GDP, 1847–2017

	1847	*1870*	*1890*	*1930*	*1947*	*1970*	*1990*	*2007*	*2017*
North	**23.20**	**24.73**	**26.84**	**34.51**	**25.71**	**18.44**	**19.16**	**14.68**	**12.42**
Tumbes	0.17	0.29	0.37	0.29	0.32	0.31	0.45	0.26	0.22
Piura	2.67	3.24	3.13	17.37	11.61	6.65	4.65	2.95	2.55
Lambayeque	3.19	6.42	5.12	4.68	3.51	3.08	3.44	2.23	2.11
La Libertad	5.03	4.47	7.01	5.67	4.40	3.96	3.80	3.96	3.42
Cajamarca	5.11	4.99	5.50	3.08	2.46	1.81	1.85	2.28	1.66
Amazonas	2.13	1.34	1.01	0.52	0.50	0.50	0.79	0.75	0.66
San Martin	2.55	2.59	2.17	1.04	1.15	0.81	1.11	1.05	1.07
Loreto	2.34	1.40	2.53	1.87	1.74	1.32	3.07	1.20	0.74
Centre	**34.35**	**37.63**	**40.98**	**44.80**	**56.91**	**68.57**	**67.95**	**73.08**	**74.27**
Ancash	7.59	8.62	9.62	5.37	4.48	3.95	2.62	2.08	1.77
Lima	13.77	15.68	15.78	26.45	41.52	54.85	57.44	63.72	65.15
Ica	1.50	3.87	3.12	4.31	3.89	3.39	2.08	2.24	2.72
Pasco	3.07	2.77	1.89	1.14	0.73	0.79	0.69	0.59	0.35
Junín	2.75	2.08	4.62	4.65	4.04	3.67	3.22	2.52	2.60
Huánuco	2.54	3.06	3.26	1.75	1.44	1.23	1.15	0.80	0.81
Ucayali	3.13	1.56	2.69	1.13	0.81	0.68	0.75	1.14	0.88
South	**42.44**	**37.63**	**32.18**	**20.69**	**17.39**	**12.99**	**12.89**	**12.24**	**13.31**
Arequipa	7.08	6.59	8.35	6.21	4.74	3.64	4.31	4.83	5.31
Moquegua	1.43	0.88	1.47	0.59	0.47	0.45	0.96	0.83	0.56
Tacna	1.66	2.48	2.19	1.76	1.33	1.56	1.04	0.92	0.75
Arica and Tarapacá	0.73	2.96							
Huancavelica	2.67	2.89	2.25	1.73	1.48	1.26	1.10	0.67	0.57
Ayacucho	4.85	4.72	3.16	1.91	1.58	1.30	0.89	0.84	0.96
Apurimac	3.50	3.70	2.17	1.70	1.38	0.78	0.64	0.38	1.22
Cusco	10.75	7.62	5.77	2.92	3.07	1.74	1.91	1.76	2.07
Madre de Dios	2.33	1.19	1.84	0.67	0.42	0.20	0.24	0.27	0.25
Puno	7.42	4.60	4.98	3.21	2.92	2.06	1.81	1.75	1.62

Sources: Seminario et al. (2019) and Seminario (2015). Own elaboration

The data shows that the relative importance of the different departments has changed over time. Despite this, the department of Lima has always concentrated on the most important fraction of economic activity. In 1847, the economic activity of the North was concentrated in the departments of Cajamarca (5.1% of the national GDP) and La Libertad (5.0%), in the Centre in Lima (13.8% of the national GDP) and Ancash (7.6%), and in the South in Cusco (10.8% of the national GDP) and Puno (7.4%). However, in 2017, the economic activity of the North was located in the departments of La Libertad (3.4%) and Piura (2.6%), in the Centre in Lima (65.2%) and Ica (2.7%), and in the South in Arequipa (5.3%) and Cusco (2.1%). However, we can better understand the evolution of inequality between departments using several indicators of regional inequality.

4.1 *Regional Inequality*

In this section, we discuss the long-term evolution of regional inequality in Peru using the value of the Williamson's Coefficient (WC) weighted with the population. To achieve this objective, we use the series of population and GDP estimated by Seminario et al. (2019) to calculate the GDP per capita of the Peruvian departments and regions for the period 1847–2017.

Figure 10.2 shows a persistent increase in the WC for the period 1847–2017. The value of the WC at the beginning of the reference period, 1847, reached a value of 0.41. Then, it dropped to 0.40 in 1856 and increased back again to 0.57 in 1878. In the twentieth century, the trend continued upward. In 1914, it reached a value of 0.69 and a maximum of 0.86 in 1934. After a period of stabilization, between 1934 and 1957, the value of WC decreased continually until 1989. Since then, the WC increased again to achieve values close to 0.70 at the end of the period.

The evolution of regional inequality in Peru contains three cycles related to the structure and dynamics of the Peruvian export sector: (1) 1847–1879, (2) 1879–1989; (3) 1989 until today.

This first cycle of regional inequality can be divided into two phases: The Guano Era and the Saltpetre Exports Era. During the Guano Era, the most dynamic area was the Central Coast (Ica, Lima, and the Coast of Ancash) where the main deposits of guano and saltpetre were located. The government concentrated most of the public investment in railways with the purpose of facilitating the exploitation of guano. During the second

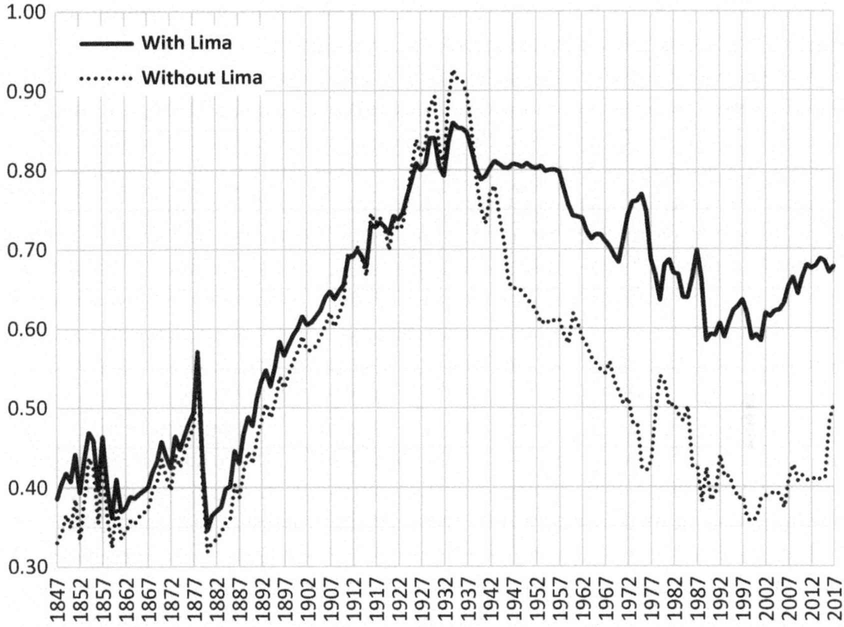

Fig. 10.2 Regional Williamson Coefficient in Peru, 1847–2017. (Sources: Seminario et al. (2019) and Seminario (2015). Own elaboration)

phase, the Saltpetre Exports Era, the inequality grew again caused by the economy diversification policies of the Peruvian government. These policies benefited the Northern Coast (modernization of sugar plantations, suppression of slavery, increase of investment financed with the guano surplus, and the promotion of international migration). In this cycle, the WC index increased from a value of 0.39 in 1847 to 0.57 in 1878. Three factors seem to play a fundamental role in the increasing inequality: (1) the location on the Coast of new Peruvian export products developed after the Independence (guano and saltpetre); (2) the crisis in the silver mining extraction that was only overcome in the late nineteenth century with the construction of a railway linking the Cerro de Pasco mines to the port of Callao; and (3) the public investment policy at the end of the nineteenth century privileged the construction of railways on the Central Coast, and the modernization of sugar plantations on the Northern Coast. However, with the War of the Pacific, the foundations of this export-oriented economy were destroyed, and the economic crisis decreased inequality.

The second cycle of regional inequality followed the trend described by Williamson (1965) and pushed by migration, industrialization, and urbanization. This phase began with the economic recovery after the War of the Pacific. A new export sector was built around the export of agricultural products from the Northern Coast, non-ferrous metals from the Central Sierra, rubber from the Amazon, and wool from the South. The great diversity of products mitigated the geographic concentration of economic activity in the nineteenth century. However, the growing population of Lima and the beginning of industrialization worked in opposite directions. During the first years of the cycle, the forces that prevailed were those that increased regional inequality. Between 1885 and 1934, the WC went from a value of 0.40 to 0.86. During the construction of the Panamericana highway in the 1930s and 1940s, the increasing internal migration to Lima and changes in the regional structure of public and private investment contributed to the reduction of regional inequality.

The third cycle of regional inequality corresponds to the recovery of the Peruvian economy that followed the crisis of the import substitution model and the external debt crisis. In this cycle, the WC increased from 0.59 in 1989 to 0.68 in 2017. The factors that have caused this increase are linked to the strong development of mining, export agriculture, and the dynamics of public investment in large infrastructure projects.

Figure 10.2 also shows the value of the WC excluding the department of Lima. We did this exercise because when considering the department of Lima, the WC increases its value. Therefore, this index allows us to measure the influence of Lima in the national results. As we can see, the trajectory of the WC follows even more intensely the characteristics of the national cycle.

4.2 *Regional Convergence*

Regional inequality can also be analysed using convergence analysis. The hypothesis of economic convergence aims to prove that poorer regions grow faster than richer ones. The existence of convergence can be proved when finding a negative relationship between the initial value of the GDP per capita and the growth rate. Figure 10.3 plots the growth rate of GDP per capita and the level of initial GDP per capita for the period 1847–2017.

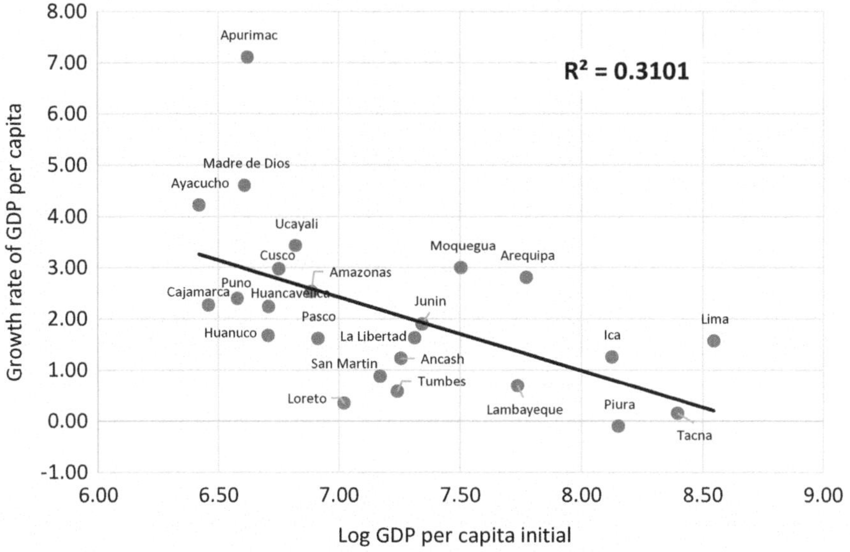

Fig. 10.3 Convergence between the regions of Peru, 1847–2017. (Sources: Seminario et al. (2019) and Seminario (2015). Own elaboration)

This figure suggests that Peru experienced a process of regional income convergence between 1847 and 2017.

Seminario et al. (2019) also found regional income convergence considering sub-periods. However, the value of the beta convergence rate depends on the methodology and the control variables. For example, when using quantile regressions, the regional convergence rates of the lower-income quantile (poor regions) is low, while the convergence rate of the regions belonging to the upper quantile (rich regions) is high. This result suggests the presence of convergence clubs in Peru (Delgado and Rodríguez 2014, 2015; Odar 2002; Cermeño 2002). Therefore, future research on regional income convergence should use methodologies to find this modality of convergence.

The evolution of regional inequality can also be analysed using development indicators (e.g. GDP per capita). Table 10.3 contains information on GDP per capita of the regions relative to the national GDP per capita. Although regional inequality in 1847 was not as pronounced, GDP per capita in the South was slightly lower than the national average. The

Table 10.3 GDP per capita regional (Peru = 100)

	1847	*1870*	*1890*	*1930*	*1947*	*1970*	*1990*	*2007*	*2017*
North	**108**	**96**	**102**	**122**	**87**	**63**	**64**	**50**	**42**
Tumbes	152	142	129	73	70	55	65	36	31
Piura	83	71	79	308	174	106	73	48	44
Lambayeque	178	193	224	167	115	82	83	55	55
La Libertad	115	113	113	94	75	69	66	67	56
Cajamarca	106	72	76	41	32	26	32	45	30
Amazonas	173	110	84	49	49	35	52	55	49
San Martin	121	115	100	57	65	49	46	39	35
Loreto	62	45	89	63	56	47	99	37	21
Centre	**112**	**110**	**121**	**132**	**156**	**150**	**140**	**145**	**148**
Ancash	99	92	105	77	71	73	59	54	45
Lima	187	176	200	229	258	203	183	187	188
Ica	286	197	160	214	170	129	81	86	108
Pasco	93	117	124	76	51	60	65	57	38
Junin	69	43	72	87	78	71	68	56	64
Huanuco	99	113	112	48	41	39	39	29	31
Ucayali	57	37	69	40	46	69	54	72	58
South	**89**	**94**	**80**	**55**	**51**	**52**	**60**	**60**	**66**
Arequipa	118	132	157	148	119	94	104	115	129
Moquegua	98	89	171	106	91	83	163	141	103
Tacna	208	195	231	331	222	227	108	88	73
Arica and Tarapacá	167	308							
Huancavelica	87	78	70	45	41	50	61	40	38
Ayacucho	100	103	59	32	31	38	38	37	46
Apurimac	98	88	57	40	38	33	36	26	87
Cusco	85	93	69	37	43	32	41	41	48
Madre de Dios	59	40	68	38	37	54	67	68	59
Puno	67	56	53	36	36	35	37	38	35

Sources: Seminario et al. (2019) and Seminario (2015). Own elaboration

richest region was the Centre by concentrating 31.3% of the population and generating 34.9% of the GDP. The importance of the Central region rose dramatically during the Republican era due to the growth of Lima and the concentration of mineral production in the *intendencia* of Tarma. In 2007, the Centre of Peru accounted for 50.3% of the population and generated 73.1% of GDP. In this same period, the participation of the northern region in the total population slightly increased from 22% to 29.1%, and its economic importance decreased by 38.8%.

Likewise, regional inequality can be analysed using Maps 10.2 and 10.3. Map 10.2 shows the regional economic development in the nineteenth century. The darker grey regions are the regions with a GDP per capita that exceeds the mean of the distribution plus one standard deviation. The second darker tone represents those that have a GDP per capita between the mean and the mean plus a standard deviation. The lighter shaded ones correspond to the territories with a GDP per capita level below the average (between the mean and one standard deviation below the mean).

On the one hand, Map 10.2 shows the spatial distribution of economic activity in 1847. In this map, we see that the Amazon regions (Loreto, Ucayali, and Madre de Dios) were the poorest regions, while regions of the coast (Lambayeque, Lima, Ica, and Tacna) were the richest ones as a consequence of the location of the deposits of guano and saltpetre. On the other hand, Map 10.2 also includes the distribution of GDP per capita in 1890. One of the most noticeable changes is the transition of the Amazon regions, which transitioned from being very poor to poor. Also, we observe that the regions of Puno and Apurimac transitioned from

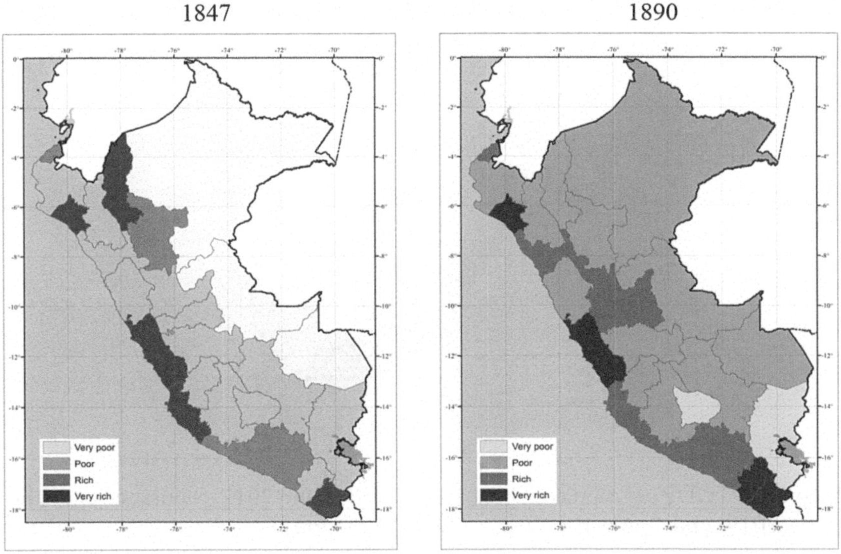

Map 10.2 GDP per capita by region, 1847 and 1890. (Sources: Seminario et al. (2019) and Seminario (2015). Own elaboration)

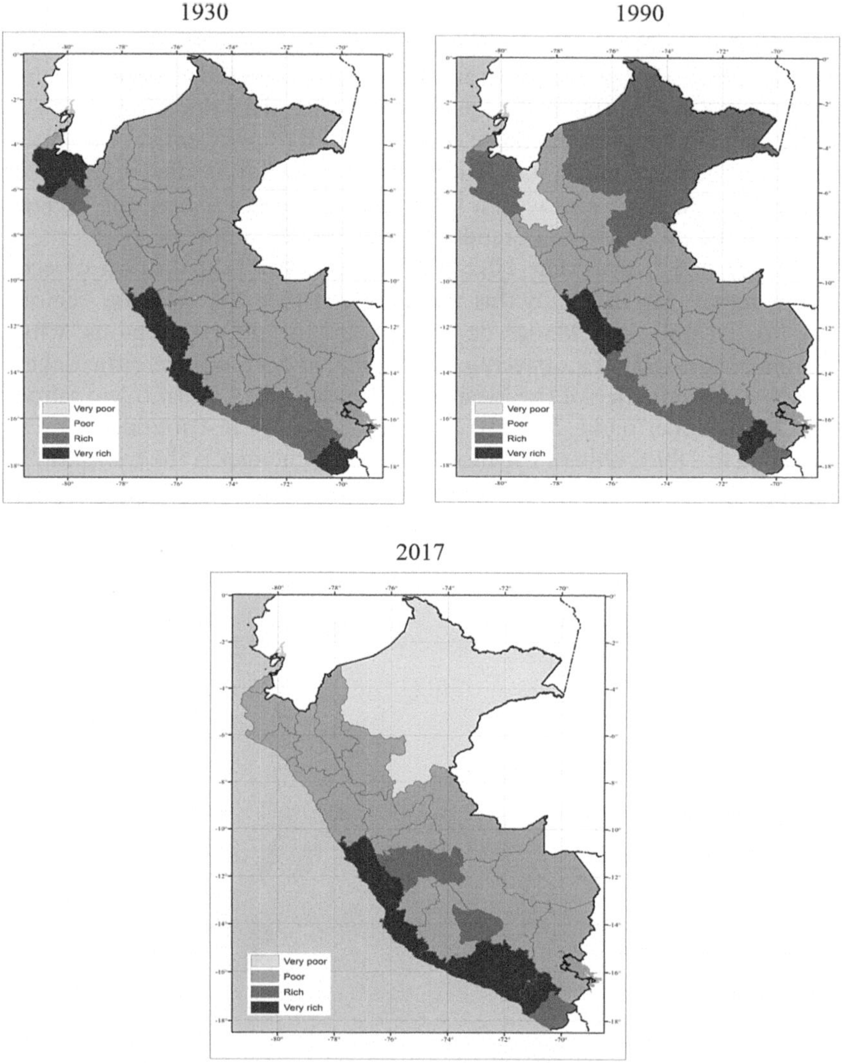

Map 10.3 GDP per capita regional—1930, 1990, and 2017. (Sources: Seminario et al. (2019) and Seminario (2015). Own elaboration)

poor to very poor. The departments of the Central highlands (Pasco and Huánuco) and the department of La Libertad transitioned from poor to rich. Here the factor that explains the transition is the modernization of the sugar departments (La Libertad) and the mines of the Central highlands (Pasco).

Map 10.3 shows the regional economic development in the twenty and twenty-first centuries. On the one hand, Map 10.3 presents the distribution of the GDP per capita in 1930. One of the most important features observed in this map is the disappearance of the very poor regions and the reduction of regions belonging to the upper tail of the distribution (rich and very rich). The most notorious change is perceived in the Northern Coast, with the incorporation of Piura to the group of very rich regions, a consequence of the exploitation of oil and the cultivation of cotton. On the other hand, Map 10.3 shows the distribution of the GDP in 1990. This map shows that the region of Loreto had the best performance, by transitioning from being very poor in 1850, to poor in 1930, and finally rich in 1990. The map also shows that the number of very rich regions has decreased from four in 1930 to two in 1990. The transition from the department of Loreto to the very rich regions is explained by the exploitation of oil in the Amazon. Finally, Map 10.3 corresponds to the distribution of GDP per capita in 2017. This map shows that the coastal regions of Central and Southern Peru belong to the upper tail of the distribution. Likewise, the department of Loreto transitioned from being rich in 1990 to very poor in 2017, due to the depletion of oil deposits. The department of Apurímac was also incorporated into the group of rich regions due to the opening of new copper mines. Similar transition was experienced by the department of Junín.

5 The Forces Behind Regional Inequality in Peru

Using the GDP statistics by department estimated by Seminario et al. (2019), we have shown that economic inequality increased during the second half of the nineteenth century and the first half of the twentieth century. During this period, the WC value transitioned from 0.41 in 1850 to a maximum value of 0.86 in 1934, equivalent to an increase of 74.6%. We also found that Lima highly influenced national inequality indicators (see Fig. 10.2). However, we can better understand the evolution of regional inequality in Peru if we analyse the evolution of the three major transversal regions: North, Central, and South. According to Table 10.2, in 1847, the South was the most important economic region, because it concentrated on 46.7% of the population and generated 42.4% of GDP. However, its importance has changed over the years. In 2017 the southern region only accounted for 20.0% of the population and generated 13.3% of the GDP.

On the one hand, Fig. 10.4a shows the annual distribution of the economic activity by region between 1847 and 2017. In 1847, the South (42.4%) contributed most to GDP, followed by the Centre (34.6%) and the North (23%). Soon after the end of the War of the Pacific, the Centre surpassed the South. While the Centre continued increasing its economic dynamism, the South continued reducing its importance in the Peruvian economic activity. After the Financial Crisis of 1929, the North began to reduce its participation in the GDP and the Centre became the most predominant region of the country.

On the other hand, Fig. 10.4b shows that the GDP per capita followed a similar pattern as total GDP. The annual GDP per capita growth rate of Lima (Centre region) was 2.9% between 1847 and 1878, higher than the ones in Trujillo (northern region), 1.6%, and the South, 2.1%. At the beginning of the Guano Era, around 1847, Lima had 1.62 times the national average GDP per capita, and by the end of this period, in 1878, this ratio increased to 1.96. During this period, the GDP per capita of Trujillo and the South decreased, while the GDP per capita of the Central Sierra (Tarma) increased. The trends that prevailed during the Guano Era reflect the action of three forces: the location of the guano deposits in the Central and Southern Coasts, the crisis of the silver mine in Cerro de Pasco, and the public investment policy.

The economic collapse caused by the War of the Pacific generated a convergence of the GDP per capita similar to that experienced after the independence. Due to the War of the Pacific, the Peruvian GDP per capita fell by 50.1% between 1878 and 1883. The loss of the saltpetre deposits located on the southern coast and the location of the battles and the destroyed infrastructure were the main reasons why the consequences of the war were different across the country. As a result, the average annual reduction rate of the GDP per capita was higher in Lima (9.8%), Trujillo (8.6%), and the South (8.4%) than the one in Tarma (7.1%).

A new phase began with the economic recovery that came after the war and prevailed throughout the Aristocratic Republic (1895–1929). During

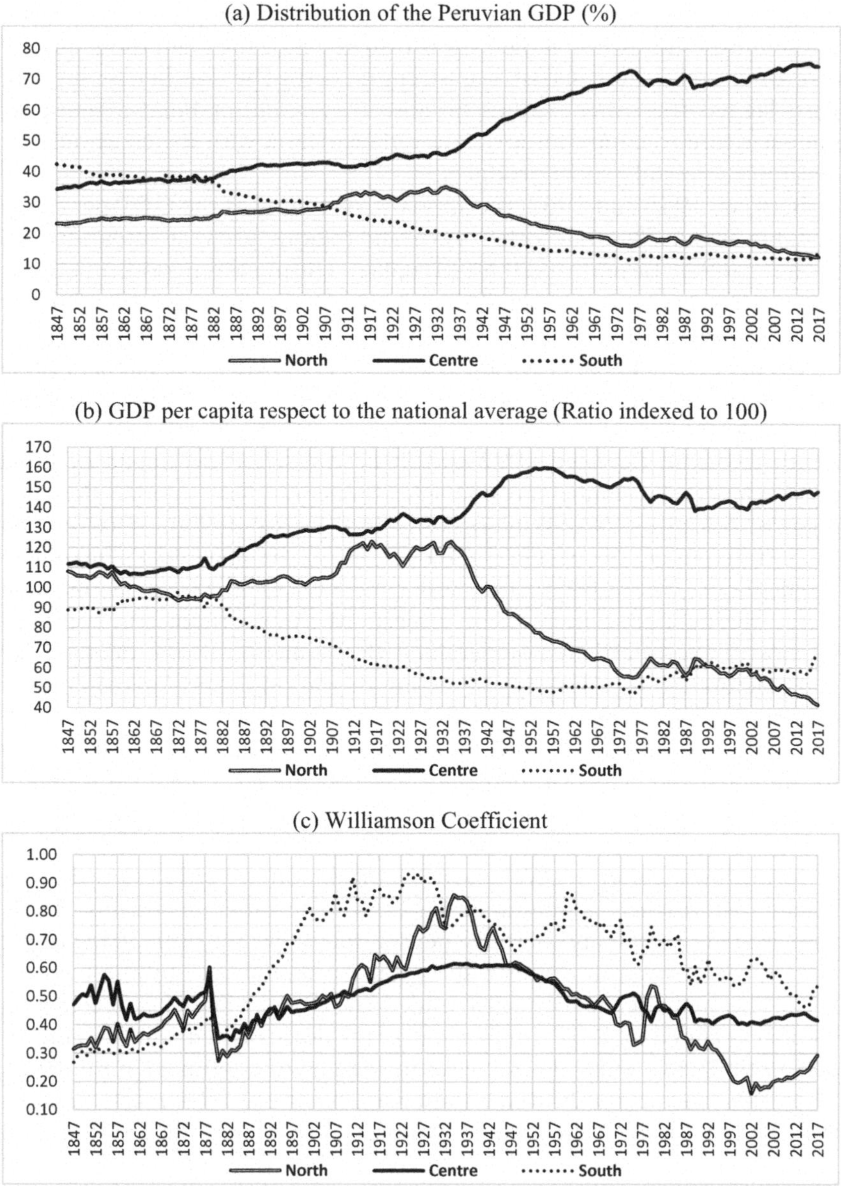

Fig. 10.4 Economic activity and regional inequality: North, Centre and South, 1847–2017 (%). (**a**) Distribution of the Peruvian GDP (%). (**b**) GDP per capita respect to the national average (Ratio indexed to 100). (**c**) Williamson Coefficient. (Sources: Seminario et al. (2019) and Seminario (2015). Own elaboration)

this period, the modernization of Lima's manufacturing industry began, the mining of the Central Sierra was restructured, the plantation agriculture of the Northern Coast was strengthened. The southern region of Peru lagged the other regions because they couldn't build a transport infrastructure to communicate the southern Sierra with the coast, neither develop successful export products.

Between 1945 and 1968, the annual growth rate of the GDP per capita in Lima was 1.3% while other Peruvian regions grew at rates of 0.9% (South), 0.9% (Tarma), and 0.8% (Trujillo). During this period, an import substitution policy was adopted that contributed to increase the GDP per capita in Lima.

On the one hand, between 1975 and 1992, the GDP per capita of Lima grew at an average annual rate of −0.9%, while other Peruvian regions grew at lower negative rates: Central Sierra (−0.4%), North (−0.7%), and South (−0.3%). Between 1992 and 2017, the GDP per capita of Lima grew at an average annual rate of 1.4%, a higher rate than in other Peruvian regions: South (1.3%), Trujillo (1%), and Tarma (0.9%). What caused these differential effects? First, the decrease in the demand for manufactured goods, whose production was concentrated in Lima. Second, the metal mining public investment projects in the northern and southern regions of Peru partially compensated the reduction in the demand for manufactured goods. Finally, the strong migration to the Amazon region due to the drugs (coca).

Likewise, analysing the WC for the North, Centre, and South of Peru we find that the cycles of inequality have begun and ended on different dates. In Fig. 10.4c, we observe that in the South the WC reached a maximum level in 1924, in the Centre in 1934, and in the North in 1936.

In the South, after the WC reached a maximum in 1911, a slow descent began that reached a minimum in 1948. Thereafter, inequality slowly increased until 1960 and started a new period of decline until 2014. In the North, there was a movement analogous to that shown by the national WC. The increase in inequality ended in 1936, while the decrease in inequality ended in 2002. In the Centre, the decrease in inequality continued until 1948, while the increase in inequality continued until 1989. Thereafter, inequality showed a stationary behaviour. This result suggests that the behaviour of the inequality indicator combines the action of two types of forces: (a) those associated with the cycles of exploitation of certain raw materials that tend to predominate in southern Peru and

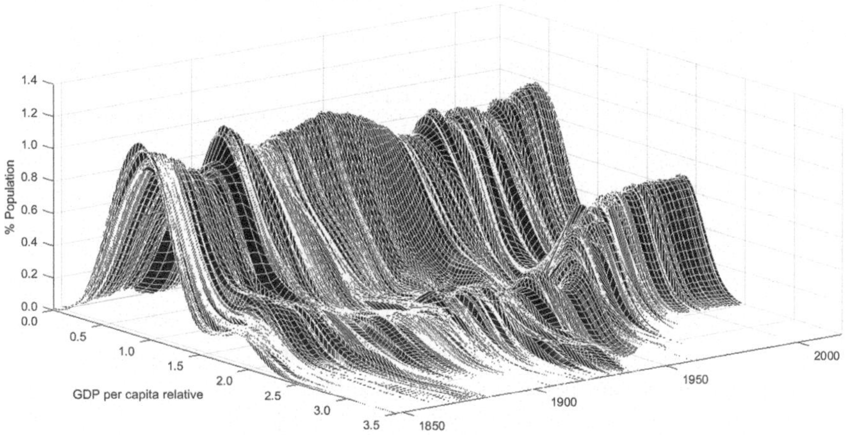

Fig. 10.5 Distributive evolution of GDP per capita in Peru, 1850–2017. (Sources: Seminario et al. (2019) and Seminario (2015). Own elaboration)

(b) those associated with the urbanization and modernization process, which would predominate in the north and centre of Peru.

Finally, Fig. 10.5 shows the functional distribution of GDP per capita of the regions of Peru from 1847 to 2017. The most notable feature is the appearance and consolidation of a bimodal function. That is, there is evidence of a certain polarization in the regional Peruvian distribution of income. According to Seminario et al. (2019), one of the possible reasons why bimodality is present in GDP per capita is the presence of bimodality in the population. Therefore, it is necessary that studies on regional inequality consider population expansion factors.

According to Seminario et al. (2019), several geographic variables have significant impacts on the growth rates of the regions of Peru. Therefore, future research on the determinants and impacts of regional inequality could consider the effects of geographic variables. Moreover, it is necessary to use empirical methodologies that give results according to the functional distribution of the data (Seminario et al. 2019; Díez-Minguela et al. 2017; Tirado et al. 2015; Yamamoto 2007; Quah 1993).[8]

[8](1) agricultural area (populated area of Chala, Yunga Maritime, Quechua, Suni, River Yunga, High Jungle, and Low Jungle); (2) livestock area (populated area of Puna, Janca, and Glaciers); (3) altitude (average height of the populated centres—PCs—by department); (4)

6 Conclusions

The goal of this chapter was to analyse the evolution of regional inequality in Peru between the years 1847 and 2017.

On the one hand, using the series of national GDP per capita, we identify four cycles in the economic evolution: (1) 1821–1883, (2) 1883–1932, (3) 1932–1991, and (4) 1992, until today. The first cycle, from 1847 to 1878, focused on the export of guano and saltpetre. The second cycle, from 1895 to 1929, focused on the export of metal mining and agricultural products. The third cycle, from 1945 to 1976, is associated with the impulse of the export of mining and fishing products. Finally, the fourth cycle that began in 1992 corresponds to the period of neoliberalism.

On the other hand, using the series of GDP per capita of the Peruvian departments and the WC weighted with the population, we can distinguish three cycles of regional inequality: (1) 1847–1879, (2) 1879–1989; (3) 1989 until today.

This first cycle of regional inequality can be divided into two phases: the Guano Era and the Saltpetre Exports Era. In this cycle, the WC index increased from a value of 0.39 in 1847 to 0.57 in 1878. Three factors seem to play a fundamental role in the increasing inequality: (1) the location on the coast of new Peruvian export products developed after the Independence (guano and saltpetre); (2) the crisis in the silver mining extraction that was only overcome in the late nineteenth century with the construction of a railway linking the Cerro de Pasco mines to the port of Callao; and (3) the public investment policy at the end of the nineteenth century privileged the construction of railways on the Central Coast, and the modernization of sugar plantations on the Northern Coast.

The second cycle of regional inequality followed the trend described by Williamson (1965) and pushed by migration, industrialization, and urbanization. This phase began with the economic recovery after the War of the Pacific. During the first years of the cycle, the forces that prevailed were those that increased regional inequality. Between 1885 and 1934, the WC went from a value of 0.40 to 0.86. In 1934, the WC reached a maximum value.

distance to the sea (average distance of the PCs to the sea by department); (5) distance to the main port (average distance of the PCs to the nearest port by department); (6) population by PC (total population divided by the amount of PCs by department), and (7) growth of the populated area between 1795 and 2017.

The third cycle of regional inequality corresponds to the recovery of the Peruvian economy that followed the crisis of the import substitution model and the external debt crisis. In this cycle, the WC increased from 0.59 in 1889 to 0.68 in 2017. The factors that caused this increase are linked to the strong development of mining, export agriculture, and the dynamics of public investment in large infrastructure projects.

The ascending phase of WC lasted until 1878, while in the twentieth century it lasted until 1934. The ascending phase that was characteristic of the nineteenth century produced an increase in the WC of 32 percentage points, while that corresponding to the twentieth century, 23 percentage points. During the ascending phase of the WC in the twentieth century, the upper tail of the distribution tends to expand because the benefits of the growth process are concentrated in a small group of departments that belong to the upper and upper-middle quartiles of the GDP per capita distribution. In the middle of the twentieth century, growth was basically concentrated in three economic poles: Lima, mining areas, and the Northern Coast. The spatial continuity of these zones produced externalities that were concentrated in the zone but that could not expand towards the poorest territories located in the south and in the highlands of the north. When inequality begins to fall, there is a double modality of the distribution due to a discrete increase in the homogeneity of the departments that belonged to the upper quartile and the upper-middle quartile.

The study also suggests that it is important to consider the scale at which the process occurs since the examination of the trajectory of inequality within regions does not necessarily follow the national trend. We have shown that the influence of the WC of Lima on the inequality indicator can be substantial when examining the trajectories of the inequality that occurs within the departments. In southern Peru, the phase of increasing inequality phase ends ten years earlier than in the north of the country and in the centre region ten years later. The trajectory of WC between regions suggests that the process occurred at different speeds depending on the region considered.

References

Bonilla, H. (1981). Historia del Perú t. VI. Perú Republicano. Entre la Independencia y la Guerra con Chile. Editorial Juan Mejía Baca Lima-Perú.

Centro de Estudios de Población y Desarrollo (CEPD) (1972). *Informe demográfico del Perú.* Lima: Centro de Estudios de Población y Desarrollo.

Cermeño, R. (2002). *Growth convergence clubs: evidence from Markov-switching models using panel data.* Divisin de Economa, CIDE, Mexico.

Contreras, C., Cosamalón Armas, J., Deustua, J., Monsalve, M. and Salinas, A. (2011). *Economía de la primera centuria Independiente. Compendio de Historia Económica del Perú.* Tomo 4. Lima: Banco Central de Reserva del Perú & Instituto de Estudios Peruanos.

Contreras, C. and Cueto, M. (2013). Historia del Perú Contemporáneo. 5° Edición, Lima: Instituto de Estudios Peruanos (IEP).

Contreras, C. (2009). La crisis mundial de 1929 y la economía peruana. Capítulos de Libros PUCP/Chapters of PUCP books, 21–56.

———. (2014). Compendio de historia económica V: la economía peruana entre la gran depresión y el reformismo militar, 1930–1980.

Dancourt, O., Mendoza, W. and Vilcapoma, L. (1997). Fluctuaciones económicas y shocks externos: Perú 1950–1996. Documentos, Pontifica Universidad Católica del Perú (PUCP).

Delgado, A. and Rodríguez, G. (2014). *Convergencia en Los Departamentos Del Perú: ¿inclusión O Exclusión en El Crecimiento de la Economía Peruana (1970–2010)?* Pontificia Universidad Católica del Perú. Departamento de Economía.

———. (2015). Structural Breaks and Convergence in the Regions of Peru: 1970–2010. *Review of Development Economics*, 19(2): 346–357.

Denevan, W. M. (1980). La población aborigen de la Amazonia en 1492. *Amazonia Peruana*, 3(5): 3–41.

Díez-Minguela, A., González-Val, R., Martinez-Galarraga, J., Sanchis, M. T. and Tirado, D. A. (2017). The long-term relationship between economic development and regional inequality: South-West Europe, 1860–2010. *European Historical Economics Society (EHES)*, Working paper 119.

Gonzales de Olarte, E. (1998). El Neoliberalismo a la peruana: Economía Política del ajuste estructural, 1990–1997. Lima: Consorcio de investigación económica; Instituto de Estudios Peruanos.

Hunt, S. J. (1984). *Growth and Guano in Nineteenth Century Peru.* Research Program in Economic Development, Princeton University, New Jersey, Discussion Paper No. 34.

———. (2011). *La formación de la economía peruana: distribución y crecimiento en la historia del Perú y América Latina.* Lima: Pontificia Universidad Católica del Perú.

Instituto Nacional de Estadística e Informática (INEI). (1995). *Producto Bruto Interno por departamentos, 1970–1995.* Lima: INEI.

———. (1996). *Producto Bruto Interno por departamentos, 1970–1995.* Lima: INEI.

———. (2001). *Producto Bruto Interno por departamentos, 1994–2001.* Lima: INEI.

Kubler, G. (1952). The Indian Caste of Peru, 1795–1940: A Population Study Based Upon Tax Records and Census Reports. *Smithsonian Institution, Institute of Social Anthropology*, No. 14.

Maletta, H. (1985). *Requerimientos de mano de obra en la agricultura peruana.* Lima: Centro de Investigación de la Universidad del Pacífico.

Mendoza, W. (2013). Contexto Internacional y Desempeño Macroeconómico en América Latina y el Perú: 1980–2012. Documento de trabajo N° 351. Pontifica Universidad Católica del Perú (PUCP).

Odar, J. C. (2002). Diferencias departamentales de crecimiento. Un análisis de convergencia para Perú: 1961–1996. *Apuntes: Revista de Ciencias Sociales*, (47): 5–57.

Portocarrero, S., Beltrán, B., Romero, P. and Elena, M. (1992). *Compendio estadístico del Perú, 1900–1990.* Lima: Universidad del Pacífico.

Quah, D. (1993). Empirical cross-section dynamics in economic growth. *European Economic Review*, 37(2–3): 426–434.

Seminario, B. (2015). *El desarrollo de la economía peruana en la era moderna: precios, población, demanda y producción desde 1700.* Lima: Universidad del Pacífico.

Seminario, B. and Zegarra, M. A. (2014). Las tendencias de largo plazo de la desigualdad regional en el Perú, 1827–2007. *Documento de Discusión CIUP* DD1403.

Seminario, B., Zegarra, M. A. and Palomino, L. A. (2019). Estimación del PIB departamental y análisis de la desigualdad regional en el Perú: 1795–2017. *Documento de Trabajo*, IDB-WP-1016.

Tirado, D. A., Díez-Minguela, A. and Martinez-Galarraga, J. (2015). A closer look at the long-term patterns of regional income inequality in Spain: the poor stay poor (and stay together). *European Historical Economics Society (EHES)*, Working paper 87.

Thorp, R. and Bertram, G. (2013). Perú 1890–1977: crecimiento y políticas en una economía abierta. Apéndice 1: "Estimación del valor de las principales exportaciones: 1880–1910". Lima: Universidad.

Williamson, J. G. (1965). Regional inequality and the process of national development: a description of the patterns. *Economic Development and Cultural Change*, 13(4, Part 2), 1–84.

Yamamoto, D. (2007). Scales of regional income disparities in the USA, 1955–2003. *Journal of Economic Geography*, 8(1): 79–103.

CHAPTER 11

Patterns of Regional Income Distribution in Uruguay (1872–2012): A Story of Agglomeration, Natural Resources and Public Policies

Julio Martinez-Galarraga, Adrián Rodríguez Miranda, and Henry Willebald

1 Introduction

In the final decades of the nineteenth century, during the early stages of the First Globalization, Uruguay was among the wealthiest countries in the world. In its best year (1873), Uruguay occupied the fourth position in the gross domestic product (GDP) per capita world ranking, with values above those of the UK (#5), the undisputed industrial leader at that

J. Martinez-Galarraga
Departament d'Anàlisi Econòmica
Universitat de València, València, Spain
e-mail: julio.martinez-galarraga@uv.es

A. Rodríguez Miranda • H. Willebald (✉)
Universidad de la República, Montevideo, Uruguay
e-mail: adrianrm@iecon.ccee.edu.uy; hwillebald@iecon.ccee.edu.uy

D. A. Tirado-Fabregat et al. (eds.), *Time and Space*,
Palgrave Studies in Economic History,
https://doi.org/10.1007/978-3-030-47553-6_11

time, with a level similar to that of the US (#3) and somewhat below other Western Offshoots such as New Zealand (#2) and Australia (#1) (Bolt et al. 2018). Today, however, Uruguay ranks around number 60, with an income per capita comparable to countries located in the European periphery such as Romania and Turkey. From this perspective, the economic development of Uruguay may be described as a reversal of fortune, although this long-term trajectory is not very different from that followed by other Latin American countries.

The key to the economic success of Uruguay in the second half of the nineteenth century lies in the specialization in the production and export of primary goods. Natural resources in Uruguay are abundant, and most of the land is suitable for agricultural production. More than 95% of the total territory corresponds to grassland, steppe and open shrub land (Willebald and Juambeltz 2018), and, in fact, almost all the territory is apt for rearing livestock. One of the most classical characterizations of Uruguay corresponds to Reyes Abadie (1966), who described the country as a combination of prairie, border and harbour. In other words, Uruguay was a region well endowed with natural resources suitable for cattle breeding and with the best port in South America, which made Montevideo the

We acknowledge financial support from CSIC-UDELAR (*Comisión Sectorial de Investigación Científica—Universidad de la República*) I+D Program and Mobility and Academic Exchange Program, as well as from ANII Territorial Equity Fund (*Fondo Sectorial de Equidad Territorial de la Agencia Nacional de Investigación e Innovación*). We would also like to thank Micaela Araujo, Pablo Castro, Mariana García, Sebastián Goinheix and Sabrina Siniscalchi for their collaborations in previous works that were valuable inputs for this research. We also thank for the comments and suggestions made in several seminars and conferences: *Primer Encuentro sobre la Reconstrucción de los PIBs regionales en América*, December, 2013; *IV Congreso Latinoamericano de Historia Económica*, Universidad Jorge Tadeo Lozano, Bogotá, Colombia, July, 2014; *Tercer Foro Bienal Iberoamericano de Estudios del Desarrollo*, Montevideo, Uruguay, April, 2015; XVII World Economic History Congress, Kyoto, Japan, August, 2015; *V Congreso Latinoamericano de Historia Económica*, Universidade de São Paulo, Brasil, July, 2016; XVIII World Economic History Congress, Massachusetts Institute of Technology (MIT), Boston, the US, International Economic History Association, August, 2018; *VI Congreso Latinoamericano de Historia Económica*, Universidad de Santiago, Chile, July, 2019. We would like to thank especially to Marc Badia-Miró, Luís Bértola, Reto Bertoni, Jean Pascal Bassino, Pablo Galaso, José Perez-Cajías, Esteban A. Nicolini, Carolina Román and Daniel A. Tirado-Fabregat. Julio Martinez-Galarraga acknowledges financial support from the Projects ECO2015-65049-C12-1-P and PGC2018-095821-B-I00 (MCIU/AEI/FEDER, UE). We are responsible for all errors that still remain.

main 'exit door' of commodities from the River Plate to the international markets.

Uruguay gained independence from the Crown of Spain in 1828. Traditionally, the country was the frontier between two empires: Spain and Portugal. This feature extended after independence with other protagonists—Argentina and Brazil—but with similar characteristics: Uruguay constituted a buffer state between two immense countries. The new country occupied an area of 176,215 square kilometres, which, to put it in comparative perspective, is twice the size of Portugal or more than four times the size of the Netherlands and Switzerland.

While in terms of size Uruguay is larger than many European countries, its population has traditionally been very small. At the time of independence, its population was close to 75,000 inhabitants; it reached a million around the turn of the twentieth century, a period in which the country received large inflows of migrants as other Western Offshoots did. Today the population amounts to 3.5 million (around 90% of European descent).[1] A large portion of this population lives in the capital city, Montevideo, which is home to 1.3 million people and concentrates around 40% of the country's current total population. The high concentration of population, working force and transportation infrastructures in Montevideo explains why some contemporary authors claimed that Montevideo acted as a 'suction pump' of the country and stressed the extreme territorial imbalance that this meant for the economic development (Martínez Lamas 1930).

In the long run, the Uruguayan economy has exhibited an irregular trajectory that alternates periods of significant productive expansion with others of deep depressions, as well as periods of openness with others of constrained international trade. While growth episodes and recessions occurred equally in open or closed periods (Bértola and Porcile 2000), the local historiography has traditionally split the contemporary history of Uruguay into three phases associated with different 'development patterns' (Bértola 2008; Oddone 2010). These phases are linked to the changes in the productive structures and trade regimes, that is to the different degrees of specialization and integration in international markets.

First, from the last quarter of the nineteenth century to the 1920s, the economy showed increasing exports and the development of a domestic market (Bulmer-Thomas 2003). This growth model, based on the

[1] This makes Uruguay a country with very low density of population, close to 20 inhabitants per square km, a level similar to that of Sweden or ten times smaller than Italy.

production of a few primary products, was quite successful and, as seen, allowed the country to obtain welfare levels close to those of the core economies. This positive period came to an end with the Great Depression, which had severe adverse effects on an open economy such as the Uruguayan, and the meagre performance lasted until the mid-1930s.

After the World War II, the economy presented a new period of steady economic growth characterized by an increasing participation of the state in the economy, the implementation of a (truncated) process of Import Substitution Industrialization (ISI) and improvements in personal income distribution. However, the positive evolution had finished by the end of the 1950s, and the economy entered a long period of 'stagflation' that lasted until the beginning of the 1970s.

During the first half of the 1970s, in a context of deep social and political change, the economy experienced important adjustments that resulted in a new development pattern. Increasing trade openness, financial liberalization and new regional trade agreements gave place to a new phase of economic expansion that lasted until the end of the twentieth century in a sort of re-globalization period. The beginning of the twenty-first century was, however, dominated by one of the worst crises in Uruguay's history. Since 2003, the economy has nonetheless largely recovered through a sound involvement in the international commodity markets, significant changes in the organization of primary production and the regulation of the labour market.

In this context, the aim of this chapter is to analyse the long-term evolution of the Uruguayan economy from a different angle, adopting a regional perspective. In so doing, we first present estimates of regional GDP for the 19 provinces (*departamentos*) that make up Uruguay nowadays. Our estimates correspond to 16 benchmark years throughout roughly a century and a half, from 1872 to 2012. This information allows us to evaluate the main patterns of regional income inequality from the globalization of the Atlantic economy in the late nineteenth century until today. Further, the regional GDP database offers the possibility to examine the following: the magnitude of the relevance of Montevideo and its evolution over time; the impact of different trade regimes on the levels of regional inequality; the effect of public policies during the state-led industrialization on the spatial distribution of economic activity; or the evolution of the economies of the borders with Argentina and Brazil.

To this end, the chapter is structured as follows. First, we briefly survey the main features of the Uruguayan economy from colonial times to the present (Sect. 2). Then, we define the spatial unit of analysis and outline the estimation methodology and sources (Sect. 3). Next, we present the main results and discuss our findings (Sect. 4). Finally, as conclusion, we hypothesize about the potential forces behind the evolution of regional inequality in Uruguay in the long run (Sect. 5).

2 Historical Background

Over the last century and a half, the Uruguayan economy experienced recurrent ups and downs. While GDP per capita multiplied by six between the 1870s and today, this increase did not prevent the growth of the gap between Uruguay's income per capita and that of the most developed economies in spite of a promising beginning. In the 1870s, Uruguay was among the wealthiest countries in the world, close to the US levels, as Fig. 11.1 shows. From then on, divergence was plainly visible and Uruguay rapidly lost ground. On the eve of the World War I, the relative fall with respect to the US economy had been substantial (40%) and continued afterwards throughout the twentieth century until it reached an all-time minimum during the 2002 crisis (20%). In this context of relative decline,

Fig. 11.1 Uruguay GDP per capita relative to US GDP per capita, 1870–2015. (Source: Maddison project database)

we next present a brief summary of the evolution of the Uruguayan economy, with a particular focus on its insertion in international markets and on the different policies and productive models promoted by the State.

In colonial times, during the sixteenth and seventeenth centuries, the River Plate was not a particularly attractive region, distantly located in the far south of the Spanish Empire and lacking economically interesting resources to exploit, such as spices or precious metals. One of the first European settlements in Uruguay (*Banda Oriental*, according to its colonial name) was Colonia del Sacramento, a Portuguese military fortress founded in 1680, located across from Buenos Aires, whose foundation dates from 1580. Montevideo, also a fortress, was founded by the Spaniards in 1724 on the River Plate coast, almost 180 km from Colonia del Sacramento towards the East.

Uruguay was on the border between the Spanish and Portuguese empires, a condition which would be decisive for the creation of an independent state in 1828, with an active British participation (Bértola 2008). Before independence, migrant flows from Spain were significant, and they founded several towns with the aim to restrain the Portuguese advances on the Spanish imperial possessions. The dissolution of the Jesuit Missions in the last quarter of the eighteenth century also meant the arrival of numerous indigenous communities (*guaraníes*) (González and Rodríguez 1990), and the inflow of African slaves, arriving from Brazil (in the North) or directly from Africa, was important too (Borucki et al. 2004). After independence, immigration was promoted by liberal governments, which argued that populating the territory meant increasing the wealth of the nation and the military power of the State. They also claimed that it contributed to defining the borders with the neighbouring nations.

Memoirs and historical chronicles agree on the exceptional conditions of Montevideo's harbour (Mulhall and Mulhall 1892), which constitutes the best natural seaport in this area of the continent. The harbour promptly became the end point of trans-Atlantic routes into the region. It was, therefore, the support for the Spanish navy in the colonial period and for strong international trade interests—particularly British and French—in the independent period, in addition to promoting a thriving commercial elite (Barrán and Nahum 1973). European immigration settled mainly in Montevideo, where its presence was significant since colonial times (in 1860, almost half of its inhabitants were foreigners and, in 1908, almost a third were). In regional terms, the centre of the economic activity was

Montevideo—highly specialized in administrative and trade activities—and the rest of the territory enjoyed a huge natural wealth related to abundant land and livestock.

Two major transformations paved the road for economic modernization in the 1870s: the wire fencing of rural lands and the arrival of immigration flows composed of progressive rural producers related, fundamentally, to wool production (Barrán and Nahum 1967, 1971). This new rural class was predominant in the Littoral of the Uruguay River and extended its influence to the south in the River Plate coastal region, which coincides with the most productive lands of the territory (Millot and Bertino 1996). In the rest of the country, the rural traditionalism continued prevailing over technical and business innovations.

The following two decades were characterized by an ongoing improvement in the state communications and administrative systems which, however, had to coexist with considerable resistance to the central authority of provincial governments and several internal conflicts. Usually, scholars consider 1904 the year of the last internal armed uprising and the definitive consolidation of the state as the national authority. In fact, this meant the triumph of the port city (Montevideo) over the rest of the territory, and it converted the state into the constructor of the 'social order' (Arocena 1992). In short, this period could be associated with the consolidation of Montevideo as the commercial, industrial and administrative centre.

In addition, the improvement in infrastructure and transport in the decades prior to World War I favoured the integration of the domestic market. In this process, the connection of the inland provinces with coastal locations, mainly with the port of Montevideo from which most exports were sent to international markets, played a decisive role, and railways were particularly important. Although the railway construction started relatively late—the first stretch was opened in 1869, with a delay partly due to the impact of a civil war called *Guerra Grande*—by 1913, Uruguay had one of the densest railway networks in the continent which accounted for 2577 km (Díaz 2017). The railway system, which was privately owned by a few British companies, was designed in a centralized way, so it mainly connected distant points with the capital.[2] In this process of expansion of the domestic market, in the first decades of the twentieth century, in addi-

[2] Although the Uruguayan railway system helped to integrate the national market, their economic impact seems to have been much lower than in other countries based on the lim-

tion to Spanish and Italian immigrants, the inflow of immigrants from Middle East and East Europe increased.[3]

The historical characterization of Uruguay as an agrarian economy since the nineteenth century is essentially based on the type of integration in the international commodity markets (jerky, leather, wool and beef). However, this type of agrarian trade specialization required the extended presence of activities that supported the commercialization of these products, such as transport and storage, logistic, financial and professional services, and public services. In addition, Uruguay experienced a dynamic urbanization process that rapidly transformed Montevideo, the administrative capital of the country, into the head of a macrocephalic country. Under these conditions, it is not surprising that the share of services on GDP was 45% in the years before World War I. In this evolution, the 1920s are conceived as a transition period between two development patterns (Bertino et al. 2001).

The Great Depression adversely affected an open economy like Uruguay (Jacob 1977, 1981), but also represents, in later years, the beginning of a process of industrialization of the country. In the early 1930s, the industrialization process began without state planning. However, later, there was a very active participation of the state in different areas of the economy. In fact, the ISI, more appropriately called state-led industrialization (Bértola and Ocampo 2012), had strong dynamism in the 1940s. The protectionist policy aimed at promoting the industrialization of the country, combining import taxes and fiscal exemptions with a multiple exchange rate system and the direct participation of the state in the manufacturing industry (Azar et al. 2004; Garcia Repetto 2017). Huge changes in the bargaining policy, and in particular the installation of wage councils (1943–1968), represent another important transformation of these decades. In this period, there were very favourable international conditions to support this development model due to the World War II postwar context. These conditions refer to the prior accumulation of international reserves during the conflict and the impressive improvement in the trade terms related to the Korean War. In summary, the state-led industrialization in Uruguay can be characterized by high levels of protection and incentives for manufacturing and agriculture (industrial crops),

ited amount of social savings it generated on the economy and the low profitability obtained by the railway investments (Díaz 2017).

[3] The entry of immigrants came to a halt in the 1930s but resumed after World War II.

rising real wages, decreasing economic inequality and increasing public spending (Bértola 1993, 2008).

However, the model described above based on state-directed industrialization soon faced many limitations that determined its decline since the late 1950s (Arnabal et al. 2013; Bértola 1993; Finch 1980). An interpretation of the economic crisis which the economy faced from the 1960s onwards points out that state intervention promoted the growth of a non-competitive industrial sector and inhibited capital accumulation in agriculture, affecting the comparative advantage of the economy (OPP 1972). However, the intervention of the state was decisive for promoting the diversification of the economy and for creating better conditions for economic growth and equality (Bértola 1993), but it never solved the structural restrictions. The protectionist policy, typically conceived with short-term character, resulted in protecting the low technological dynamism of the local firms, the entrepreneurs' scarce interest and education in technical issues, the comfortable self-confinement in the internal market, as well as the absence of workforce qualification policies.

The 1960s were characterized by economic stagnation and high inflation which extended into the 1970s, when a coup d'état and the institutionalization of a military government promoted a renewed modality of development (Astori 2001). As a result of the economic stagnation, from 1960 onwards, Uruguay became a source of emigrants more than a destination for immigrants (Pellegrino 2014). The worsening of the economic situation and the establishment of a military dictatorship in 1973 would explain the increase in emigration. Bilateral trade agreements with Argentina and Brazil and the liberalization of the financial market (exchange rates and capitals) characterized the new growth strategy (Notaro 1984) typified by a re-globalization or non-traditional export-led growth (Oddone 2010).

The progressive openness of the economy, the promotion of international integration programmes (Mercosur) and the financial liberalization continued, as a general pattern, in the 1990s (after the democratic restoration in 1985). From 1993 to 1998, the country showed a new process of economic growth. During this period, activities related to the insertion in the Mercosur were favoured, turning Uruguay into a financial and logistics centre for neighbouring countries, with an important development of tourism and exports to Argentina and Brazil. But, at the same time, it had a negative bias towards agro-exports destined to the rest of the world. This production model favoured Montevideo and the southern coastal provinces, especially Maldonado and Colonia, but it benefitted much less the central and northern provinces of the country (Rodríguez Miranda 2006).

Therefore, economic growth in the 1990s was based on production oriented to services and exports to Mercosur, founded on a stable exchange rate relationship with the two large neighbours, Argentina and Brazil. The devaluation of Brazil's Real in 1999 and the Argentinean crisis of 2001 broke that model, and both led to financial and economic collapse in 2002 (Mordecki 2017). Thus, the beginning of the twenty-first century was dominated by one of the most severe crises, with significant fiscal and trade imbalances, financial bankruptcies, a strong decrease in real incomes and renewed impulses to emigration (reaching almost 150,000 people in 2000–2008) (Pellegrino 2010).[4]

Since 2003, the economy has nonetheless decisively recovered with a significant presence in the international commodity markets and important changes in the organization of primary production (Errea et al. 2011). Within a very favourable international context of commodity prices, this new agricultural export boom benefitted many inland provinces, in addition to those in the South and on the border with Argentina. New primary and agro-industrial developments were exploited to their maximum potential, such as in the lumber sector (northeast of the country), the pulp industry (in the West), soybean production (in the West and the South, under the influence of investments from Argentina) and the meat industry in almost the whole country (Rodríguez Miranda et al. 2017).

In this period, policy instruments to support competitiveness have multiplied. In addition to the traditional export, capacity in entrepreneurial management and sectoral instruments as well as innovation and investment promotion created a denser policy structure to encourage advanced industries (e.g. biotechnology and pharmaceutical) (Bértola et al. 2014). Simultaneously, an increasing interest in the local development of different regions of the country has been notorious, including specific legal norms and public policies aimed at promoting productive and social changes in the interior provinces (Rodríguez Miranda 2014). As a result of economic growth, in the last decade, there has been a reversal of the negative migration trend, with new immigrant waves arriving from Latin

[4] By the end of the twentieth century, almost a half-million Uruguayans resided outside the national territory (Cabella and Pellegrino 2005).

American countries (Dominican Republic, Venezuela, Colombia) while there is also a substantial return of former emigrants.

3 GDP Estimates at the Province Level: Sources and Methods

In order to assess the long-term evolution of economic development in Uruguay from a regional perspective, we obtained estimates for 16 benchmark years from 1872 to 2012. For the years 1872, 1884, 1890, 1895, 1900, 1908, 1936, 1955, 1975, 1986, 1990, 1995, 2000 and 2005, our own estimations were taken into account, while for 1961 and 2012, official available data were considered. The latter two correspond to official data produced by state bodies (BROU and OPP-INE-BCU, respectively), but only that referred to 2012 (OPP 2016) had the support and advice of the Central Bank of Uruguay (the institution that elaborates the National Accounts). The territorialized information of GDP that we obtained refers to the current 19 provinces.

Since the eighteenth century, different regional divisions have been created in Uruguay, following economic and political criteria (Zubillaga 1977; Yagüe and Díaz-Puente 2008). Initially, the governors of the provinces (*intendentes*) were political leaders appointed by the national government, and, to a large extent, this responded to the need to prevent the local powers from rising up against the power of the country's capital. Only after the Constitution of 1918, the provincial governments began to be elected and enjoyed certain autonomy, with exclusive responsibilities that were established by law in 1935 (Arocena and Marsiglia 2017). The current administrative division was configured at the end of the nineteenth century with the last changes in political boundaries.[5]

The final provincial division of Uruguay, as it is shown in Map 11.1, configures spaces of diverse dimensions. The province of Montevideo is the smallest one as it occupies just 530 square km, and the biggest, Tacuarembó, has an area of around 15,500 square km. As a coastal country, 8 out of the 19 provinces have access to the sea, 6 of them share the border with Argentina—separated by a river which may be easily

[5] In 1880, the provinces of Río Negro and Rocha were created from the subdivision of (then larger) Paysandú and Maldonado, respectively. In 1884–1885, Artigas, Flores, Rivera and Treinta y Tres were created from the territories corresponding to Salto, San José, Tacuarembó, Cerro Largo and Lavalleja, respectively.

Map 11.1 Provinces (*departamentos*) of Uruguay. (Source: Own elaboration based on Servicio Geográfico Militar (http://www.sgm.gub.uy))

crossed—and 4 of them with Brazil—an extensive land border. Moreover, the country has mild weather with abundant rain, so the mostly flat terrain is run by large and mighty rivers, the Uruguay River, which is a natural border with Argentina being the longest one.

Our estimation of Uruguayan regional GDP is based on a strategy that, in broad terms, combines: (1) direct estimations for some sectors and years when data are available; (2) the methodology developed by Geary and Stark (2002) (hereafter G-S); and, finally, (3) the use of specific criteria to distribute national sectoral value-added (VA) in some particular activities. The choice of our benchmarks is subject to the availability of information (mainly census data). In this instance, although the availability of population censuses in Uruguay is to some extent limited, the publication of agrarian censuses, with territorialized information about production was more frequent and we also have industrial censuses that allow a direct estimation of regional production.[6] All in all, the database combines information from three previous studies that estimate regional GDPs for Uruguay in different historical periods (Castro and Willebald 2019; Martinez-Galarraga et al. 2019; Rodríguez Miranda and Goinheix 2018).[7]

The benchmarks are historically meaningful. The first estimates corresponding to 1872–1908 represent a period of strong dynamism related to the First Globalization. Castro and Willebald (2019) propose regional GDP estimates for six years and 12 economic sectors in a study that combines several estimation techniques, including the information in the Agrarian Censuses, the standard G-S methodology and the use of alternative procedures (e.g., trading license taxes) to distribute national values.[8]

Estimates from 1908 to 1975 capture the evolution of the regional economies in Uruguay from the last years of the First Globalization, going through the interwar years, the beginning, the zenith and the end of the state-led industrialization, and up to the mid-1970s, with the outbreak of the oil crisis and the establishment of the military government. In this case, the estimates come from the study by Martinez-Galarraga et al. (2019). These authors combine again direct production estimates, the G-S methodology and distribution keys elaborated from official reports to

[6] Population Censuses: 1852, 1860, 1908, 1963, 1975, 1985, 1996, 2011. Agrarian Censuses: 1852, 1872, 1900, 1908, 1916, 1924, 1937, 1943, 1951, 1956, 1966, 1970 and 1980 (there are three additional censuses for 1990, 2000 and 2011, but we used other sources for the estimation). Industrial census: 1936 (there are three additional industrial censuses for 1975, 1988 and 1997, but we used other sources).

[7] The full details of the estimation procedures and the sources used in each one of the years included in this study can be found in these works.

[8] The economic sectors considered are: 'Agriculture'—livestock and crops—'Mining', 'Construction', 'Manufacturing', 'Utilities', 'Wholesale and retail trade', 'Government', 'Financial intermediation', 'Education, health, and other community, social and personal services', 'Transport and storage', 'Communications' and 'Real estate activities'.

obtain GDP for Uruguay's provinces, in this case, disaggregated in 11 economic sectors.[9]

In the 1970s, there followed a new period of openness, financial liberalization and international regional integration, whose base was developed during the military government and extended until the 1990s. Then, Uruguay suffered in 2001–2002 the most serious economic crisis in the last 100 years, and emerged in a new international context in the twenty-first century. This period is captured with the GDP estimates presented by Rodríguez Miranda and Goinheix (2018). In this study, the standard methodology developed by G-S is applied to data from household surveys (wages and employment) to estimate industries and services, with some adjustments to the G-S method for specific sectors specially for some capital-intensive industrial branches. To estimate agriculture VA, the authors build value indices for different provincial product baskets taking as base year the official estimates available for 2008 (OPP 2016). Additionally, direct estimation is made in some particular sectors (e.g. mining and energy) and distribution keys are used in other cases (e.g. fishing and forestry). The authors present annual estimates for ten economic sectors, and we take as benchmark years those corresponding to (around) five-year periods: 1986, 1990, 1995, 2000, 2005 and 2012.[10]

Finally, our estimations require two additional data series: total and sectoral GDP for Uruguay in current prices and population by province. We use Uruguay's GDP series disaggregated for 11 economic sectors, provided in Román and Willebald (2019), annually, from 1870 to 2017. In turn, population censuses offer provincial data for census years (*Instituto Nacional de Estadística*) and recent estimates offer new annual series of total population (Nathan 2014; Pellegrino n.d.).[11] To obtain provincial figures for the missing years, when necessary, we interpolate the intercensal years and rescale to these recent estimates of total population.

[9] This work includes the following sectors: 'Agriculture', 'Manufacturing', 'Utilities', 'Construction', 'Wholesale and retail trade, restaurants and hotels', 'Transport', 'Communications', 'Financial intermediation', 'Real estate activities', 'Government', 'Education, health, social work, and other community, social and personal service activities'.

[10] 'Agriculture (livestock, crops and forestry) and fishing', 'Mining', 'Manufacturing', 'Construction', 'Utilities', 'Restaurants and hotels', 'Transport and logistics', 'Telecommunications', 'Services to companies, real estate and financial', 'Other services (including public administration)'.

[11] We would like to thank Professor Wanda Cabella for this suggestion.

4 Results: Stylized Facts of Regional Income Distribution in Uruguay

4.1 *Montevideo: A Suction Pump?*

From an economic—as well as demographic—perspective, the relevance of Montevideo is one of the most remarkable features of the regional history of Uruguay. The distribution of Uruguay's GDP by province (Table 11.1) shows a very high concentration of economic activity in Montevideo, even higher than the population density. It currently accounts for more than half of Uruguay's GDP (51.3%). Besides Canelones, which represents a significant proportion of the national income, close to 10%, only Maldonado and Colonia reach values around 5% of Uruguay's GDP. The remaining provinces show in general a small participation that barely amounts to 3% and an evolution characterized by a sustained declining share over time.

The prominent role of Montevideo is thus one of the main stylized facts that emerge from Table 11.1, although in the long term some fluctuations can be observed. During the decades of the First Globalization, the share of Montevideo in the national GDP was lower, yet with a large share around 45–48%.[12] Importantly, in the interwar years (1908–1936) an increase in the concentration of economic activity in Montevideo occurred, reaching a share close to 55%. This share hardly changed in the next decades (1936–1961), during the years of the state-led industrialization. However, by 1975, Montevideo had again increased its participation in Uruguay's GDP, and from then until 2000 the share oscillated between 57% and 59%, reaching an all-time maximum in 2000. Interestingly, after the severe economic crisis and the beginning of a new agro-export growth model with state policies to support competitiveness, the first decades of the twenty-first century have witnessed a substantial reduction of almost eight points in the share of Montevideo, which stands, as seen, currently around 51% (a value similar to that of the interwar years).

[12] In 1890, this share increased to 54% probably as a result of the consumption and speculative boom that preceded the financial and economic crisis of that year. This was nonetheless a transitory shock, and the share of Montevideo returned to 47% in 1895.

Table 11.1 Regional shares in Uruguayan GDP (%) (Source: Own estimates)

Province	*1872*	*1884*	*1890*	*1895*	*1900*	*1908*	*1936*	*1955*	*1961*	*1975*	*1986*	*1990*	*1995*	*2000*	*2005*	*2012*
Artigas	2.9	2.6	2.1	2.7	2.5	1.7	1.8	1.5	1.5	1.2	1.3	0.9	1.2	0.9	1.5	1.5
Canelones	3.7	4.0	3.4	4.3	4.0	6.3	5.8	7.2	7.9	8.2	6.8	8.1	8.7	10.2	7.8	9.4
Cerro Largo	3.4	3.5	2.9	3.3	2.9	2.5	2.1	1.9	2.0	1.7	1.9	1.3	1.7	1.4	1.9	1.8
Colonia	4.6	5.7	5.3	5.3	7.4	5.4	3.9	3.8	4.1	3.7	1.9	3.2	3.8	2.8	4.2	4.7
Durazno	3.0	3.5	2.7	3.1	3.2	2.1	1.8	1.9	1.7	1.8	1.9	1.2	1.5	1.0	1.4	1.4
Flores	1.5	1.9	1.7	1.8	1.8	1.2	1.1	1.2	0.9	0.7	1.1	1.0	0.8	0.9	0.7	0.8
Florida	2.5	2.6	2.2	2.8	2.9	3.7	3.1	2.8	2.5	2.1	2.4	1.5	1.6	1.5	1.5	1.9
Lavalleja	1.6	1.3	1.2	1.3	1.9	1.9	1.6	2.0	1.7	1.9	2.3	1.4	1.3	1.4	1.2	1.6
Maldonado	3.0	2.6	2.0	2.4	2.5	1.2	2.2	2.8	3.1	3.0	3.1	6.1	4.7	5.0	5.4	5.6
Montevideo	45.4	45.6	54.2	46.9	45.1	48.1	54.5	53.3	54.8	57.3	54.0	57.9	57.6	58.9	56.0	51.3
Paysandú	5.7	5.5	4.0	4.3	4.2	4.5	3.7	3.2	3.3	2.8	5.1	2.7	2.6	2.4	2.5	2.8
Río Negro	2.2	2.7	2.4	2.8	2.6	2.9	2.4	2.0	1.6	1.9	2.2	1.6	1.5	1.4	1.8	2.3
Rivera	1.8	1.5	1.4	1.7	1.6	1.7	1.7	1.7	1.7	1.6	2.4	1.4	1.7	1.9	2.3	2.1
Rocha	2.2	1.8	1.7	2.2	2.3	1.7	1.7	2.1	1.7	1.7	1.6	1.5	1.4	1.3	1.5	1.8
Salto	4.8	4.2	3.4	4.0	4.1	3.2	2.8	2.7	2.7	2.5	4.4	3.4	3.3	2.8	3.0	2.7
San José	2.0	2.0	1.7	2.3	2.3	4.0	3.3	3.0	2.6	2.3	2.0	2.0	1.9	2.2	2.5	2.9
Soriano	3.7	3.6	2.9	3.5	3.6	4.1	2.7	3.2	2.7	2.2	2.7	2.1	2.0	1.6	2.0	2.4
Tacuarembó	3.9	3.4	2.8	3.2	2.9	2.5	2.4	2.4	2.3	2.1	2.1	1.9	1.7	1.5	1.7	1.9
Treinta y Tres	2.1	2.2	1.8	2.1	2.1	1.3	1.4	1.4	1.3	1.2	1.0	0.9	1.0	1.0	1.0	1.2
Uruguay	*100.0*	*100.0*	*100.0*	*100.0*	*100.0*	*100.0*	*100.0*	*100.0*	*100.0*	*100.0*	*100.0*	*100.0*	*100.0*	*100.0*	*100.0*	*100.0*

4.2 *Regional Inequality: A Convergence Story?*

Combining our estimates of regional GDPs and population, we use GDP per capita at the province level to explore the long-term evolution of regional inequality in Uruguay. Methodologically, we follow the approach suggested in the empirical literature on economic growth (Barro and Sala-i-Martin 1991). Thus, we focus on the existence of economic convergence/divergence across regions and over time, examining the hypothesis of σ-convergence, that is, if for a given set of economies the dispersion or inequality in terms of per capita income tends to decrease/increase over time.

To measure the dispersion of per capita income over time, we first compute a simple coefficient of variation (SCV), a widely used indicator in the empirical growth literature. To consider the potential effects on the results that may arise from differences in the size of the provinces in demographic terms, we also present the population-weighted coefficient of variation (WCV) (Williamson 1965). If the WCV is above the SCV, it implies that the most populated provinces are in the extremes of the income distribution. In the case of Uruguay, considering the provinces' population seems to be crucial given that Montevideo concentrates a large share of the county's population. Figure 11.2 presents the long-term evolution of regional inequality in Uruguay.[13]

While both indicators, the SCV and the WCV, depict a similar trend over time, some differences in the levels of inequality can nonetheless be appreciated. In general, the SCV is slightly below the WCV, indicating that the most populated provinces have tended to have higher GDP per capita over time and that the least-populated provinces have tended to be less dynamic.[14] If we focus on the WCV, we see that the years of the First Globalization were characterized by high levels of regional inequality and by a general yet rather slight trend towards the reduction of disparities.[15] Further, this trend intensified during the interwar years and continued from then on until the early 1960s, when a historical minimum in regional inequality levels in Uruguay was reached. Thus, the period of sustained

[13] Similar results are obtained if alternative inequality indicators (Gini, Theil, MLD) are used.

[14] There are some exceptions though. In the 1950s and 1960s, both indicators show similar levels, and in the late 1980s the SCV sheds higher values than the WCV.

[15] The peak in 1890 might be related with the economic boom that preceded the financial and productive crisis of that year.

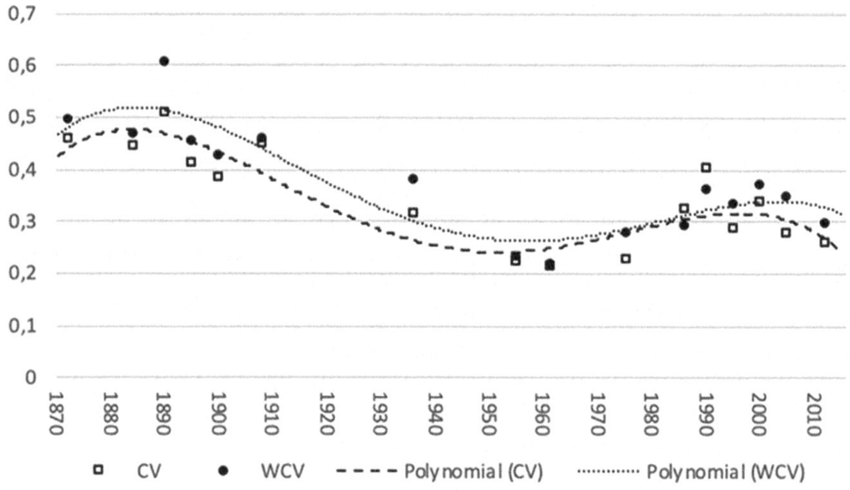

Fig. 11.2 Regional inequality in Uruguay (GDP per capita), 1872–2012. (Source: Own elaboration)

convergence, from the last decades of the nineteenth century to the 1960s, covered the agro-export model corresponding to the era of the First Globalization, the troublesome interwar years and also the period of economic growth, industrialization and increasing state intervention during the 1940s and 1950s.

However, after this long-term trajectory of convergence, regional inequality increased significantly and reached again high levels in the 1990s, close to those registered at the beginning of the twentieth century, at the end of the First Globalization. What is nonetheless particularly interesting in the case of Uruguay is the evolution of territorial disparities in the twenty-first century. Figure 11.2 shows a clear reversal of the trend in the 2000s after the most severe economic crisis of Uruguay and the new agro-export growth model. This means that the U-shaped evolution that ended with high regional inequality in the 1990s has given way to a new process of regional income convergence.

4.3 *Persistence, Mobility, Reversals of Fortune and Other Stories*

Having presented the general trends of the distribution as a whole, to gain further insights, we next focus on the evolution of income per capita for the individual provinces. Table 11.2 shows the Uruguayan provinces according to their relative GDP per capita (Uruguay = 100) in all our benchmark years. On the one hand, some persistence at the top and the bottom can be seen, with some provinces consistently occupying these positions. However, a significant degree of mobility is also observed with provinces rapidly improving their relative position or falling behind. Based on this evidence, we classify Uruguay's provinces into five different groups: (1) persistently rich; (2) persistently poor; (3) middle income; (4) reversal of fortunes; (5) convergent.

First, Montevideo and Río Negro are two persistently rich provinces. The leadership of Montevideo is evident as, on average, it exceeded the mean of the country by 45%, showing the highest ratio in 1890 (190) and the lowest in 1961 (120). As regards the evolution, it was more clearly above the average in the period between 1872 and 1936 (54% to 90%), than from then on (from 20% to 41%). Nowadays, the GDP per capita of Montevideo exceeds the average of Uruguay by 30 percentage points. The other rich province is Río Negro. This province traditionally had an economic structure based on agriculture, but the combination of abundant natural resources, low population density and the historical presence of big industrial firms could explain the relatively high income per capita in the province from the nineteenth century until the 1950s. Afterwards, its income per capita evolved around the average of the country until the beginning of the twenty-first century, when a new increasing trend related to new investment in pulp industry started.

At the other extreme, we find the persistently poor provinces. At the beginning of our period of study they were between 25% and 60% below the national average; today they are still between 15% and 40% below. This group includes provinces in the centre and north-east of the country (Cerro Largo, Durazno and Treinta y Tres) and those bordering Montevideo (Canelones and San José). On the one hand, the former three are among the regional economies with the lowest level of productive diversification in the country until today (Rodríguez Miranda et al. 2017) and historically specialized in extensive livestock production in low-quality soils.[16] This implies a relatively low income per capita in historical perspective.

[16] The incorporation of rice crops in the second half of the twentieth century meant certain degree of diversification.

Table 11.2 Relative GDP per capita for Uruguayan provinces, 1872–2012 (Uruguay = 100) (Source: Own estimates)

Province	*1872*	*1884*	*1890*	*1895*	*1900*	*1908*	*1936*	*1955*	*1961*	*1975*	*1986*	*1990*	*1995*	*2000*	*2005*	*2012*
Artigas	167	132	97	120	106	68	78	70	71	58	57	40	50	39	62	65
Canelones	41	45	39	49	47	75	62	72	80	70	54	62	63	70	52	58
Cerro Largo	63	70	60	70	63	59	59	63	72	64	72	49	65	54	70	69
Colonia	79	100	95	97	137	103	82	90	101	92	49	84	99	75	113	125
Durazno	74	84	67	76	78	53	61	83	82	91	100	67	86	58	76	79
Flores	103	125	110	119	118	79	92	117	91	82	131	117	102	113	91	96
Florida	49	53	47	61	65	84	91	102	101	89	105	69	73	70	73	92
Lavalleja	32	26	24	27	39	38	45	69	64	81	112	68	67	75	63	88
Maldonado	73	72	59	74	83	42	84	116	130	109	96	171	120	119	122	109
Montevideo	168	162	190	162	154	162	146	123	120	129	122	133	135	141	137	130
Paysandú	117	124	94	104	108	122	101	90	96	79	146	77	75	69	73	82
Río Negro	168	178	149	166	149	150	124	105	91	106	131	99	94	86	108	138
Rivera	122	78	65	69	58	50	53	55	56	53	79	45	54	59	73	66
Rocha	116	80	68	80	79	52	65	89	79	79	71	66	65	58	70	84
Salto	90	84	70	84	89	71	68	71	74	69	120	92	88	74	79	71
San José	46	46	40	51	52	91	86	92	83	72	64	66	61	70	78	87
Soriano	65	72	63	79	86	107	78	103	88	78	100	79	76	62	78	95
Tacuarembó	111	87	70	77	67	55	63	76	75	70	76	68	63	53	63	67
Treinta y Tres	74	76	64	76	76	48	62	75	76	71	60	59	65	65	69	81

On the other hand, Canelones and San José are quite different cases. They have the particularity of showing a high heterogeneity within their respective territories. In a large part of the territory, there is a very diversified agricultural economy, where, in addition to livestock, farm products, dairy industry and vineyards stand out. These diversified agricultural developments benefit from the proximity to Montevideo (the big market), as predicted by the well-known von Thünen model, which should contribute to placing these provinces in a favourable position in the national context. However, especially since the 1980s, dormitory cities and villages have developed on the border with Montevideo and within its metropolitan influence, including informal settlements, with a population that works in low-productivity jobs and largely located in Montevideo.[17] Then, the border areas with Montevideo host a large population but have a relatively low value generation in the territory (i.e. the local gross VA per capita is low).

In fact, large capitals in Latin America tend to grow in such a way that their metropolitan areas, far from benefitting from better development possibilities, suffer from worrying processes of residential segregation, deprivation of basic services and fragmented urban models. This phenomenon is explained by the importance of the informal land and housing market in Latin America, which generates an expansion of the city based on residential segregation and urban fragmentation (Ward 2009). This informal market is developed by private promoters in a context of low-income popular classes that are expelled from urban areas with good services. This process generates monocentric metropolitan areas with substantial socio-territorial and labour market inequalities, which give rise to greater mobility of the poor and favours the encapsulation of the rich (Rodríguez Vignoli 2008). All these factors do not allow making the most of the agglomeration economies that the theory points out as beneficial for regional economic development. Hence, spatial spillovers due to proximity to Montevideo did not seem to have generated a positive net effect for these provinces. On the contrary, both have traditionally shown relatively low per capita income and remain so.

[17] With information from the Continuous Household Surveys of the *Instituto Nacional de Estadística* for the years 2011 to 2013, it can be seen that approximately 32% of the population of Canelones works in Montevideo and the same occurs with 16% of the population of San José. On the contrary, less than 2% of the population of Montevideo works in Canelones and only 0.2% in San José. This flow of commuters of Canelones and San José occurs only regarding Montevideo and it is practically inexistent with the other provinces.

A third group of provinces can be characterized as middle-income group. This group is composed of five provinces located in the Littoral and in the south of the country (Colonia, Flores, Paysandú, Salto and Soriano). They have enjoyed the best soils of the territory, so intensive agricultural activities have developed there in the course of the twentieth century (crops, dairy industry), providing a large supply of foodstuffs. In addition to this agricultural specialization, these provinces were also favoured by the establishment of modern means of transport and communications, the historical influence and accessibility to a large urban centre such as Buenos Aires—sometimes as nearby as Montevideo, especially in the nineteenth and the first decades of twentieth century—and the influx of progressive immigrants.

While these three first groups are characterised by a marked persistence, other provinces have experienced a remarkable mobility over time. A fourth group of provinces includes those that experienced a clear reversal of fortune: they started with relatively high income but eventually became poor provinces. While these provinces exceeded by more than ten points the national average in the 1870s, by 1908, at the end of the First Globalization, they were already below that average (30–50%). This was indeed a negative and rapid reversal of fortune from rich to poor provinces. Further, they remained there for most of the twentieth century. This group includes the northern provinces of the country (Artigas, Rivera and Tacuarembó) and Rocha, on the border with Brazil in the East. In the late nineteenth century, the combination of large natural resources, large herds (livestock and sheep) and low population density made it possible to generate significant amounts of VA distributed among few inhabitants. However, this specialization in cattle and the absence of structural changes soon proved their limitations for long-term growth. As early as the beginning of the twentieth century, cattle production gave signs of stagnation and no alternative activities were developed.

Finally, a last group includes the convergent provinces, which in this case experienced a somewhat positive reversal of fortune that allowed them to reduce the gap and even catch up with the average of the country. This group includes Florida, Lavalleja and Maldonado. The most outstanding case is Maldonado, a province that started the twentieth century—together with Lavalleja—as one of the poorest provinces but, nonetheless, occupied the top positions of the ranking from the 1980s onwards. Maldonado based its success on the specialization in tertiary activities (fundamentally services) and big pushes of the construction industry (from the 1970s) linked to tourism and financial sectors (Rodríguez Miranda and Goinheix 2018). Florida and Lavalleja both followed a similar evolution, with a sustained improvement from 1908 until the 1970s, but then lost ground mainly after the late 1980s, and recovered again with the new century after the 2001 crisis. It should be noted that, even though the income per capita improved over the period, these two provinces have remained below the country's average. Florida converged thanks to its specialization in intensive agriculture (mainly dairy industries and industrial crops). Lavalleja had several characteristics that could put it in the same position as the poor provinces of the country. However, its small population and productive diversification (with some relevant sectors at a national scale like cement, soft drinks and milling) allowed improving the income per capita of the region (Rodríguez Miranda et al. 2017).[18]

4.4 *The Changing Economic Geography of Uruguay*

From a geographical point of view, at the beginning of the 1870s, the Uruguayan economy was turned towards the North, with the only exception of Montevideo in the South (Map 11.2). As mentioned before, in colonial times and the first post-independence decades, Montevideo became the main economic centre including the port, financial services, commerce, and political and military power. However, in the north of the country there was a great source of wealth since it had a huge stock of cattle. The combination of these resources and a small population explains the high income per capita. Additionally, at a time when distances and traditional land transport were an important limitation, the economy of the North was not so dependent on Montevideo, and was closely linked to the nearest markets located on the coast of the Uruguay River—along the border with Argentina—and in the south of Brazil.

In the Uruguayan historiography, the features of the occupation of the territorial space in the century previous to 1850 have been discussed. The most traditional literature considered Montevideo the centre of gravity of the territory based on the idea that the expansion of the markets (and population) occurred from Montevideo to the rest of the territory.

[18] Lavalleja, together with Treinta y Tres and Rocha, is under the influence of Maldonado, which has become an urban centre of reference and received migration from the eastern region of the country (Martínez et al. 2016).

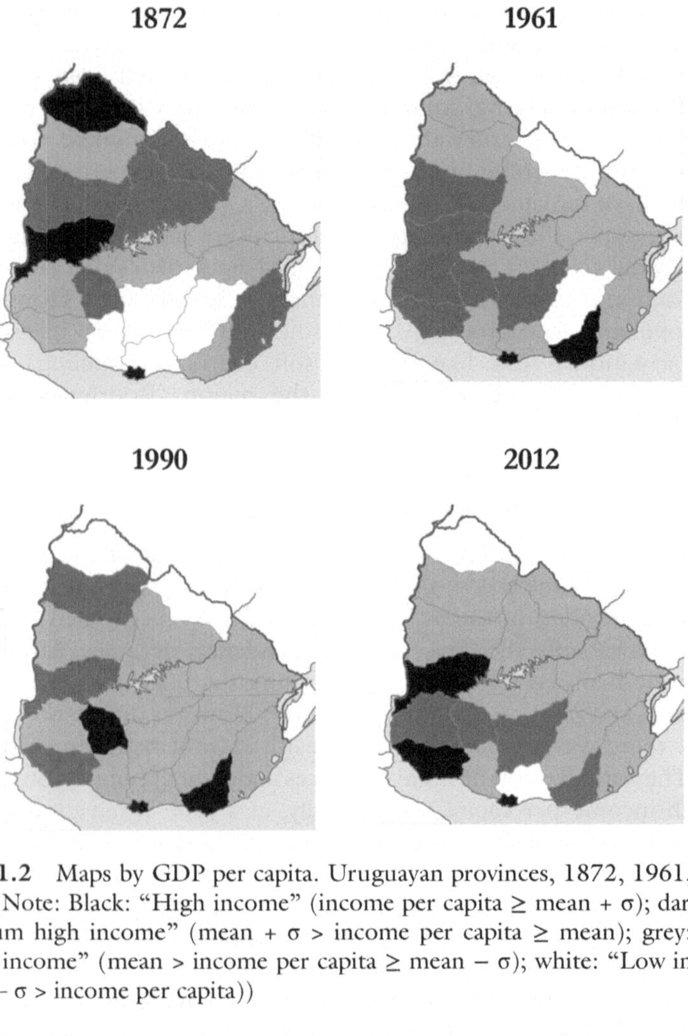

Map 11.2 Maps by GDP per capita. Uruguayan provinces, 1872, 1961, 1990, 2012. (Note: Black: "High income" (income per capita $\geq$ mean + σ); dark grey: "Medium high income" (mean + σ > income per capita $\geq$ mean); grey: "Low middle income" (mean > income per capita $\geq$ mean − σ); white: "Low income" (mean − σ > income per capita))

However, Moraes (2008) argues that this process included, in addition to this axe named *sur-atlántico*, another axe named *norte-misionero*, which comprised active product and factor markets, and historically represented the long-run influence of the *Misiones Orientales* in the north of (current) Uruguay. Our results support this latter representation, which seems to reflect appropriately the regional characterization of Uruguay in the early decades of the First Globalization.

During the last third of the nineteenth century, the Uruguayan economy gravitated to the West (Littoral) and South. Therefore, in the beginning of the twentieth century, the provinces with high incomes per capita were more dispersed in the territory. The Littoral region—on the Uruguay River, along the border with Argentina—constituted an area which, according to the local historiography, was characterized by progressive agrarian producers, modern methods of production and a definite 'capitalist mentality' (Barrán and Nahum 1978). In the first decades of the twentieth century (1908–1936), the geographical pattern continued changing and the South presented the highest economic dynamism. Thus, the structure inherited from the First Globalization progressively decanted towards the South. Here, the emergence of Maldonado stands out and will be consolidated.

On this spatial structure the state-led industrialization will operate. As we have seen, it had an equalizing effect in terms of convergence, which also results in a greater dispersion of economic activity in space. This result reinforces the idea that industrialization in Uruguay did not have adverse consequences in terms of regional inequality. At the end of the ISI process, the majority of the provinces presented a middle GDP per capita, and only two provinces—Rivera and Lavalleja—were typically poor (Map 11.2, 1961). In general terms, we observe a geographical pattern in which the provinces with the highest incomes are located in the Littoral and in the South, forming a sort of 'L' shape, similar to that identified in the end of the century (Rodríguez Miranda 2006).

Since then, no noteworthy changes in the economic geography of Uruguay have been observed. With the exception of some "islands of progress", the rest of the provinces have remained around the country's average or relatively poor. Some scattered rich provinces in the South (Montevideo), West (Colonia), East (Maldonado), centre (Flores) and Littoral (Río Negro) have consolidated their positions, although their dynamism has varied over time. In general, the provinces with the lowest per capita income are those located in the border with Brazil and the adjacent provinces to Montevideo.

5 What Explains the Evolution of Regional Inequality over Time?

In the previous pages, we presented the main patterns in regional income inequality in Uruguay since the late nineteenth century. In what follows, we hypothesize about the forces that might be behind such patterns. To do this, we rely on different theoretical strands. On the one hand, the neoclassical trade theory argues that regional incomes differ because of differences in factor endowments and factor prices. Yet, the increase in trade and factor movements leads to factor price equalization across regions and convergence.[19]

On the other hand, geography can also influence the distribution of regional income. Two different views are usually considered: 'first nature' and 'second nature' geography. The first concept refers to pure geography elements, such as the environmental, ecological or physical conditions of countries (Gallup et al. 1999). 'Second nature geography' is represented by New Economic Geography (NEG) models in which agglomeration forces may give rise to the concentration of economic activity and, consequently, lead to an uneven distribution of income across locations (Fujita et al. 1999).[20] In short, NEG argues that market integration could initially lead to regional divergence, although in more mature stages of the process, when trade costs are sufficiently low, the trend may be reversed and convergence may appear (Puga 1999).

This non-monotonic evolution seems to be more in line with the historical experience. Williamson (1965) argues that throughout the economic development process regional inequality exhibits an inverted U-shaped pattern: in the early stages of modern economic growth, industrial activity concentrates in specific locations while the rest of the regions remain largely agricultural, and, therefore, income inequality across regions increases. However, over time, these disparities eventually tend to disappear through the spread of industrialization and the homogenization of economic structures across regions.

[19] It should be noted, however, that market integration may also lead to divergence because regions may differ in factor endowments and differences in regional specialization may increase (Slaughter 1997). In any case, factor price equalization (FPE) theorem requires a long list of strict assumptions (Samuelson 1949) to hold the conclusions.

[20] These models assume imperfect competition, increasing returns to scale and reductions in transport costs, which may generate pecuniary externalities in firms and workers' location choices.

In the case of Uruguay, we have shown that the evolution of regional inequality was characterized by regional convergence throughout the century that goes from the early 1870s to the 1960s. From then on, regional inequality experienced an increasing trend for almost three decades. However, after the severe economic crisis of 2001–2002, divergence came to a halt and territorial disparities began to decrease again. The Uruguayan experience, therefore, does not reproduce the U-inverted pattern suggested by Williamson (1965), which, actually, appears in a good number of early industrialized countries in Western Europe and the US. The marked specialization in primary production and the absence of a strong industrialization process since the nineteenth century—that is, the slow advance of structural change—may explain this result.

In this respect, some additional issues may be highlighted. First, the performance of Uruguay in terms of the evolution of spatial disparities is, to a large extent, comparable to that followed by the Scandinavian countries, characterized also by abundant natural resources, low population density and late industrialization. These countries show a pattern of regional inequality in which convergence was the norm since the late nineteenth century until the oil crisis in the 1970s when divergence big time arrived (Enflo et al. 2014; Rosés and Wolf 2019). Second, industrialization—developed under the umbrella of the state after the 1930s—did not foster regional imbalances, but the opposite. Third, if we put in a more global perspective the divergence recorded since the 1970s, Uruguay does not represent an exception, given that in most countries regional convergence came to a halt in the 1980s and, in general, divergence began to emerge (Lessmann 2014). What makes the Uruguayan experience different with respect to those European cases is that after the 2001–2002 economic crisis, divergence came to a halt and territorial disparities began to decrease again. This new period of convergence, thus, differentiates the country from the general pattern of increasing regional divergence in the last decades.[21]

What forces might have shaped this evolution of regional inequality in Uruguay? One of the main findings arising from the evidence presented is the large share that Montevideo represented over time, both demographically and economically. It is possible to hypothesize that the advantages derived from its geography played a role in the early economic success of

[21] The effect of the Great Recession was, at least in the south of Europe, the opposite (see Díez-Minguela et al. 2018, for Spain, and Petrakos and Psycharis 2016, for Greece).

Montevideo. In particular, access to the sea and the fact that the city was built around a natural harbour with excellent conditions may explain the concentration of the economic activity (and people) in the capital. This 'first-nature-geography' characteristic conferred Montevideo a privileged access to international markets, and this natural advantage became crucial throughout the nineteenth century as international trade thrived, particularly during the years of the First Globalization.

Agglomeration, or 'second-nature-geography' forces, thus reinforced the initial natural advantages enjoyed by Montevideo. In this process, a good number of services related to the flourishing trade activities emerged (banking, finances, transport and commerce) and, likewise, manufacturing and construction activities concentrated in the capital as its population increased. Montevideo then became an important urban agglomeration in the area, a sizeable market for final goods itself, and, to put it in Marshallian terms, a large market of skilled-labour.[22]

While Montevideo concentrated a great share of production and population, regional inequality slightly decreased from the late nineteenth century to World War I, and this trend became more pronounced during the interwar years. This result points to the existence of other relevant forces that were able to offset the NEG-type agglomeration forces described above. Here, the arguments provided by the traditional trade theory may help explain regional convergence. The availability of natural resources makes almost the whole of Uruguay a country apt for agrarian production. This comparative advantage, in a period in which trade was booming in the Atlantic economy—and considering the limited size of the domestic market—explains that most of the agrarian production, mainly from animal origin (jerky, leather, wool and beef), was oriented towards exports. Under these circumstances, all regions specialized in primary production and benefitted from international trade. Furthermore, the integration of the domestic market through the construction of the railways that connected the inland and landlocked provinces of Uruguay with the port of Montevideo reduced trade costs and reinforced regional convergence during the First Globalization and the interwar years. Towards the World War

[22] A similar argument could be put forward, although to a lower extent, to explain the economic dynamism in these years of the western provinces of the country located on the Uruguay River. They enjoyed a double advantage: on the one hand, they could rely on coastal shipping (which increased in volume up to 1912) and, on the other hand, they benefitted from a good access to the Argentinian market, and particularly to Buenos Aires.

I, the railway system was practically completed and, since the 1920s, the motor transport (passenger and freight transport) evidenced a true transport revolution (Bertino et al. 2005). This innovation reinforced the previous evolution and was vital for the expansion of the internal market in the next development stage.

Nonetheless, the state also played an important role in promoting the development of agricultural value chains in this period. An example of this is the law about the creation of Agronomic Experimental Stations in 1911 (second presidency of José Batlle y Ordóñez), which permitted in the following decades the development of public–private partnership and research capabilities applied to improve the competitiveness of production in the inland provinces. Some decades later, there is another significant example, with the creation, in 1935 by law, of the National Milk Producers Cooperative (Conaprole), which favoured the consolidation of the national dairy industry that has supported important dairy basins in several provinces until now.

Interestingly, after the troublesome years of the Great Depression, regional economic convergence continued at a considerable pace. Despite the existence of the aforementioned state initiatives, it was not until the late 1930s and for at least the next two decades that Uruguay experienced the highest degree of state intervention in the economy, during the so-called Import Substitution Industrialization (ISI) period. In addition to the production for the domestic market that sought to substitute imports, due to the size of the Uruguayan economy, important industries were largely based on primary products—leather, wool, beef—and oriented to foreign markets. Consequently, the location of natural resources was, frequently, also a strategic factor. In a context where the railway system had already developed and transport costs between some inland regions and Montevideo's port were relatively low, industry had an important development in some provinces where agricultural raw materials were located. Therefore, a policy that altered the relative prices favouring specific industrial branches—and the existence of local entrepreneurs or foreign investors willing to carry out these activities—could explain why some industries may have had an incentive to set up business far away from the main urban agglomeration in the country (e.g. Paysandú, Río Negro, Colonia).[23]

[23] Even the agriculture sector benefitted from the government support of several industrial crops (sunflower, sugar cane, flax) (Finch 1980).

In other words, in the case of Uruguay, state intervention in the economy through economic policies, legislation and direct participation as a producer meant that the ISI policies opened business opportunities for provinces other than Montevideo. As a result, in these decades of industry promotion, the spatial location of production was affected by the degree of state intervention through economic policy, with important implications. This result shows that, contrary to other experiences (especially in the core countries), industrialization in Uruguay led to a more even distribution of economic activities across space. Therefore, it implies that the state-led industrialization policy, between the 1930s and the 1960s, was an equalizing force for regional income distribution as it also was for personal income distribution (Bértola 2005).

By the end of the 1950s, the decline of a strategy based on the substitution of imports was evident, and the balance of political and social forces significantly changed (Bértola 1993). In 1958, the Nacional Party (or *Blanco* Party) allied with important rural sectors won the national elections after 90 years representing the second national political force (behind the *Colorado* party). This was the beginning of an economic liberalization process that, nonetheless, would advance slowly during the 1960s (Finch 1980).[24] The multiple exchange system was eliminated, trade and exchange controls were dismantled, and tariffs to exports and imports were restructured. This was the beginning of a gradual and irregular process that would culminate with the definitive change of model in the 1970s.

The new growth model in the 1970s was based on a lower degree of state intervention, with a greater emphasis on the development of the financial and services sectors. On the one hand, the pattern of international trade was largely oriented towards neighbouring countries, with bilateral agreements, which ended in the 1990s with the signing of the Mercosur treaty. This was detrimental for extra-regional trade, which had been one of the sources of economic growth with equalizing power between provinces in the previous stage. Without the preceding levels of protection, many of the agro-industrial developments (textiles, clothing, leather, food) that had formerly prospered in the inland provinces of the country began to decline. This situation was aggravated by the 1982 financial crisis and the external debt crisis that characterized the 1980s (the 'lost decade').

[24] The passing of the Law No 12,670 called Law of Exchange and Monetary Reform represented the most important legal milestone in this period (December, 1959).

In the 1990s, the deepening of globalization in the world and the influence of the Washington Consensus in Latin America generated a new stage in the national economic growth model based on a low degree of state intervention in the economy. Governments followed a strategy aimed at making Uruguay 'a country of services', trying to position the country as a financial services centre for Argentine companies, as well as a seaside resort tourist centre (aimed at the Argentine tourist) and a logistic hub for Mercosur (related to the port of Montevideo). In turn, in addition to the state's withdrawing from active policies to promote the productive development of agro-industrial value chains, macroeconomic policies created adverse conditions for the competitiveness of Uruguayan agricultural and agro-industrial products in international markets (*extra* Mercosur) (Mordecki 2017; Oddone 2010).

This clearly benefitted productive activities based in Montevideo, as well as few regional economies such as Maldonado and Colonia, with close ties with the Argentinean economy (through tourism, financial services and construction). GDP grew until 1998 but in a context of increasing regional inequality, which boosted at the end of the 1990s and reached levels similar to those registered at the beginning of the twentieth century. Then, this economic model, biased towards services and highly dependent on Mercosur, finally collapsed with the devaluation and financial crises of Brazil and Argentina in 1999 and 2001, respectively.

After Uruguay's worst economic crisis in 2001–2002, a new process of regional income convergence started driven by the boom in commodity prices. This could be related to the important changes experienced by the economy, with a new extra-Mercosur orientation of exports (with China's transformation into the main trading partner and significant diversification of markets) and a new set of policies to promote export competitiveness. In fact, in the 2000s, the Uruguayan economy maintained a sustained growth trajectory, characterized by a new wave of public–private institutions to promote innovation and competitiveness, especially in agro-export chains, and the adoption of policy actions that positively affected transversally different productive sectors (Bértola et al. 2014; Pittaluga et al. 2014). Some examples of these policies are the development of a tracking and traceability system for the entire meat industry (from production process to retail packs) and the creation of the National Milk Institute, the National Logistics Institute and the export promotion agency called *Uruguay XXI*. In addition, two relevant laws referring to local and regional development were passed. One related to territorial planning at the subnational level and the other related to political decentralization (Law No. 18308: Territorial Planning and Sustainable Development, 2008; Law No. 18567: Law on Political Decentralization and Citizen Participation, 2009). Therefore, while the very favourable international prices in commodity markets must be pointed out, public policies would once again be behind the more balanced regional growth, this time promoting the addition of value to agro-industrial export products and production-related services.

Consequently, our results show that the evolution of regional disparities in Uruguay has been strongly related to the country's integration in international markets in the different phases of globalization, but in an interaction with the type of productive model and policies that the state promoted in each period. Therefore, the First Globalization and the new stage at the beginning of the twenty-first century, which favoured a strong integration of the country into international commodity markets, tended to favour the reduction of regional inequality. However, this occurred within the framework of important public policies that promoted technological improvements and competitive access to international markets in the agro-export sectors.

From the 1970s to the 2001–2002 crisis, within the framework of a neoliberal conception of the economy, as we indicated above, no favourable conditions were generated for agricultural and agro-industrial exports to world markets (other than Brazil and Argentina). The financial liberalization (which began in the early 1970s), the country's strong insertion in international financial markets and the integration into Mercosur (in the 1990s) following a strategy to position the country as a regional centre for financial and logistic services, ended up reinforcing regional inequality.

In any case, our analysis of Uruguay clearly suggests that countries in the periphery may have experienced a different pattern of spatial development and regional inequality over time compared to that of the core countries. And, even within the peripheral countries, regional economic development have shown different patterns as the present book evidences for the Latin American countries.

References

Arocena, J. (1992). El Estado, la descentralización y la iniciativa local en Uruguay. In D. Raczynsky and C. Serrano (Eds.), *Políticas Sociales, Mujeres y Gobierno Local*. Santiago de Chile: CIEPLAN.

Arocena, J. and Marsiglia, J. (2017). *La escena territorial del desarrollo. Actores, relatos y políticas*. Montevideo: Taurus.

Arnabal, L., Bertino, M. and Fleitas, S. (2013). Una revisión del desempeño de la industria en Uruguay entre 1930 y 1959. *Revista de Historia Industrial*, 53, 143–173.

Astori, D. (2001). Estancamiento, desequilibrios y ruptura, 1955–1972. In Instituto de Economía, *El Uruguay del Siglo XX. La Economía*. Uruguay, Montevideo: Editorial Banda Oriental-Instituto de Economía.

Azar, P., Bertino, M., Bertoni R. and Garcia Repetto, U. (2004). ¿De quiénes, para quiénes y para qué? Impuesto cambiario y subsidios en el Uruguay (1937–1959). *Boletín de la Asociación Uruguaya de Historia Económica*, 3, 20–32.

Barrán, J. and Nahum, B. (1967). *Historia Rural del Uruguay Moderno, 1851–1885*. Uruguay, Montevideo: Ediciones de la Banda Oriental.

———. (1971). *Historia Rural del Uruguay Moderno. Tomo II: 1886–1894*. Montevideo: Ediciones de la Banda Oriental.

———. (1973). *Batlle, los estancieros y el Imperio Británico, Tomo I: El Uruguay del Novecientos*. Uruguay, Montevideo: Ediciones de la Banda Oriental.

———. (1978). Historia Rural del Uruguay Moderno. Tomo VII: Agricultura, crédito y transporte bajo Batlle (1905 – 1914). Montevideo: Ediciones de la BandaOriental.

Barro, R.J. and Sala-i-Martin, X. (1991). Convergence across States and Regions. *Brookings Papers on Economic Activity*, 22 (1), 107–182.

Bertino, M., Bertoni, R., Tajam, H. and Yaffé, J. (2001). La larga marcha hacia un frágil resultado. 1900–1955. In *El Uruguay del Siglo XX. La Economía*. 9–63. Montevideo: Ediciones Banda Oriental – Instituto de Economía.

———. (2005). *La economía del Primer Batllismo y los años veinte. Historia Económica del Uruguay – Tomo III*. Montevideo: Fin de Siglo.

Bértola, L. (1993). *La industria manufacturera uruguaya 1913–1961: un enfoque sectorial de su crecimiento, fluctuaciones y crisis*. Uruguay, Montevideo: Facultad de Ciencias Sociales de la Universidad de la República y Centro Interdisciplinario de Estudios sobre el Desarrollo.

———. (2005). A 50 años de la curva de Kuznets: crecimiento económico y distribución del ingreso en Uruguay y otras economías de nuevo asentamiento desde 1870. *Investigaciones de Historia Económica*, 1 (3), 135–176.

———. (2008). An overview of the economic history of Uruguay since the 1870s. *EH Net Encyclopedia*. Retrieved from http://eh.net/encyclopedia/article/Bertola.Uruguay.final

Bértola, L., Isabella, L. and Saavedra, C. (2014). *El ciclo económico de Uruguay, 1998–2012*. Programa de Historia Económica y Social, Facultad de Ciencias Sociales, Universidad de la República, Working Paper No. 33. Retrieved from http://cienciassociales.edu.uy/wp-content/uploads/sites/6/2015/05/DT_PHES_No-33-Uruguay-1998-2012.pdf

Bértola, L. and Ocampo, A. (2012). *The economic development of Latin America since independence*. Oxford, UK: Oxford University Press.

Bértola, L. and Porcile, G. (2000). Argentina, Brasil, Uruguay y la economía mundial: una aproximación a diferentes regímenes de convergencia y divergencia. In Bértola, L. (Ed.) *Ensayos de Historia Económica. Uruguay y la región en la economía mundial 1870–1990*. 53–90. Montevideo: Trilce.

Borucki, A., Chagas, K. and Stalla, N. (2004). *Esclavitud y Trabajo. Un estudio sobre los afrodescendientes en la frontera uruguaya (1835–1855)*. Montevideo: Pulmón Ediciones.

Bolt, J., Inklaar, R., de Jong, H. and van Zanden, J.L. (2018). *Rebasing 'Maddison': new income comparisons and the shape of long-run economic development*. Maddison Project Working Paper, 10. Retrieved from https://voxeu.org/article/rebasing-maddison

Bulmer-Thomas, V. (2003). *The economic history of Latin America since independence* (2nd ed.). Cambridge: Cambridge University Press.

Cabella, W. and Pellegrino, A. (2005). *Una estimación de la emigración internacional uruguaya entre 1963 y 2004*. Unidad Multidisciplinaria, FCS-UdelaR, Working Paper 70. Retrieved from https://www.colibri.udelar.edu.uy/jspui/bitstream/20.500.12008/4634/1/DT%20MULTI%2070.pdf

Castro, P. and Willebald, H. (2019). *Producto regional en Uruguay durante la Primera Globalización (1872–1908): menor desigualad y convergencia entre regiones*. Instituto de Economía, Facultad de Ciencias Económicas y de Administración, Universidad de la República, Working Paper.

Díaz, G. (2017). Railway investment in Uruguay before 1914: profitability, subsidies, and economic impact. *European Review of Economic History*, 21, (3), 280–301.

Díez-Minguela, A., Martinez-Galarraga, J. and Tirado-Fabregat, D. (2018). *Regional Inequality in Spain 1860–2015*. Cham: Palgrave Studies in Economic History.

Enflo, K., Henning, M. and Schön, L. (2014). Swedish regional GDP 1855–2000: estimations and general trends in the Swedish regional system. *Research in Economic History*, 30, 47–89.

Errea, E., Peyrou, J., Secco, J. and Souto, G. (2011). *Transformaciones en el agro uruguayo: nuevas instituciones y modelos de organización empresarial*. Montevideo: Universidad Católica del Uruguay.

Finch, H. (1980). *Historia económica del Uruguay contemporáneo*. Montevideo: Banda Oriental.

Fujita, M., Krugman, P., Venables, A.J. (1999). *The Spatial Economy. Cities, Regions, and International Trade*. Cambridge (MA): MIT Press.

Gallup, J. L., Sachs, J. D., Mellinger, A. D. (1999). "Geography and Economic Development." *International Regional Science Review*, 22(2), 179–232.

Garcia Repetto, U. (2017). El contralor de exportaciones e importaciones en Uruguay (1941–1959). *Revista Uruguaya de Historia Económica*, 7(11), 43–72.

Geary, F. and Stark, T. (2002). Examining Ireland's post-famine economic growth performance. *The Economic Journal*, 112, 919–935.

González, R. and Rodríguez, S. (1990). Guaraníes y paisanos. *Colección Nuestras Raíces*, 3. Montevideo: Nuestra Tierra.

Jacob, R. (1977). *El Uruguay en la crisis de 1929: Algunos indicadores económicos.* Montevideo: Fundación de Cultura Universitaria.

———. (1981). *Uruguay 1929–1938: Depresión ganadera y desarrollo fabril.* Montevideo: Fundación de Cultura Universitaria.

Lessmann, C. (2014). Spatial inequality and development. Is there an inverted-U relationship? *Journal of Development Economics*, 106, 35–51.

Martínez, E., Delgado, M. and Altmann, L. (2016). *Sistema urbano nacional del Uruguay.* Montevideo: Facultad de Arquitectura, Diseño y Urbanismo de la Universidad de la República and Ministerio de Vivienda, Ordenamiento Territorial y Medio Ambiente.

Martinez-Galarraga, J., Rodríguez Miranda, A., Siniscalchi, S. and Willebald, H. (2019). La distribución regional de la producción en Uruguay, 1908–1975: propuesta metodológica y fuentes. Instituto de Economía, Facultad de Ciencias Económicas y Administración, Universidad de la República, Working Paper, 13/19.

Martínez Lamas, J. (1930). *Pobreza y Riqueza del Uruguay.* Montevideo: Palacio del Libro.

Millot, J. and Bertino, M. (1996). *Historia Económica del Uruguay. Tomo II (1860–1910).* Montevideo: Fundación de Cultura Universitaria.

Moraes, M.I. (2008). *La Pradera Perdida. Historia y economía del agro uruguayo: una visión de largo plazo, 1760–1970.* Montevideo: Linardi y Risso.

Mordecki, G. (2017). Uruguay en democracia: treinta años de evolución económica, 1985–2015. Instituto de Economía, Facultad de Ciencias Económicas y Administración, Universidad de la República, Working Paper 8/17.

Mulhall, M.G. and Mulhall, E.T. (1892). *Handbook of the River Plate, comprising the Argentine Republic, Uruguay, and Paraguay.* Buenos Aires: M.G. and E.T. Mulhall, London: Kegan Paul Trench and Co.

Nathan, M. (2014). Empalme de las estimaciones y proyecciones de población anual por sexo y edad de INE-CELADE Rev. 1998 e INE Rev. 2013. *mimeo.*

Notaro, J. (1984). *La política económica en el Uruguay, 1968–1984.* Montevideo: CIEDUR.

Oddone, G. (2010). *El Declive. Una Mirada de la Economía de Uruguay del Siglo XX.* Montevideo: Linardi y Risso.

OPP—Oficina de Planeamiento y Presupuesto. (1972). *Plan nacional de desarrollo, 1973–77.* Montevideo: Presidencia de la República.

———. (2016). *Producto Interno Bruto Regional 2008–2011. Metodología.* Montevideo: Oficina de Planeamiento y Presupuesto (OPP), Dirección de Descentralización e Inversión Pública.

Pellegrino, A. (n.d.). Un ensayo de estimación de la población de Uruguay 1885–1962. Programa de Población, Facultad de Ciencias Sociales, UdelaR, Working Paper.

———. (2010). *La Población de Uruguay. Breve caracterización demográfica.* Montevideo: UNFPA Uruguay and Doble clic Editores.

———. (2014). *Migraciones.* Montevideo: Colección Nuestro Tiempo. Libro de los Bicentenarios.

Pittaluga, L. Rius, A., Bianchi, C. and González, M. (2014). *Public-Private Collaboration on Productive Development in Uruguay.* IDB Working Paper Series, 501.

Petrakos, G. and Psycharis, Y. (2016). The spatial aspects of economic crisis in Greece. *Cambridge Journal of Regions Economy and Society*, 9 (1), 137–152.

Puga, D. (1999). The rise and fall of regional inequalities. *European Economic Review*, 43 (2), 303–334.

Reyes Abadie, W. (1966). *La Banda Oriental: pradera, frontera, puerto.* Montevideo: Ediciones de la Banda Oriental.

Rodríguez Miranda, A. (2014). *Desarrollo económico y disparidades territoriales en Uruguay.* Cuadernos de Desarrollo Humano 3. Montevideo: UNDP Uruguay.

———. (2006). *Desarrollo Territorial Endógeno. Teoría y aplicación al caso uruguayo.* Instituto de Economía, Facultad de Ciencias Económicas y Administración, Universidad de la República, Working Paper 2/16.

Rodríguez Miranda, A. and Goinheix, S. (2018). *Estimación del VAB departamental en Uruguay y evolución en el período 1981–2011.* Instituto de Economía, Facultad de Ciencias Económicas y Administración, Universidad de la República, Working Paper 3/18.

Rodríguez Miranda, A., Galaso, P., Goinheix, S. and Martínez, C. (2017). *Especializaciones productivas y desarrollo económico regional en Uruguay.* Instituto de Economía, Facultad de Ciencias Económicas y Administración, Universidad de la República, Working Paper 7/17.

Rodríguez Vignoli, J. (2008). Movilidad cotidiana, desigualdad social y segregación residencial en cuatro metrópolis de América Latina. *EURE* (Santiago), 34 (103), 49–71.

Román, C. and Willebald, H. (2019). *Structural change in a small natural-resource intensive economy. Switching from productive diversification to re-primarization?.* Instituto de Economía, Facultad de Ciencias Económicas y Administración, Universidad de la República, Working Paper.

Rosés, J.R. and Wolf, N. (2019). *The economic development of Europe's regions: a quantitative history since 1900.* New York: Routledge.

Samuelson, P.A. (1949). International Factor-Price Equalisation Once Again. *The Economic Journal*, 59, 181–197.

Slaughter, M.J. (1997). Economic Development and International Trade. *American Economic Review*, 87 (2), 194–199.

Ward, P. (2009). Unpackaging residential segregation: the importance of scale and informal market processes. *Investigaciones Geográficas*, 70, 114–134.

Willebald, H. and Juambeltz, J. (2018). Land frontier expansion in settler economies (1830–1950): Was it a Ricardian process?. In Pinilla, V. and Willebald, H. (Eds.) *Agricultural development in the world periphery. A global economic history approach*. Ch. 17, Palgrave Studies in Economic History, 439–466. London: Palgrave Macmillan.

Williamson, J.G. (1965). Regional Inequality and the Process of National Development: A Description of Patterns. *Economic Development and Cultural Change*, 13, 3–47.

Yagüe, J. and Díaz-Puente, J. (2008). Tres siglos de planificación regional en Uruguay: lecciones de experiencia para afrontar los retos de desarrollo en el siglo XXI. *Estudios Geográficos*, 69, 264, 247–280.

Zubillaga, C. (1977). Algunos antecedentes sobre acondicionamiento territorial en Uruguay (1611–1911). In *Cuadernos del CLAEH, 4. Regionalización. Un aporte al estudio de caso uruguayo*. Montevideo: CLAEH.

CHAPTER 12

Was the Oil Sown Evenly? Long-Term Patterns of Regional Inequality in Venezuela (1881–2011)

Giuseppe De Corso and Daniel A. Tirado-Fabregat

1 Introduction

According to the International Monetary Fund, in 2016 the gross domestic product (GDP) per capita for Venezuela was around \$13,000 (PPP, 2011 international \$), putting it in sixth position in the income rankings of the nine Latin American countries analysed in this volume. This is far below the position it reached in the 1980s. At that time, of all the countries in the area, Venezuela's GDP per capita was exceeded only by

Authors thank the help and advice received from Pablo Astorga, Henry Willebald, Alicia Gómez-Tello, Alfonso Herranz and Marc Badia. Only the authors are responsible of all remaining errors.

G. De Corso
Universidad Jorge Tadeo Lozano, Bogotá, Colombia
e-mail: giuseppeb.decorsos@utadeo.edu.co

D. A. Tirado-Fabregat (✉)
Departament d'Anàlisi Econòmica, Universitat de València, València, Spain
e-mail: Daniel.Tirado@uv.es

D. A. Tirado-Fabregat et al. (eds.), *Time and Space*,
Palgrave Studies in Economic History,
https://doi.org/10.1007/978-3-030-47553-6_12

Argentina. The country's recent decline should not, therefore, disguise the fact that Venezuela was one of the most developed societies in Latin America in the twentieth century. Proof of this can be found by analysing a synthetic indicator such as the Human Development Index, which shows us that Venezuela reached the end of the century with a score that was in the middle of those of the six biggest countries of Latin America (below those of Argentina, Chile and Mexico but over the levels reached by Peru, Colombia and Brazil) and much higher than the average for the Latin America region as a whole (Astorga et al. 2005; UNDP 2000).

In fact, the position held by Venezuela at that time was the result of a historical development process that enabled the country's standard of living, as measured by GDP per capita, to increase sixfold in the course of just over a century. One of the key elements that explain this evolution is oil, which had a huge impact on the country's economic future. From 1925, the year in which oil exports exceeded coffee exports for the first time, this item accounted for 90% of the value of Venezuela's exports. It also generated on average more than 75% of the state's tax revenue. In addition to this, until the collapse of oil prices in 1986, the growth in exports was accompanied by a gradual increase in their real value, which ultimately enabled the country to underwrite a notable economic development process. As Astorga (2000) points out, crucial to this process was the action of the state, anxious to appropriate an increasing proportion of the income generated through the export of natural resources exploited by foreign companies (Shell Oil, Gulf, Standard Oil) in order to channel it into the diversification of the country's economy.

The action that the state should take was set out by Arturo Uslar Pietri in an editorial in the Caracas newspaper *Ahora* on 14 July 1936 entitled *Sembrar el petróleo (Sowing the oil)*. He wrote: "The only wise policy that we should follow to save the economy is to convert mining revenues into loans for agriculture, encourage modern scientific farming, import stud animals and animal feeds, replant forests, build all the reservoirs and channelling systems necessary to secure irrigation … mechanize and industrialize the land, create cooperatives for certain crops and smallholdings for others." These ideas were taken up by the new government led by General López Contreras, which chose to increase public sector intervention and involvement in transferring oil-generated revenue for the purposes of developing and diversifying Venezuela's production structure (e.g. by approving the new customs tariff in 1936 and setting up the Banco Industrial Venezolano with 60% public ownership). After the World War

II, the Pérez Giménez government (1953–1958) intensified this trend towards greater public intervention and set the country on the path already taken by other countries in the area. The Import Substitution Industrialization (ISI) policies promoted by the United Nations Economic Commission for Latin America and the Caribbean (ECLAC) took on a character of their own in Venezuela and would dominate the political scene until the final decade of the twentieth century.[1]

Within this framework of exploring Venezuela's economic growth process, the foundations of which were the exploitation of natural resources and increased public intervention aimed at developing production activities to reduce the country's dependence on oil, the aim of this chapter is to analyse the Venezuelan economy from a regional, long-term perspective, thus contributing to our knowledge of the evolution of economic inequality between the states that make up the Republic of Venezuela.

Analysing the case of Venezuela from a regional perspective is particularly relevant when we bear in mind that its economic development was based on the exploitation of certain natural resources basically found in just a small part of the territory. It might therefore be said that the conditions were such that economic growth was a process with the potential to generate serious territorial imbalances. Then again, the export of hydrocarbons generated the resources (income and public revenues) to activate the general development of the country. Thus, the increasing government action taken to redistribute income by protecting different production sectors or implementing programmes involving public investment or subsidies to private companies (ISI policies) could have affected the relative growth of the states of Venezuela in ways that have yet to be analysed in depth. In other words, the case of Venezuela could serve to illustrate the potential impact of public policies on territorial equilibrium, and as far as we are aware, this approach has seldom been used to assess the effects of ISI policies in Latin America.

In order to contribute to our knowledge of these aspects, this chapter presents new estimates for GDP and GDP per capita for the period 1881–2011 for the 23 states and Distrito Capital which, together with the

[1] Rubio-Varas (2015) offers a detailed analysis of the view of Venezuelan policymakers (and economists) on the use of wealth extracted from oil resources depletion and of its implications on the depreciation of national natural capital.

Dependencias Federales, today make up the Republic of Venezuela.[2] Given that the Banco Central de Venezuela (BCV) does not compile figures either for regional GDP or for the most recent period, calculating and presenting this new evidence is in itself an important contribution to our knowledge of the country's economic reality. At the same time, it is a necessary step enabling us to study the impact of the long-term growth processes on territorial inequality.

The study is divided into four sections. In the first, in order to set out the main stages of economic development in Venezuela, we provide a brief overview of the country's history in political, institutional and economic terms. In the second, we explain the methodology followed to calculate these new regional GDP estimates. We then present the main results and describe the broad stages in the evolution of regional economic inequality in Venezuela between 1881 and 2011. And in the final section we review this evidence in the light of its possible determinants within the framework of the main stages of the country's economic development process.

2 Historical Background

After the dissolution of Gran Colombia, the present-day Republic of Venezuela was founded in 1830 by the General José Antonio Páez with the support of what would later be called the conservative oligarchy.[3] The economic policy followed during the nineteenth century could broadly be described as liberal, aimed at connecting the domestic market with the Atlantic economy. The basic idea was to reproduce in Venezuela the patterns of development characteristic of Europe, in particular England, leaving the markets to decide on the mechanisms for determining prices and quantities. A balanced fiscal policy was predominant during this period, along with a trade policy aimed at increasing exports. At the same time, the foundations were laid for a banking and financial system suitable for the development of the national economy. In particular, during the Guzmán Blanco period (1870–1888), coinciding with the start of the first wave of globalization, a modernization policy was implemented based on

[2] The *Dependencias Federales* comprise twelve groups of virtually unpopulated islands. For this reason, these territories have not been considered when reconstructing regional GDP.

[3] Between 1819 and 1830, the territory of the Republic of Venezuela was a part of the Gran Colombia (that included the present day Colombia, Venezuela, Ecuador and Panama), the first union of independent estates in Latin America, presided by Simón Bolívar.

increasing openness to the world market. This liberal model remained in place virtually throughout the second half of the nineteenth century and continued until, at least, the first decade of the twentieth century.

In terms of production, these years were characterized by the spread of coffee cultivation, coffee being Venezuela's main export product at the time, although cocoa and other goods made up a significant proportion of the country's exports and accounted for an average of around 47% of the total between 1830 and 1899. The Venezuelan coffee economy grew relatively strongly in the first half of the nineteenth century, during the early years of the Republic and the 1870s. The hectares of agricultural land given over to production rose from around 43,000, of which 4,500 were devoted to coffee, to 270,000, of which 108,000 were coffee plantations in 1875. This meant an increase of 104,000 hectares in roughly 40 years. In 1900, approximately 450,000 hectares were under production, of which 190,000 were devoted to the chief export. Coffee eventually occupied half the land under production, with around 250 million trees distributed across 33,000 plantations by the first decade of the twentieth century, accounting for 50–70% of exports.[4]

Boosted by this period of integration into the international economy and its growing production and exports, Venezuela started on a path of timid economic growth in which the state, as in most of the continent's liberal regimes, played a residual role. The liberal governments essentially set the rules for the markets, developing the institutional frameworks needed for them to function. During these years the Venezuelan governments established the conditions necessary to appeal to foreign capital attracted by the idea of exploiting the territory's natural resources. Foreign investment grew exponentially, drawn to the mining sector and public services such as transport and those involved in the urbanization of the country's cities (water supplies and, later, electrification). Thus, the financial and technical strength of various foreign companies allowed different railway projects to be undertaken with the aim of providing the country with a transport system to link some of the regions and, more importantly, the agricultural and mining production centres with the port system.[5]

[4] Rangel (1974).

[5] Venezuela's first railway, the Bolívar line, was opened in 1877 and covered the route between the Aroa mines in the state of Yaracuy and the port of Tucacas. This was followed in 1883 by the line connecting Caracas with the port of La Guaira. However, the biggest railway project was the Great Venezuela Railway, also known as the German railway due to the nationality of the companies that won the tender. Opened in 1894, it carried goods and

Ultimately unsuccessful plans were also made to attract European immigrants, the monetary system was unified by creating the currency known as the venezolano, later renamed the bolívar, and a law was passed introducing free compulsory education. Venezuela was gradually creating a domestic market for goods and capital in a context of thorough integration into what was known as the Atlantic economy (O'Rourke and Williamson 1999).

The increasing insertion of the Venezuelan economy into the international goods, capital and labour markets encouraged the beginning of a gradual economic growth process. It was in this context that a set of regional economies took shape, aimed at the export market[6] by way of the ports in which the big trading companies run by foreigners (the English, Italians and Germans) operated. The first of these "economic development areas" comprised the state of Zulia and the Andes, which mainly produced coffee for the US market and used the port of Maracaibo. The second was the Caracas-Valencia corridor with access to the sea in Puerto Cabello and La Guaira, the principal export products of which were coffee, cocoa, skins and copper, destined mainly for the European market. The third area was located in the east of the country and comprised the state of Bolívar and the coastal states of Anzoátegui, Monagas and, most importantly, Bermúdez (now known as Sucre). Bolívar had a big river port in Ciudad Bolívar, which was a centre of mineral wealth with gold from the mines in Callao, but also skins and cattle. This waterway gave products access to the sea via the state of Monagas. The main markets for these products were also European. And from the port of Carúpano, the state of Bermúdez exported products such as asphalt to the United States and cocoa to Europe.

By the end of the nineteenth century, however, the liberal model of economic development in Venezuela was beginning to show signs of strain, with no new possibilities of capital accumulation, unchanging levels of exports per capita, and a very low annual rate of population growth (1891–1926) that barely reached 0.7%. Just as in other nearby countries, the limits of a growth model based on producing and exporting natural

passengers between the central coastal states, from Valencia to Caracas. The so-called German railway was nationalized in 1946 and closed in 1966.

[6] For the evolution of the Venezuelan economy at national and regional levels after the colonial period, see Rangel (1974), Izard et al. (1992), Astorga (2003), Baptista (2006), Cartay (1988) and De Corso (2013).

resources were becoming evident. Besides, the construction of the new state and the investments made over these years had incurred a high level of debt that ended up crippling public finances.[7]

However, unlike with other economies in the area, the exploitation of oil resources utterly transformed the country's economic outlook and served as the basis for a new stage of economic growth that would continue until the last quarter of the twentieth century. The downside of this was the virtual disappearance of autonomous regional economies, since the country as a whole now depended on the *situado constitucional*, that is the income obtained from issuing oilfield exploration and exploitation licences.

Oil meant a complete break with the past and linked the Venezuelan economy to the world market—and especially to the United States—as an energy supplier. Foreign investment, product per capita and income per capita took off in the mid-1920s as oil production and exports grew. This allowed the country's income per capita to increase rapidly and converge with that of its biggest trade partner—the United States—reaching 45% of US income per capita in 1974 (Fig. 12.1).

Broadly speaking, the evolution of Venezuela's oil economy[8] in the twentieth century can be broken down into three general periods. The first was one of rapid growth that lasted from around 1925 until 1958 and was characterized by a big increase in revenues and public spending, the use of oil revenues for public and private investment, and exports. This rapid growth was naturally the result of the initial shock of the arrival of oil production and investment in an economy with a low standard of living and little revenue. The second period, from 1958 to 1974, with a lower rate of growth more typical of a mature oil economy, was characterized by a balanced economic situation, a prudent tax regime, low inflation and a strong currency pegged to the dollar through oil. Finally, despite the temporary blip of the oil boom of 1974–1978, the final period from 1978 to 2011 was characterized by stagnation in both oil production, as measured in barrels per inhabitant, and the country's GDP per capita. Apart from the period of oil price growth during 2004–2012, the trend has been for Venezuela to lose ground to the US economy in terms of GDP per capita.

[7] The refusal or inability to meet the debts incurred with Great Britain and Germany led these powers to blockade Venezuelan ports in 1902.

[8] For information on Venezuela's oil economy, see Baptista (2010) and Carrillo Salazar (2004).

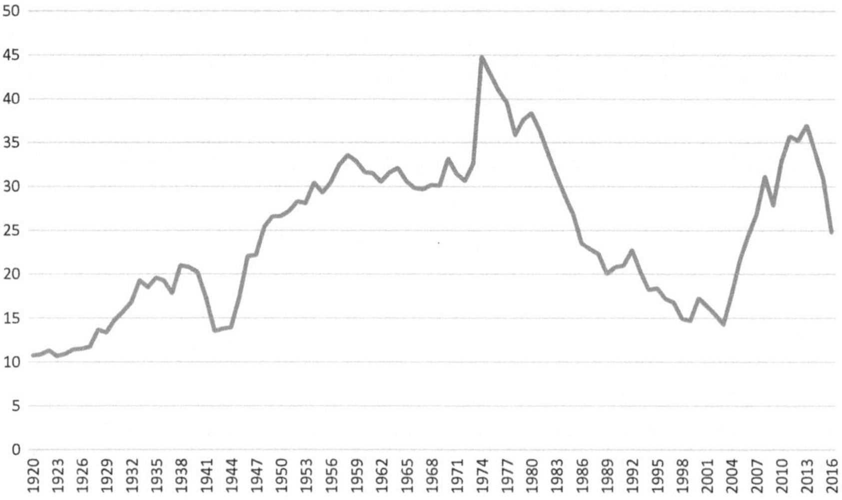

Fig. 12.1 GDP per capita of Venezuela as a percentage of GDP per capita of the United States, 1920–2016. (Source: Bolt et al. 2018)

The big increase in GDP per capita that characterized the period 1925–1978 as a whole also meant a radical change in the availability of resources on the part of the state and in its conception of the role it should play in the country's economic development. For the first time it was acknowledged that public intervention was needed for the economic development of Venezuela. From 1936 the governments of the Republic acted as the driving force behind the diversification of the national production structure. Thus, in 1937 the government of General López Contreras set up the Banco Industrial de Venezuela, which was 60% state-owned and whose purpose was to grant loans for business initiatives that were considered top priority. These years were also crucial in the creation of a new institutional framework to help shape government action on the economy. It is in this period that a number of significant laws were passed, including the Customs Tariff Act of 1936, the Income Tax Act of 1942 and the new Hydrocarbons Act of 1943. In addition, the Banco Central de Venezuela was set up in 1939, and in 1940 a new law regulating the country's banking system was introduced.[9] Finally, public action also

[9]Although the monetary unification of the country dates back to the second half of the nineteenth century, it was not until 1940 that the Banco Central de Venezuela gained the

included the regulation of social aspects. The Employment Act was passed in 1936, and in 1940 new laws were introduced to regulate education and develop a public social security system. Oil revenues were used as the basis for developing new production sectors and, through public spending, were able to reach more of the population. This interest in distributing and *sowing* oil revenue would continue over time. During the first oil boom (1974–1978), the surplus from oil revenues accumulated in the Fondo de Inversiones de Venezuela (Venezuela Investment Fund—FIV) was channelled into big industrialization projects in the areas of basic industries and communications. More recently, extraordinary oil revenues were deposited in the Fondo Conjunto Chino Venezolano (Chinese-Venezuelan Joint Investment Fund—FCCV) and the Fondo de Desarrollo Nacional (National Development Fund—Fonden), whose aims were similar to those of the FIV.[10]

However, it is in the period after the World War II that the political call to *sow the oil* really took off and Venezuela followed in the wake of other Latin American economies by introducing import substitution industrialization (ISI) policies. Starting in 1952, the military dictatorship of Pérez Jiménez extended direct state action in economic development to cover two important areas. A great deal of public investment was committed to building infrastructures for hydroelectric production and communications,[11] while emphasis was also placed on developing strategic industrial sectors such as steel, petrochemicals and electricity. In addition to this and supported by high levels of protection, encouragement was given to the development of sectors of light industry aimed at domestic consumption, which achieved very significant growth rates during the 1950s and 1960s.[12]

monopoly to issue money. Before that there were five issuing banks: the Banco de Venezuela (the predecessor of the BCV), the Banco Mercantil and the Banco de Caracas, all based in Caracas, plus two based in the state of Zulia, the Banco Comercial de Maracaibo and the Banco de Maracaibo, which was the oldest bank in the country, established in 1882. As well as centralizing money issuance, the new law set up bodies to regulate the financial sector and supported the creation of the Banking Council and the Banking Supervisory Authority, in charge of overseeing the system.

[10] A detailed account of the role of state in Venezuelan industrialization in Astorga (2000).

[11] During the 1950s and 1960s, a number of big infrastructure investment projects were carried out, including the Valencia-Caracas motorway and the initial stages of what would become the third biggest hydroelectric complex in the world, the Simón Bolívar power station, located in the state of Bolívar and using water from the Orinoco.

[12] It is significant that the Venezuelan food sector today has major brands very well-known to domestic consumers that basically came into being from the 1930s onwards and which

Moreover, the size of this domestic market received a huge boost between 1951 and 1960 with the arrival in Venezuela of around one million emigrants from southern Europe (Spain, Portugal and Italy), who would settle mainly in the states of Carabobo, Miranda and Distrito Capital and whose active participation in trade and small and medium-sized industry boosted growth in these regions. Oil revenues did not only drive public finances; through public spending and state regulation, they also helped bring about the gradual transformation of the Venezuelan economy.

Starting in the mid-1970s, the international economic crisis had a serious effect on crude-producing economies like Venezuela's. Once the extraordinary boom in oil prices came to an end, oil production stagnated and the growth of public resources was undermined by an unstable geopolitical economic framework, thereby weakening the foundations of the country's ISI model. As a result, the rate of GDP growth slowed down to such an extent that Venezuela's GDP per capita returned to pre-war levels relative to US GDP. Despite the nationalization of the big steel and oil companies under the first government of Carlos Andrés Pérez (1975–1979), the ISI model showed serious limitations to continue to drive economic growth. Attempts to improve efficiency levels in public-sector and part-public companies failed and the big Venezuelan firms were unable to compete in the exterior market even with the help of a devalued bolívar and direct state subsidies for exports.

The second government of Carlos Andrés Pérez (1989–1993) was characterized by its introduction of a far-reaching programme to privatize companies owned or part-owned by the state and by macroeconomic adjustment. Like other economies in the area, from the end of the 1980s the Venezuelan economy returned to a path marked by decreased government intervention in the production apparatus and market liberalization. However, after 1999 the so-called Bolivarian Revolution reactivated the policy of intervention in the public sector. Supported by the continuous growth in oil prices between 2004 and 2012, *Chavismo* returned to the heyday of intervention and applied very similar economic policies to those applied in the period 1974–1978. But once this upward trend came to an

cornered the domestic market in the years during which these *sow the oil* policies were in place. Striking examples include Cervezas Polar (1941), Ron Pampero (1938), Pepsico Venezuela (1939), Chocolates Savoy (1941), Industrias Iberia (1952) and Alimentos Remavenca, now Alimentos Polar (1954). A shared characteristic is that most of them were set up in different areas of Distrito Capital and spread into neighbouring states such as Lara, Aragua and Miranda.

end, the Venezuelan economy's structural problems reappeared and the development model was plunged into crisis. This calls into question the model's viability, especially if it appears to be undermined by a bitter geopolitical conflict that deprives Venezuela of its main market, the United States.

3 Long-Term Patterns of Regional Income Inequality: Sources and Methods

Before we present our new evidence on the evolution of regional inequality in Venezuela, we need to explain some of the basic aspects involved in how this evidence was calculated, that is the way the territory is divided, our primary sources and previous work consulted, and the methodology we followed to estimate the aggregate figures for regional GDP.

As far as the first of these aspects is concerned, the territorial division of Venezuela has been subject to various political and constitutional changes. Different constitutions have introduced a variety of territorial divisions. The 1811 constitution, for example, defined seven federal provinces (Margarita, Mérida, Cumaná, Barinas, Barcelona, Trujillo and Caracas), while the 1830 constitution established 11 provinces (Cumaná, Barcelona, Margarita, Caracas, Carabobo, Coro, Maracaibo, Mérida, Barinas, Apure and Guayana), which were themselves divided into cantons and parishes. However, it was the constitution of 1864 that introduced the term 'state', which was used instead of province, and organized the country into 20 states, a territorial division not very different from that of today. These states were Apure, Aragua, Barcelona, Barinas, Barquisimeto, Carabobo, Caracas, Cojedes, Coro (now Falcón), Cumaná (now Sucre), Guárico, Guayana (now Bolívar), Maracaibo (now Zulia), Maturín (now Monagas), Mérida, Margarita (now Nueva Esparta), Portuguesa, Táchira, Trujillo and Yaracuy.

Although the 1881 constitution changed the pre-existing territorial division by grouping the 20 states of 1864 into 9 big states, the first Cipriano Castro government and the constitution of 1901 reinstated the division of the territory into 20 states, although this time the territorial borders were those laid down in the Law of 1856. The constitution of 1909, during the first presidency of Juan Vicente Gómez, basically re-established the political-territorial division that existed in 1864. The 20 states were restored, but added to them were Distrito Federal, two Territorios Federales and the Dependencias Federales.

The administrative division of Venezuela today comprises 23 states (Amazonas, Anzoátegui, Apure, Aragua, Barinas, Bolívar, Carabobo, Cojedes, Delta Amacuro, Falcón, Guárico, Lara, Mérida, Miranda, Monagas, Nueva Esparta, Portuguesa, Sucre, Táchira, Trujillo, Vargas, Yaracuy and Zulia), Distrito Capital (the former Distrito Federal of Caracas) and the Dependencias Federales (12 groups of islands). These are subdivided into 335 municipalities and 1116 parishes. Bearing in mind that for most of the period analysed the territorial division differs little from today's and that the sources make it possible to produce estimates at this level of territorial disaggregation, this is the administrative division that we use retrospectively for the whole of the period analysed (Map 12.1).[13]

As for the methodology followed to estimate the regional figures for economic activity, a number of attempts were made during the last century to construct local accounts, but the highly centralized decision-making of the Caracas bureaucracy made this impossible. Faced with a lack of official information, we have used various research papers to cover this gap in documentation.

First, the work carried out by Gloria Abilahoud for the BCV in 1953 provided GDP estimates in current terms for each of the federal entities in 1950. Similarly, in its report for 1961 the International Institute for Research and Training for Harmonized Development (IRFED) included estimates of regional GDP. However, of greatest interest to us is the work produced by Valecillos (1998) under the auspices of the BCV, the methodology for which was based on calculating the average income received by workers and the operating surpluses of the various federal entities by branch of activity. This information is cross-checked against information in the various population censuses and the industrial censuses of the *Oficina Central de Estadística e Informática* (OCEI), today the *Instituto Nacional de Estadística* (INE). On the basis of this information, Valecillos presents regional GDP estimates for the census years from 1961 onwards.

[13]The estimation does not include the Guayana Esequiba, a 159.500 square kilometre territory subject to a long-lasting border dispute with Guyana government. This area appears coloured in grey in Map 12.1.

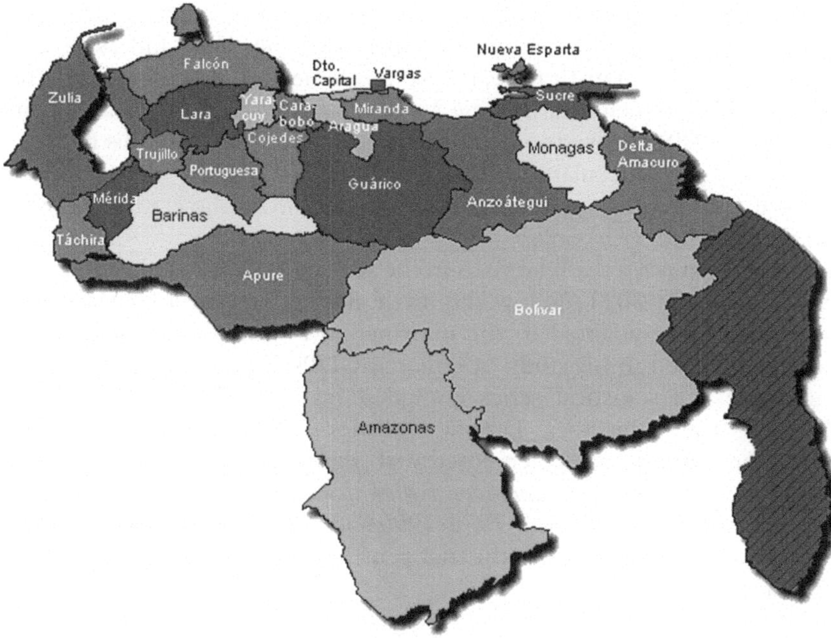

Map 12.1 Map of the states of Venezuela

These works gave us a starting point for the new evidence we present in this study.[14] The information provided here extends the temporal spread of the estimates and homogenizes the information contained in existing estimates by gathering vast amounts of regional information from the various regional and national statistical yearbooks for the nineteenth century. As a result, we can provide estimates of regional and GDP per capita for the following base years: 1881, 1891, 1920, 1926, 1936, 1950, 1961, 1971, 1981, 1990, 2001 and 2011, which coincide with census years. More specifically, we used the Geary–Stark method to draw up the estimates for 1891, 1920 and 1936, obtaining the necessary information from national and regional statistical yearbooks, along with the active population from the censuses for those years.[15] This information was supplemented for 1920 and 1936 with data compiled by the Ministry of Public

[14] Details of the methodology used can be found in De Corso (2013).
[15] Geary and Stark (2002).

Works, including the Industrial Census for 1936, information from the Treasury in the shape of its Annual Reports for 1936, 1937 and 1938, and figures from the Statistical Yearbook for Venezuela for 1944 and the BCV's publication entitled *Ingreso Nacional de Venezuela*. Drawing up an estimate for 1881 proved to be more difficult, and therefore this figure is somewhat more speculative. We carried out an indirect estimation of regional GDPs using tax information and data from the census of 1881 and the statistical yearbooks.

The estimates for the final years in the series (1950, 1961, 1971, 1981, 1990, 2001 and 2011) follow the methodology proposed by Valecillos, since this can be adapted to the information available and was used by Valecillos himself in his study of regional GDPs. In this case the sources used were the statistical series compiled by the BCV for the period 1940–1999 and the Socio-Labour Statistics of Venezuela, 1936–1990. This information was supplemented with that supplied by Valecillos in a subsequent work entitled *Impactos regionales del crecimiento y la contracción económica en Venezuela, 1936–1990* and with information published in various agricultural and industrial censuses and economic reports for 2001 and 2011.

All the statistical information is presented in constant bolivars at 1984. To this end the nominal magnitudes have been converted into real magnitudes using the national deflator. As mentioned earlier, the level of territorial disaggregation at which the information is presented corresponds to today's political-territorial division.

4 Long-Term Patterns of Regional Income Inequality: New Data and Stylized Facts

In the light of this new evidence, the following pages contain an analysis of the evolution of the regional economies throughout Venezuela's historical development process. First, we analyse the relative GDP of the different regions, that is the part of Venezuela's GDP produced in each region. The results of this exercise can be seen in Table 12.1, from which we can extract various conclusions. The first is that at the starting date, 1881, most of the production was already concentrated in the three economic centres located on the country's coastline. The biggest of these, which comprised today's states of Distrito Capital, Carabobo, Miranda and Vargas, accounted for roughly a quarter of Venezuela's GDP. The

Table 12.1 Regional GDP as a percentage of national GDP

	1881	*1891*	*1920*	*1926*	*1936*	*1950*	*1961*	*1971*	*1981*	*1990*	*2001*	*2011*
Distrito Capital	7.94	11.85	17.15	19.44	23.99	22.88	20.9	17.15	12.38	8.65	9.94	11.13
Amazonas	0.17	0.19	0.17	0.41	0.06	0.04	0.06	0.1	0.21	0.11	0.2	0.29
Anzoátegui	5.7	5.33	3.3	2.76	2.44	6.65	6.03	5.21	6.23	5.96	5.95	5.95
Apure	0.85	0.77	0.99	0.81	0.83	0.79	0.73	0.82	0.68	1.18	1.26	1.31
Aragua	5.39	5.64	4.77	4.1	4.11	3.02	3.69	4.94	4.91	6.01	6.26	6.49
Barinas	2.7	2.39	1.46	1.12	0.8	0.89	1.37	1.43	1.53	1.6	1.86	2.11
Bolívar	2.52	2.71	4.28	3.89	3.55	1.69	2.83	3.99	3.62	7.02	5.56	4.25
Carabobo	6.95	7.85	7.91	7.46	7.29	6.14	5.96	6.55	7.07	7.44	8.15	8.8
Cojedes	3.82	3.24	1.72	1.22	0.49	0.66	0.49	0.52	0.58	0.55	0.7	0.84
Delta Amacuro	0.4	0.36	0.3	0.28	0.27	0.33	0.11	0.26	0.21	0.17	0.24	0.32
Falcón	5.32	4.64	3.16	3.21	2.78	2.73	2.65	5.46	5.47	6.97	4.84	2.97
Guárico	8.3	7.41	3.1	2.38	1.69	1.99	1.58	1.85	1.74	1.66	1.71	1.77
Lara	8.74	7.94	6.77	6.27	5.06	4.11	4.45	3.39	3.35	3.2	4.32	5.35
Mérida	3.73	3.29	3.24	2.9	2.52	1.82	1.48	1.58	1.55	1.27	1.88	2.45
Miranda	6.36	6.11	6.56	5.49	4.92	6.86	10.35	10.24	11.8	10.91	12.14	13.27
Monagas	2.55	2.68	2.83	2.43	2.74	2.89	1.93	2.4	3.13	5.6	4.9	4.28
Nueva Esparta	1.72	1.6	1.73	1.63	1.32	0.62	0.35	0.52	0.83	0.93	1.21	1.47
Portuguesa	4.37	3.78	1.21	0.98	0.85	1.41	1.64	1.82	1.67	1.6	1.87	2.12
Sucre	3.58	3.24	4.18	4.5	4.08	2.71	2.16	2.07	1.94	1.58	1.89	2.17
Táchira	3.89	3.65	4.8	4.59	4.16	2.86	2.32	2.34	2.34	1.99	2.92	3.77
Trujillo	6.75	5.84	4.27	3.78	2.98	2.1	1.53	1.61	1.34	1.25	1.55	1.83
Yaracuy	3.66	3.19	2.46	2.01	1.42	1.15	1.25	1.16	1.1	1.04	1.29	1.51
Zulia	3.38	4.69	10.41	14.66	17.12	21.24	22.43	22.48	24.73	22.39	18.2	14.16
Vargas	1.22	1.62	3.22	3.68	4.53	4.42	3.69	2.11	1.53	0.92	1.16	1.39
Venezuela	100	100	100	100	100	100	100	100	100	100	100	100

Source: Main text

western region accounted for another 25%, mainly attributable to Zulia, but also to Lara and Falcón and the coffee states of Táchira, Mérida and Trujillo. Finally, the smaller east coast area accounted for 15% of production, which was concentrated mainly in the states of Anzoátegui, Monagas and Sucre.

The most striking element about the way the location of economic activity in Venezuela evolves over the first stage of economic development (1881–1936) is the great advance of the Caracas area. At its peak, Distrito Capital alone concentrates 24% of the country's output, increasing its initial share more than threefold. The next most striking element is the boom in Zulia, where the growth in oil production pushes its share of GDP up from an insignificant 3.4% in 1881 to 17.1% in 1936. With the advances made by these two states, there were few territories that could maintain their share of national GDP over this period.

The growth dynamic of the region in which oil production is concentrated continues through the period 1936–1981. By this time the state of Zulia accounts for 25% of Venezuelan GDP. Offsetting this is Distrito Capital, which sees its share fall by half. However, what makes this period stand out is the fact that a new state, Miranda, is added to the exclusive list of territories that have a larger than 10% share of national GDP. With 11.8% it joins Zulia and almost catches up with Distrito Capital. It is clear that the expansion of Caracas, which receives considerable migrant flows, means that its associated economic activity extends beyond its borders and spreads into neighbouring states. Finally, advances in the development of natural resources (oil and natural gas) in the Orinoco region enabled the states of Monagas and Anzoátegui to join the list of territories that gained weight during these years in terms of their share of Venezuela's GDP. Finally, the last period covered (1981–2011) shows the relative decline of Zulia, whose contribution to the country's GDP decreases by 10 percentage points, and the relative recovery of the Caracas area, in particular due to the state of Miranda's continuing differential growth.

So far we have taken into account GDP inequality across regions, but there are other ways of considering the regional distribution of income. In this respect, we present information on the evolution of territorial inequality in terms of GDP per capita. Figure 12.2 depicts the long-term evolution of a regional income dispersion index—the population-weighted

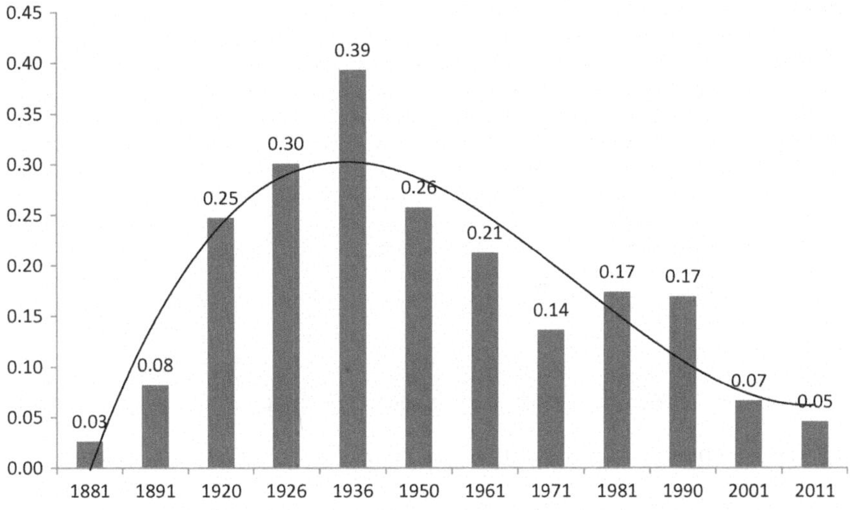

Fig. 12.2 Weighed coefficient of variation (WCV). (Source: Main text)

coefficient of variation of GDP per capita in the regions of Venezuela—which could be considered a measure of σ-convergence.[16]

We see that there was a trend of increasing regional income inequality in Venezuela between 1881 and 1936. This was followed until 1971 by a period in which this inequality gradually decreased. The process suffered a reversal during the 1980s when the ISI model collapsed. However, the convergence of regional income per capita resumed from 1990 and continued. Over the long term, regional income inequality presents an inverted U-shaped pattern with inequality increasing between 1881 and 1936, that is, during the early part of the economic development process when the Venezuelan economy was becoming increasingly integrated into international markets and there was little public intervention. From then until the international economic crisis of the 1970s, which in the case of Venezuela marks the end of ISI policies and a gradual return to a liberal development model, territorial inequality in Venezuela was characterized by a continuous process of decreasing regional differences. The liberal surge at the end of the 1980s and during the 1990s marked a backward

[16] For a full development of the concepts of σ-convergence and β-convergence, see Barro and Sala-i-Martin (2003).

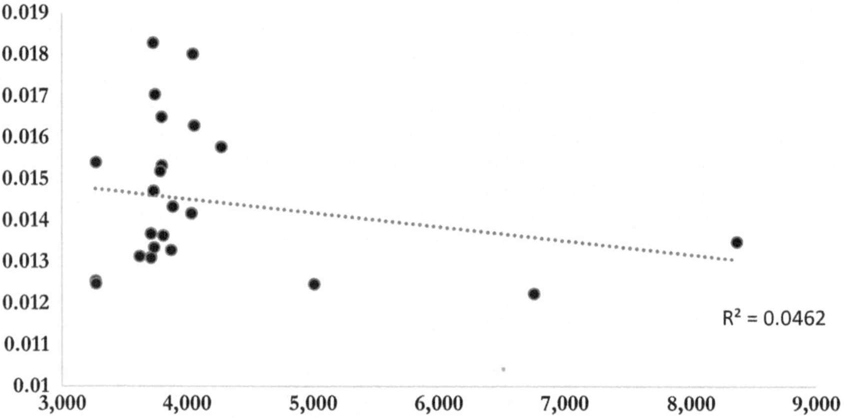

Fig. 12.3 GDP per capita in 1881 vs. GDP per capita growth rate 1881–2011. (Source: Main text)

movement along the road to decreasing inequalities that was only recovered in the last two points in time analysed, which correspond to the Bolivarian Revolution.

A complementary approach to the σ-convergence methodology for investigating regional convergence processes is based on growth regressions, in which the rate of growth of income per capita between two periods is explained by its initial level. A negative correlation between growth and initial income implies a tendency for poor regions to catch up with rich ones. The convergence concept associated with these regressions is known as β-convergence.

Such an exercise is presented in Fig. 12.3, where it can be seen that the poorer regions in 1881 tended to grow faster than the richer regions over the next 130 years (i.e. from 1881 to 2011). However, if we split the period analysed into the two main trends outlined by the temporal evolution of the weighted coefficient of variation, that is, the growth in inequality between 1881 and 1936 and the decrease between 1936 and 2011, we obtain very different results (Figs. 12.4 and 12.5). During the first period, there is no confirmed presence of β-convergence between the regions of Venezuela. More likely the reverse, on average, since the initially poor regions tended to grow more slowly than the initially rich ones. In this case, however, the average behaviour is conditioned by the evolution of a

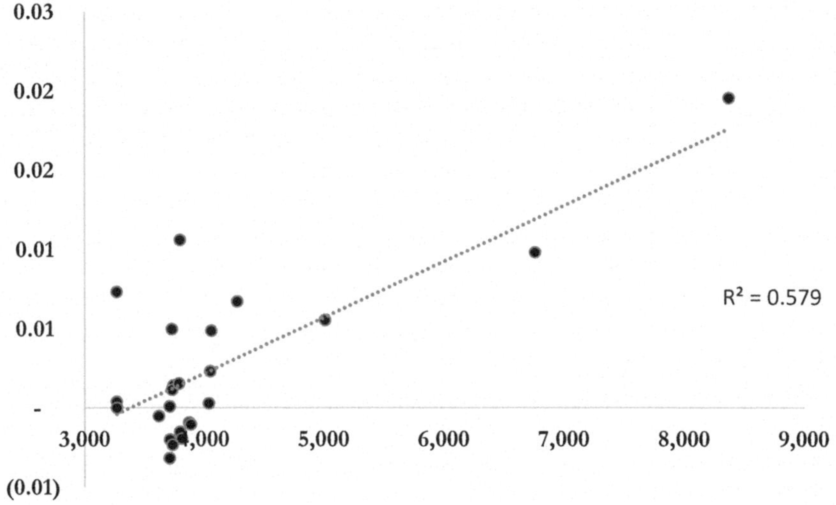

Fig. 12.4 GDP per capita in 1881 vs. GDP per capita growth rate 1881–1936. (Source: Main text)

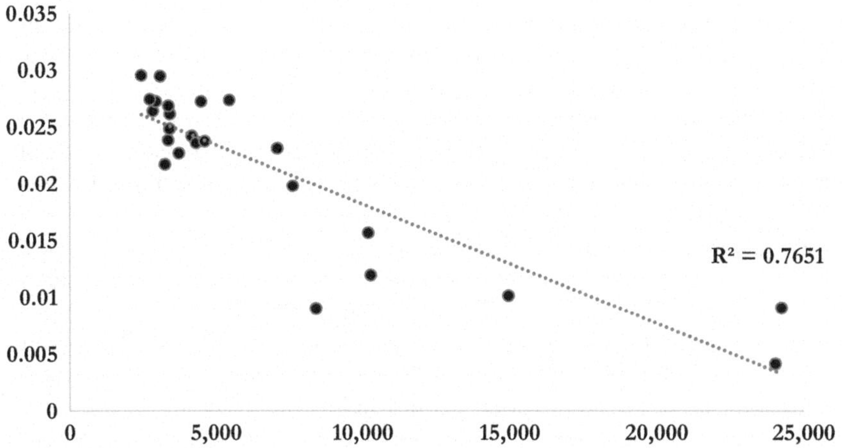

Fig. 12.5 GDP per capita in 1936 vs. GDP per capita growth rate 1936–2011. (Source: Main text)

small group of regions. Thus, for the period 1881–1936, the growth of inequality can basically be explained by the higher growth rates of GDP per capita in two territories: Distrito Capital and Vargas. It is the central coastal area of Venezuela, along with the oil-producing Zulia region, that achieves the highest levels of growth and, given its high initial income per capita, marks the advance of regional inequality.

Nevertheless, during the period 1936–2011, it is the initially poor regions that grow more quickly on average than the rich regions, sketching out a pattern of β-convergence. This is linked to the behaviour of a greater number of territories which, although with varying individual experiences, share the fact that their growth rates are significantly inversely related to their initial income levels.

The evidence relating to the evolution of inequality conceals the behaviour of individual territories. Therefore, in order to give a more detailed idea of regional inequality, Table 12.2 contains information on the relative income per capita of Venezuela's regions (with the average being equal to one). A new stylized fact emerges from the table: the regional rankings varied very little during these 130 years. The leaders and laggards maintained their positions despite major changes in overall income dispersion. According to almost all the different benchmarks, Distrito Capital, Carabobo and Vargas occupied the top positions in the regional income rankings. The exception to this picture of stability is Zulia, home to most of the country's oil production. In 1881, it occupied an intermediate position in the ranking but took the top position in 1961, 1971 and 1981. However, it has fallen back in the course of the last 30 years, gradually dropping in the rankings in the last three points of time considered (1991, 2001 and 2011).

Zulia's dynamic of rise and relative decline over the periods that comprise Venezuela's economic development process can be seen most clearly if we compare its GDP per capita with that of the country's top region, Distrito Capital (Fig. 12.6). In the first period up to 1936, GDP per capita in Distrito Capital was twice that of Zulia. The beginnings of the dynamism associated with oil exports do not help Zulia close in on the country's richest region. However, after 1936 the boom in oil exports takes just a few years to make Zulia the territory with the highest GDP per capita, twice that of Distrito Capital in the final period of this stage. This dynamic goes into reverse from the 1990s and, after the Bolivarian Revolution, Zulia again records income levels far below those of Distrito Capital. This decline is mainly due to the depletion of its oilfields and the

Table 12.2 Regional GDP per capita (Venezuela = 100)

	1881	*1891*	*1920*	*1926*	*1936*	*1950*	*1961*	*1971*	*1981*	*1990*	*2001*	*2011*
Distrito Capital	203	271	323	335	353	243	192	137	118	100	143	176
Amazonas	79	50	114	117	123	24	50	61	81	42	75	61
Anzoátegui	91	86	71	68	66	173	155	136	161	148	129	125
Apure	79	73	56	53	50	56	61	66	64	88	88	88
Aragua	98	130	109	109	111	100	116	120	97	114	114	122
Barinas	94	83	59	55	50	70	97	82	83	80	79	80
Bolívar	121	106	144	146	150	84	130	134	95	166	121	92
Carabobo	104	103	140	143	148	159	154	131	117	109	112	121
Cojedes	90	80	46	42	36	80	66	73	76	65	73	80
Delta Amacuro	79	106	54	51	48	62	32	71	65	43	65	60
Falcón	92	72	55	51	45	67	77	177	191	249	168	101
Guárico	88	92	57	54	49	76	63	77	78	73	72	73
Lara	98	91	68	65	61	70	90	67	62	57	74	93
Mérida	94	81	58	55	49	54	54	60	59	48	70	91
Miranda	98	94	83	82	80	157	207	158	146	124	138	153
Monagas	90	78	101	102	103	104	77	106	142	254	182	146
Nueva Esparta	90	86	68	66	63	52	38	58	74	75	86	92
Portuguesa	90	85	51	47	42	73	79	81	69	59	68	74
Sucre	90	76	62	59	55	51	53	58	58	50	64	74
Táchira	92	78	72	75	67	59	57	60	62	53	78	99
Trujillo	92	86	53	49	43	48	46	56	54	54	67	82
Yaracuy	91	81	50	46	40	55	72	68	65	58	68	77
Zulia	92	119	193	203	218	239	240	228	260	213	162	118
Vargas	164	194	313	328	350	243	193	136	118	78	103	121
Venezuela	100	100	100	100	100	100	100	100	100	100	100	100

Source: Main text

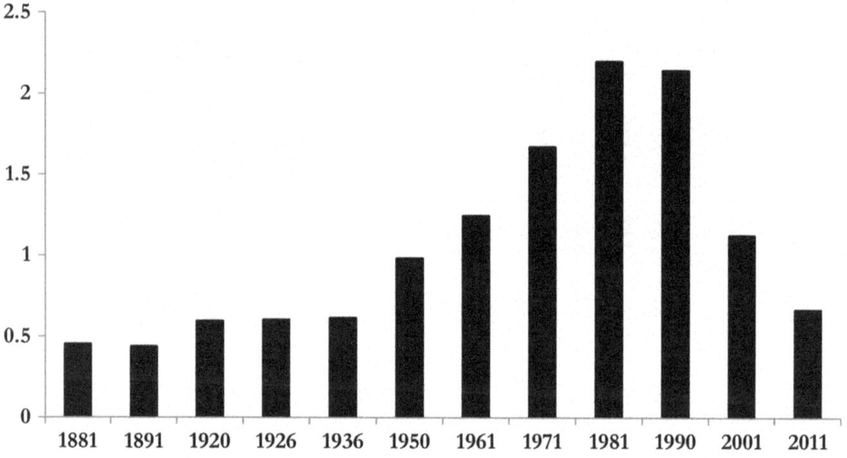

Fig. 12.6 Zulia GDP per capita as a share of Distrito Capital GDP per capita. (Source: Main text)

government's decision to focus on developing the *Faja Petrolífera del Orinoco* (Orinoco Oil Belt—FPO), from which half the country's production is extracted today. It is no surprise that, as was the case at other times in Venezuela's recent history, the regional elites in Zulia have shown that they are not happy with this dynamic.

The other side of the coin is the large group of regions that usually rank among the poorest and consistently record below-average levels of GDP per capita. Over these 130 years, regions of the interior such as Apure, Barinas, Táchira and Portuguesa are always around the bottom of the rankings. It might, therefore, be possible to identify a pattern whereby, with some exceptions, the coastal regions and especially those in central and western areas have experienced the highest levels of development in the country, while those in the interior have languished at the bottom of the table. In other words, there seem to be indications that a map of regional economic development in Venezuela does exist, with the geographical position of the territories indicating relative income levels, and this map seems to remain stable regardless of which period of history is being studied.

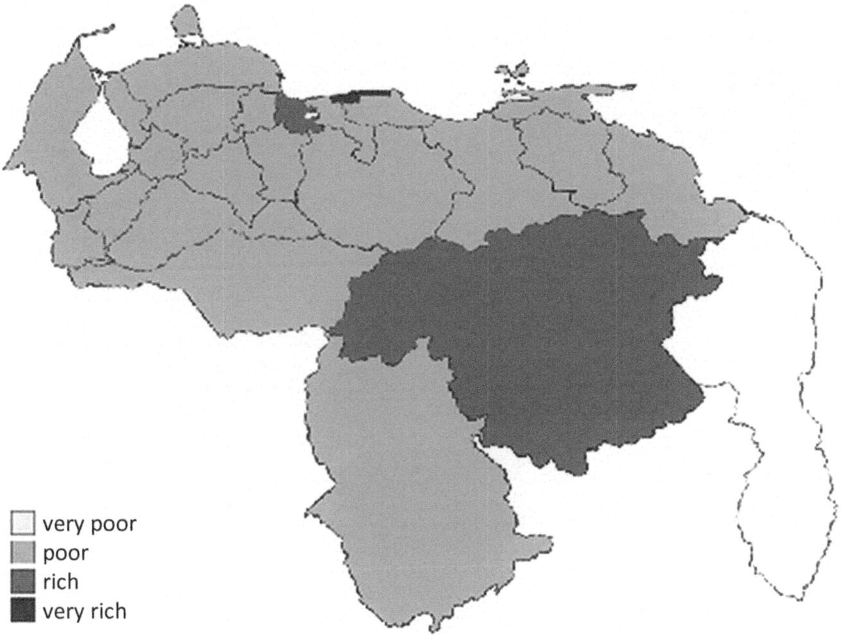

Map 12.2 Regional GDP per capita in 1881. (Source: Main text)

Maps 12.2, 12.3, 12.4 and 12.5 provide information on the geography of regional economic development in Venezuela.[17] There are four shades of grey used in the maps: very dark, dark, light and very light (which only appears on Map 12.5).[18] The very dark grey denotes regions with a GDP per capita that exceeds the average for the distribution plus one standard deviation. Dark grey denotes those with a GDP per capita between the average and the average plus one standard deviation. The lighter grey territories all have below-average levels of income (either between the average and one standard deviation below it (light) or below this threshold (very light)). Following this coding, Map 12.2 for 1881 shows that levels

[17]The authors are grateful to Alicia Gómez-Tello for the maps presented in the text. The shapefiles used to construct these GIS maps are from Porto Tapiquén (2015a, b, c).

[18]On the various maps, there is an unshaded area to the east. This is Guayana Esequiba, or Región Esequibo that is a disputed territory that Venezuela is claiming from Guyana. Although it does not legally belong to Venezuela, it usually appears on the country's physical and political maps bearing the legend *Disputed Territory*.

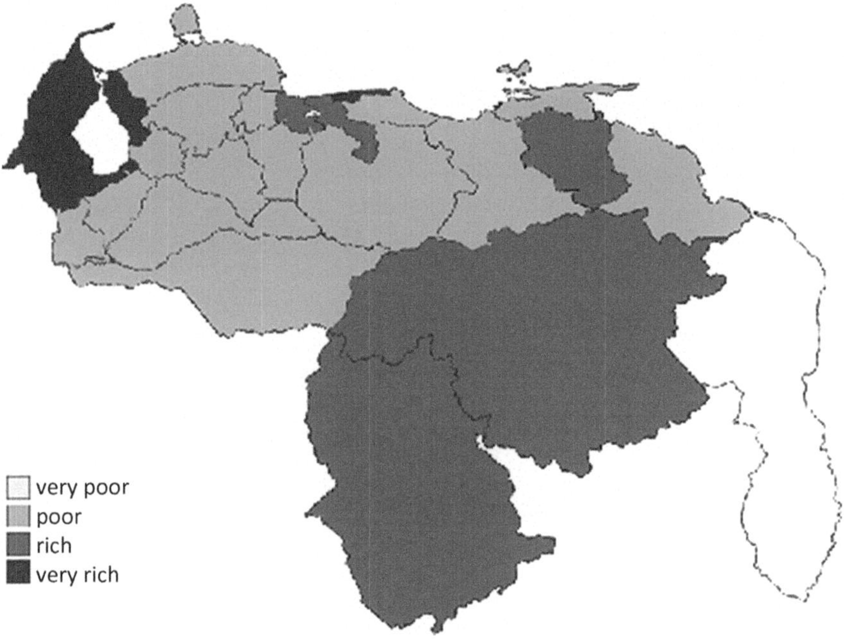

Map 12.3 Regional GDP per capita in 1936. (Source: Main text)

of territorial inequality were relatively low. Many regions were to be found in the intermediate area of the distribution. However, we can also make out a certain geographical pattern showing the richest regions gathered around the area delimited by Carabobo and Distrito Capital. Beyond this area only the Bolívar region, noteworthy at this time for its gold deposits, had above-average levels of GDP per capita.

The end of the so-called liberal period is considered to be 1936, and the situation at this point in time is shown in Map 12.3. We can see that two significant changes have taken place since the previous map for 1881. The first is that territorial inequality has increased, with more regions in the upper tail of the distribution, and the second is that, in geographical terms, the map shows that the coastal locations are leading the field. In particular, we see that three extensive coastal areas contain the country's most developed territories. These consist of the Zulia region, which benefits from its growing oil exports, the area around the central Caracas-Valencia corridor that extends to the coastal region of Vargas, and one

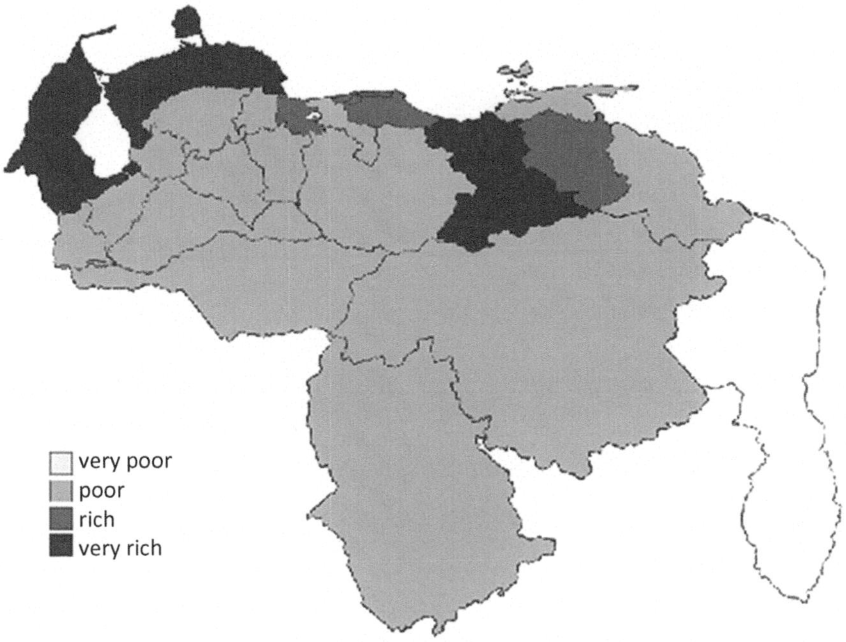

Map 12.4 Regional per capita GDP in 1981. (Source: Main text)

final somewhat poorer region situated on the eastern coast that is characterized by providing access to the sea for the mineral resources of the Bolívar region and which comprises today's states of Sucre, Monagas and Anzoátegui.

Map 12.4 for 1981 outlines the geography of the decreasing inequality revealed by the synthetic indicators. However, this is not due to a levelling of income between all territories. In fact, the map shows that there is a deeper division between the coast and the interior. Nevertheless, we do see indications of a process whereby the coastal regions move closer to each other in terms of income. Zulia now occupies the top position in the ranking and income levels in the oil states of the Orinoco belt on the country's east coast are closing in on those of the more developed states on the central coast. The *sowing of oil* therefore enabled not only the relative growth of those states that specialized in its production and transformation, but also the growth of the central coastal regions, which were

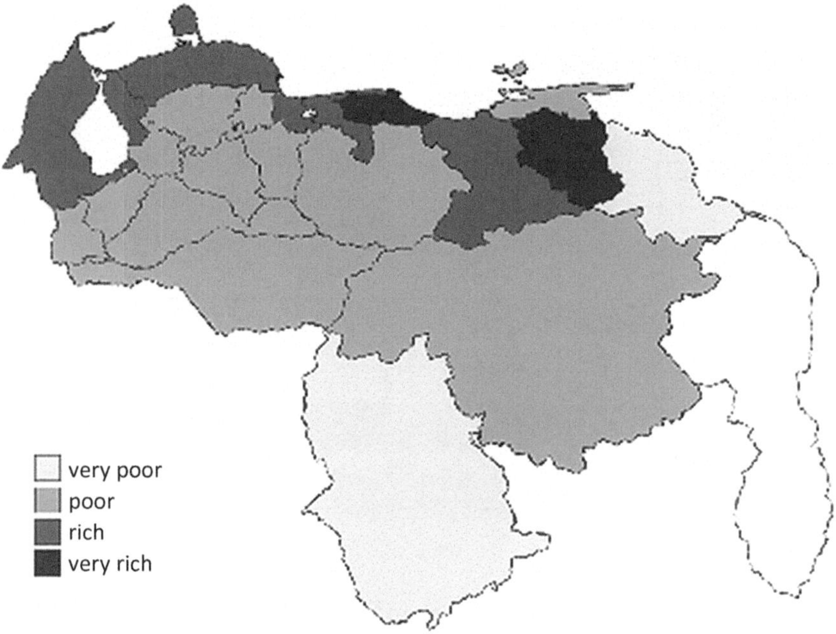

Map 12.5 Regional GDP per capita in 2011. (Source: Main text)

often involved in the production of consumer goods to supply the domestic market.

The last point in time considered (2011, Map 12.5) shows the continuation of the generalized decrease in inequality that began in 1936. However, its impact on the economic geography is only nominal. In 2011, there is still a marked division between the coastal regions and those of the interior. Indeed, this division is possibly even clearer because we can see that there has been an increase in the number of states on the central Venezuelan coastline that occupy the upper positions in the income rankings. This would therefore indicate a regional convergence process dominated by a polarization between income levels in the coastal regions and those in the states of the interior. Nevertheless, among the top positions we can detect the relative growth of territories in the Orinoco Belt, in which an increasing proportion of the country's hydrocarbon production has been concentrated over recent years.

5 The Forces Behind Regional Inequality in Venezuela

To summarize, the descriptive evidence on regional income inequality in Venezuela presented in the previous section showed that its long-term evolution follows an inverted U-shaped curve. It was also shown that this evolution followed a pattern that broadly coincides with the main changes in direction marked by Venezuelan economic policy over the last 130 years. Finally, throughout the text we find evidence as to which regions have played the biggest roles in the country's economic development. We have seen the pressure that exists between two groups of regions, those on the coast and those of the interior, the former generally being more developed than the latter, and the stellar roles played by two territories that have competed for economic leadership: Caracas area and the state of Zulia.

Bearing all these details in mind, in this section we intend to construct some hypotheses to explain the forces that have shaped this reality by considering the predictions that emerge from different theoretical trade and growth models. We need to be aware that, according to neoclassical trade theory, disparities in initial regional income per capita are caused by spatial differences in the distribution of endowments (e.g. natural resources, factors of production and infrastructure). The increase in trade and factor movements across regions (i.e. the integration of regional markets) may lead to changes in this initial distribution of income. According to the neoclassical trade model, this process brings about factor price equalization across regions, and thus per capita GDP convergence.

However, increasing market integration may also lead to increasing regional specialization, and thus regional inequality, because regions differ in their factor endowments.[19] The new economic geography literature also explains this inverted U-shaped evolution of regional income inequality. Market integration in these models can lead to the spatial agglomeration of economic activity in regions with the biggest markets due to the presence of increasing returns (Krugman 1991). This agglomeration of economic activity results in increasing regional inequality. However, migration and congestion costs counterbalance this process and eventually generate a process of delocalization for certain economic activities, and this may lead to regional income convergence.[20] We will therefore take as our start-

[19] Slaughter (1997).
[20] See, for example, Puga (1999).

ing point this conceptualization of the possible determinants of territorial economic inequality and its evolution during the country's national development processes in order to construct some hypotheses to explain what happened in Venezuela over the period of our study.

Modern economic growth in Venezuela is considered to have begun in the second half of the nineteenth century. This process was initially enhanced by the country's increasing involvement in a globalized Atlantic economy and the integration of its national markets for goods and factors of production. The economic development process was accompanied by a substantial increase in regional inequality, which continued until 1936. This was due to two concomitant forces: the growing integration of the Venezuelan economy into the international economy, and the incomplete—since it did not affect the whole territory—process leading to the creation of some kind of national market.

In this first stage (1881–1936), Venezuela was undergoing a regional process of production specialization associated with the export of agricultural goods, mainly coffee, although also cocoa and natural resources such as gold and oil. The export structure at this time was relatively diversified, and this allowed various regions to participate in the processes involving foreign markets. However, the result of this vocation for export was that the highest income levels were achieved in the areas from which products left the country, where activities complementary to the export trade could also be conducted. These included not only port activities such as stevedoring and ship maintenance services, but also associated services such as finance, currency exchange and customs. This dynamic began to generate differences between the coastal regions and those of the interior, which did not benefit to such a degree from national progress.

In addition to this, of all the coastal regions the central area occupied a privileged position. Apart from the fact that it was actually on the coast, which in itself was a key element in a context of increasing openness to the exterior, another advantage was that it attracted the lion's share of the big investments made during the period, including the railway connecting the state of Carabobo with Distrito Capital and its nearest coastline, the state of Vargas. The conditions were therefore in place for this territory to also attract much of the production and trade activity needed to supply the country's main concentration of population. A first-nature geographical cause in the shape of its position on the coast and a second-nature cause in the shape of the infrastructures that gave the central coastal area a bigger market would be the fundamental elements to enable us to understand the growing division between the coast and the interior, and within the coastal area itself, the increasing share in terms of both GDP and GDP per capita of the capital's area of influence. These two elements together would explain the increase in territorial inequality shown by the synthetic indicators presented earlier.

As we know, this pattern changed due to the unexpected boom in the production and export of hydrocarbons. This enabled the main producing region, Zulia, to rapidly rise up the GDP and GDP per capita rankings of the states of Venezuela. In addition, the growing development of oil resources in the Orinoco Belt (Monagas and Anzoátegui) gradually raised these coastal territories of eastern Venezuela to positions of privilege in the national rankings. This lottery of natural resources marked the evolution of territorial inequalities. However, this period is also characterized by the government's intention to redistribute the income generated by exports by investing in the diversification of the country's production structure. From a regional point of view, it could be argued that the *sow the oil* economic policies could have made it easier for the profits from the oil boom to be distributed to more parts of the territory. Public spending and protectionist policies for various industrial sectors aimed at import substitution acted almost as territorial cohesion policies and, despite the magnitude of a growth based mainly on the exploitation of natural resources, the Venezuelan economy did not record greater increases in territorial inequality. Indeed, the reverse was true, since inequality followed a downward trend between the Great Depression and the oil crisis.

However, not all the non-producing regions benefitted to the same degree from public policies. State-supported activities were often located in the same states that produced the oil. One example is the location of the country's main petrochemical industry in Anzoátegui, a region that was already experiencing notable growth in connection with crude oil production. And the import substitution policies encouraged the growth of a variety of companies that produced consumer goods for the domestic market, and naturally these tended to be concentrated in territories with the greatest market potential.[21] Given the conditions at the start, the basic

[21] Although this is not usually emphasized in the new economic geography literature, the state also generates revenues that sustain demand in certain territories and might therefore act as territorial cohesion policies by providing public employment (administration, security, education and health). Public employment went from representing 4.5% of the country's active population in 1936 to 17.6% in the ten-year period 1970–1980 (Baptista 2010). One hypothesis could be that, given the size of the public sector, which was much bigger than

availability of infrastructures (improved over these years by the construction of roads and motorways) and the size of the population they served, these activities clustered in the coastal area of Caracas and in the neighbouring territories from Carabobo to Vargas via Miranda.[22] In other words, the *sow the oil* policies contained the advance of inequality between the coastal territories in a context in which, in their absence, inequality might have increased due to the boom in the oil-producing regions. However, they did not serve to stop the growing division, or we could say polarization, in terms of both GDP and GDP per capita between the country's coast and its interior.

Over the period 1981–2011 Venezuela experienced a variety of economic situations and constitutional frameworks. The extraordinary increases in oil prices (1973–1979 and 2004–2012) enabled the state to step up the action it took regarding the economy, including the nationalization of partly state-owned companies in the second half of the 1970s and after the Bolivarian Revolution. However, during the 1980s and especially the 1990s, the government had to restrict the extent of its direct action in the country's production economy in the international context of decreasing oil prices. Such unforeseen situations also affected the evolution of territorial inequality, which stopped decreasing between 1980 and 1990 and then started again, but more slowly during the period 1991–2011 than during the period 1936–1981. In this final period, the recovery of oil revenues meant that the two big coastal territories in which hydrocarbon production was concentrated, Zulia in the west and Anzoátegui-Monagas in the east, maintained their privileged positions. In particular, however, the policies implemented by the Bolivarian governments involved the relative rise of the big economic area comprising—from west to east—Carabobo, Miranda, Aragua, Distrito Capital and Vargas. Overall, the relative rise of a greater number of states in this region, which make up the biggest domestic market in Venezuela, has made it possible for territorial economic inequality in the country to continue decreasing. Nevertheless,

considered normal for the level of economic development achieved at the time, together with the geographical concentration of this economic development in Distrito Capital and its surrounding areas, it would be reasonable to consider this element as a possible explanatory factor for the evolution of regional inequality in Venezuela between 1936 and 1981.

[22] Among the pioneering contributions to the new economic geography, Krugman and Livas Elizondo (1996) analyse the role played by import substitution policies in the formation of the great metropolises of Latin America.

the gap in GDP per capita levels between the interior and coastal areas has become even wider.

In short, territorial economic inequality in Venezuela has followed an inverted U-shaped curve. However, although inequality today is no greater than it was in 1881, along the road a huge gap has opened up between the GDP per capita levels of the coastal regions and those of the interior. This dynamic is the result of two elements. The first of these is the export of natural resources, basically hydrocarbons. The production of these is limited to a few locations across the territory, and this has benefitted just a few coastal territories (first-nature geographical cause). The second is the actions of the state. Although they have not always had the desired results, government spending policies brought about the conditions whereby some territories were able to take advantage of their geographical location, in this case to supply the domestic market, thus boosting their relative growth (second-nature geographical cause). In this sense, it might be said that *Venezuela sowed the oil, but unevenly.*

Bibliography

Astorga, P. (2000). The industrialisation in Venezuela: the problem of abundance. In: Cárdenas, E., Ocampo, J.A., and R. Thorp (eds.), *Industrialisation and the State in Latin America: The Black Legend and the Post War Years.* New York: Macmillan.

———. (2003). La economía venezolana en el siglo XX. *Revista de Historia Económica*, 21, 3, 623–653.

Astorga, P., Berges, A. R. and Fitzgerald, V. (2005). The standard of living in Latin America during the twentieth century. *Economic History Review*, 58 (4), 765–796.

Baptista, A. (2006). *Bases Cuantitativas de la Economía Venezolana 1830–2002.* Caracas: Fundación Polar.

———. (2010). *Teoría Económica del Capitalismo Rentístico.* Caracas: Banco Central de Venezuela.

Barro, R. J., Sala-i-Martin, X. (2003). *Economic growth.* New York: McGraw Hill.

Bolt, J., Inklaar, R., Herman, D. J., van Zanden J. L. (2018). *Rebasing 'Maddison': New Income Comparison and the Shape of Long-Run Economic Development*, https://ideas.repec.org/p/gro/rugggd/gd-174.html.

Carrillo Salazar, J. (2004). *Oil and Development in Venezuela during the 20th Century.* London: Praeger.

Cartay, R. (1988). *Historia Económica de Venezuela 1830–1900.* Valencia, Venezuela: Vadell Hermanos Editores.

De Corso, G. (2013). El crecimiento económico de Venezuela, desde la oligarquía conservadora hasta la revolución bolivariana: 1830–2012. Una visión cuantitativa. *Revista de Historia Económica*, 31, 321–357.

Geary, F. and Stark, T. (2002). Examining Ireland's Post-famine Economic Growth Performance. *Economic Journal*, 112, 919–935.

Izard, M. et al. (1992). *Política y Economía en Venezuela. 1810–1991*. Caracas: Fundación John Boulton.

Krugman, P. (1991). Increasing returns and economic geography. *Journal of Political Economy*, 99 (3), 483–499.

Krugman, P. and Livas Elizondo, R. (1996). Trade policy and the third world metropolis. *Journal of Development Economics* 49 (1), 137–150.

O'Rourke, K. H. and Williamson, J. G. (1999). *Globalization and History: the Evolution of a Nineteenth Century Atlantic Economy*. Cambridge, Massachussetts: MIT Press.

Porto Tapiquén, C. E. (2015a). *Estados de Venezuela*. Porlamar, Venezuela: Orogénesis Soluciones Geográficas. http://tapiquen-sig.jimdo.com.

———. (2015b). *Línea Costera de Venezuela*. Porlamar, Venezuela: Orogénesis Soluciones Geográficas. http://tapiquen-sig.jimdo.com.

———. (2015c). *Límites Internacionales de Venezuela*. Porlamar, Venezuela: Orogénesis Soluciones Geográficas. http://tapiquen-sig.jimdo.com.

Puga, D. (1999). The rise and fall of regional inequalities. *European Economic Review*, 43 (2), 303–334.

Rangel, D. A. (1974). *Capital y Desarrollo La Venezuela Agraria*. Caracas: Faces UCV.

Rubio-Varas, M. (2015). Oil illusion and delusion: Mexico and Venezuela over the twentieth century, in Badia, M., Pinilla, V. and Willebald, H. (eds.) *Natural resources and economic growth: learning from History*, Routledge Explorations in Economic History. London and New York: Routledge.

Slaughter, M. (1997). Per-capita income convergence and the role of international trade. *American Economic Review* 87, 194–199.

UNDP (2000). *Human Development Report, 2000*, New York, United Nations Publications.

Valecillos, H. (1998). *Impactos regionales del crecimiento y la contracción económica en Venezuela, 1936–1990*. Caracas, Venezuela: Banco Central de Venezuela.

Primary Sources

Central Bank of Venezuela. Statistical Series for Venezuela 1950–1999, volume 1-A National Accounts and Economic Reports 2000–2013 (Banco Central de Venezuela. Series Estadísticas de Venezuela 1950–1999, tomo I-A Cuentas Nacionales, e Informes Económicos 2000–2013).

Ministry of Public Works Statistical Yearbooks (Anuarios Estadísticos del Ministerio de Fomento), 1877–1944 with various interruptions. Biblioteca del Banco Central de Venezuela.

National Income of Venezuela (Ingreso Nacional de Venezuela) (1949) Banco Central de Venezuela.

National Institute of Statistics Venezuela (Instituto Nacional de Estadísticas Venezuela, INE). Population censuses from 1881 to 2011, Vital statistics 1944–2012, Vital statistics for Zulia and Táchira 1950–2011, in the Statistics Yearbooks. The material was published as a special edition on CD ROM in 2012. In print the data are available from 1873 to 1981.

PODE. The People's Ministry of Petroleum (Ministerio del Poder Popular para el petróleo) at http://www.minpet.gob.ve/index.php/es-es/comunicaciones/pode.

Treasury: Report and Account (Ministerio de Hacienda Memoria y Cuenta) for 1936, 1937 and 1938.

Venezuelan Home Office (Ministerio de Relaciones Interiores) and Administrative Service for Identification, Migration and Aliens (SAIME – Servicio Administrativo de Identificación, Migración y Extranjería) (2015). Point of Information. Situation of Colombian citizens in Venezuela.

Venezuelan Home Office: Report and Account (Ministerio de Relaciones Interiores de Venezuela: Memoria y Cuenta) 1961–2000.

CHAPTER 13

Spatial Inequality in Latin America (1895–2010): Convergence and Clusters in a Long-Run Approach

Marc Badia-Miró, Esteban A. Nicolini, and Henry Willebald

1 Introduction

Scholars seeking to write about the economic history of Latin American face the challenge of offering any type of generalizations about a group of territories with such a marked range of disparities. Latin America, which

M. Badia-Miró
Departament d'Història Econòmica, Institucions, Política i Economia Mundial
Universitat de Barcelona, Barcelona, Spain
e-mail: mbadia@ub.edu

E. A. Nicolini
CIEDH—Universidad del Norte Santo Tomás de Aquino, Tucumán, Argentina

INVECO—Universidad Nacional de Tucumán, Tucumán, Argentina

H. Willebald (✉)
Universidad de la República, Montevideo, Uruguay
e-mail: hwillebald@iecon.ccee.edu.uy

D. A. Tirado-Fabregat et al. (eds.), *Time and Space*,
Palgrave Studies in Economic History,
https://doi.org/10.1007/978-3-030-47553-6_13

constitutes a large part of the American continent, stretches across all the globe's climate zones from the Straits of Magellan in the South to the border of Mexico with the US in the North. It is crossed by huge mountain chains, deserts (both hot and cold) and jungles, forming a complex physical environment that encompasses huge differences in its flora and fauna and in its natural resource endowments. This diversity has witnessed the emergence of many autochthonous cultures throughout the history of the Americas, many of which have achieved a relatively high level of economic development. From the eighteenth century onwards, however, these cultures have been exposed to the far-reaching transformations ushered in by colonization, massive flows of migration, economic integration (both internal and international) and the expansion of world capitalism. Yet, despite these differences, it is possible—as Bértola and Ocampo (2012) recognize—to conceptualize an economic history of Latin America as a unique region and to identify certain characteristics and patterns that are common to all the economies and societies of the continent.

More specifically, Bértola and Ocampo (2012) identify four aspects that characterize the long-term trajectory of the economic history of Latin America. The first concerns its rate of economic development, which over the past two centuries has fluctuated at a level around that of the world average; yet, a comparison of its GDP per capita with that of the West reveals a long-run deterioration exemplifying a marked process of economic divergence. The second concerns the economic instability caused by its patterns of productive specialization and attributable to the fact that its natural resources are constantly exposed to the fluctuations of the world's commodities and financial markets. The third aspect is characterized by the slow pace at which the region has adopted modern political and economic institutions, resulting in considerable instability in its implementation of economic policies and development paradigms that have directed (or misdirected) the long-term performance of the region. The fourth concerns the high degree of inequality that has come to characterize the region, leaving Latin America among the most unequal regions in the world.

This chapter examines these aspects in greater detail but does so from within the novel perspective afforded by historical economic geography and, by so doing, it is able to offer new insights into the economic history of Latin America. More specifically, it provides new evidence about three long-term features of the Latin American economy: the evolution of the dispersion of regional average incomes, the existence of economic convergence and the formation of geographical clusters of rich or poor economic regions. In relation to the first of these, the chapter explores the origins of the current situation whereby some regions of Latin America present levels of income and development similar to those recorded in Europe—the case of the richer regions of Brazil, Mexico and Chile—while others present levels of development in terms of education or life expectancy that are similar to those found in regions of Africa—the case of some regions in Peru and Bolivia. In examining the second feature, the chapter probes the relationship between processes of regional economic growth and the economic conditions prevailing at the end of the nineteenth century. Finally, in relation to the third feature, the chapter analyses the way in which the geographical characteristics shared by neighbouring regions generated similar patterns of economic development and levels of average income.

The discussion presented in this chapter is based on a newly assembled data set that includes estimates of regional gross domestic product (GDP) per capita for Argentina, Bolivia, Brazil, Chile, Colombia, Mexico, Peru, Uruguay and Venezuela from the end of the nineteenth century to the beginning of the twenty-first. The data set enables an exploration to be made of the evolution of income inequality and the dynamics of regional growth, considering, for the first time, a group of Latin American countries at both the national and subnational levels, complemented by a broader international dimension.

Here, in relation to the evolution of regional income disparities, our background assumption is that the trajectory taken is in line with that described by Williamson (1965), that is, that differences in regional incomes during the process of economic development exhibit an inverted U-shaped pattern. This reflects increasing inequality in the initial stages of industrialization, due to the spatial concentration of economic growth, and decreasing inequality (i.e. convergence, as the growth of the poorest regions outstrips that of the richest) thereafter, due to rapid growth in the lagged regions in the long run. However, our evidence for the whole region contradicts Williamson's hypothesis and provides some interesting insights for understanding the convergence process in Latin America.

Thus, first, while regional inequalities have declined in the long run, the trend has not always been decreasing. During the period of export-led growth until World War I, the main driving force behind the reduction in inequality was the 'between component' of the regional income distribution, that is, the gap between countries narrowed, as they incorporated into global markets. After a short period of rising inequality between 1913 and 1925, there was a gradual reduction over the next 45 years to 1970.

In the following three decades, inequality remained largely stable, reaching what were historically low levels. More recently, during the early 2000s, another decline was recorded, due to the fall in the 'between component', reflecting the latest commodity price boom. In short, against a general backdrop of decreasing regional inequality, the periods of economic openness and lower state intervention in the economies—that is, from the First Globalization to the early 1930s and from the 1980s onwards—were dominated by a reduction in the income gaps between Latin American countries. In the period of inward-looking growth and state-led industrialization, the reduction in regional inequality responded to a more balanced distribution of income within the countries.

Second, and as expected from a decreasing trend in inequality, a clear pattern of regional convergence across Latin America can be observed, albeit that in some periods there is some divergence between the regions within the same country. This pattern allows us to conjecture that the spatial inequality in Latin America has responded historically to factors that extend beyond political divisions and national policies and is, probably, more closely associated with factor endowments and international and local market relations.

Third, and finally, after mapping the GDP per capita of the Latin American regions at the subnational level, we identify, in line with the previous results, a persistent feature: the highest incomes per capita correspond to the extremes of the continent (i.e. the richest regions lying in Mexico—to the North—and in Argentina and Chile—to the South), while the lowest correspond to the central region, extending from the tropical zones of Amazonia to the Pacific Ocean. Given this pattern, we sought to identify the existence of clusters of rich and poor regions within the nine countries or along their borders. According to our analysis, we were able to identify clusters of rich regions in the south and clusters of poor regions in the centre with one highly relevant characteristic: this conformation of clusters transcends national boundaries. Thus, the rich clusters correspond to certain regions of Argentina and Chile, while the poor clusters correspond to regions of Brazil, Bolivia and Peru.

The rest of this chapter is organized as follows. Following on from this introduction, we present our long run-approach to the study of regional inequality in Latin America (Sect. 2), propose convergence exercises (Sect. 3) and identify regional clubs in the continent (Sect. 4). Finally, we discuss our results and conclude (Sect. 5).

2 Regional Inequality in Latin America: A Long-Run Approach

The data set used here is drawn from the specific chapters in this book dedicated to the individual countries. These chapters include details of the individual methodologies employed, while a specific discussion of the similarities and differences between these estimations can be consulted in the methodology chapter.[1] In using this original data set, we faced an initial restriction attributable to the huge size differences between the regional divisions making up the sample. To overcome this obstacle, we used the regional divisions for Argentina, Brazil, Bolivia, Chile (as opposed to former provincial divisions), Mexico, Peru and Venezuela, and we grouped the Colombian and Uruguayan departments into large regions.[2] To further homogenize country data, we fixed benchmark years—1895, 1913, 1925, 1935, 1950, 1960, 1970, 1980, 1990, 2000 and 2010—interpolating the shares from each national benchmark and rescaling GDP figures according to calculations for Maddison's International Geary-Khamis US dollars (2011 base).[3] Data for Colombia are available since 1925

[1] For a detailed description of the methodology used to build the data, see Araoz et al. (2020); Badia-Miró (2020); Bucciferro and Ferreira (2020); De Corso and Tirado-Fabregat (2020); Martinez-Galarraga et al. (2020); Meisel-Roca and Hahn de Castro (2020); Peres-Cajías (2020); Aguilar-Retureta et al. (2020); Seminario et al. (2020). For an analysis of the accuracy of the methodology used in each chapter, see Diez-Minguela and Sanchis-Llopis (2020).

[2] For Colombia, we have considered: Antioquia, Atlántico, Bolívar (Bolívar, Sucre, Córdoba), Boyacá (Boyacá, Casanare), Caldas (Caldas, Quindío, Risaralda), Cauca, Chocó, Cundinamarca (Bogotá D.C., Cundinamarca, Meta), Huila, Magdalena (Cesar, La Guajira, Magdalena), Nariño, Norte de Santander, Santander, Tolima, Valle, (Valle del Cauca) and Others (Amazonas, Arauca, Caquetá, Guainía, Guaviare, Putumayo, San Andrés y Providencia, Vaupés, Vichada). For Uruguay, we have considered: Metropolitan (Canelones, Montevideo), South-West (Colonia, Río Negro, San José, Soriano), East (Lavalleja, Maldonado, Rocha, Treinta y Tres), Centre (Durazno, Flores, Florida) and North (Artigas, Cerro Largo, Paysandú, Rivera, Salto, Tacuarembó).

[3] For a more detailed analysis of the methodology used originally in this instance to compare European countries, see Rosés and Wolf (2018). Neither methodology (as used for Latin American or Europe) considers potential differences in relative internal prices or price differences between countries that might not have remained stable in the long run. Previous evidence shows that this oversimplification might conceal relevant variations within those countries with regions that are richer in natural resources.

(guestimates until 1950), and, for Bolivia, data are available since 1950. Data for Argentina in 2010 are unavailable.[4]

Some regions of the Latin American countries studied—particularly those in Amazonia, the Andes and the south of Argentina and Chile—have operated at some time as frontier economies. In some, abundant land and natural resources, together with low population density, generated high incomes during the period of First Globalization, though at levels that cannot be compared with those of the rich districts of the industrialized countries. Similarly, regions whose wealth was based on the exploitation of natural resources have been referred to as what Gollin et al. (2016) call 'consumption cities', that is, regions whose economies consist primarily of non-tradable services. This suggests that the differences between regions with high and low levels of GDP per capita were wider than those observed in industrialized countries, or even those in other countries in the European periphery. Figure 13.1 shows the differences between the GDP per capita of the top 90% Latin American regions and the bottom 10%. Although the trend is clearly decreasing, the ratio levels move between 12 and 4, quite distinct from the predominant ratios of 2 recorded for the OECD countries (Bluedorn et al. 2019).

To advance further in our analysis of the evolution of inequality across regions, we can usefully test Williamson's hypothesis of an inverted U-shaped pattern, with rising income inequality in the early stages of development followed by convergence thereafter. First, using a mean log deviation (MLD) index to observe dispersion, we decomposed the inequality into two components ('between' and 'within' indexes) to understand the drivers of this evolution and to identify the main stylized facts. The 'within' component incorporates inequality in each country (i.e. without considering average income differences across countries), whereas the 'between' component serves as a weighted measure of inequality across average national incomes (i.e. without considering inequality within each country). We define the MLD as:

$$MLD = \frac{1}{N}\sum_{i=1}^{n} Ln\left(\frac{\mu}{x_i}\right), \qquad (13.1)$$

[4] The latest homogenized figures available for Argentinian were from 2004.

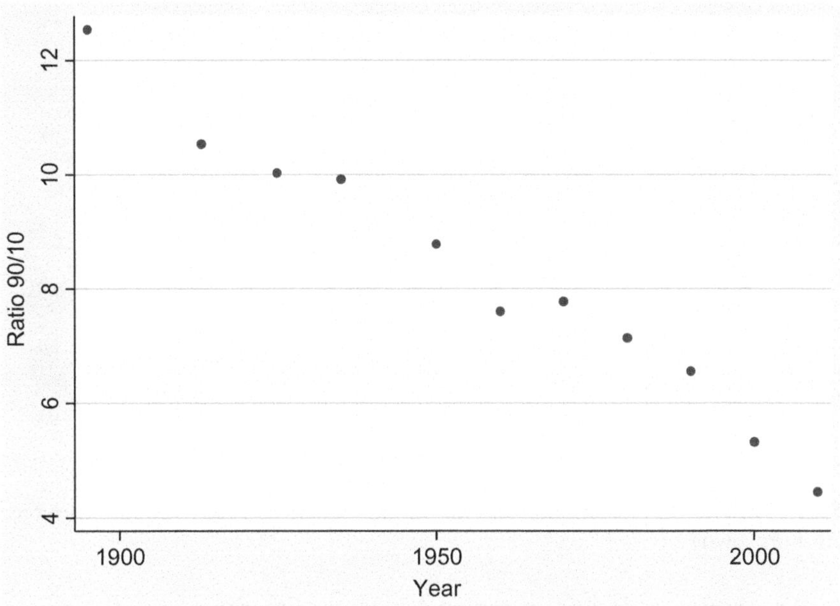

Fig. 13.1 Ratio between top 90% and bottom 10% regional GDP per capita. (Source: Authors' own)

where i is the region; n is the total number of regions; x_i is the GDP per capita for each region; and μ is the GDP per capita of the whole unit of analysis. From equation (13.2), we can decompose MLD as:

$$MLD = MLD_{Within} + MLD_{Between} = \sum_{j=1\ldots} \frac{n^j}{N} MLD^j + \sum_{j=1\ldots} \frac{n^j}{N} \ln\left(\frac{\mu}{\mu^j}\right), \tag{13.2}$$

where N is the total number of regions; $j = 1,2,3\ldots$ tells us whether a province belongs to one country or another; μ is the average GDP per capita for the whole region; and μ^j is the average GDP per capita in each country. The results are shown in Fig. 13.2.[5]

[5] In our case, when measuring total inequality, the unit of analysis comprises the nine Latin American countries studied herein (i.e. Argentina, Bolivia, Brazil, Chile, Colombia, México, Peru, Uruguay and Venezuela) or each of these countries considered separately when measuring national inequality.

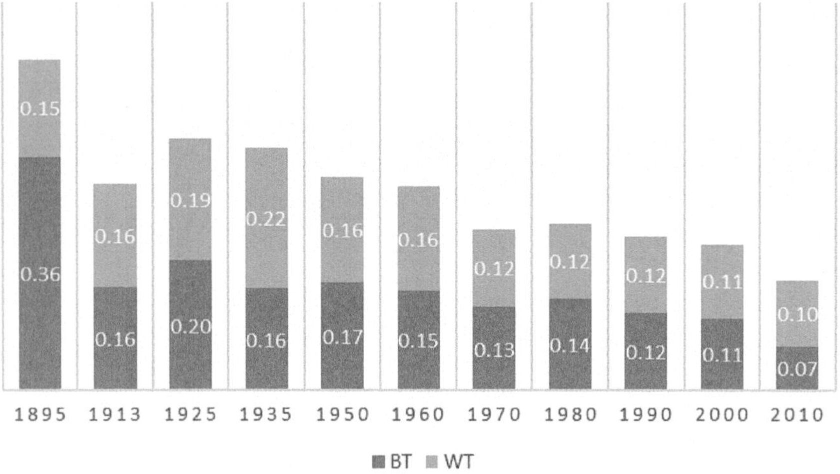

Fig. 13.2 MLD components in Latin America, 1895–2010. (Source: Authors' own)

We observe a decline in regional income disparity across the whole period. However, this decline presents two different stages. First, the decline before World War I was driven by convergence between countries, supported by export-led growth and the integration of Latin American economies into the world economy. During the 1920s, the recovery of international trade after World War I, the rise of protectionism in most European countries, the effects of the commodity lottery, the expanding size of domestic markets and the increasing relevance of the US in the region (displacing the historical influence of the UK) put a brake on the 'between' component of convergence. In the case of the 'within' component, several complementary forces interacted during this period. Thus, on the one hand, some countries adopted an incipient growth model based on an expanding domestic market and the protection of industry. These emerging forces of agglomeration served to increase regional inequality. On the other hand, other countries were affected by the post-war recovery and hit by increases in commodity prices and the expansion of exporting regions, factors that also drove the expansion of inequality.

Since the 1930s, a gradual reduction in total regional inequality can be observed. The 'between' component has declined almost monotonically since the 1920s with only a small increase between 1935 and 1950. The 'within' component increased between 1913 and 1935 and then declined monotonically until 2010. The contribution of 'between' inequality to the decline in overall inequality was clearly greater in the periods 1925–1935 and 2000–2010 with a reduction of four points of inequality over both decades. In these periods, most of the countries were open to international markets and engaged in export-led strategies of development.

The largest reductions in 'within' inequality occurred between 1935 and 1950 and between 1960 and 1970 and coincided with a period of collapse in international markets—during World War II—and the expansion of manufacturing and the upturn in the domestic economy during the 1960s. These results stand in marked contrast with those observed in industrialized countries. Thus, while in Europe industrialization and domestic market integration generated regional dispersion because of the major role played by the manufacturing sector, in Latin America industry appeared as a counterweight to the expansion of those regions endowed with natural resources.

The trends we report also contrast with findings in previous studies. When Badia-Miró et al. (2018) considered the evolution of regional inequality in the Southern Cone, a decreasing trend until 1940 and a marked increase between 1950 and 1960 were observed. These differences can be attributed to the fact that in the Southern Cone, the period of export-led growth seems to have caused a notable reduction in both the 'between' and 'within' components of regional inequality. Yet, if we consider the whole of Latin America, export-led growth coincided with the highest levels of regional inequality, levels that did not change from the end of the nineteenth century to World War I, driven by both the 'between' and 'within' components. In the Southern Cone, World War I and the Great Depression ushered in a period of reduction in inequality, driven above all by the 'between' component: that is, the countries underwent a process of convergence during this period. In the 1940s and 1950s, during World War II and the period of import substitution industrialization (ISI) in the larger countries, levels of regional inequality remained stable. During the 1960s and 1970s, when ISI spread to most countries, regional inequality fell, specifically as regards the 'within' component, that is, industrialization, contrary to expectations, reduced dispersion within each country. From the 1990s onwards, dispersion fell again, driven now by the 'between' component. In short, the debt crisis, the liberalization of the Latin American economy during the 1990s and the commodity boom in the early twenty-first century reduced inequality between countries, against a backdrop of the lowest levels of regional inequality.

However, the trajectory outlined for the entire region was far from being a general pattern. Figures 13.3, 13.4 and 13.5 highlight notable differences by country, coinciding only in the fact that the levels of spatial inequality were among the highest in the world. Figure 13.3 describes the evolution of the three largest economies: Argentina, Brazil and Mexico. In the cases of Brazil and Mexico, we observe a sort of inverted-U shaped pattern, peaking, however, in different periods. In the case of Mexico, regional inequality describes more of a W-shaped pattern, with the peaks occurring between 1935– and 1950 and around the year 2000. In Brazil, the inverted-U is clearer with a peak in 1950 and a decline in inequality thereafter. In Argentina, there was a reduction in inequality in the first decades of the twentieth century, a marked increase until 1960 and then a stabilization at quite high levels. Most of the growth in this country's

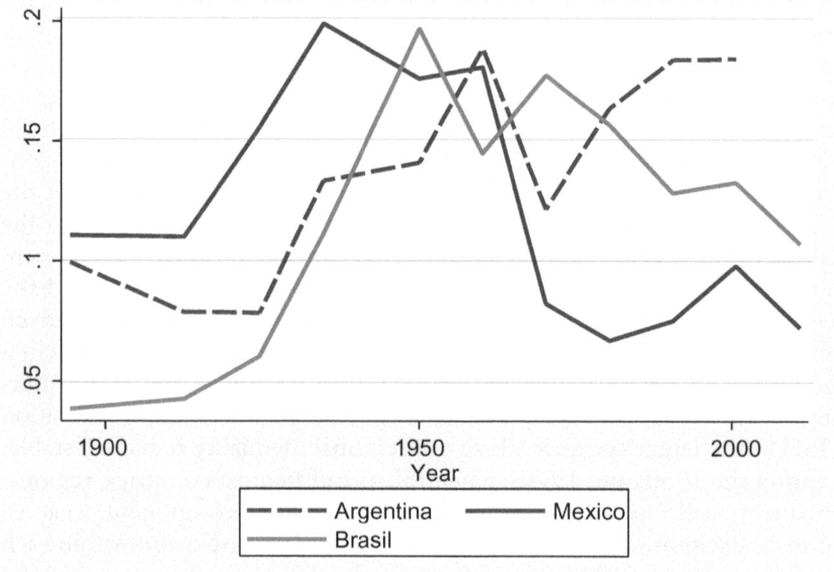

Fig. 13.3 Regional inequality by countries (MLD), 1895–2010. (Source: Authors' own)

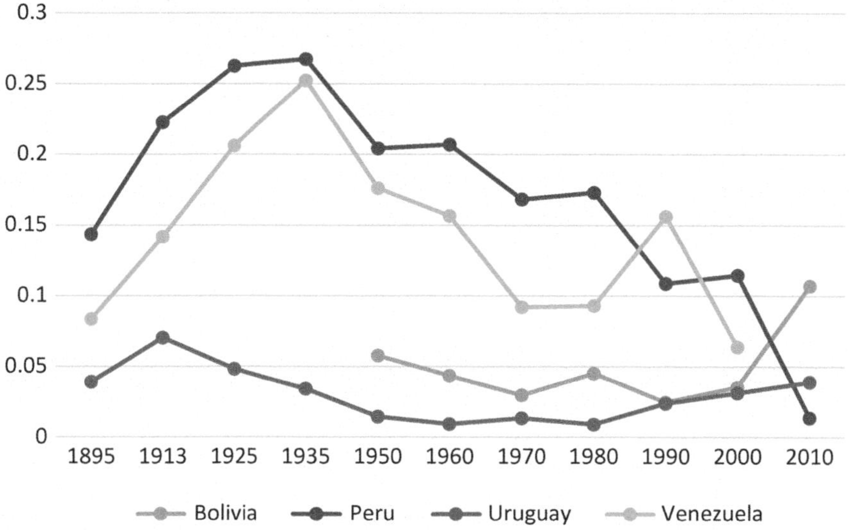

Fig. 13.4 Regional inequality by countries (MLD), 1895–2010. (Source: Authors' own)

industrial sector in the middle decades of the century until the 1970s occurred in districts that were previously among its richest (in particular, the Capital Federal and the province of Buenos Aires) while the expansion of oil production benefited other very rich provinces in Patagonia; the absence here of an inverted-U shape is unsurprising given that in the 1970s the country's growth rates plummeted and the processes of industrial growth and structural change of the previous decades were rapidly reversed.

The drivers behind the evolution of the Mexican case were the comparative advantages associated with natural resource location, changes in access to international markets, and the differences across regions in economic structure and agrarian productivity. Regional differences emerged during the First Globalization and the 1930s, with the expansion of the country's richer regions due to increased global demand. Between the 1940s and 1980s, regional disparities fell. This trend was most intense after 1960 due to the expansion of the domestic market and the collapse of what had been the richer regions. More recently, in the 1980s and the

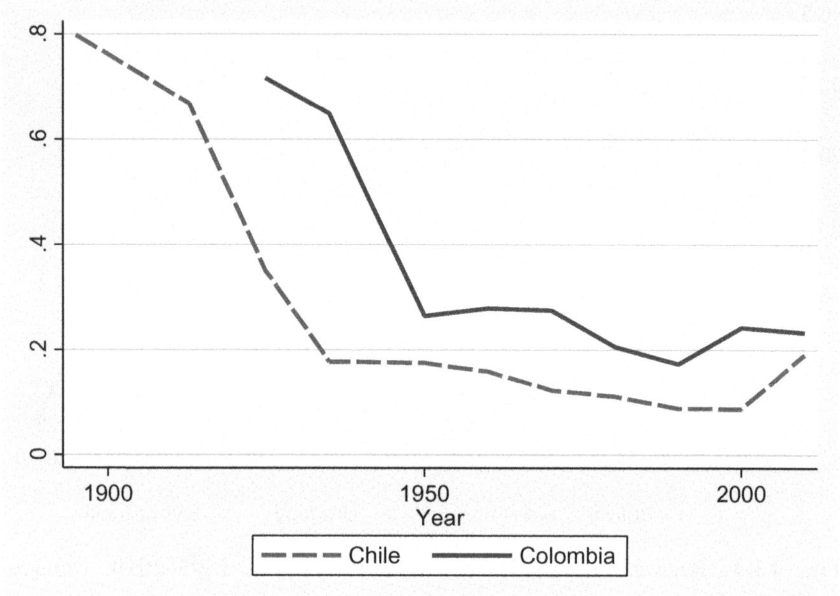

Fig. 13.5 Regional inequality by countries (MLD), 1895–2010. (Source: Authors' own)

1990s, the proximity of the northern regions to the US has fostered their economic growth.[6]

The expansion in regional inequality in Brazil up to 1950 was the result of market integration, the rise of its southern regions and the take-off of Sao Paulo pushed by its early industrialization. ISI policies reinforced this pattern. The liberalization of the economy that began in the 1980s has reduced regional inequality at the same time as those regions with good ties to the international markets have expanded (Bucciferro and Ferreira 2020).

Figure 13.4 illustrates the evolution taken by regional inequality in Bolivia, Peru, Uruguay and Venezuela. In the case of Peru and Venezuela, we observe an inverted-U shaped pattern. In the case of the former, the drivers were migration, industrialization and urbanization, which drove

[6]For the Mexican case, we have calculated the regional GDP figures without taking into account the oil sector. For a detailed explanation, see Aguilar-Retureta et al. (2020).

the expansion of Lima as the country's main centre (Seminario et al. 2020). In the case of Venezuela, the pattern is attributable to the integration of the country into the international markets and to differences in regional specialization (De Corso and Tirado-Fabregat 2020). Bolivia and Uruguay show lower levels of regional inequality, their patterns being due, in the case of Bolivia (Peres-Cajías 2020), to the shift in location of the main economic activities from La Paz to Santa Cruz and, in that of Uruguay, to market integration and the extension of the country's public economic policy (not only of an industrial character but also that concerned with prices, agriculture and the creation of a social welfare state during the middle decades of the century) (Martinez-Galarraga et al. 2020).

Figure 13.5 shows two outliers. Chile and Colombia underwent a marked reduction in regional inequality from the highest levels observed at the beginning of the sample (late nineteenth century in the case of Chile, early 1920s in that of Colombia). For Chile, as Badia-Miró (2020) points out, the explanation can be found in the end of the nitrate cycle (concentrated in just a few regions) and the emergence of the copper cycle (dispersed in several regions). For Colombia, domestic market integration reduced the initial economic dispersion. However, until 1950, regional GDP per capita estimates in this country should be considered as guestimates. If we only consider the evolution since 1950, we observe a declining pattern until 1990 and a slight rise thereafter. As such, Colombian regions did not converge during the second half of the twentieth century, due to the fact that its richer provinces remained as the leading regions throughout the whole of this period (Meisel-Roca and Hahn de Castro 2020).

3 Convergence and Divergence of Latin American Regions

A convergence analysis serves as a good complement to the insights generated from monitoring the evolution of regional inequality (as presented in the previous two sections). Here, we specifically examine the process of unweighted convergence. Following Rodrik (2013), our empirical model is based on a simple specification in which the growth rate of GDP per capita is a function of the distance between the steady-state level and the initial level of GDP per capita and other characteristics specific to each country. The econometric specification takes the form:

$$\hat{y}_{it} = \alpha + \beta \ln y_{it} + \gamma D_i + \varepsilon_{it}, \quad (13.3)$$

where $\hat{y}_{it}$ is the growth rate of GDP per capita in region i in each time frame (identified by t); y_{it} is the level of GDP per capita at the beginning of the time frame in that region; and D_i is some characteristic of region i (typically in our exercise, one belonging to a particular country) (Rodrik 2013). The choice of this specification implies focusing on the concept of unconditional convergence in the sense that we do not control for factors that may eventually generate different steady-state levels of income per capita (i.e. education, institutional quality, availability of natural resources, etc.). The inclusion of variable D_i opens up the possibility of testing the hypothesis of the existence of some ad hoc, previously defined, convergence clubs; if D_i identifies the regions within a country, the implicit hypothesis would be that the regions within that country converge to a different level of capital in the steady state to that which the other regions converge.[7]

The convergence analysis was performed for the whole period (1895–2000) and for three sub-periods: the first (1895–1925) covers essentially the second half of the period of globalization and the incorporation of most of the countries of Latin America into the international goods and productive factor markets; the second (1935–1970) allows us to determine the consequences of the period of government-led industrialization on regional economic growth; and the third (1980–2000) concentrates on the changes recorded following the end of the process of inward-looking development and the onset of the period of liberalization in the 1970s and 1980s.

The number of regions included in each regression depends on data availability at the national level. Thus, the series of subnational GDPs only start in 1925 for Colombia and in 1950 for Bolivia. Likewise, we have no data for the first sub-period for some regions in other countries. Thus, we do not incorporate Region XI (Chile) and FNT (Colombia) into the data set until 1950.

Our results clearly point to a slow, but an unmistakably robust, process of regional convergence in all four of the time spans considered.[8] When we include national dummies (i.e. assuming the same convergence rate for the whole sample but allowing for growth rates across countries), some

[7] Convergence is usually characterized using the speed of convergence defined as $v = -\ln(1 + T\beta)/T$.

[8] The 'usual' rate of convergence is 2% per year (Sala-i-Martin 1996). An estimated convergence parameter of −0.005 implies a speed of convergence of 0.7%.

countries present significantly higher levels of GDP in the steady state in some periods (regression results available from the authors upon request); yet, the convergence speed remains basically unchanged with respect to the specification without dummies.

Figure 13.6 shows the general results of the convergence analysis for the period 1895–2000 with growth rates of GDP per capita on the vertical axis and the initial level of GDP per capita on the horizontal axis. As discussed, Bolivia and Colombia are not included in this analysis for reasons of data availability. An initial inspection of the graph shows the clear alignment of the Latin American regions along the negatively sloping diagonal, which is consistent with the results obtained in the econometric analysis (Table 13.1). What the figure also highlights is that the regions of the same country tend to concentrate in particular areas of the graph; for instance, all the regions of Argentina lie in the bottom-right corner of the graph (high initial level of GDP per capita but low average growth), while

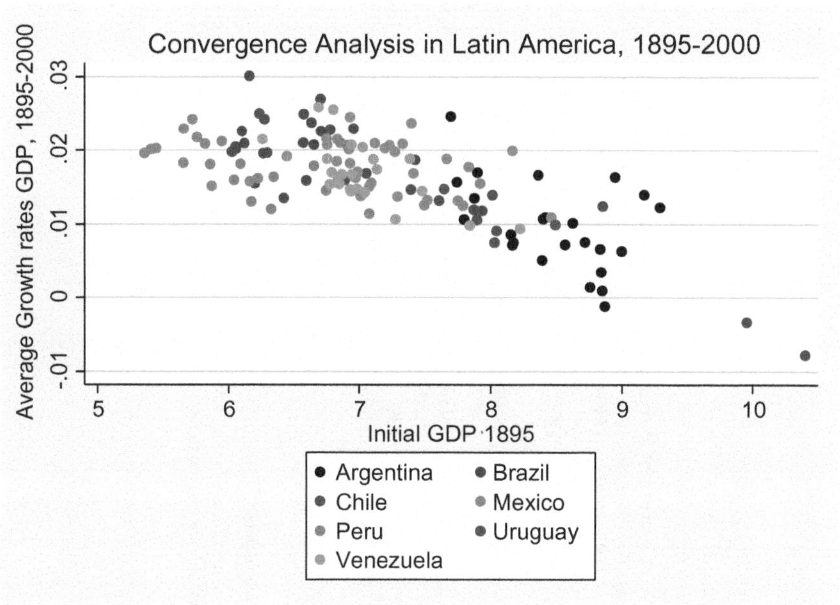

Fig. 13.6 Convergence analysis in Latin America, 1895–2000. (Source: Authors' own)

Table 13.1 Convergence regression of Latin American regional growth (OLS)

	1895–2000	*1895–2000*	*1895–1925*	*1895–1925*	*1935–1970*	*1935–1970*	*1980–2000*	*1980–2000*
	(1)	*(2)*	*(1)*	*(2)*	*(1)*	*(2)*	*(1)*	*(2)*
$Lngdppc_t$	−0.005	−0.005	−0.007	−0.006	−0.009	−0.011	−0.010	−0.006
	(−12.54)**	(−8.74)**	(−5.40)**	(−3.33)**	(−8.62)**	(−10.64)**	(−6.56)**	(−3.78)**
Constant	0.049	0.053	0.057	0.050	0.095	0.108	0.092	0.060
	(18.43)**	(10.24)**	(6.25)**	(3.16)	(11.99)**	(11.86)**	(7.02)**	(3.66)**
N	139	139	139	139	154	154	165	165
R-adj	0.531	0.605	0.170	0.44	0.324	0.657	0.204	0.581

*$p < 0.1$

**$p < 0.05$

(1) Regional convergence

(2) Regional convergence including national dummies to allow for different intercepts (i.e. assuming the same convergence rate for the whole sample but allowing different levels of growth rates across countries)

most of the regions of Brazil and Peru lie in the top-left corner (low initial level of GDP but high growth rates). This pattern is consistent with the marked reduction in the 'between' component of inequality in the period illustrated in Fig. 13.2. The regressions for individual countries show that over the course of the twentieth century there was convergence within countries in the cases of Argentina, Chile, Peru, Mexico and Venezuela, whereas there was no statistically significant convergence in Brazil and Uruguay.[9] The fact that there was convergence across regions in most of the countries is consistent with the reduction of the 'within' component of inequality illustrated in Fig. 13.2.

In the period 1895–1925, during which most countries became incorporated into the global markets of goods, services and productive factors, we find, when taking all the Latin American regions together, that the speed of convergence was slightly higher than the average for the twentieth century both in the regressions with and without national dummies. In the regression without dummies, an estimated parameter of −0.007 implies a speed of convergence of 0.8%; in the regression with dummies, it implies a speed of convergence of 0.7%. The only statistically significant national dummy variable is that of Peru, where a positive sign suggests that all the regions in the other countries had, given their initial level of per capita GDP, similar growth rates to that of Uruguay (the omitted country), while the regions of Peru grew faster conditional to their GDP in 1895.

Figure 13.7 shows, once again, that in the period of globalization there was an inverse relation between initial levels of GDP and growth rates and that the regions of the same country tend to concentrate in specific areas of the graph: Peru and Brazil in the top left, the countries of the Southern Cone (Argentina, Chile and Uruguay) in the bottom right and Mexico in the centre. Additionally, when we run convergence regressions for individual countries, we find that in the period 1895–1925 only Argentina and Chile present 'within' convergence, while Brazil, Uruguay (with only five observations), Venezuela, Mexico and Peru do not present any statistically significant convergence. These results are consistent with the reduction in overall regional inequality during the period. The increase in the 'within'

[9] In the chapters dedicated herein to Brazil and Uruguay, the authors are able to report the existence of regional convergence because they consider the period 1870–2010. Here, in order to work with a homogenized database, we consider the period 1895–2000 and, for this period, convergence was not statistically significant.

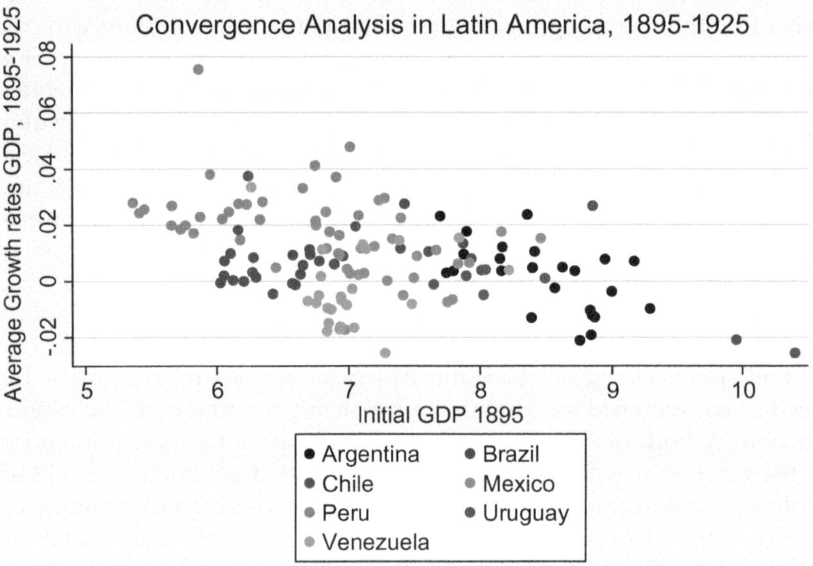

Fig. 13.7 Convergence analysis in Latin America, 1895–1925. (Source: Authors' own)

component of inequality between 1895 and 1925 can be explained by the fact that the increase in inequality and the non-convergence in most of the countries—in particular, of big countries like Brazil—more than offset the reduction in inequality (and convergence) in Argentina and Chile.

If we combine the results of the convergence regression for all the regions with those of the regression for each country separately, it becomes apparent that the convergence observed across the regions is in fact a convergence across countries together with a small variability in levels of per capita GDP within countries. In other words, in a graph with levels of GDP per capita on the horizontal axis and growth rates of GDP per capita on the vertical axis, most of the regions of a given country would lie very close to each other and close to the national average. Moreover, these national averages would tend to converge. Thus, it is possible to observe convergence across regions even though the regions within each country diverge.

In the 35-year period of state-led industrialization (1935–1970), the speed of convergence increased to 1.1 and 1.4%, the national dummies

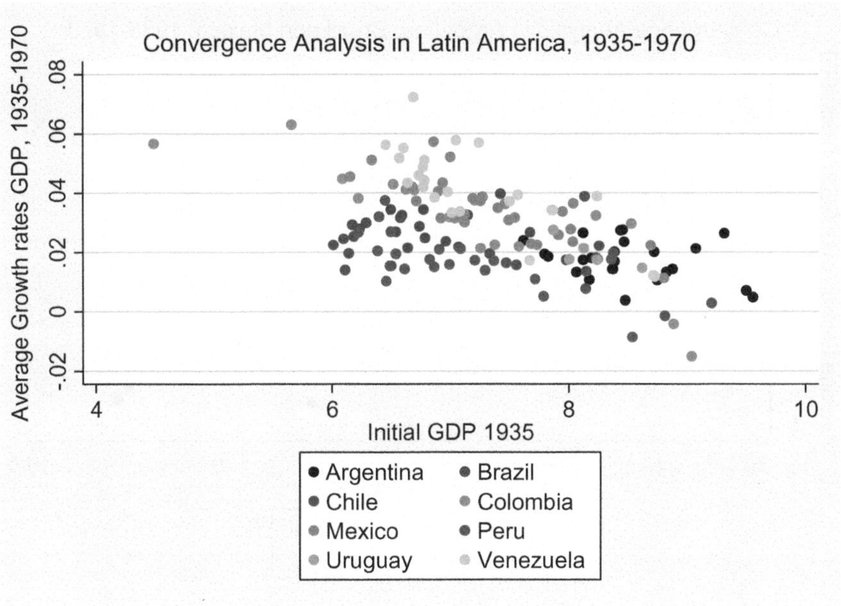

Fig. 13.8 Convergence analysis in Latin America, 1935–1970. (Source: Authors' own)

suggesting that the growth rates of all the regions (conditional on their initial level) were similar to those in Uruguay, with the exception of Venezuela, which presented growth rates that were more than one percentage point (p.p.) higher, and Peru, which presented growth rates one p.p. lower than those of the baseline country.

Figure 13.8 once again shows that in this period the regions of the same country tend to concentrate in specific areas of the graph—thus, those of Argentina, Chile and Uruguay lie in the bottom right and those of Colombia, Venezuela and México in the top left. Natural resource specializations, specifically, that of oil during the 1940s and 1950s, accounts for the high growth of what were formerly the poorer regions.[10] In

[10]As mentioned, Colombian GDP figures between 1925 and 1950 are guestimates from bank deposits, which has resulted in a bias of the country's low density and low urbanized regions. The two points in the top left of Fig. 13.8 correspond to the regions of Boyacá and Other regions (comprising Amazonas, Arauca, Caquetá, Guainía, Guaviare, Putumayo, San

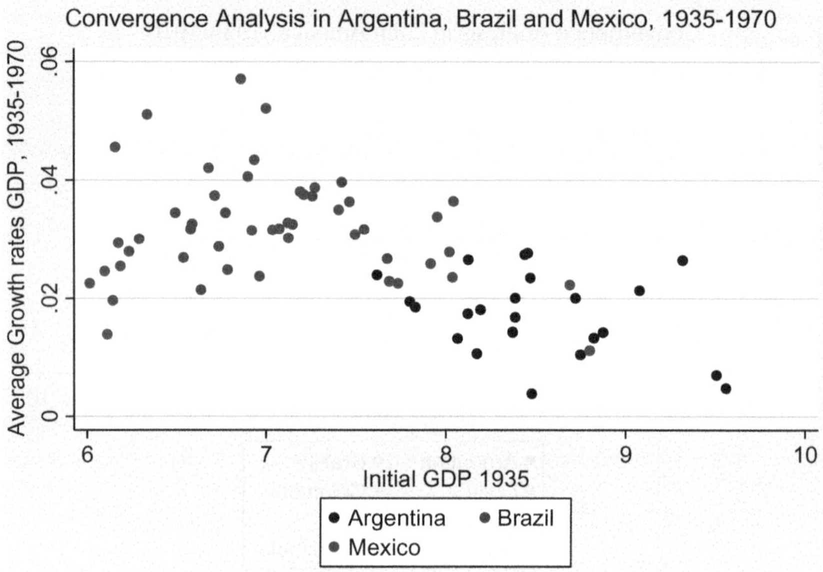

Fig. 13.9 Convergence analysis in Argentina, Brazil and Mexico, 1935–1970. (Source: Authors' own)

contrast, the early industrialized regions of the big countries lie in the bottom right. If we restrict our analysis to those big countries where ISI was most intense—that is, Argentina, Brazil and Mexico, when considering all the regions of these three countries together, we find that there was indeed convergence, while the only country presenting statistically significant convergence was Mexico. These results are quite unexpected as they indicate that industrialization in the richer countries in this period (Europe and the US) increased levels of regional inequality and, hence, of divergence (Felice 2012; Rosés et al. 2010).

Figure 13.9 shows that between 1935 and 1970 the poorest states of Mexico (Oaxaca and Guerrero) presented very high growth rates, growing faster than the richest states in the same country and generating convergence within Mexico. In Brazil, the poorest regions (Ceará, Paraíba

Andrés y Providencia, Vaupés and Vichada). These regions present unrealistic GDP per capita figures and should be considered as outliers.

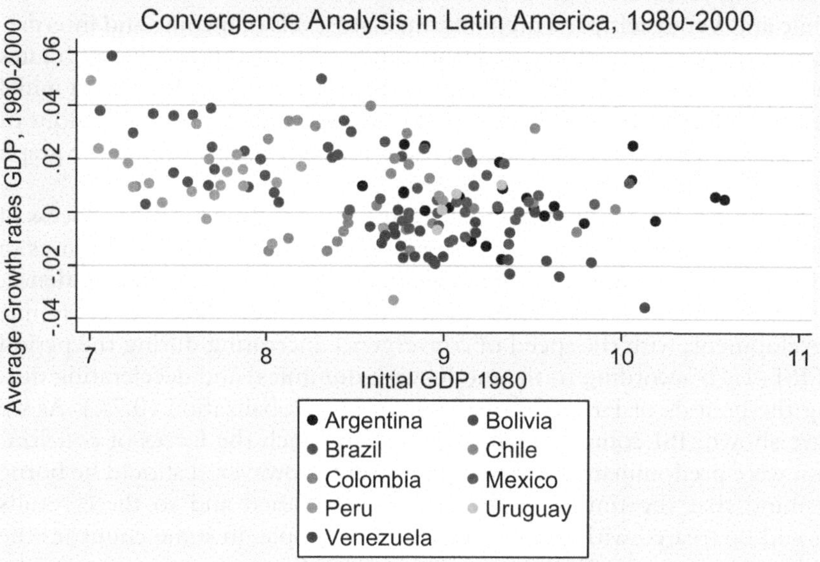

Fig. 13.10 Convergence analysis in Latin America, 1980–2000. (Source: Authors' own)

and Piauí) presented disappointingly low rates of growth, lower, that is, than the rates of both the poorest Mexican states and the richest regions in Brazil. In contrast, most of the provinces in Argentina were relatively rich and presented relatively low growth rates, while the poorer regions did not grow faster than their richer counterparts (there is no statistically significant convergence within Argentina).

In the last period (1980–2000), after the debt-crisis, the 'lost decade' and the liberalization of the 1990s, the speed of convergence remained high but slightly lower than in the previous period (1.1% in the model without national dummies and 0.7%. in the regressions with these dummies).

Figure 13.10 shows that, in the period after 1980, Latin America's poorest regions were in Peru, Bolivia and Brazil[11] with most of them

[11]Thirty-eight of the 41 poorest regions in 1980 were in Bolivia (9), Brazil (10) or Peru (19). The other three were in Chile (1) and Colombia (2).

presenting relatively high growth rates. Most of the regions in Mexico, Chile and Venezuela presented intermediate levels of income and intermediate growth rates; within this group, Chile presented higher growth rates than Mexico, while Venezuela had the lowest rates. Levels of both initial wealth and growth rates fluctuated around the average for the regions of Colombia, while those of Argentina lie principally to the right of the graph with high initial levels and low growth rates.

In short, considered as a whole, Latin America shows a clear process of regional economic convergence, which is consistent with our findings in terms of the evolution of regional inequality. Based on our evidence, regional disparities were reduced during the three stages of economic development, with the speed of convergence increasing during the period of ISI (1.4% according to the model with dummies) and decelerating during the periods of First Globalization and re-globalization (0.7%). As we have shown, ISI coincided with a period in which the forces of equalization were predominant and acted intensively. However, it should be borne in mind that the timing of the ISI process varied and so these results should be treated with some caution. For example, in some countries the process began in the 1930s, while in others it did not commence until the 1950s. Likewise, in some countries the process began to decline in the 1960s, but in others it extended into the 1980s.

Thus, considering Latin America as a whole, its regions underwent a general process of economic convergence; yet, in some instances, we have detected national processes of non-convergence in each of the three subperiods. These results are evidence of the existence of regional economies that could operate beyond the limitations of national borders and whose particular factor endowment was more determinant than their national condition. In the next section, we are able to identify clusters of poor and rich regions, corresponding to 'clubs' whose members included regions from different countries.

4 The Emergence of Regional Clubs in Latin America

The fact that traditional analyses of regional inequality fail to consider the geographical dimension—that is, the distance between the units of analysis—is particularly unfortunate, because the evolution of income per capita in a region can be strongly influenced by the economic activity in a neighbouring region (via trade, migration, technological spillovers, infrastructure, etc.). Figure 13.11 shows the evolution of the spatial pattern of

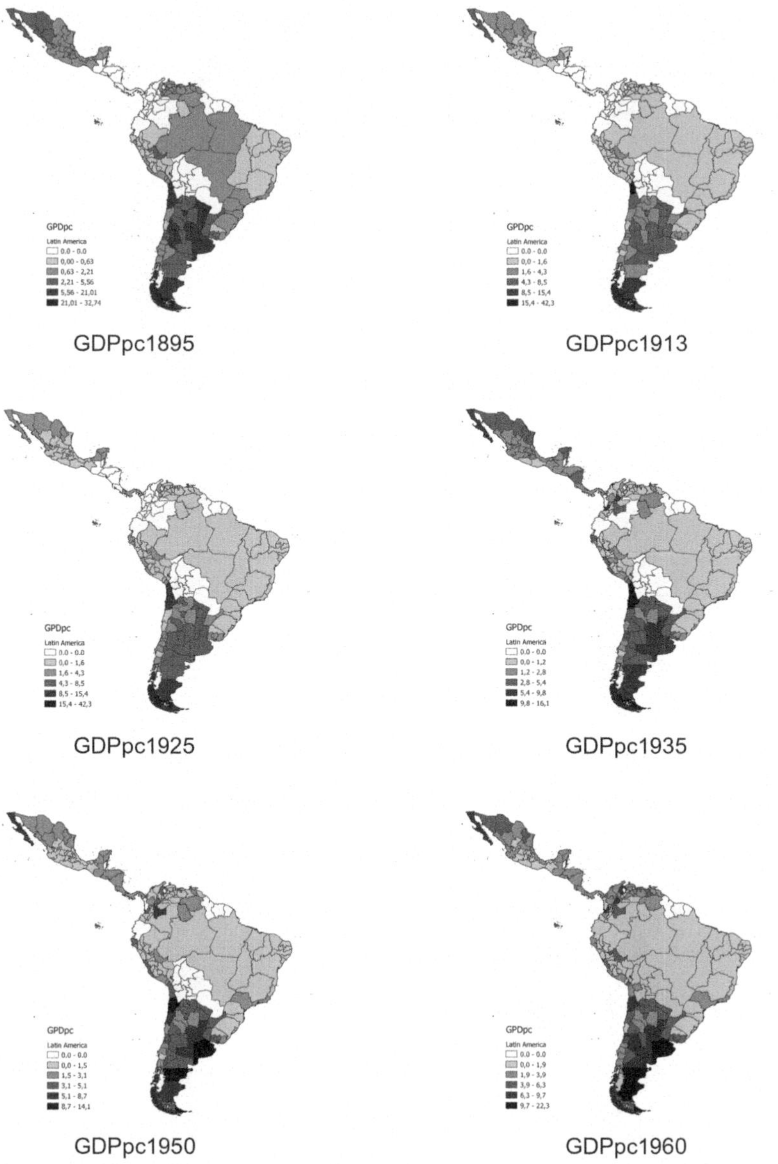

Fig. 13.11 Regional GDP per capita in Latin America, 1895–2010. (Source: Authors' own)

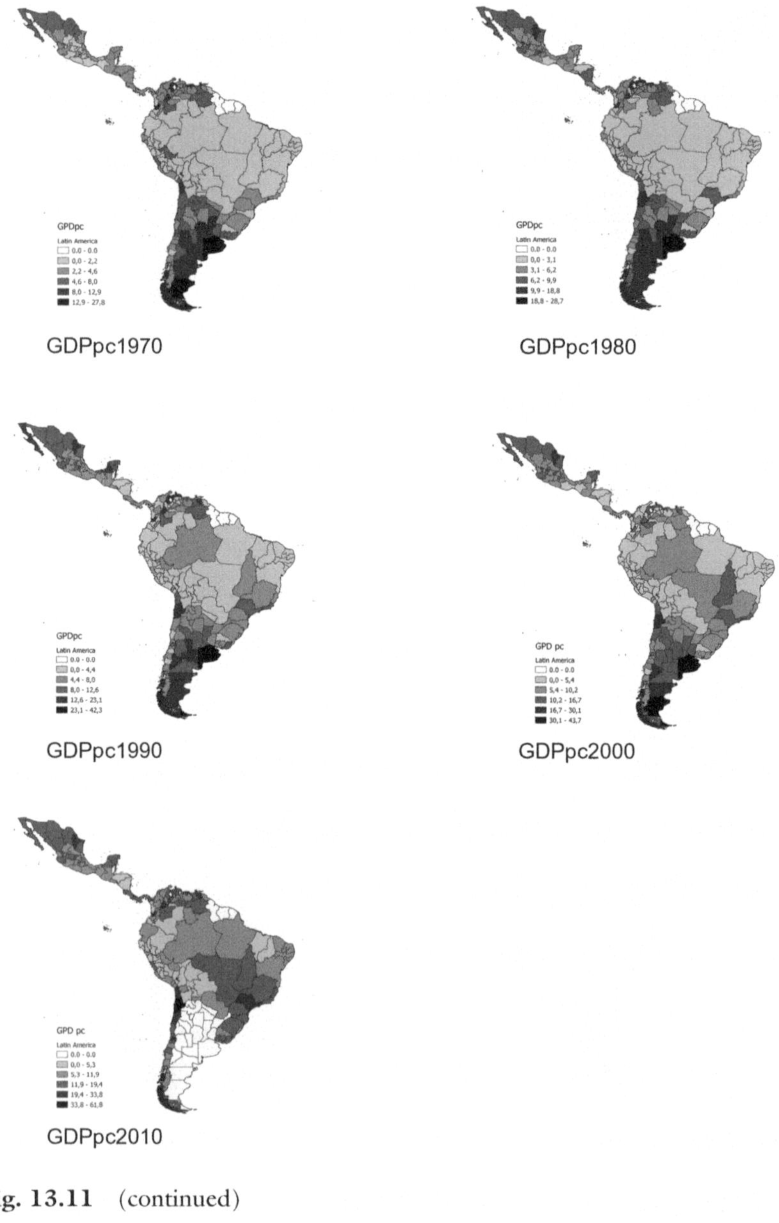

Fig. 13.11 (continued)

regional GDP per capita in Latin America between 1895 and 2010.[12] The richer regions were those in the North (Mexican regions close to the US border) and the South (Argentinian, Chilean and Uruguayan regions). Other regions endowed with natural resources became richer thanks to upturns in their respective commodity price cycles (oil in the case of Venezuela and nitrates in that of northern Chile). Other leading regions, from the beginning of the period, included the dynamic economies of Colombia, Peru and Brazil, most coinciding with the country's regional capitals which, in turn, benefitted from expanding processes of urbanization and industrialization, the latter associated with the efforts of the period of ISI (Cundinamarca, Lima, Rio de Janeiro and Sao Paulo). In contrast, the lowest levels of regional GDP per capita corresponded to the low-density regions located along the Amazon River, regardless of the countries considered. Since 1950 (i.e. when data became available), the Bolivian, Brazilian, Peruvian and Colombian regions of the interior (and the Paraguayan regions too, when added to the sample) presented similar levels of GDP per capita until 1990. Since then, Amazonas (Brazil), which has specialized in industry (taking advantage of the free trade zone), and Ucayali and Madre de Diós (Peru), two low-density regions specialized in the export of resources (mainly agrarian commodities), have managed to break from their long history as regions with low levels of GPD per capita.

The Uruguayan border is another interesting case. The GDP per capita of its northern regions is at similar levels to that of its neighbouring Brazilian state (Rio Grande do Sul), while the GDP of its southern regions, including Montevideo, are similar to that of Entre Rios, the neighbouring state in Argentina, but lower than the levels observed in Buenos Aires and the Distrito Federal.

The case of Mexico is also noteworthy. While the impact of the proximity of the US border in boosting the growth of its northern regions is evident, there is also a perceptible continuity between the low GDP per capita levels of its southern regions and the levels observed in Guatemala.

[12] When no data are available for the regions of a country, we consider the GDP per capita for the whole country (i.e. Bolivia and Colombia before 1950 and 1925, respectively, and Central American Republics and Paraguay for the entire period). In the case of Argentina for 2010, we have considered no data.

Finally, it should be noted that the comparison provided is a regional one. This means that in some cases, the poorer regions of one country may, at the same time, be among the richer regions when considering Latin America as a whole. This is specifically the case of some Argentinian and Chilean agrarian regions in the interior, which appear as lagging regions from a country perspective facing difficulties to take advantage of the growth experienced in the leading regions.

In order to verify statistically the presence of clusters of rich regions in the south and poor regions in the centre, we ran a simple test to obtain a local Moran's I coefficient for all the regions making up the sample. Plotting the results of this test on a map, we can verify the existence of a statistical relationship between the regional GDP per capita of any region and the level of GDP per capita in its neighbouring regions (Fig. 13.12). Specifically, we are interested in the spatial dimension of this coefficient, so as to identify the existence of clusters of rich or poor regions inside the nine countries or, as we expect, the existence of clusters across borders.[13]

From the end of the nineteenth century to the 1970s, we can identify two clearly differentiated clusters of regions in Latin America. The 'club' of the poor regions (shaded in light grey) occupies the centre of Latin America, corresponding largely to Amazonia, stretching from the Atlantic to the Pacific Oceans and including the regions of several countries (Brazil, Bolivia, Peru and Colombia). The 'club' of the rich regions (shaded in dark grey) occupies territories in the south of Latin America and includes provinces of Argentina and Chile. These two clusters were first observed at the end of the nineteenth century and expanded thereafter into neighbouring areas, both 'clubs' reaching their maximum extent around 1970. One explanation for the location of economic activity and income concerns the preponderance of 'first nature' factors, that is, relative to temperate regions, tropical regions are hindered in their development by higher disease burdens and limitations on agricultural productivity (Gallup et al. 1999). Based on our evidence, the richest regions emerged in temperate zones, where agriculture (both livestock and crops) flourished and the

[13] We considered a distance matrix in which the cells of two regions take the number one when contiguous and zero otherwise. For further details about spatial-autocorrelation analysis, see Anselin (2010), and Anselin and Rey (2009). We employed maps for the period 1895–2000. The 2010 outcomes are not considered due to the lack of data for Argentina, which could bias results given the size of the country. Data for Colombia are not available between 1895 and 1925 and for Bolivia before 1950. When data were not available, we considered the GDP per capita for the whole country.

Fig. 13.12 Local Indicators of Spatial Autocorrelation (LISA) maps, 1895–2000. (Source: Authors' own)

connection with international markets was achieved and proved profitable at an early date. The possible impact of geography on development and the relatively low levels of development of tropical regions can also be mediated through relative factor endowments and inequality (Sokoloff and Engerman 2000), settlement characteristics and the variability of institutional arrangements (Acemoglu et al. 2002). This explains, at least partially, the relative backwardness of the regions in Bolivia, Brazil, Peru and Colombia that are members of the 'club' of poor regions.

After the 1970s, however, the distinction between rich and poor regions faded, which is evidence of the decreasing influence of 'first nature' factors and, we would argue, of the increasing importance of 'second nature' factors. New economic geography shows that, when trade costs fall, increasing returns to scale emerge, and agglomeration economies become important, the case here of the growing relevance of cities such as Sao Paulo, Rio de Janeiro, La Paz and Lima. In the case of Latin America, domestic trade costs were relatively high compared to those of the international trade of those regions with good transport infrastructure. The fall in transport costs becomes evident with the expansion of both railway and highway networks in the early twentieth century and during state-led industrialization (Bértola and Ocampo 2012). Product differentiation reinforced this pattern and saw Latin America take on a highly differentiated spatial organization of economic activity even when the overriding physical geography remained undifferentiated. The urbanization, modernization and integration of many regions in the centre of Latin America saw the dissipation of the 'club' of poor regions, in a process that was consistent with the evolution of inequality as described herein. The models of new economic geography illustrate the possibility of self-organizing spatial patterns of production based on agglomeration effects rather than on differences in climate, ruggedness, rainfall, ecology and transport costs.

The 'first' and 'second nature' factors combined with the impact of economic policy and, in particular, with that of the productive, trade and income policies that were implemented in Latin America after the end of the nineteenth century (Bértola 2020). During the First Globalization (from 1890 to the 1920s), the most significant policies were those directed at consolidating the state and its conditions as a (true) central power, enforcing property rights and promoting investment in infrastructure (mainly railways), logistics (ports) and utilities (communications, electricity, potable water and sewage). This set of policies facilitated the exploitation of natural resources which proved invaluable in helping the countries of Latin America engage in international trade. In terms of productive policy, tariffs played a key role. In conservative countries, with a protectionist tradition dating from colonial times, the use of tariffs as productive promotional tools was usual. In more liberal regions, tariffs represented an essential component of their tax income, but increasingly they were used as a systematic protection of domestic industries.

Following the crisis of 1929 and during the Great Depression of the decade that followed, the Latin American countries were forced to be much more active in terms of their productive, trade and income policies. Initially, they reacted spontaneously as they sought to recover the external equilibrium against the backdrop of a dramatic decline in international trade. After World War II, more systematic and planned industrialization policies were considered and implemented. However, in those years, regional development was not a question of any particular concern. It would not be until the 1960s that explicit attempts were made to develop some regional economies, above all through the creation of free zones, as in Brazilian Amazonia, Northern Mexico and Northern Chile, the construction of major infrastructure works (such as the Pan-American Highway in Peru and extensive highways in Argentina) and far-reaching changes in political administration (such as the creation of Brasilia as Brazil's new capital). In each of these cases, geopolitical considerations were always present. These changes in economic policy design were arguably responsible for the progressive dissolution of the 'club' of poor regions—and the reduction in regional inequality—that our evidence highlights. Policies promoting local and regional development in recent decades have been underpinned by a range of different ideas. The interest generated is also the result of the recognition that the prevalent development models have been unable to modernize wide regions of the continent.

5 Conclusions

While regional disparities in Latin America continue to be among the highest in the world, there has been a narrowing of this gap in the course of the twentieth century. Industrialization, exploitation of natural resources, trade and regional development policies in a context of domestic and regional market integration have combined to produce this pattern of regional economic convergence; however, the intensity of the process has varied depending on the specific nature of the historical period.

Initially, during the period of export-led growth, convergence between countries accounted for most of the reduction in spatial inequality. Subsequently, during periods characterized by the expansion of policies of manufacturing and regional development—above all in the larger and already more industrialized countries (i.e. Argentina, Brazil and Mexico), but also in those that invested in their industrial sectors in the 1950s and 1960s—a reduction was recorded in the inequality within countries, but the disparities between them were maintained, representing the most intense period of convergence (in contrast with the experience of the industrialized countries). Later, during the oil crisis in the 1970s and the debt crisis in the 1980s, regional differences were maintained, although the evolution of individual countries was diverse (e.g. the oil-exporting regions expanded, while urbanized and industrial regions fell into decline in parallel with the collapse of ISI policies and the progressive opening up of markets). And, finally, the re-globalization in the 1990s and the expansion of commodity prices at the beginning of the twenty-first century resulted in a new fall in inequality levels, both between and within countries.

However, above and beyond all these economic trends and factors, the local occurrence of natural resources affected the evolution of many regions. The impact of these resources over time was directly dependent on the evolution of that particular natural resource, that is, whether its exploitation enjoyed continuity over time or whether it was exhausted in a matter of years. In most cases, the wealth of these regions did not spread to neighbouring regions.

But the result has not been a simple process of convergence of the regions of Latin America. What we observe is the emergence of clusters of regions, most markedly so during the ISI years, in the 1960s and 1970s, with similar levels of GDP per capita: thus, on the one hand, we find agglomerations of rich regions in the extremes—in the North, adjacent to the border with the US, and, in the South, around the Argentine capital and of those that are most abundant in natural resources; on the other hand, we find agglomerations of poorer regions along the Amazon River in Brazil, Colombia and Peru. Later, the clusters of rich regions were maintained while those of poor regions dissipated, which points to the progressive predominance of factors of a secondary nature—that is, those different to climate, rainfall, the ruggedness of the terrain and accessibility problems—together with a public policy that increasingly focused on the regional problems ignored by previous development policies (mainly since the 1960s).

References

Acemoglu, D., Robinson, J. A., Johnson, S., and Robinson, J. A. (2002). Reversal of Fortune: Geography and Institution in the Making of the Modern World Income Distribution. *The Quarterly Journal of Economics, 117*(4), 1231–94.

Anselin, L. (2010). Local Indicators of Spatial Association-LISA. *Geographical Analysis, 27*(2), 93–115.

Anselin, L., and Rey, S. J. (2009). *Perspectives on Spatial Data Analysis*. Springer.

Araoz, M. F., Nicolini, E. A., and Talassino, M. (2020). Growth and convergence among Argentine provinces since 1895. In D. A. Tirado-Fabregat, M. Badia-Miró, and H. Willebald (Ed.), *Time and Space: Latin American Regional Development in Historical Perspective*. Palgrave Macmillan.

Aguilar-Retureta, J., Badia-Miró, M., and Herranz-Loncán, A. (2020). Regional GDP in Mexico, 1895–2010. In D. A. Tirado-Fabregat, M. Badia-Miró, and H. Willebald (Ed.), *Time and Space: Latin American Regional Development in Historical Perspective*. Palgrave Macmillan.

Badia-Miró, M. (2020). Spatial inequality in Chile in the long run: a paradox of extreme concentration in absence of agglomeration forces (1890–2017). In D. A. Tirado-Fabregat, M. Badia-Miró, and H. Willebald (Ed.), *Time and Space: Latin American Regional Development in Historical Perspective*. Palgrave Macmillan.

Badia-Miró, M., Nicolini, E. A., and Willebald, H. (2018). Growth and regional disparities in South America, 1890–1960. *Journal of Interdisciplinary History, 49*(1), 117–139.

Bértola, L. (2020).Productive and regional development policies in Latin America since 1890. In M. Badia-Miró, D. A. Tirado-Fabregat, and H. Willebald (Ed.), *Time and Space: Latin American Regional Development in Historical Perspective*. Palgrave Macmillan.

Bértola, L., and Ocampo, J. A. (2012). *The Economic Development of Latin America since Independence*. Oxford, United Kingdom: Oxford University Press.

Bluedorn, J., Lian, W., Novta, N., and Timmer, Y. (2019). Widening Gaps: Regional Inequality within Advanced Economies. Available in https://blogs.imf.org/2019/10/09/widening-gaps-regional-inequality-within-advanced-economies/ (accessed 26/01/2020).

Bucciferro, J. R., and Ferreira, P. C. G. (2020). The Evolution of Regional Income Inequality in Brazil, 1872–2015. In D. A. Tirado-Fabregat, M. Badia-Miró, and H. Willebald (Ed.), *Time and Space: Latin American Regional Development in Historical Perspective*. Palgrave Macmillan.

De Corso, G., and Tirado-Fabregat, D. A. (2020). Was the oil sown evenly? Long-term patterns of regional inequality in Venezuela (1881–2011). In D. A. Tirado-Fabregat, M. Badia-Miró, and H. Willebald (Ed.), *Time and Space: Latin American Regional Development in Historical Perspective*. Palgrave Macmillan.

Diez-Minguela, A., and Sanchis-Llopis, M. T. (2020). Comparing different estimation methodologies of regional GDPs in Latin American countries. In D. A. Tirado-Fabregat, M. Badia-Miró, and H. Willebald (Ed.), *Time and Space: Latin American Regional Development in Historical Perspective*. Palgrave Macmillan.
Felice, E. (2012). Regional convergence in Italy, 1891–2001: testing human and social capital. *Cliometrica, 6* (3), 267–306.
Gallup, J. L., Sachs, J. D., and Mellinger, A. D. (1999). Geography and Economic Development. *International Regional Science Review, 22*(2), 179–232.
Gollin, D., Jedwab, R., and Vollrath, D. (2016). Urbanization with and without industrialization. *Journal of Economic Growth, 21*(1).
Martinez-Galarraga, J., Rodríguez Miranda, A., and Willebald, H. (2020). Patterns of regional income distribution in Uruguay (1872–2012): a story of agglomeration, natural resources and public policies. In D. A. Tirado-Fabregat, M. Badia-Miró, and H. Willebald (Ed.), *Time and Space: Latin American Regional Development in Historical Perspective*. Palgrave Macmillan.
Meisel-Roca, A., and Hahn de Castro, L. W. (2020). Regional Economic Inequality in Colombia, 1926–2018. In D. A. Tirado-Fabregat, M. Badia-Miró, and H. Willebald (Ed.), *Time and Space: Latin American Regional Development in Historical Perspective*. Palgrave Macmillan.
Peres-Cajías, J. A. (2020). From West to East: Bolivian Regional GDPs since the 1950s. A story of Natural Resources and Infrastructure. In D. A. Tirado-Fabregat, M. Badia-Miró, and H. Willebald (Ed.), *Time and Space: Latin American Regional Development in Historical Perspective*. Palgrave Macmillan.
Rodrik, D. (2013). Unconditional Convergence in Manufacturing. *The Quarterly Journal of Economics, 128*(1), 165–204.
Rosés, J. R., Martinez-Galarraga, J., and Tirado-Fabregat, D. A. (2010). The upswing of regional income inequality in Spain (1860–1930). *Explorations in Economic History, 47*(2), 244–257.
Rosés, J. R., and Wolf, N. (Ed.). (2018). *The Economic Development of Europe's Regions. A Quantitative History since 1900*. Routledge.
Sala-i-Martin, X. (1996). Regional cohesion: evidence and theories of regional growth and convergence. *European Economic Review, 40*(6), 1325–1352.
Seminario, B., Zegarra, M. A., and Palomino, L. (2020). Peruvian regional inequality: 1847–2017. In D. A. Tirado-Fabregat, M. Badia-Miró, and H. Willebald (Ed.), *Time and Space: Latin American Regional Development in Historical Perspective*. Palgrave Macmillan.
Sokoloff, K. L., and Engerman, S. L. (2000). History Lessons: Institutions, Factors Endowments, and Paths of Development in the New World. *The Journal of Economic Perspectives, 14*(3), 217–32.
Williamson, J. G. (1965). Regional Inequality and the Process of National Development: A Description of the Patterns. *Economic Development and Cultural Change, 13*(4), 1–84.

CHAPTER 14

Regional Inequality in Latin America: Does It Mirror the European Pattern?

Julio Martinez-Galarraga, Esteban A. Nicolini, Daniel A. Tirado-Fabregat, and Henry Willebald

1 Introduction

The World Bank devoted its *World Development Report* of 2009 to the geography of economic development.[1] It analysed the evolution and determinants of inequality at different levels of territorial disaggregation (international, national and local), using the trajectories of regional

[1] World Bank (2009).

J. Martinez-Galarraga (✉) • D. A. Tirado-Fabregat
Departament d'Anàlisi Econòmica, Universitat de València, València, Spain
e-mail: julio.martinez-galarraga@uv.es; Daniel.Tirado@uv.es

E. A. Nicolini
CIEDH—Universidad del Norte Santo Tomás de Aquino, Tucumán, Argentina

INVECO—Universidad Nacional de Tucumán, Tucumán, Argentina

H. Willebald
Universidad de la República, Montevideo, Uruguay
e-mail: hwillebald@iecon.ccee.edu.uy

D. A. Tirado-Fabregat et al. (eds.), *Time and Space*,
Palgrave Studies in Economic History,
https://doi.org/10.1007/978-3-030-47553-6_14

inequality followed in the past by today's developed countries to draw conclusions as to their possible evolution in developing countries. The report documented the past experiences of countries such as France, Spain, Japan, the Netherlands and Canada, postulating that these pointed to the existence of a number of stylized facts about territorial inequality that could be extrapolated to developing countries.

The first fact was that the long-term evolution of territorial differences in income or living standards was characterized by an initial increase in inequality followed by a period of stabilization and, finally, a stage of income convergence. The report concluded that "*there are no reasons to expect greatly different patterns today*". Although it noted that the circumstances now faced by developing countries are not the same as those that shaped the future of today's developed countries over a hundred years ago—the report explained that international markets are bigger nowadays due to greater international economic integration and that domestic markets are smaller because there are more national borders—it concluded that "*the general patterns of concentration and convergence are likely to remain the same for today's developing countries as they were for early developers*".

The second involved the determinants of the evolution of territorial inequality over the course of the development processes and thus the economic policy recommendations that could be formulated by learning from the past. In this respect the report was clearly inspired by the conceptual framework set out by Williamson (1965)—who was in turn influenced by Kuznets (1955)—and held that industrial activity in the early stages of modern economic growth tended to be concentrated in particular locations while all other areas remained mainly agricultural. This led to an increase in per capita income inequality across regions, although these disparities would eventually disappear in the long term. Therefore, regional economic disparities were closely related to the uneven spread of industrialization, and increasing inequality in the early stages of modern economic growth could be explained by the specialization and divergence of economic structures. With further integration of national markets and the homogenization of economic structures would come a gradual decrease in regional disparities.

Thus, the World Development Report 2009 provided an economic foundation upon which to base hypotheses on the evolution of territorial inequality over the course of the economic development processes along with long-term evidence to support them. However, a decade after its publication it seems that both its characterization of the evolution of inequality and, possibly, its optimistic view that developing countries might achieve a territorially inclusive growth path were mistaken. The opening sentence of a recent article by Iammarino et al. (2018) could perhaps serve as a summary of what academics, institutions and the media think about the extent of territorial inequality today and the problems it generates: "*In the new millennium inequality among regions has turned sharply up. Regional economic divergence has become a threat to economic progress, social cohesion and political stability in Europe.*" They added, "*This is not uniquely a European problem but one common to many countries, both developed and developing.*"[2]

There has therefore been a new surge of interest in seeking to understand the economic foundations of territorial inequality and to build new evidence on which to carry out an empirical analysis of the hypotheses deriving from them.

As far as these economic foundations are concerned—after decades in which analyses were carried out essentially from empirical bases—Barrios and Strobl (2009), following the growth model put forward by Lucas (2000), proposed a theoretical framework for exploring the evolution and determinants of regional economic inequality. According to this framework, regional inequality emerges as a consequence of technology shocks (i.e. industrialization) concentrated in particular locations. Due to region-specific factor endowments and/or institutions, technology shocks are assumed only to occur in certain regions. These *lucky* regions will start to grow more quickly, and this will lead to spatial inequality. Other regions will gradually catch up due to the spread of technology or because of factor flows (capital, labour). The authors thus provide a theoretical foundation in line with classic contributions on regional economic growth including those originating from neoclassical growth theory (Barro and Sala-i-Martin 1991; Barro et al. 1995).[3]

The importance of the uneven distribution of technology acquisition in explaining inequality between regions is complemented by the hypothesis that the fundamentals of location (such as natural resources, safe harbours,

[2] One example of the media's interest in the spread of territorial inequality and its possible political implications is the in-depth report published in The Economist (2016). As for institutional interest, EUROSTAT produces an annual report on the problems associated with the issue: the *European Regional Yearbook*.

[3] Barrios and Strobl (2009) also supply an economic basis for the relative growth dynamics identified by the literature on the technology gap and catch-up (Abramovitz 1994).

proximity to rivers, etc.) play a vital role in the spatial profile of economic activity (Maloney and Caicedo 2016). This relative productivity advantage resulting from the characteristics of location correlates with the probability of a positive technology shock being experienced in the context of a model such as Barrios and Strobl's (2009) and may give rise to persistence and path dependence, especially when accompanied by increasing returns to scale in certain production sectors (Krugman 1991).

This conceptualization opens up the possibility that new waves of technology change could trigger new phases of rising inequality, regardless of initial levels of per capita income. It could also be concluded that today's scenario of technology change marks the beginning of the new upsurge in territorial inequality identified in the literature. And that this upsurge could affect developed as well as developing countries.

A growing number of empirical investigations have analysed how regional economic inequality has evolved in the course of national economic development processes. Of these, two stand out in particular. First, the above-mentioned work by Barrios and Strobl (2009) econometrically tested the inverted-U hypothesis using regional data from a sample of developed economies for the period 1975–2000. The authors found evidence that strongly supported the idea of an inverted U-shaped curve showing the relationship between regional inequality and economic development. This is in line with the characterization in the World Bank's report of 2009. And second, the paper by Lessmann (2014), the aim of which was to account for different levels of development, used panel data for 56 developed and emerging economies for the period 1980–2009 to prove that spatial inequalities are increasing again today.[4]

However, both of these studies analysed the evolution of regional inequality using cross-sectional or panel data with information covering relatively short historical periods that basically involved looking at how regional inequality evolved in the most developed countries. As Lessmann (2014: 36) himself admits: "*The major problem for this kind of research is that it is essential either to have historical data for single countries or to include poorer countries in a cross-country data set, since the theories of Kuznets and Williamson point at the deep structural changes associated with the industrialization process.*" A more suitable approach would therefore be to explore the evolution of regional inequality over the entire course of

[4] Similar results have also been found by Lessmann and Seidel (2017).

the economic development process, looking at the long-term dynamics of countries from the beginnings of modern economic growth.

The long-term evidence for many European countries, as compiled by Wolf and Rosés (2019), indicates that regional inequality may indeed have followed an inverted U-shaped evolution that began with the onset of contemporary economic growth and continued until the 1980s. In the context of Europe, this dynamic would certainly be associated with the industrialization of a limited number of regions in countries such as Belgium, France, Great Britain, Italy, Portugal and Spain, in which prosperous territories were characterized by the fact that they enjoyed various accumulating factors (e.g. human capital and infrastructure) and locations that enabled them to benefit from the agglomeration effects associated with industrial production. The initial increase in regional inequality would therefore be connected to the industrialization process, after which the spread of industry across regions would make convergence possible. According to this long-term dynamic, many European economies could today be facing the beginning of another upward path resulting from a new technology shock in a context of increasing globalization.

However, many of the histories of Latin American countries presented in this volume show that, unlike with industry in Western Europe, it was the possibility of exporting commodities or natural resources that first acted as a lever for growth, mainly at the time of the first globalization. Then in the stages when growth was driven by industry, generally in the context of state-led industrial policies after 1930, territorial imbalances did not increase. If anything, the contrary was true. Therefore, the historical study of the evolution and explanatory factors of territorial inequality in Latin America from a long-term perspective adds new elements to those already established by the literature.

The following pages are devoted to comparing the long-term patterns of regional income inequality in Latin America—as described in earlier chapters—and Europe. The construction of a new data set on historical regional incomes in Europe (Díez-Minguela et al. 2020) and Latin America (this volume) makes it possible for us to compare the evolution of regional income inequality over the course of national economic development processes on both continents. Such an analysis will help to fill a gap in the literature and establish whether the most widespread characterization of the evolution and determinants of regional inequality reflects only what happened in the most developed countries, or whether on the contrary it also applies to what happened in other areas of the world. Also, a detailed knowledge of past events in the nine Latin American economies analysed in this volume will enable us to see whether the past experience of Europe provides a template suitable for marking out the possible evolution of territorial inequality in this group of developing countries.

This, then, is the main aim of our comparison between the Latin American and European experiences. The text is divided into five sections. Following this introduction, Sect. 2 presents the data set that will enable us to carry out the analysis. Section 3 provides a comparative description of the long-term evolution of regional economic inequality in Europe and Latin America. Section 4 follows the methodological approach first used in papers such as those by Barrios and Strobl (2009) and Lessmann (2014) to characterize and analyse the patterns of territorial inequality in Europe and Latin America. Finally, in order to aid our understanding of the recent evolution of territorial inequality on both sides of the Atlantic, Sect. 5 discusses the differences between the two sets of experiences.

2 Long-Term Patterns of Regional Inequality in Europe and Latin America: The Data Set

Recent developments in European economic history have provided researchers with a new opportunity to explore the long-term evolution of regional income inequality. The articles collected in Wolf and Rosés (2019), for example, analyse the long-term patterns of inequality for a varied group of European countries between 1900 and 2010. Nevertheless, in order to have a time frame allowing us to study the evolution of territorial inequality from the very start of the economic growth processes in Europe, way back in the nineteenth century, we have gathered regional data on population and gross domestic product (GDP) for the period 1860–2010 to use as a sample.[5]

This information has been collected for four countries of South West Europe (France, Italy, Portugal and Spain) at a scale of territorial disaggregation corresponding to NUTS2 in the EUROSTAT classification

[5] Our data set on regional GDP per capita borrows from previous research. For France, we obtained data from Combes et al. (2011), Díez-Minguela and Sanchis (2019) and Rosés and Sanchis (2019); the data for Italy came from Felice (2011, 2015), for Portugal, from Badia-Miró et al. (2012), and for Spain, from Martinez-Galarraga et al. (2015) and Tirado et al. (2016). We are grateful to Marc Badia-Miró, Emanuele Felice, Jordi Guilera, Pedro Lains and Joan R. Rosés for sharing unpublished data with us.

system.[6] With a possible maximum of 16 decadal reference time points per country (16 for Spain, 15 for Italy, 13 for Portugal and 12 for France), we have constructed an unbalanced panel data set.[7] We use per capita GDP in a common unit—1990 Geary-Khamis US$—to evaluate national and regional income.[8] Once the national average incomes have been obtained (Maddison Project Database), we use estimates of historical regional GDP to allocate a share of national GDP to each NUTS2 region. Using also the data on regional population taken from population censuses, we then compute regional per capita income. While this enables us to make inter-regional comparisons across countries, it does not allow for any adjustments to regional prices. To help overcome this lack of variation, we go some way to tackling the problem of differences in the cost of living across regions by using national deflators.[9]

In this way we obtain information on today's NUTS2 regions for all four countries: France (22 regions), Italy (20), Portugal (5) and Spain (17). The data set therefore comprises 64 regions in four countries covering a total area of 1,543,265 square km, that is, over 35% of the area covered by the EU-28. In terms of population, the number in our sample

[6] Over the years, South West Europe has come to be considered an economic area in its own right insofar as it is taken into account as such in current EU development policy and in historical works such as the *Cambridge Economic History of Modern Europe* (Broadberry and O'Rourke 2010). From a comparative perspective, the detailed study of this macroregion has two advantages as far as this chapter is concerned: first, the Latin character of these countries should enable us to achieve greater institutional proximity between them and the Latin American sample; and second, with the exception of France, the time it took before the region started on the path of economic development means that the evidence presented here, like in the case of Latin America, covers most of the time frame of the process.

[7] For Spain, the sample covers all reference time points. Because of limitations in the estimates, the number of time points available for the other countries is lower. For Italy, there are no data for 1860 prior to unification, for Portugal the estimates do not begin until 1890, and for France the two decades between 1870 and 1890 are missing, as is 1940, during the World War II.

[8] Figures for per capita GDP in 1990 Geary-Khamis US$ for France, Italy, Portugal and Spain are from the Maddison Project Database (Bolt and Van Zanden 2014). Figures for national population for 1860–1990 are from the original Maddison database, and for 1990–2010 from the Total Economy Database.

[9] To account for price differences, EUROSTAT created the purchasing power standard (PPS). This is calculated by comparing the prices of a representative basket of goods and services across countries. It does not, however, account for within-country price dispersion, which means that the price levels used for Spain and all its regions are those of the capital city/region of Madrid.

rises from 83 million in 1860 to 180 million in 2010, that is, roughly 35% of the total EU-28 population at both dates and more than 25% of the EU-28's GDP. The data set includes regions that form part of the economic core of Europe (Île-de-France, Northern Italy) along with others that form part of the economic periphery of the southernmost areas of the continent.

Turning to Latin America, the articles included in this volume have made it possible for us to build a data set comprising regional figures for population and GDP for nine countries (Argentina, Bolivia, Brazil, Chile, Colombia, Mexico, Peru, Uruguay and Venezuela). For this sample, we have compiled data for a maximum of 11 common reference time points (1895, 1913, 1925, 1935, 1950, 1960, 1970, 1980, 1990, 2000 and 2010) covering the main stages of economic development in Latin America.[10] However, this is mixed coverage since we were unable to obtain information for all these reference time points for all nine countries that make up the data set. Data for all 11 points were obtained for Brazil, Chile, Mexico, Peru, Uruguay and Venezuela, 10 points for Argentina, but only 7 for Bolivia and Colombia. This is therefore an unbalanced panel data set.

Again we use per capita GDP in a common unit—1990 Geary-Khamis US$—obtained following the same procedure we used for the European sample involving the use of national deflators.[11] Unlike with Europe, in the case of Latin America there is no homogeneity regarding the size and number of regions into which the data are broken down.[12] Bearing in mind suggestions made by the authors of the various chapters on particular countries, we decided to use the following territorial disaggregation: Argentina (24 regions), Bolivia (9), Brazil (20), Chile (13), Colombia

[10] Our data set on regional GDP per capita borrows from research presented by various authors in this volume. For Argentina we use data from Araoz et al. (2020), for Bolivia data from Peres-Cajias (2020), for Brazil data from Bucciferro and Ferreira da Souza (2020), for Chile data from Badia-Miró (2020), for Colombia data from Meisel and Hahn de Castro (2020), for Mexico data from Aguilar-Retureta et al. (2020), for Peru data from Seminario et al. (2020), for Uruguay data from Martinez-Galarraga et al. (2020) and for Venezuela data from de Corso and Tirado-Fabregat (2020). We are extremely grateful to all these authors for sharing their research with us.

[11] GDP per capita for Argentina, Bolivia, Brazil, Chile, Colombia, Mexico, Peru, Uruguay and Venezuela in 1990 Geary-Khamis US$ were also retrieved from the Maddison Project Database (Bolt and Van Zanden 2014).

[12] See the chapter on methodology (Díez-Minguela and Sanchis 2020) for details regarding the size of the regions considered in the case of each country included in this volume.

(16), Mexico (32), Peru (25), Uruguay (19) and Venezuela (24). Our data set therefore comprises 182 regions in nine countries covering a total area of 18,630,000 square km, which is approximately 93% of Latin America. In terms of population, the sample comprises 523 million inhabitants at 2010, that is, around 84% of the total population of Latin America.

3 Long-Term Patterns of Regional Inequality in Europe and Latin America: Descriptive Evidence

We measure regional inequality using a population-weighted coefficient of variation (the Williamson coefficient of variation, WCV), which is computed as follows:[13]

$$\mathrm{WCV} = \sqrt{\sum_{i=1}^{n}\left(\frac{y_i}{y_m}-1\right)^2 \cdot \frac{p_i}{p_m}} \qquad (14.1)$$

where *y* and *p* denote per capita GDP and population, and *i* and *m* denote regional and national values, respectively. The higher the WCV values, the higher is the inequality.

Table 14.1 shows the long-term evolution of regional inequality in the four countries of South West Europe. The general trend appears to be towards rising inequality in the early stages of modern economic growth. While this inequality does at some point start to decrease, its timing varies from country to country. France and Spain show signs of regional convergence from the early twentieth century, after which time disparities gradually decrease.[14] In Italy and Portugal, after an initial rise in inequality, the convergence process eventually begins at a later date, in the 1950s in Italy and the 1970s in Portugal. By 1980 the inverted U appears to be fully formed in all four countries, meaning that over the previous three decades regional catch-up had been completed or even gone into reverse (apart from in Portugal). France stands out due to the sharp increase in regional inequality that took place between 1980 and 2010. Indeed, the figures

[13] See Williamson (1965), Ezcurra and Rapún (2006), Rodríguez-Pose (2012) and Lessmann (2014). The use of a weighted index is particularly suitable in the case of Latin America given the huge differences in size between regions in different countries.

[14] Estimates for regional GDP (at current prices) for 1920 could have an upward bias because of World War I's impact on prices.

Table 14.1 Regional inequality (WCV) South West Europe

	1860	*1870*	*1880*	*1890*	*1900*	*1910*	*1920*	*1930*	*1940*	*1950*	*1960*	*1970*	*1980*	*1990*	*2000*	*2010*
France	0.35				0.37	0.30	0.32	0.30		0.33	0.31	0.25	0.23	0.26	0.27	0.32
Italy		0.17	0.19	0.17	0.20	0.20	0.23	0.26	0.30	0.36	0.29	0.24	0.25	0.25	0.25	0.25
Portugal				0.21	0.23	0.25	0.38	0.28	0.34	0.36	0.41	0.43	0.26	0.27	0.24	0.21
Spain	0.30	0.29	0.32	0.34	0.42	0.39	0.48	0.40	0.35	0.34	0.36	0.27	0.22	0.22	0.24	0.24

Source: Diez-Minguela et al. (2020)

presented in Table 14.1 suggest the hypothesis that those countries that are the first to reach peak regional inequality, such as France and Spain, are also the first to experience a change of trend towards greater inequality. In Italy, on the other hand, inequality has remained stable since 1980, and in Portugal—the last of these countries to reach maximum inequality—it is still on its downward trend.

The evidence relating to Latin America (see Table 14.2) is more complex. The levels of inequality calculated for the first reference time point, which is 1895 for seven of the nine cases considered, are higher than those observed for South West Europe. Only the levels recorded for Argentina and Brazil come close to those calculated for the European country with the highest levels of inequality at the end of the nineteenth century, that is, Spain. In all other cases the figures for Latin America are markedly higher than those for Europe. Chile stands out in this respect with a maximum WCV value that exceeds 1, while the values for Mexico, Peru, Uruguay and Venezuela are around 0.5. In some cases, such as Chile and Argentina, this result is related to unusually high levels of GDP per capita in a small number of regions with very low population density but well endowed with certain natural resources (Magallanes in Chile, Tierra del Fuego and Santa Cruz in Argentine Patagonia). If we plot these values on the historical trajectory of Latin America, we will see that the start of the national development processes—for the most part resulting from the boom in exports of agricultural products and mineral resources—gave rise to greater inequality here than the incipient industrialization that formed the basis of economic development did in South West Europe.

Table 14.2 Regional inequality (WCV) Latin America

	1895	*1913*	*1925*	*1935*	*1950*	*1960*	*1970*	*1980*	*1990*	*2000*	*2010*
Argentina	0.31	0.25	0.30	0.38	0.42	0.45	0.53	0.62	0.56	0.60	
Bolivia					0.18	0.21	0.17	0.24	0.21	0.33	
Brazil	0.30	0.29	0.37	0.56	0.68	0.60	0.64	0.52	0.45	0.47	0.41
Chile	1.28	0.93	0.88	0.54	0.42	0.43	0.39	0.36	0.32	0.35	0.54
Colombia					0.53	0.59	0.63	0.61	0.58	0.62	0.63
Mexico	0.52	0.54	0.67	0.84	0.74	0.82	0.49	0.47	0.51	0.58	0.51
Peru	0.55	0.70	0.79	0.85	0.81	0.74	0.68	0.68	0.59	0.59	0.66
Uruguay	0.46	0.45	0.41	0.38	0.27	0.21	0.25	0.27	0.36	0.37	0.30
Venezuela	0.50	0.64	0.77	0.86	0.61	0.52	0.43	0.50	0.51	0.33	0.26

Source: See footnote 10

During this initial stage, which comes to an end at around the reference time point of 1935 (or 1950), the dynamic followed by inequality in most of the Latin American countries is similar to that followed in Europe, with WCV values increasing steadily in the cases of Argentina, Brazil, Mexico, Peru and Venezuela. The two exceptions are Chile, which starts from a high level of territorial inequality and follows a downward trajectory throughout this period, and Uruguay, which is characterized by the relative stability—although declining—of the indicator.

Although this dynamic of inequality has a number of points in common with that of Europe, there are at least two things that make it different. The first is the value reached by the historical maximum for the period (this being recorded in either 1935 or 1950). The peak levels for the Williamson coefficient are much higher in Latin America.[15] The second is the point at which this trend reverses, which is generally later in Latin American countries, especially compared to France and Spain. The upward trend in inequality only comes to a halt at the reference time point of 1935 in the cases of Mexico, Peru and Venezuela and 1950 for Brazil.[16]

Another interesting element is that in most cases, from 1935/1950 until the crisis of the 1970s (the impact of which can be seen in the reference time point of 1980), the trend observed in Latin American economies is towards a decrease in territorial inequality. Again, this behaviour is similar to that observed in South West Europe. The difference is to be found in the explanatory factors. In the case of Latin America, the beginnings of industrialization, driven by import substitution policies, would have acted as a balancing element. In other words it might be said that, given that the regions with the highest GDP per capita were those that had grown on the basis of exports of primary products from either agriculture or mining, the spread of industrialization—along with increasing state participation in the economy in the shape of price and employment policies that completely changed relative returns—served in many cases to slow down territorial inequality rather than make it stronger, which is what had happened in the case of South West Europe.

A good example of this would be Venezuela. The policies aimed at *sowing the oil* that were introduced in the 1940s encouraged the relative

[15] The region also recorded high levels of personal inequality. Territorial inequality can therefore be seen as another historical dimension of a characteristic typical of this group of countries.

[16] In the case of Argentina, the trend continues upwards until 1980.

growth of those regions along the country's central coastline, helping to close the gap between these and the oil-exporting region of Zulia. In Colombia on the other hand, the industrial development driven by import substitution policies to a certain extent strengthened the leadership of the country's central regions, which were already among the most prosperous due to their specialization in the production and export of coffee. Another exception would be Argentina, where industrial growth was mainly concentrated in the city and province of Buenos Aires, which were already areas with high GDP per capita because of their traditional dedication to providing livestock and farming products and services.

Finally, the trajectories followed by inequality after the end of import substitution policies up to the 2010 reference time point are varied. In some cases, the path continues to be dominated by a decrease in territorial imbalances (Venezuela), but in others we see a change in trend and an increase in territorial inequality (Mexico, Chile and Uruguay). This would coincide with the introduction of the new institutional and economic policy framework that favoured economic liberalization and integration with international goods and factor markets. In these cases, we again find a strong parallel between what happened in Latin America and what happened in European countries. However, the factors behind the two dynamics are different.

The hypothesis put forward by Williamson (1965), endorsed by much of the literature, points to the existence of a relationship between levels of inequality and its evolution over the course of the development processes, in parallel with the introduction of changes in production structures. The following paragraphs will therefore focus on an analysis of whether or not a relationship exists between economic development and regional disparities. This is summarized in the scatter plots shown in Figs. 14.1 and 14.2.

In the case of South West Europe (Fig. 14.1), the inverted U-shaped relationship between development and regional inequality is clear to see, although a number of country-specific features need to be highlighted. First, the upward trend of the inverted U-curve is absent in the case of France. This could be due to the fact that modern economic growth in this early-industrialized country began before 1860, the first year for which we have estimates of GDP per capita (and there is a gap in the data from then until 1900). Second, when there are high levels of GDP per capita, regional disparities show different patterns. In the case of France, for example, there is a notable increase in spatial inequality, whereas in Italy and Spain the convergence process did not come to a halt until later

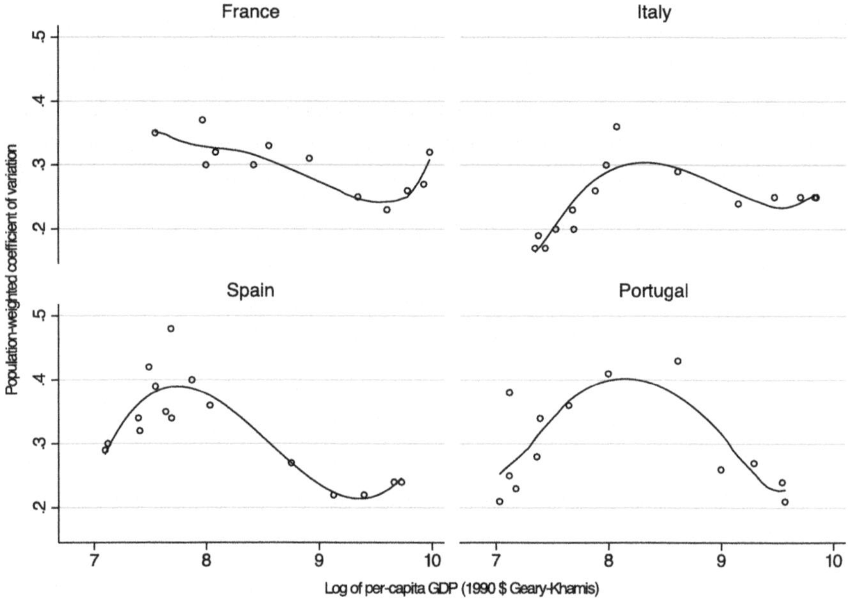

Fig. 14.1 Regional income dispersion (WCV) and GDP per capita (South West Europe, 1860–2010). (Source: Díez-Minguela et al. 2020)

stages of development, leading to the stabilization of (or a slight increase in) regional disparities. And finally in Portugal, although the inverted U-shape is clearly visible, there is (still?) no evidence of growing regional inequality in recent decades. This initial analysis would indeed appear to indicate the existence of a non-monotonic bell-shaped curve over the course of the development process in the countries of South West Europe, although this is followed by mixed evidence regarding the evolution of regional inequality in subsequent stages of economic growth.

The dynamic followed by the countries of the Latin American sample (Fig. 14.2) is more heterogeneous. We can establish three groups of countries with different behaviours. The first, comprising Argentina and Bolivia, is characterized by the uninterrupted spread of inequality throughout the economic development process. The second comprises Uruguay and Chile. The trend in these two countries is for inequality to decrease over the course of the economic development process, although in both cases there seems to be an increase when higher levels of income in the

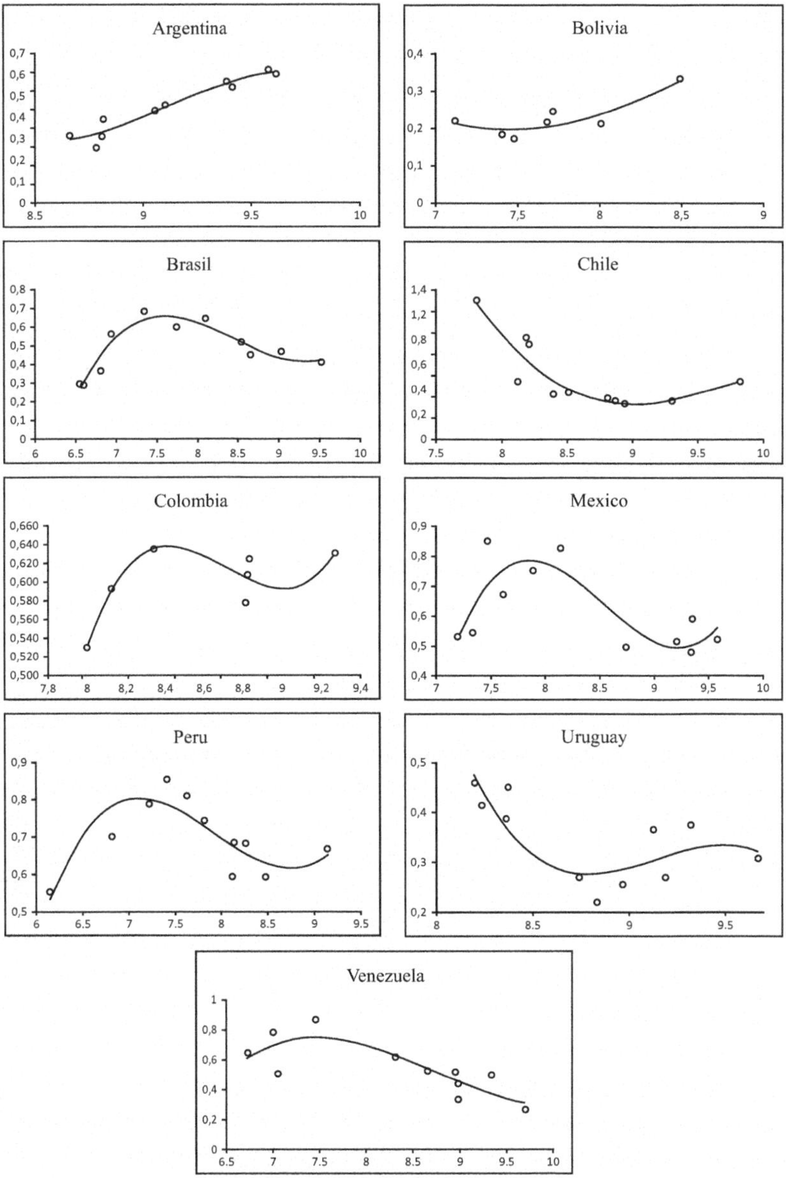

Fig. 14.2 Regional income dispersion (WCV) and GDP per capita (Latin America, 1895–2010). (Source: Own elaboration based on footnote 10)

12,000–15,000 US$ bracket are involved. The third and largest group is made up of Brazil, Colombia, Mexico, Peru and Venezuela. For all these countries, the descriptive evidence shown in the graphs in Fig. 14.2 enables us to identify the presence of an inverted U-shaped relationship between territorial inequality and levels of development. Also, with the exception of Venezuela, in all these territories we see an increase in inequality for high levels of GDP per capita, although there is no common pattern regarding the level of income at which this new trend begins.

All this would seem to indicate the existence of a non-monotonic bell-shaped curve over the course of the development processes in three of the four countries of South West Europe and five of the nine countries of Latin America in our sample. There is also mixed evidence as to how regional inequality evolves in the later stages of economic growth. To look at these issues in greater detail, the next section contains an econometric analysis whereby we empirically test the relationship between economic development and regional inequality.

4 The Relationship Between Regional Inequality and Economic Growth: Econometric Analysis

We can begin to test the relationship between regional inequality and economic development (as measured by GDP per capita) by running a simple parametric OLS regression for our sample of four South West European countries (France, Italy, Portugal and Spain) and nine Latin American countries (Argentina, Bolivia, Brazil, Chile, Colombia, Mexico, Peru, Uruguay and Venezuela).

The parametric specification we follow is similar to that put forward by Barrios and Strobl (2009) and Lessmann (2014), taking the following form:

$$\mathrm{WCV}_{it} = \alpha + \sum_{j=1}^{k} \beta_j Y_{it}^j + \sum_{m=1}^{q} \gamma_m X_{mit} + \varepsilon_{it} \quad i = 1,2,\ldots,N, t = 1,2,\ldots,T \tag{14.2}$$

where WCV_{it} is the Williamson coefficient of variation (i.e. the population-weighted coefficient of variation) of national GDP per capita for country i at time t; Y_{it} is the logarithm of GDP per capita at country level, which enters the regression in a polynomial form of degree j; and X_{mit} represents q different control variables at country level. ε_{it} is the error term. Like

Lessmann (2014), we include all the observations and run pooled regressions for the period 1860–2010.

The control variables are similar to those used in earlier empirical work on spatial inequalities. They include the number of regions by country (NUTS2 regions in the case of Europe and the various regional scales provided in the chapters on Latin American countries in this volume) and country size in square kilometers. This means that we can control for the differences in size of the regions, which can be considerable as regards both the NUTS2 of Europe and the regions of Latin America. We also include a measurement of trade openness for each country. As far as this aspect is concerned, various investigations have empirically established that there is a relationship between trade and regional inequality (Rodríguez-Pose 2012; Ezcurra and Rodríguez-Pose 2014; Hirte and Lessmann 2014). We therefore include a national trade openness ratio—which can be defined as the sum of imports and exports as a share of GDP—to measure how trade has evolved since the wave of globalization that took place in the late nineteenth century (O'Rourke and Williamson 1999).[17]

The main coefficients of interest are the β_j. We consider different polynomial functions with K values from 1 to 3 in order to capture any non-linearity in the relationship between WCV_{it} and Υ_{it}. In the case of $k = 2$ (a quadratic function), we expect $\beta_1 > 0$ and $\beta_2 < 0$, which would indicate an inverted U-shaped relationship between spatial inequality and economic development in line with Williamson (1965). A cubic term is included in some specifications to control for a possible increase in inequality at high levels of development after the inverted-U pattern has fully taken shape (Amos 1988; Lessmann 2014). Tables 14.3 and 14.4 show the results of the OLS estimation of Eq. (14.2) for South West Europe and Latin America, respectively.

In the case of Europe, the first column corresponds to a simple bivariate regression that finds a negative but non-significant relationship between GDP per capita and regional inequality as measured by the WCV. Column 2 shows not only the level of GDP per capita but also its square term in order to capture any non-linearity in its relationship with inequality. The

[17]This is a standard measurement used in the empirical literature to capture trade openness (Frankel and Rose 2002), although some authors have proposed alternative indicators (Alcalá and Ciccone 2004; Hirte and Lessmann 2014). The data on trade openness ratios are taken from Federico and Tena-Junguito (2016).

Table 14.3 Parametric estimates (pooled regressions) South West Europe 1860–2010

	(1)	*(2)*	*(3)*	*(4)*	*(5)*
ln(GDPpc)	−0.020	0.573*	0.602	−0.067	13.994***
	(0.016)	(0.241)	(0.279)	(0.323)	(2.197)
ln(GDPpc)^2		−0.035*	−0.036	0.004	−1.642***
		(0.014)	(0.016)	(0.021)	(0.239)
ln(GDPpc)^3					0.064***
					(0.008)
Number of regions			0.067	−0.100	−0.136
			(0.164)	(0.262)	(0.245)
Country size			0.096**	0.102***	0.111***
			(0.017)	(0.013)	(0.012)
Openness ratio				−0.000	−0.001
				(0.002)	(0.002)
Observations	56	56	56	56	56
R^2	0.075	0.177	0.379	0.408	0.565

Notes: Coefficient (robust standard errors clustered by country). Dependent variable: Williamson coefficient of variation (population-weighted CV). Significant at *10%, **5% and ***1%. All models include a constant. Columns (4) and (5) include additional control variables (The Krugman specialization index in particular, which captures the presence of agglomeration economies, and the government expenditure/GDP ratio, which accounts for the magnitude and evolution of a country's redistributive capacity. The variables generally used in the literature are described in Barrios and Strobl (2009) and Lessmann (2014))

estimated coefficients are significant at 10%, with the GDP coefficient being positive while the square value of GDP shows a negative effect on the WCV. This is consistent with an inverted U-shaped relationship between spatial inequality and development, although both coefficients become non-significant when our set of controls is included (columns 3 and 4). When we consider a third-degree polynomial function (column 5), we obtain robust evidence of the inverted U-shaped relationship between GDP per capita and regional inequality. Moreover, the estimated coefficient of the cubic term is positive and significant. As in Lessmann (2014), this would imply that spatial inequality increases once the inverted-U pattern is completed.

As regards the control variables, the only significant coefficient in all the regressions (columns 3 to 5) corresponds to country size, indicating that the bigger the country the higher the level of regional inequality. The other geographical controls are in no case significant, which means that there is no heterogeneity in the territorial classification of the various

Table 14.4 Parametric estimates (pooled regressions) Latin America, 1895–2010

	(1)	*(2)*	*(3)*	*(4)*	*(5)*
ln(GDPpc)	−0.057**	0.311	0.766*	16.817***	17.97***
	(0.024)	(0.426)	(0.399)	(4.165)	(3.575)
$\ln(GDPpc)^2$		−0.023	−0.052**	−2.071***	−2.219***
		(0.026)	(0.024)	(0.518)	(0.445)
$\ln(GDPpc)^3$				0.084***	0.089***
				(0.021)	(0.018)
Number of regions			0.008***	0.007***	
			(0.003)	(0.002)	
Country size			0.000	0.000*	0.000***
			(0.000)	(0.000)	(0.000)
Openness ratio			0.000	0.000	−0.001
			(0.000)	(0.001)	(0.001)
Country dummies	No	No	No	No	Yes
Observations	92	92	85	85	85
R^2	0.025	0.066	0.259	0.417	0.617

Notes: Coefficient (robust standard errors clustered by country). Dependent variable: Williamson coefficient of variation (population-weighted CV). Significant at *10%, **5% and ***1%. All models include a constant

countries. As for the economic variables, we find no statistically significant relationship between globalization, as measured by the rate of openness, and levels of regional inequality.

Moving on to the case of Latin America, the first column in Table 14.4 corresponds to a simple bivariate regression between GDP per capita and regional inequality, again measured by the WCV. Unlike the results obtained for the European sample, in this case the relationship is negative and also significant. Column 2 shows both the level of GDP per capita and its square term so as to capture any non-linearity in its relationship with inequality. The GDP coefficient is positive and the square value of GDP shows a negative effect on the WCV. This is consistent with an inverted U-shaped relationship between spatial inequality and economic development, but the estimated coefficients are not significant. However, both coefficients become significant when we include our set of controls (column 3),[18] and thus we obtain robust evidence of the inverted U-shaped

[18]The number of observations in this case falls to 85 given the lack of available data for calculating the openness rate for Bolivia.

relationship between GDP per capita and regional inequality. In addition, when we consider a third-degree polynomial function (column 4), the estimated coefficient of the cubic term is positive and significant at 1%. This means that spatial inequality increases at the highest levels of income.[19]

As far as the control variables are concerned, in the case of Latin America both the number of regions (columns 3 and 4) and country size (column 4) are significant, meaning that the bigger the country and the more regions considered, the greater the level of regional inequality. As pointed out earlier, there is no homogeneity in the size of the regions, and so there is no direct relationship between the number of regions considered and the size of the country. Both elements could therefore be significant when estimating levels of inequality.

Finally, in order to verify the existence of an idiosyncratic effect for each country, column 5 of Table 14.4 includes the results of considering the existence of fixed country effects.[20] It can be seen that in this case the estimate's fit improves considerably, while the estimated signs and values of the parameters show no notable changes. Like in the case of Europe, the economic variable (rate of openness) is also non-significant. In neither of the samples, therefore, do we find a statistically significant relationship between globalization, as measured by the rate of openness, and levels of regional inequality.[21]

[19] To be more specific, the estimated coefficients would mean that inequality would on average increase up to a GDP per capita level of 1074 US$ and then decrease until a GDP per capita level of 15,367 US$ is reached, after which it would rise again. These values are consistent with the income levels at which maximum and minimum levels of inequality are reached in various countries of the sample (Fig. 6.2).

[20] The analysis of Latin American countries does not include other economic control variables such as the Krugman specialization index or the government expenditure/GDP ratio because it was not possible to construct them for all the countries and all the reference time points that make up the sample. This is why it makes more sense to consider the inclusion of a dummy variable to capture any differential effect associated with the country.

[21] One explanation for this could be that, as Hirte and Lessmann (2014) point out, since globalization involves the integration of the goods, capital and labour markets, the effects of increasing international integration in the capital and labour markets might perhaps be compensating for any cost in terms of regional inequality caused by the growth in trade. It should also be considered that the effects of increased integration on territorial inequality are not analysed in this exercise. In other words, the picture given of the possible relationship between both variables is static and non-dynamic.

5 Discussion

The aim of the present study was to analyse the evolution of regional inequality over the course of the historical economic development processes in 4 countries of South West Europe—France, Italy, Portugal and Spain—and 9 countries of Latin America—Argentina, Bolivia, Brazil, Chile, Colombia, Mexico, Peru, Uruguay and Venezuela. A new data set of regional per capita GDP for these 13 countries was constructed for the purpose. The study's time frame begins in 1860 for the European sample and 1895 for the Latin American. On the basis of this new evidence, we were able to carry out a comparative analysis of the long-term evolution of regional inequality in Europe and Latin America. It was also our intention to identify for both sets of countries the existence of a common relationship between regional income inequality and economic growth.

In general terms, the study has found that regional income inequality has followed what appears now to be an N-shaped evolution over the course of economic development in both South West Europe and Latin America. This result, which was obtained using parametric regressions with polynomial functions for income, is robust to the inclusion of confounding factors that could have an effect on regional inequality. Studying the evolution of inequality in these two areas thus reinforces one of the ideas that the recent literature, as we mentioned in the introduction, now considers to be stylized facts. However, the new evidence presented in this volume along with that already compiled for South West Europe (Díez-Minguela et al. 2020) provides a level of detail that makes it possible to identify a varied group of elements that make the two sets of experiences different from each other, thereby questioning some of the conclusions reached in previous investigations.

The first distinguishing element is the initial level of regional inequality. At the beginning of their respective development processes, the countries of Latin America showed higher levels of inequality than those of Europe. From this starting point, the phase of increasing inequality, which generally speaking took place between the end of the nineteenth century and the interwar years in both Europe and Latin America, only emphasizes this characteristic. The historical maximums recorded for territorial inequality in Latin America have no comparable counterpart in Europe. The reason for this might be found in the factors that drove economic growth in the two sets of countries. The increase in inequality in Europe was based on the high territorial concentration of industry. Inequality in Latin America, on the other hand, grew mainly due to the specific geography of the natural resources (i.e. geography of first nature), which in many cases were also highly concentrated in spatial terms and formed the basis of an economic growth model that relied especially on the export of raw materials. Extreme cases of regional inequality caused by the increasing exploitation of natural resources would be Venezuela and Chile. In the first of these, for example, GDP per capita in the oil-producing region of Zulia at one point rose to 2.5 times the national average, while in Chile per capita GDP in the northern regions (Tarapacá and Antofagasta) was over three times the national average due to nitrate exports.

Nevertheless, both continents underwent a period of convergence between the aftermath of the Second World War and the crisis of the 1970s. This decrease in inequality was more marked in the group of European countries, and indeed three of the four countries analysed recorded their historical minimums in the 1980s. However, in at least five of the nine Latin American countries analysed, the levels of inequality calculated for the end of this convergence stage were still above those recorded at the very start of the economic development process. This was therefore a period of decreasing inequality which in Latin America did not allow the huge gap between the richest and poorest regions to be narrowed to the same extent as it was in Europe.

Apart from its different intensities, there may be other explanatory factors associated with this dynamic. In the case of Europe, it seems to have been the spread of industrialization and structural change to a growing number of regions that contributed to the decrease in inequality. This would no doubt have been helped by the sizeable migratory flows from poorer to richer regions at a time when international economic integration was increasing although still limited. In the case of Latin America, however, it was the marked change in economic policy—known as import substitution industrialization (ISI)—that in various cases was the driving force behind the regional convergence process. Industrial policy and government investment in the provision of infrastructures to encourage domestic market integration allowed some territories to become economic centres of their respective countries, thereby weakening the privileged position of the traditionally wealthier exporting regions, which in many cases were also those endowed with abundant natural resources. The existence of a common pattern in the evolution of inequality in both continents does not therefore mean that the reasons behind this pattern were the same.

The crisis of the 1970s and changes in the international political and economic consensus in the 1980s signalled the beginning of a new stage in the evolution of inequality on both sides of the Atlantic. In Europe, the collapse of the convergence processes affecting regional production structures in combination with the new technology shock in a context of increasing international economic integration brought to a halt the narrowing of the gap between richer and poorer regions. However, the upsurge in inequality in this case is not as strong as that experienced in Latin America. In Europe, the existence of a large public sector—associated with the development of the welfare state—and supranational economic institutions has limited the spread of regional inequality through social spending and transfers between territories.[22]

Meanwhile, in Latin America the liberalism typical of the 1980s, as enshrined in the Washington Consensus, favoured reinsertion into the international goods and factor markets and led to the unequal growth of those regions best endowed with resources. This new wave of globalization was not accompanied by widespread public sector action to offset the upsurge in regional inequality. Given these conditions, the growth of inequality in this new phase of the historical development process in Latin America is more acute than that recorded in South West Europe. It is no surprise that in this new institutional and economic context, some Latin American countries have explored left-wing political experiences which, through the use of social spending programmes, have aimed to limit the growth of personal inequality and generate balancing effects between territories. In consonance with these policy initiatives, countries such as Brazil and Venezuela have recorded very limited growth in regional inequality over the last 25 years. The case of Uruguay, on the other hand, involves an economic model based on the export of primary products—reintroduced following the serious impact of the economic crisis of the early twenty-first century—accompanied by a whole raft of public policies aimed at making insertion into the international markets easier through competitiveness, but at the same time helping to reduce regional inequality.

[22] A parallel to this evolution can be found in the dynamic of interpersonal income inequality, which has also increased since the late 1970s (Milanovic 2016; Atkinson et al. 2011). Gluschenko (2017) shows how the weighted indexes of territorial inequality widely used in the literature—such as the Williamson index—approximate the interpersonal inequality of the whole population.

With a view to the future, globalization along with technology change is a key aspect of special relevance to the economies of Latin America. Globalization is not a neutral element insofar as it affects regional inequality, and this has been shown by a growing corpus of international literature. A number of recent studies have performed detailed analyses of the positive relationship between trade and regional economic inequality within particular countries.[23] The evidence from these empirical studies confirms that this effect exists, which means that greater exposure to trade, although possibly of benefit to national economies in aggregate terms, could generate winners and losers among the regions.

In summary, it can be agreed that the recent growth in territorial inequality is a global phenomenon of concern to both developed and developing countries. However, if we look carefully at the historical, institutional, political and economic circumstances that have shaped what at first sight seems to be a common evolution, the conclusion is that Latin American countries should be more concerned about the issue than Europe. Not only are their initial levels of territorial inequality very different, but their future evolution may be too. History shows us that the new technology shock and stronger patterns of Latin American specialization in the production and export of natural resources (especially when they are concentrated in just a few regions) makes it possible to predict that territorial inequality will continue to grow for quite some time. And even more so if these societies continue to lack the political (and economic) clout needed to implement public policies aimed at promoting economic growth and improving production structures in the more disadvantaged regions.

Therefore, in complete contrast to the ideas put forward by a number of international bodies such as the World Bank, as mentioned at the very beginning of this chapter, from the work presented in these pages it follows that the text from the World Development Report that we quoted in the introduction should be amended to read: "*the general patterns of concentration and convergence are <u>NOT</u> likely to remain the same for today's developing countries as they were for early developers*". Or, to be more

[23] Empirical tests that prove the existence of this relationship can be found in Rodríguez-Pose (2012), Rodríguez-Pose and Gill (2006), Ezcurra and Rodríguez-Pose (2014) and Hirte and Lessmann (2014). An exception is Milanovic (2005), who analyses the five most populated countries in the world (Brazils, China, India, Indonesia and the United States) from approximately 1980 to 2000 and finds no link between trade openness and regional inequality.

specific, that the evolution of territorial inequality in Latin America does not necessarily have to follow the same path as in Europe. This is an implication for economic policy that, based on an analysis over the long term, should be taken into account when dealing with regional inequality in Latin America.

References

Abramovitz, M. (1994). Catch-up and convergence in the postwar growth boom and after. In: Baumol, W., Nelson, R. and E. Wolff (eds.), *The convergence of productivity: cross-national studies and historical evidence.* Oxford: Oxford University Press), 86–125.

Aguilar-Retureta, J., Badia, M. and Herranz-Loncán, A. (2020). Regional GDP in Mexico, 1895–2010. In: Badia, M., Tirado, D. A. and H. Willebald (eds.), *Time and Space – Latin American Regional Development in Historical Perspective.* Palgrave Studies in Economic History. Cham: Palgrave Macmillan.

Alcalá, F. and Ciccone, A. (2004). Trade and productivity. *Quarterly Journal of Economics*, 129, 2, 613–646.

Amos, O. J. (1988). Unbalanced regional growth and regional income inequality in the latter stages of development. *Regional Science and Urban Economics*, 18, 4, 549–566.

Araoz, F., Nicolini, E. A. and Talassino, M. (2020). Growth and convergence among Argentine provinces since 1895. In: Badia, M., Tirado, D. A. and H. Willebald (eds.), *Time and Space – Latin American Regional Development in Historical Perspective.* Palgrave Studies in Economic History. Cham: Palgrave Macmillan.

Atkinson, A. B., Piketty, T. and Saez, E. (2011). Top incomes in the long run of history. *Journal of Economic Literature*, 49, 1, 3–71.

Badia-Miró, M. (2020). Spatial inequality in Chile in the long run: a paradox of extreme concentration in absence of agglomeration forces (1890–2017). In: Badia, M., Tirado, D. A. and H. Willebald (eds.), *Time and Space – Latin American Regional Development in Historical Perspective.* Palgrave Studies in Economic History. Cham: Palgrave Macmillan.

Badia-Miró, M., Guilera, J. and Lains, P. (2012). Regional incomes in Portugal: industrialisation, integration and inequality, 1890–1980. *Revista de Historia Económica*, 30, 2, 225–244.

Barrios, S. and Strobl, E. (2009). The dynamics of regional inequalities. *Regional Science and Urban Economics*, 39, 5, 575–591.

Barro, R. and Sala-i-Martin, X. (1991). Convergence across states and regions. *Brooking Papers on Economic Activity*, 1, 107–182.

Barro, R., Mankiw, G. and Sala-i-Martin, X. (1995). Capital mobility in neoclassical models of growth. *American Economic Review*, 85, 1, 103–115.

Bolt, J. and Van Zanden, J. L. (2014). The Maddison Project: collaborative research on historical accounts. *Economic History Review*, 67, 3, 627–651.

Broadberry, S. and O'Rourke, K. H. (2010). *The Cambridge economic history of modern Europe*. Cambridge: Cambridge University Press.

Bucciferro, J. and Ferreira da Souza, P. (2020). The Evolution of Regional Income Inequality in Brazil, 1872–2015. In: Badia, M., Tirado, D. A. and H. Willebald (eds.), *Time and Space – Latin American Regional Development in Historical Perspective*. Palgrave Studies in Economic History. Cham: Palgrave Macmillan.

Combes, P. P., Lafourcade, M., Thisse, J. F. and Toutain, J. C. (2011). The rise and fall of spatial inequalities in France: a long-run perspective. *Explorations in Economic History*, 48, 2, 243–271.

de Corso, G. and Tirado-Fabregat, D. A. (2020). *Was the oil sown evenly?* Long-term patterns of regional inequality in Venezuela (1881–2011). In: Badia, M., Tirado, D. A. and H. Willebald (eds.), *Time and Space – Latin American Regional Development in Historical Perspective*. Palgrave Studies in Economic History. Cham: Palgrave Macmillan.

Díez-Minguela, A., Gonzalez-Val, R., Martinez-Galarraga, J., Sanchis, M. T. and Tirado, D. A. (2020). The long-term relationship between economic development and regional inequality: South-West Europe, 1860–2010. *Papers in Regional Science*, 9, 3, 479–508 .

Díez-Minguela, A. and Sanchis, M. T. (2019). Regional income inequality in France: What does history teach us? *Historical Methods: Journal of Quantitative and Interdisciplinary History*, 52, 1, 1–14.

———. (2020). Comparing different estimation methodologies of regional GDPs in Latin American countries. In: Badia, M., Tirado, D. A. and H. Willebald (eds.), *Time and Space – Latin American Regional Development in Historical Perspective*. Palgrave Studies in Economic History. Cham: Palgrave Macmillan.

(The) Economist (2016). Rage against the Dying of the Light. Regional inequality is becoming too dangerous too ignore. *(The) Economist*, 17 December, 70–71.

Ezcurra, R. and Rapún, M. (2006). Regional disparities and national development revisited: the case of Western Europe. *European Urban and Regional Studies*, 13, 4, 355–369.

Ezcurra, R. and Rodríguez-Pose, A. (2014). Trade openness and spatial inequality in emerging countries. *Spatial Economic Analysis*, 9, 2, 162–182.

Federico, G and Tena-Junguito, A. (2016), World trade, 1800–2015, VoxEU.org, 7 February.

Felice, E. (2011). Regional value added in Italy, 1891–2001, and the foundation of a long-term picture. *Economic History Review*, 64, 3, 929–950.

———. (2015). *Ascesa e declino. Storia economica d'Italia*. Bologna: il Mulino.

Frankel, J. A. and Rose, A. (2002). An estimate of the effect of common currencies on trade and income. *Quarterly Journal of Economics*, 117, 2, 437–466.

Gluschenko, K. (2017). Measuring regional inequality: to weight or not to weight? *Spatial Economic Analysis*, 13, 1, 36–59.

Hirte, G. and Lessmann, C. (2014). Trade, integration, and interregional inequality. *CESifo Working Papers Series* 4799.

Iammarino, S., Rodríguez-Pose, A. and Storper, M. (2018). Regional inequality in Europe: evidence, theory and policy implications. *Journal of Economic Geography*, 19, 2, 273–298.

Krugman, P. 1991. Increasing returns and economic geography. *Journal of Political Economy*, 99, 3, 483–499.

Kuznets, S. (1955). Economic growth and income inequality. *American Economic Review*, 45, 1, 1–28.

Lessmann, C. (2014). Spatial inequality and development. Is there an inverted-U relationship. *Journal of Development Economics*, 106, 35–51.

Lessmann, C. and Seidel, A. (2017). Regional inequality, convergence, and its determinants. A view from outer space. *European Economic Review*, 92, 110–132.

Lucas, R. E. (2000). Some macroeconomics for the 21st Century. *Journal of Economic Perspectives*, 14, 1, 159–168.

Maddison Project Database: http://www.ggdc.net/maddison/maddison-project/data.htm

Maloney, W. F. and Caicedo, F. V. (2016). The persistence of subnational fortune. *Economic Journal*, 126, 598, 2219–2445.

Milanovic, B. (2005). Half a world: regional inequality in five great federations. *Journal of the Asia Pacific Economy*, 10, 4, 408–445.

———. (2016). *Global inequality: a new approach for the age of globalization*. Cambridge: Harvard University Press.

Martinez-Galarraga, J., Rodriguez-Miranda, A. and Willebald, H. (2020). Patterns of regional income distribution in Uruguay (1872–2012): a story of agglomeration, natural resources and public policies. In: Badia, M., Tirado, D. A. and H. Willebald (eds.), *Time and Space – Latin American Regional Development in Historical Perspective*. Palgrave Studies in Economic History. Cham: Palgrave Macmillan.

Martinez-Galarraga, J., Rosés, J. R. and Tirado, D. A. (2015). The long-term patterns of regional income inequality in Spain, 1860–2000. *Regional Studies*, 49, 4, 502–517.

Meisel, A. and Hahn de Castro, L. W. (2020). Regional Economic Inequality in Colombia, 1926–2018. In: Badia, M., Tirado, D. A. and H. Willebald (eds.), *Time and Space – Latin American Regional Development in Historical Perspective*. Palgrave Studies in Economic History. Cham: Palgrave Macmillan.

O'Rourke, K. H. and Williamson, J. G. (1999). *Globalization and history. The evolution of a nineteenth-century Atlantic economy.* Cambridge: The MIT Press.

Peres-Cajias, J. (2020). From West to East: Bolivian Regional GDPs since the 1950s. A story of Natural Resources and Infrastructure. In: Badia, M., Tirado, D. A. and H. Willebald (eds.), *Time and Space – Latin American Regional Development in Historical Perspective.* Palgrave Studies in Economic History. Cham: Palgrave Macmillan.

Rodríguez-Pose, A. (2012). Trade and regional inequality. *Economic Geography*, 88, 2, 109–136.

Rodríguez-Pose, A. and Gill, N. (2006). How does trade affect regional disparities? *World Development*, 34, 7, 1201–1222.

Rosés, J. R. and Sanchis, M. T. (2019). A long run perspective on French regional income inequalities, 1860–2010. In: Wolf, N. and J. R. Rosés (eds). *The economic development of Europe's regions. A quantitative history since 1900.* London: Routledge.

Seminario, B., Zegarra, M. A. and Palomino, L. (2020). Peruvian regional inequality: 1847–2017. In: Badia, M., Tirado, D. A. and H. Willebald (eds.), *Time and Space – Latin American Regional Development in Historical Perspective.* Palgrave Studies in Economic History. Cham: Palgrave Macmillan.

Tirado, D. A., Díez-Minguela, A. and Martinez-Galarraga, J. (2016). Regional inequality and economic development in Spain, 1860–2010. *Journal of Historical Geography*, 54, 87–98.

Total Economy Database: https://www.conference-board.org/data/economydatabase/

Williamson, J. G. (1965). Regional inequality and the process of national development: a description of the patterns. *Economic Development and Cultural Change*, 13, 4, 1–84.

Wolf, N. and J. R. Rosés (eds.) (2019). *The economic development of Europe's regions. A quantitative history since 1900.* London: Routledge.

World Bank (2009). Reshaping Economic Geography. *World Developmet Report.* Washington D.C.: World Bank.

Index[1]

A

Agglomeration economies, 8, 158, 159, 174, 176, 178, 179, 236, 291, 370, 392

Argentina, 4, 5, 11, 13, 19, 21–23, 21n6, 27, 29, 36, 42, 43, 45, 46, 48, 52, 56, 58, 65, 66, 67n3, 68–71, 74, 75, 85n18, 88, 90, 103, 104, 168n12, 273, 274, 279–282, 293, 295, 301, 302, 310, 345–348, 349n5, 352, 357, 359–364, 367, 367n12, 368, 368n13, 371, 372, 382, 382n10, 385–388, 386n16, 390, 395

B

Barro, Robert, 159, 159n1, 219, 287, 377

Beta-convergence or β-convergence, 85, 85n18, 86, 114–116, 114n14, 133, 144, 145, 158, 171, 172, 204, 205, 226, 227, 325n16, 326, 328

Bolivia, 4, 9, 11, 19, 21n6, 22, 23, 25n8, 26, 29, 30, 36, 37, 42, 43, 45, 47, 51, 57, 60, 66, 98–106, 98n1, 99n3, 101n4, 111, 119, 125, 126, 242, 251, 345–348, 349n5, 354–357, 363, 363n11, 367n12, 368, 368n13, 370, 382, 382n10, 388, 390, 393n18, 395

Brazil, 4, 6, 11, 13, 19–21, 21n5, 21n6, 27, 30, 34–36, 42, 43, 46, 47, 49, 51, 52, 55, 56, 59, 103–105, 131–153, 184, 215, 273, 274, 276, 279, 282, 292, 293, 295, 301, 302, 310, 345–347, 349n5, 352, 354, 359, 359n9, 360, 362, 363, 363n11, 367, 368, 370, 372, 382, 385, 386, 390, 395, 397, 398n23

Bulmer-Thomas, Victor, 49, 161, 163, 273

[1] Note: Page numbers followed by 'n' refer to notes.

D. A. Tirado-Fabregat et al. (eds.), *Time and Space*, Palgrave Studies in Economic History, https://doi.org/10.1007/978-3-030-47553-6

C

Cafe, 6, 30, 35, 49, 108n8, 133, 135–137, 139, 140, 143, 151–153, 187–189, 203, 310, 313, 314, 324, 336, 387
Capital flows, 203
Capital markets, 71, 152, 214n5, 245
Cattle, 30, 31, 66, 67, 72, 73, 90, 164n6, 186, 251, 272, 292, 293, 314
Chile, 4, 7, 11, 19, 20, 20n3, 21n6, 22, 29–31, 33, 37, 42, 43, 46, 48, 50, 52, 57–59, 101, 101n4, 233n16, 247, 310, 345–348, 349n5, 355, 356, 359–361, 364, 367, 368, 382, 382n10, 385–388, 390, 395, 396
Clustering, 11, 13, 57, 61, 123, 204, 338, 343–372
Coefficient of variation (CV), 36, 37, 88, 89, 141–143, 184, 227, 229, 231
Colombia, 4, 7, 13, 19, 20, 21n6, 22, 37, 42, 43, 47, 50–52, 57, 60, 61, 134, 134n4, 135, 135n5, 183–207, 281, 310, 312n3, 345, 347, 347n2, 349n5, 355–357, 361, 364, 367, 367n12, 368, 368n13, 370, 372, 382, 382n10, 387, 390, 395
Concentration of manufacturing, 84, 133
Cotton, 30, 35, 56, 104, 140, 151, 242, 245, 246, 261

D

Debt crisis, 13, 71, 111, 113, 133, 152, 168, 190, 216, 256, 267, 300, 351, 363, 372
Domestic market, 4, 9, 10, 12, 49–52, 56, 89, 135, 151, 159n2, 167, 174, 177, 273, 277, 298, 299, 312, 314, 318, 318n12, 334, 337–339, 350, 351, 353, 355, 376, 396

E

Economic activity, 7–9, 22, 23, 25, 34, 36, 37, 76, 79, 90, 97–99, 98n2, 120, 125, 143, 150, 157–159, 167, 168, 175–178, 186, 190–193, 199, 204, 217, 229, 231, 233, 234, 236, 241–243, 253, 254, 256, 259, 262, 263, 274, 276, 285, 295, 296, 298, 320, 324, 335, 364, 368, 370, 378
Economies of scale, 8, 50, 90, 152, 189, 206
Endogenous growth theory, 57
Export-led growth, 13, 46, 58, 62, 102, 159, 233, 279, 345, 350, 351, 372

F

Factor flows, 377
First Globalization, 8, 47–50, 61, 139, 160, 212, 214, 214n4, 235, 271, 283, 285, 287, 288, 292, 295, 298, 302, 346, 348, 353, 364, 370, 379
First nature geography, 298
First World War (WWI), 46, 69, 88, 102, 161, 168, 174, 245, 275, 277, 278, 298, 345, 350, 351

G

Geary, F., 18n2, 31–33, 31n16, 34n17, 164, 166, 192, 218, 220, 282

Geary-Stark, 321
Globalization, 2, 61, 90, 214n4, 274, 301, 302, 312, 356, 359, 379, 391, 393, 394, 394n21, 397, 398
Golden age, 17, 44, 52
Great Recession, 17, 297n21

I
Import Substitution Industrialization (ISI), 8, 13, 71, 88, 137, 138, 143, 143n19, 144, 147, 151, 152, 158, 160, 162, 171, 174, 176, 177, 190, 203, 204, 207, 215, 217, 221, 223, 229, 233, 246, 274, 278, 295, 299, 300, 311, 317, 318, 325, 351, 354, 362, 364, 367, 372, 396
Increasing returns, 6, 89, 296n20, 335, 370, 378
Industrialization, 3, 5, 6, 8, 12, 13, 18, 42, 45, 46, 49, 51–56, 58, 59, 61, 62, 90, 103, 119, 133, 136, 147, 152, 158, 159, 159n1, 162, 171n14, 178, 190, 203, 204, 212, 214–216, 221, 236, 246, 256, 266, 274, 278, 279, 283, 285, 288, 295–297, 300, 317, 317n10, 345, 346, 351, 354, 356, 360, 362, 367, 370, 371, 376–379, 385, 386, 396
Internal migration, 196n4, 246, 256
International integration, 236, 279, 394n21
Interwar, 283, 285, 287, 288, 298, 395

L
Labour force, 164, 214, 246
Labour markets, 32, 33, 162, 164, 214n3, 218, 274, 291, 314, 394n21
Latin America, 1–14, 18–20, 23–25, 30, 37, 41–63, 65, 90, 97, 105, 134, 134n4, 135, 135n5, 184, 186, 189, 215, 243, 245, 291, 301, 310, 311, 338n22, 343–372, 375–399
Local Indicators of Spatial Autocorrelation (LISA) maps, 369

M
Maddison, Angus, 22, 44, 219, 347, 381n8
Market integration, 4, 9, 13, 32, 100, 135, 151, 214, 214n3, 217, 296, 296n19, 335, 351, 354, 355, 371, 396
Market potential, 12, 158, 176, 178, 212, 337
Mean log deviation (MLD), 287n13, 348–350, 352, 353
Meat, 66, 68, 69, 79, 85, 104, 108n8, 280
Mexico, 4, 8, 13, 19, 21n6, 26, 29, 30, 34–36, 42, 43, 47–49, 51, 54, 56, 62, 211–236, 310, 344–347, 349n5, 352, 359, 361, 362, 364, 367, 371, 372, 382, 382n10, 383, 385–387, 390, 395
Migration, 6, 9, 150–152, 196, 196n4, 198, 204, 234, 243, 246, 247, 255, 256, 264, 266, 280, 293n18, 335, 344, 354, 364
Moran's I, 368

N

Natural resources, 4, 6, 7, 9, 10, 12, 13, 45, 47, 48, 50, 53, 54, 56, 58, 61, 97–126, 158, 162, 163, 168, 170, 171, 173, 173n18, 177, 178, 198, 202–204, 206, 212, 214, 235, 250n4, 271–302, 310, 311, 313–315, 324, 335–337, 339, 344, 347n3, 348, 351, 353, 356, 367, 370–372, 377, 379, 385, 396, 398
Neoclassical growth theory, 18, 377
New Economic Geography (NEG), 12, 158, 159, 168, 176, 296, 335, 337n21, 338n22, 370
Nitrates, 7, 50, 158, 160–163, 167, 168, 172n15, 173, 176–178, 355, 367, 396

O

Oil, 7, 10, 13, 53, 54, 56, 67, 70, 75, 84, 85, 85n17, 88, 89, 89n19, 91, 103–105, 108, 108n9, 119, 138, 139, 160, 163–166, 168, 170, 177, 194, 198, 202–204, 215, 216, 219, 220, 220n11, 223, 223n12, 227, 242, 245, 246, 261, 283, 297, 309–339, 353, 354n6, 367, 372, 386
Oil crisis, 283, 297, 337, 372
Openness rate, 393n18

P

Periphery, 13, 189, 201, 207, 228, 272, 302, 348
Perú, 4, 8, 13, 19, 20, 21n6, 29, 30, 37, 42, 43, 47, 50, 52, 53, 59, 101n4, 134, 134n4, 135, 135n5, 188, 241–247, 242n1, 249–252, 250n4, 250n5, 251n7, 254, 255, 257, 261–267, 310, 345–347, 349n5, 354, 359, 361, 363, 363n11, 367, 368, 371, 372, 382, 382n10, 383, 386, 390, 395
Polarization, 7, 147, 152, 174, 265, 334, 338
Population-weighted/Williamson coefficient of variation (WCV), 37, 116, 133, 141, 142, 151, 205, 205n5, 206, 287, 325, 383, 390, 392, 393
Productivity or GDP per worker, 32
Public polices, 2–4, 14, 17, 53, 91, 126, 271–302, 311, 337, 372, 397, 398

Q

Quah, Danny, 204, 265

R

Regional development policy, 7, 13, 41–63, 132, 158, 171, 174, 371
Regional integration, 62, 284

S

Sala-i-Martín, Xavier, 158, 159, 159n1, 168, 171, 287, 356n8, 377
Second World War (WWII), 23, 44, 50, 51, 53, 61, 144, 161, 215, 215n6, 217, 246, 274, 278, 278n3, 311, 317, 351, 371, 381n7, 396
Sigma-convergence or σ-convergence, 85n18, 88, 114n14, 115–117, 133, 141, 142, 144, 151, 168, 171, 184, 205, 226, 287, 325, 325n16, 326

Simple coeffcient of variation (SCV), 287
South America, 45, 69, 184, 272
Spatial autocorrelation, 368n13
Stark, T., 18n2, 31–33, 31n16, 34n17, 164, 166, 192, 218, 220, 282
Structural change, 6, 8, 9, 12, 50–52, 58, 212–214, 221, 236, 242, 292, 297, 353, 378, 396

T
Theil Index, 227, 228
Tin, 102, 103, 118
Trade theory, 296, 298, 335
Transport costs, 7, 12, 32, 158, 159, 159n2, 189, 206, 296n20, 299, 370

U
Uruguay, 4, 9, 11, 19, 21n6, 22, 26, 26n9, 29, 30, 34, 36, 37, 42, 43, 45, 46, 52, 271–302, 345, 347n2, 349n5, 354, 355, 359, 359n9, 361, 382, 382n10, 383, 385–388, 390, 395, 397

V
Venezuela, 4, 10, 19, 20, 21n6, 22, 25, 29, 36, 42, 43, 47, 50–53, 57, 60, 281, 309–339, 312n3, 345, 347, 349n5, 354, 355, 359, 361, 364, 367, 382, 382n10, 383, 385–387, 390, 395–397

W
Williamson, Jeffrey, 2, 4, 18, 48, 139, 144, 159, 186, 227n13, 231, 256, 266, 287, 296, 297, 314, 345, 348, 376, 378, 386, 387, 391
Wool, 30, 68, 69, 167, 246, 256, 277, 278, 298, 299

The manufacturer's authorised representative in the EU is Springer Nature Customer Service Centre GmbH, Europaplatz 3, 69115 Heidelberg, Germany. If you have any concerns regarding our products, please contact ProductSafety@springernature.com

Printed and bound by CPI Group (UK) Ltd, Croydon, CR0 4YY

30/09/2026

02225645-0013